A
NATION OF
SALESMEN

Other Avon Books by
Earl Shorris

Latinos: A Biography of the People

Avon Books are available at special quantity discounts for bulk purchases for sales promotions, premiums, fund raising or educational use. Special books, or book excerpts, can also be created to fit specific needs.

For details write or telephone the office of the Director of Special Markets, Avon Books, Dept. FP, 1350 Avenue of the Americas, New York, New York 10019, 1-800-238-0658.

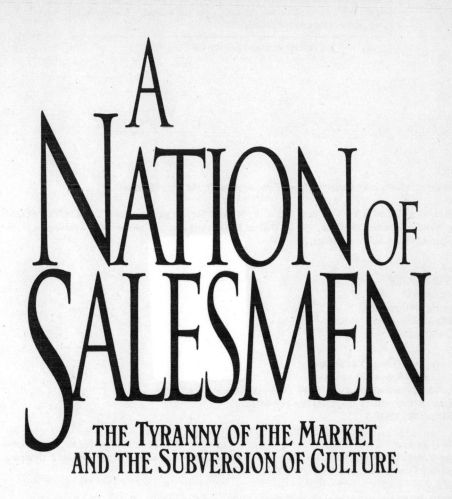

A NATION OF SALESMEN

THE TYRANNY OF THE MARKET AND THE SUBVERSION OF CULTURE

EARL SHORRIS

AVON BOOKS ◆ NEW YORK

Parts of this book, in an entirely different form, appeared in *Harper's Magazine*.

Lines from "The Man With the Blue Guitar" by Wallace Stevens reprinted from COLLECTED POEMS by Wallace Stevens. Copyright 1936 by Wallace Stevens and renewed 1964 by Holly Stevens, reprinted by permission of Alfred A. Knopf, Inc.

AVON BOOKS
A division of
The Hearst Corporation
1350 Avenue of the Americas
New York, New York 10019

Copyright © 1994 by Earl Shorris
Cover art by Robert Goldstrom
Published by arrangement with W. W. Norton & Company, Inc.
Library of Congress Catalog Card Number: 94-16580
ISBN: 0-380-72678-5

The W. W. Norton edition contains the following Library of Congress Cataloging in Publication Data:
Shorris, Earl, 1936-
    A nation of salesmen : the tyranny of the market and the subversion of culture / by Earl Shorris.
        p.   cm.
Includes index.
1. Selling—United States—History.   2. Selling—Social aspects—United States—History.
3. Salespersonnel—United States—History.   I. Title
HF5438.25.S563   1994
381'.0973—dc20   94-16580

First Avon Books Trade Printing: January 1996

AVON TRADEMARK REG. U.S. PAT. OFF. AND IN OTHER COUNTRIES, MARCA REGISTRADA, HECHO EN U.S.A.

Printed in the U.S.A.

QPM 10 9 8 7 6 5 4 3 2 1

06-02786

For
Cynthia and Maria

Contents

CONTENTS

The Plan of the Book

A writer who chooses a distant subject has the privilege of doing an explorer's work. He sets out on a journey into unmapped territory, guided only by curiosity and some strategy to keep from going around in circles. The writer as stranger expects insight to grow out of incessant surprise. Like an ancient Greek, he believes Wonder is the mother of thinking.

When the subject reaches out of personal history to choose the writer, a different kind of journey takes place. The writer travels the most familiar territory, guided only by curiosity and the hope that he will have the courage to keep his eyes open. The work is bound to be a kind of confession, one in which the writer must expect that every insight may also be an embarrassment.

This book undertakes both journeys, for I have had two careers, one as a writer and the other as a salesman. The writer has, of course, chosen to explore the salesman's territory, but the salesman has also chosen the writer. Considered in its best light, this provides a binocular view of the subject, with all the metaphorical depth such a view offers. On the other hand, there is the possibility of an ethical schism: the application of one set of rules to the personal experience and another, more rigorous ethics to researched material. The reader should be alert to the possibility that for the sake of comfort I may have fooled myself now and then.

As part of the binocular structure, there is a story at the beginning of each chapter. The stories depict the salesman in his daily life. They contain no theories, no facts or figures. I use the stories as a matter of prudence, because I think there is some danger in writing essays that do not include stories or other kinds of reportage: One risks losing the world and all of its precision.

The stories that begin the chapters are fictions, although some of them have a worldly double. One is perhaps my father; another is likely me. I have presented these doubles in deep disguise, not solely for legal reasons but to avoid deception. Fictions, as everyone knows, can never deceive, because lies presented as such are always true.

Sources

Since there is very little good data, other than novels and plays, on the various aspects of selling, I have had to rely in large part on what I have seen and been, like an anthropologist looking into a mirror. In addition to many direct observations, the book uses some personal experiences, not all of them flattering to the author.

The experiences began in 1958 and continued into the 1990s. Although the companies I knew best were AT&T, N. W. Ayer, General Motors, and the Matson Navigation Company, I had the opportunity to study selling with many organizations, both large and small, either as an employee, an agent, or a consultant:

Air New Zealand, American Broadcasting Co., Ball Corp., Bank of Tokyo, Best Fertilizers, Campbell-Ewald, Carrier, Chemical Bank, Citicorp, Dailey & Assoc., Dana, Del Monte, Democratic National Committee, DuPont, Edison Electric Institute, Feder's Jewelers, Federal National Mortgage Assn., First Boston Corp., Fletcher Richards Calkins & Holden, Folger's Coffee Co., Fuller Paint, KROD, KTSM, Kennedy Hannaford Co., Morris Plan of California, Northern California Chevrolet Dealers, Pacific Area Travel Assn., Procter & Gamble, Pureta Sausage Co., Ramsey Clark U.S. Senate Campaign, Sanders Co., Spare Tire, Sutro & Co., Tar-Gard, Toshiba, Triangle Publications (*TV Guide*), and, early on, many small retailers.

Thesis

The thesis of this book, that selling has become the determinant activity in the United States, is not complicated. The questions raised by the thesis are plain to see: If America is a nation of salesmen, who are we, each and all of us together, and are we the people and the nation we hoped to be?

The exploration of any idea about a society, even an uncomplicated idea, requires that the idea be defined analytically and historically, and then considered in relation to the politics, economics, culture, and character of the country. That is the business of the book, causing it to be divided into three parts: The first part takes up definitions and history, the second is about selling and how the United States became oversold, and the third examines the way in which the imperative character of selling in the last half of the twentieth century has caused people, especially in America, to have a new view of themselves, their freedom, and their dignity.

Of God and Gender

Gender figures among the more discomforting inconsistencies of the English language, but it needn't have been that way. The language would have been a little bit less specific and a lot less problematical if it had been, like the languages of the Maya of Mesoamerica, almost entirely androgynous. Or it could have been like a Romance language, in which everything that can be named has gender, based on both primary and secondary sexual characteristics, the secondary sexual characteristic of a word being its initial letter. *Agua,* the Spanish word for "water," ends in *a,* which makes water feminine, but it would be so awkward to say *la agua* that the rules of the language have given it, and many words like it, special dispensation. *Agua* is masculine, *el agua.* Using the same rule of graceful relations, *mano,* which has a masculine ending, is feminine, *la mano.*

Can the word *salesman* be neutered or made androgynous without violating the rule against awkwardness?

There are many possible alternatives: *salesperson, seller, vendor, purveyor.* Or *salesthem,* as in the improper use of a plural pronoun to avoid the issue of gender. A complete gender change operation produces *saleswoman, saleslady, salesgirl, salesmiss, salesmissus, salesmiz.*

None of these will really do, however, for the salesman is now often an advertisement, printed, broadcast, or written in the sky and placed before the potential customer. Any name given to the person who sells will have to apply as well to the thing that sells. Personification is a problem. If one turns to comedy, following the example of *chair* for *chairman,* the result is *sale,* as in "The sale said . . ." or "I am a sale."

The solution, of course, lies in equity, not in nouns and pronouns. It is better to fight for justice than against grammar. Treat women and men with equal dignity, and the linguistic question of gender becomes a matter of convenience rather than politics.

Religion as "relationship selling" has a place in this book, and there are two stories about people who mix business with religion, but this is not a book about proselytizing for religious purposes. Billy Graham does not have a major role in the book, nor does Tammy Bakker or Pat Robertson or the Reverend Moon or the Ayatollah Khomeini, although all of them may be described as salesmen. Not that I wasn't tempted to write at length about the selling of religion. It is a delicious subject for a writer, as Sinclair Lewis and others have demonstrated. Nevertheless, a nation of salesmen and a nation of fundamentalist preachers have little or nothing in common: Iran is not a shopping mall, and heaven is not a Chevrolet.

Some of the techniques developed by stockbrokers, advertising agencies, and carnival barkers have been used successfully by preachers of one religion or another, but the demand for heaven and the supply of hell baffle the most sophisticated market theorists. What is a fair price for salvation? Did Joan of Arc or Saint Sebastian pay too much?

It may be a lack of imagination on my part, but I cannot conceive of a great host of people trudging across all of Europe, willing to fight and die in a crusade on behalf of the videocassette player. Nor does it seem likely to me that anyone would be willing to die on the cross for the suits of Giorgio Armani or the scents of Chanel.

Finally, there is the example of confusing holy and secular pursuits: Some of the more foolish men of recent history have written books or pamphlets describing Jesus as a salesman. I felt no great urge to apply for membership in that fraternity.

Selling became

the most striking activity

of contemporary America.

—Daniel Bell,
*The Cultural Contradictions
of Capitalism*

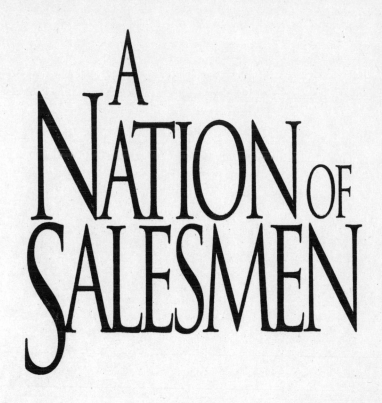

A Nation of Salesmen

Introduction

Confessions of a Day Sleeper

I was very fortunate to have a father who was a super salesperson, and who taught me the basics during my youthful, impressionable years. Through him, I learned that selling is a noble profession. . . .

—ROBERT L. SHOOK,
Hardball Selling

a salesman is an it that stinks

—E. E. Cummings

1.

Ten years ago *New York* magazine published an article about people with two careers. Although the article was not unkind to its half dozen subjects, it did imply that they were all slightly mad. One of the loonies was a well-known painter who was also chief of surgery at a major hospital. Another was the attorney and novelist Louis Auchincloss. And then there was a fellow who wrote novels and essays and had been a contributing editor of *Harper's Magazine* for more than ten years, all the while serving as a senior officer of the N. W. Ayer advertising agency. That was me.

It was a silly article, I suppose. The surgeon permitted himself to be photographed half naked in front of a wild abstract painting, presumably his work. Auchincloss, who approached the whole business with a lawyer's caution, told me later that he had refused to permit the photographer into his apartment. I allowed the photographer into my apartment, but threatened to throw him out the window of my office on the forty-first floor of Burlington House.

On the other hand, the experience had some heuristic value for me. I had written about the organization of work, but had never permitted myself to consider the meaning of the work I did. Or so I thought. I know now that I had constructed an elaborate wall of rationalizations, mostly in the form of jokes, about the selling of goods and services in America.

Advertising, I said to anyone who would listen, is not immoral, except as waste is immoral, for advertising is no more than a waste of time, effort, and money by people who might otherwise produce useful or even beautiful work. Advertising is largely useless, I said, an inefficient way to pay for the daily newspaper. It is closer to bad art than to good business.

When critics argued that advertising caused people to buy things they didn't want or need, I laughed, and pointed out to them that the best sales job the advertising business had ever done was to convince its clients and critics that advertising could control people's desires. In my best Socratic fashion, I asked whether hungry people would desire food if it were not advertised.

No one in the advertising business disputed what I said. The argument for the power of advertising had always been implied by its practitioners, but they had prudently left it to their critics to make the bald-faced claim. After all, if advertising could control people's innermost desires, it might be necessary to regulate the business or even to ban advertising altogether. No, it was not wise to make certain claims about the power of advertising; modesty was the prudent course.

Then, at the end of the 1980s, America's oldest advertising agency, Ayer, became too desperate for subtlety. Deeply in debt, losing old clients and unable to find new ones, the agency abandoned any pretense of modesty. On a sign in its main reception area, Ayer proclaimed, "We create your wants. We create your desires."

If Ayer had made advertising for a cigarette company, it would not have abandoned the industry's traditional humility, for the cigarette companies, beset by critics who claimed that billboards for Camels and other cigarettes were causing children to take up smoking, blushed at the thought of inciting desire. They insisted that advertising could do no more than lead people to switch from one brand to another.

I agreed with the cigarette companies. I had always been as modest as R. J. Reynolds about the power of advertising, but only now do I realize that my modesty and theirs had exactly the same genesis: I, too, wished to be innocent.

When I left the advertising business, I had other work to do, books and essays to write, but I could not rid myself of my own history. Slowly, at first in dreams and then in conversations, I reconsidered who I had been and what I had done.

Why should I lie to you? It is too late for lying. I awakened when I could. I needed the job. I had written a few books and a lot of essays, and they had earned a little money, but never enough to live on. As far as I knew, advertising was the easiest way to earn the most money. I started out in the business in San Francisco, and moved up steadily from full-time to half-time, and then to three hours a day, finally to ten hours a week.

It was not so easy in New York. There was an enormous pool of banality. Talented men and women were willing to work day and night to string together the most interesting and appropriate clichés. I soon realized that as a copywriter I had a fatal flaw: The kind of advertising that made people rich made me laugh. The only way I could survive was to become an executive. It was not as good as working ten hours a week, but it was not nearly so arduous as I had feared. With the lighter workload and shorter hours of a senior officer, I was able to devote most of my energies to literature.

I scheduled my soul. All day I bore the burden of other men's goods. I wanted to be autonomous, but it was not within my grasp: Dignity eluded me. Only the evenings, the silences, were mine. I owned the middle of the night.

The schedule created a confusion of metaphors. I could see clearly in the dark, but not in the day. I was a day sleeper, one of those strange creatures who live in the wrong rhythm. A moral tension arose between the man of the day and the man of the night.

One afternoon at the end of a book promotion tour in Mexico City, the wall of rationalizations that kept day and night apart was breached. I knew by the symptoms that my heart could no longer endure the secret conflict. A few months later, the attack came.

A caress from death should have been the end of innocence, but it was not. Instead, I became interested in death. I thought of its effect on politics. Death became a distraction, another way to avoid waking. Years passed. I gave up my managerial responsibilities, but I remained a day sleeper. Perhaps it was a matter of self-preservation, a way to avoid the end of dreaming, the shock of consciousness. Even after I left the business I did not believe what the rest of the world knew about the work I had done.

The end of innocence came along with the decline of N. W. Ayer and the firing of all but three of the people who had reported to me. It began in a small hearing room in the New York State Department of Employment Building, on 125th Street in Manhattan. A man who had been fired by my successor brought an age discrimination suit against the corporation.

The plaintiff was a pale man, with a cracked voice, balding and bespectacled, a studied eccentric, a Greenwich Village man: self-published poet, accomplished advertising writer, semiprofessional psychotherapist, the proprietor of the scraggles of a beard. He spoke in the precise whine of Brooklyn-born intellectuals. Once, in what must have been another world, he had walked across Europe with a rifle at the ready. This neurosis, formerly a man, had defeated panzer divisions, storm troopers, the invincible Wehrmacht. Now, dressed in his best suit and matching vest, he sought to save the last days and remaining dignity of his life. I was his chief witness, his argument, his hope.

In an age discrimination suit, it is the victim who must prove his case. He becomes a thing, meat hung on the hook of age, frightened, the quarry of the defense lawyers. All the allies of the victim are also suspect; the presumption in such cases is that the great are more righteous than the small.

The corporation's defense lawyer sat opposite me, a sweaty, pock-marked man, a kind of anti-labor lawyer who made his living by defending against age and sex discrimination suits. He had been trained as a prosecutor; now he hunted out the flaws in other men's dreams of justice.

The defense lawyer was flanked by my colleagues. The general counsel of the firm, the man who sat in the office next to mine, whispered advice to the sweaty anti-labor lawyer after every statement I made. They looked to me like lovers, putting their lips to each other's ears, hiding the secret of their intimacy behind a hand. The company lawyer was the more presentable of the two: always suntanned, the breast pocket of his coat filled with a small leather case holding only the best of cigars, this day wearing a blue shirt and a bright bow tie; the Ivy League comes to Broadway. There were many who trusted him; I had been among them.

On the other side of the defense lawyer sat my successor. A mechanical man, his face was the color of lead. In suggesting him for the job, I had made the common manager's mistake, choosing an unspectacular successor, one who would fail slowly in the job. He would be a monument to me, my ego whispered, something gray and stony, like a marker in the graveyard grass. So I was surprised by his penchant for assassination, the cruelty of it, and I sided with the victim against the firm.

The dispute was over ethics, not business. Nevertheless, I had to explain the nature of the work the man had done and how I had judged his performance. I was asked, under oath, to define my terms. Nothing could have been more demanding. The most adept of self-deceivers cannot cheat on such a test.

The hearing room was so bare, the questions so homely, the face of the man who had been fired so flaccid with shame, that illusion deserted me; the writer could no longer lie about the day sleeper. In the middle of my middle age, I opened my eyes and saw.

2.

It is nearly half a century since Arthur Miller invited us inside the soul of Willy Loman, there to weep at the tragedy of the common man. The play seems dated, vaguely comic now, not because of the language or the setting or the illusions of the hero; it is Willy's work that mocks him. *Death of a Salesman,* first produced in 1949, was still dramatically and sociologically a Depression play. America had become another country by the time Miller's play was presented, and it has become yet another country since then; no one would weep for such a salesman now.

The good man who knew his line and sold it well in three states or five, traveling in snow or rain, dragging sample cases that strained his back and required too much of his will, is gone now. The anachronism is not his velvet slippers or the parlor car of the overnight train to somewhere, it is the salesman himself; salesmen have come to power now, and a salesman in power cannot be granted a soul.

Willy Loman was a man of many flaws, the salesman as drone and dreamer, and then, in defeat, the dreamer lost to dreaming. Willy lacked style; he spoke like a man with gray stubble on his cheeks; he lived within sight of Manhattan. Willy was a dramatic problem: He was not an admirable man, and he did not work in an admirable profession. Miller was so concerned with this deviation from the idea of tragedy prescribed by Aristotle that he wrote an essay entitled "The Tragedy of the Common Man" to preface one edition of the play.

What if the salesman were a different sort of man, the antithesis of Willy Loman? Not a common man, an extraordinary one. It is possible, even likely. Salesmen are interesting people, more so than most, for almost every salesman is a psychologist and a polymath.

If salesmen were uncommon, charming, highly educated, well-traveled, truly attractive persons, what would the world think? Would e. e. cummings have said that a salesman is an "it that stinks"? Would the world, in all its cruel ways, both subtle and profound, still disdain all but the most successful salesmen?

The test of a theory is in use: At the other end of the salesman's world, in dreams at the farthest remove from Willy Loman or the metal siding and real estate hucksters of popular films, lives Tanya Rhinelander, who sells mansions beside the sea in Newport, Rhode Island. She is the inheritor of a Tolstoyan love story, the granddaughter of a Norwegian military officer who left his commission and his country to become a czarist general, all for the love of a Russian woman. A portrait of the general, dressed in white Russian splendor, looks over his granddaughter when she sits at the small writing desk in a corner of her living room.

Tanya Rhinelander was widowed recently; her children are grown and long ago moved on to their own lives. She looks more Russian now, a woman of high-fashion cheekbones who plays tennis on the hottest days and swims in the bracing autumn surf; she carries herself as if she still danced. Although her speech drawls through clenched teeth in the style associated with the best private schools, it has a directness that seems out of place among the drunks and miscreants of Newport's social world. So Mrs. Rhinelander is elegant, very good-looking, an émigré Scheherazade with only a hint of the Russian general's steely resolve underlying her perfect manners, and she sells real estate.

While it was a foregone conclusion that Land's End, the great house and grounds that had once belonged to Edith Wharton, would be sold by Mrs. Rhinelander, the general's granddaughter must sell other houses as well. She takes her turn answering the telephone at the real estate office and serving the customers who come in off the street.

"I'm not bothered in the slightest by being a salesperson," she said at the beginning of our conversation. She had taken up the work in 1978 when her late husband retired and they began to live year-round in Newport. It seemed natural enough to her, for over the years she had sold some of the houses the family had lived in. She quickly grasped the essence of selling, which was "to show the house to its best advantage." When her first customer saw the dirt floor in the basement of the house she was showing, Tanya responded immediately, "Oh, good, you can grow mushrooms." The man, who she said had a sense of humor, eventually bought a house from her.

But the customers were not all like the man who laughed about mushrooms. Although her circle is wide, she does not sell houses only to friends or acquaintances. "People don't think much of real estate brokers," she said. "They treat brokers sometimes less graciously than other professions. Since people do not pay you until a deal closes, there are those who don't show up for appointments, who run you around.

"The majority of the time people are agreeable to deal with, but there are some very trying times. People can be quite rude."

At that moment the eyes of the general's granddaughter, looking out over enviable cheekbones, glisten. The focus shifts, as if to other rooms, to the doorman/prince, the countess in the chorus, Anastasia. For no longer than it takes to raise a glass of cold white wine or administer caviar to a cracker, the aristocratic mettle fails, she is betrayed by anguish, a nineteenth-century heroine. Then without so much as a sigh, she overcomes the opinions of the impersonal world and laughs; the focus returns to this time and place; she is once again in command.

3.

If the elegant émigré of Newport and Willy Loman, the suicide from Brooklyn, are viewed by the dispassionate world of strangers as similarly undeserving of fully human status, if one can be rude to her as well as to him, it is because the world does not judge the person who sells as if he or she were a human being. Selling, the role of salesman, must have another meaning; it must have become a sign so powerful that any person, no matter how elegant or tragic, can be subsumed under it.

What meaning can it have taken on? How can an act so common, the most ordinary business of daily life, have become more powerful than a person in all of his or her human complexity? We may differ from Tanya or Willy or both by class, speech, education, and so on, but we care about them. They are enough like us that to abandon their humanity would be to abandon our own, to commit ourselves to the most profound loneliness. What could have, in effect, drawn an opaque shade over the reality of them, made them invisible as persons?

Is it the salesmen or the selling that has changed since we cried over Willy's grave? Why is it that we are now so unwilling to forgive the salesman his faults? How did the glad hand, the bad joke, the forced smile, the retread hope of the salesman at his rounds become so distasteful? Or worse, sinister? Why did I, for one, live so many years in the triangle of tension caused by the wedding of the salesman, the artist, and the sleepy whore of self-deception? What's wrong with the salesman? Who may speak about salesmen, or is it possible that only they can speak about each other?

What is a salesman, by whom has he been stripped of his soul, and why? Is the dominance of selling in our time an outgrowth of modern capitalism, or is it unavoidable, an action or interaction close to the core of human nature? These are questions the salesman needs to have answered. But first, we must know who should be included in the category of soulless creatures and what sort of commerce selling has come to be.

What is a sale? And when? Who is a salesman? What power does a salesman exert over us?

In simpler times the definition of *selling* had a certain solidity: In 1050 it was used in England in the sense of "the exchange of a commodity for money or other valuable consideration," according to the *Oxford English*

Dictionary. A millennium or so earlier, the first rabbis to write commentaries on the Old Testament discussed the ethics of the implied contract between the buyer and the seller of real property. Five centuries before the rabbis, Plato spoke of selling in this solid sense, but he also had other ideas about what might be sold. In several of the dialogues Plato tangled with the Sophists over the selling of ideas.

What is the definition now? Was there a great change of circumstances in the middle of the twentieth century, a clamorous, unheard cataclysm that revised the role of the salesman and tinkered with the content of our economic dreams? What did John Kenneth Galbraith mean when he spoke of markets and selling and "The Revised Sequence"?

As I learned in that hearing room almost ten years ago, the most difficult, discomfiting, and important problem for any salesman is to think about selling, to define the term. Only then can one hope to know who is innocent and what is necessary, who is hurt and what is wasted, whether the rise in importance of selling is a phenomenon of the maturing of the corporation or of capitalist society or the manifestation of a profound aspect of human nature. Only then can one begin to examine the place of selling in the culture and the character of the country.

Perhaps it is an unreasonable expectation, but I think this definition of the term can lead to some understanding of an essential aspect of America, for selling has achieved dominion over the world in our time, not only determining the economic spirit of the nation but deeply affecting its social, political, cultural, and moral life.

PART
1

When a salesman comes to

a fork in the road,

he takes both paths.

1

In the Beginning . . .

*Our argument is, in brief, that men have always and everywhere under-
taken the same task, and assigned to themselves the same object; all that
has differed is the means employed.*

—CLAUDE LÉVI-STRAUSS

He was born in Boston, raised in Ohio, started out on his own in California, went broke in Santa Monica, and again in San Diego, and yet again in Santa Barbara, went broke in so many towns named for saints that he swore to himself he'd never do business again with a saint, not as long as he lived. That was when he moved to Texas. He chose Odessa, because a town with a Russian name was about as far from a saint as he could get, and still be in the United States of America.

His first year in Odessa was spent working around the oil fields, but it didn't take him long to figure out that the real money was either in owning oil or in selling to the people in the business. He applied for a loan to open a store, and the local banker known as an easy touch told him, "Son, with your financial record, I wouldn't loan you money for coffee, let alone nine thousand dollars to open a I-talian food store." So he got a job in a retail shop, worked nights and weekends in a drive-in movie theater, and did people's taxes on the side. He worked every minute he could, trying to put together a stake.

In the end, it was the movie theater that turned out to be his luck. The owner developed a liver ailment that left him bright yellow and bedridden, and his wife asked if the young fellow wanted to buy him out. She said they needed a little money down, and a legally binding paper for the rest. The young fellow took her hand in his, they prayed together, and then he wrote a check to bind over the deal until they could see a lawyer.

This all happened in the heyday of the Permian Basin oil fields and the drive-in movies. It was before videotape machines, and the sexual revolution, and the oil glut, and all the other plagues that came to Midland and Odessa, Texas. The drive-in had some wonderful years. He rented the cheapest films, bought the lowest-quality frozen, partially fried chicken, sold greasy chips, stale popcorn, and Pepsi-Cola made with so little syrup that it tasted as bitterplain as seltzer. Nothing mattered to his customers but the darkness and the ability to bring a whole station wagon full of kids to the movies for only two-fifty a car. Drive-ins were for making out and for parents who had more kids than they could afford to love, feed, and leave home alone.

Some pictures drew bigger crowds than others, but he knew it was the drive-in itself that people came for. When they stopped coming, he was surprised; he thought he knew his customers.

Once they stopped, nothing short of first-run pictures would bring them back, and the rentals on those pictures were out of reach for a drive-in. He ran sales: free Pepsi with every large box of popcorn, a free hot dog for the head of the family. He booked "spicy" pictures, monster festivals, nostalgia nights. Nothing worked. He cut the schedule down to weekends only, and when the weekends went sour, he went to the hardware store and bought two pasteboard signs that said CLOSED.

For several months after the closing of the drive-in, he stayed in his house, thinking about what to do. The land wasn't worth much; he'd bought it without the mineral rights. The tiny, low-power transmitter that sent the sound to car radios wasn't worth much either. The trades were full of auctions of fryers and popcorn machines and hot dog cookers and freezers and coolers.

"Apocalypse now," he remarked to his wife, who was one of the few natives in a town full of roustabouts and carpetbaggers.

"Shame on you, making jokes about the Lord's work," she replied.

He thought nothing of it. He heard a screen door flapping in the wind, the godforsaken sound of spring in West Texas. Signs creaked. Dust rose like brown mountains on the horizon, threatening tornadoes. The house trembled in the wind. His wife read her Hal Lindsey books and listened to Jerry Falwell, Rex Humbard, Jimmy Swaggart, Pat Robertson, Kenneth Copeland, and Lindsey himself.

"If this isn't the end of the world," he told her, "you can sure see it from here."

"Yes, I can," she said.

At that moment something drew him out of the house into the premillennial wind. He stood with his eyes squinted against the stinging dust, watching all the loose things of the land gathered up by the wind, like a nuclear wind, his wife had said, like the wind of Armageddon. He heard or felt a calling, like a dream, a voice on the wind. It was as the sky clearing at the end of a storm. A reprieve, sunlight, a foretaste of rapture. He knew exactly what to do.

Seven weeks later the ads broke in the Midland/Odessa newspapers, and the radio announcements started everywhere, even on the big, hundred-thousand-watter out of Del Rio. He built a stage in front of the screen, and booked the reopening for a Wednesday night. The first cars came long before sundown. He had never before seen so many cars or such hungry people in his theater. After he blinked the lights in the snack bar to signal the start of the show, he and his wife pulled the chips and chicken out of the grease, turned off the popcorn machine, and leaned against the back wall of the snack bar to watch.

A tall, thin man, with a face as sharp as a sickle, mounted the platform, while the chorus sang and the organ played on all the car radios in every row in the brand-new, all redone, completely repainted drive-in theater. When the tall man, the Reverend Elijah Davey, reached his mark on the stage, three spotlights came on, and a triplicate shadow, twenty-one feet high, appeared on the screen.

Davey waited while the last few people hurried out of the snack bar, trailing their children behind them. The sound of the organ and the chorus faded, and there was silence in all the cars save for the sound of a child singing softly somewhere near the exit road. Davey raised his arm high and closed his fist as if he could hold the breath of the crowd in his hand.

"Jesus will win!" he shouted. And softly said again, "Jesus will win."

Another silence. Not so profound. The fist opened, the arm fell. Murmurings rose into the floodlit Texas night. It was history, everyone knew, the first words ever spoken in the first American Drive-in Church of the Awakening.

Far from the stage, at the very back of the lot, inside the bunkerlike cement block building that housed the projection room and snack bar, the owner put his arm around his wife's shoulders. His back was straight, his shoulders square; his eyes were blue and clear.

While the vats of grease crackled beneath the upraised baskets filled with half-cooked breaded chicken and french fries and the orange juice machine slowly stirred the mass of pulp and water, the owner said, " 'I'd like to sing a song of great social and political import.' "

"A religious song?" his wife asked, turning her face up to him.

He saw a solemn West Texas woman, with high cheekbones and eyes that narrowed slightly, squinting, the mark of generations born and raised in the relentless seasons of dust and sun. Her hair was pulled down and back over her ears and tied with a ribbon at the nape of her neck. She wore her snack bar duty clothes: a cotton print dress that zipped up the front, an apron with a picture of a drilling rig printed across the bib, and a pair of black fabric two-dollar-and-ninety-five-cent shoes imported from China.

"Oh, yes," he answered, and bent to touch his lips to her forehead, which he found damp and slightly cool. She smiled at the gesture. Her mouth was thin and long, the color of a newly healed wound. Wisps of hair fell across her cheek, pale renegades, the universal sign of a woman who does hard work.

He sang in imitation of the famous bourbon and hunger twang:

Oh, Lord, won't you buy me a Mercedes-Benz?

My friends all drive Porsches; I must make a-mends.

Worked hard all my lifetime; no help from my friends.

So, Lord, won't you buy me a Mercedes-Benz?

"You mustn't make fun of a preacher," his wife said. "It will bring bad luck on us."

"That was Janis Joplin. I thought you'd recognize it."

"She was a drunk and a dope fiend, and I do not approve of singing her songs while a man is preaching."

Outside, in the lot, people had begun to get out of their cars and climb up onto the hoods and fenders to get a closer look at the Reverend Elijah Davey, to be able to respond to him without the impediment of a windshield.

The owner and his wife remained inside the snack bar. Through the tiny front windows they saw someone in a heavy-looking wheelchair being lifted down from the bed of a pickup truck. Three men struggled with the chair as it came sliding down the angled truckbed, over the gate, suddenly resting in their arms. One man seemed to stumble. They rocked back and forth under the weight, an indecisive, shadowy six-legged beast.

Children came running to use the toilets on either side of the snack bar building. The owner and his wife could hear the parents hushing them, hurrying them. The fat sizzled in the vats, the slowly turning blade roiled the orange juice in its glass container, the popcorn machine was primed and waiting, the refrigerators hummed, the coffee pots simmered. Davey had promised them a two-stage program, a snack bar break before the laying on of hands.

" 'Oh, Lord, won't you buy me a Mercedes-Benz,' " the owner sang to his wife, holding his arm around her shoulder, pulling her close to him.

"He's talking about Jesus, darling. You ought to show some respect."

" 'My friends all drive Porsches; I must make a-mends . . .' "

"The Lord punishes the greedy."

"Yes, ma'am, he sends them straight to the Fortune 500."

She stepped out from under his arm, and moved toward the cooking table, where the vats of cooking grease bubbled over the heat. "Where you going?" he asked. "We didn't get the sign from Davey."

"Oh, my darling, I have received a sign. I know what to do."

"Don't overcook the chicken."

"I won't."

While he watched, she took a pot holder in each hand, and lifted up the front end of the vat that held the cooking grease. The fluid rushed to the back, spilled over onto the stainless steel tabletop, and poured slowly down into the flame below. It caught fire in a rush, a big breath of flame billowing up, almost blowing itself out. An instant later the grease that was left in the vat caught fire. It spread to the vat next to it, and on down the line until all three vats were blazing. It happened so fast she barely had time to jump out of the way.

The plastic countertop curled up from the heat and made an ugly stench. The plastic spoons, forks, and knives curled up, too. She watched for a while before she walked out the side door into the lot to attend the revival. He emptied the fire extinguisher on the burning fat, but it was no use. He tossed the empty red canister into a corner, and went outside to stand beside her. The fire department was over on the other side of town, too far from the drive-in to do any good. They didn't even bother to call.

After the heat of the fire melted the wiring inside the snack shack and projection building, the lights went out and the microphone died. Then the people turned on their headlights to illuminate the stage, and they all got out of their cars and crowded around the platform in front of the screen to listen to the Reverend Davey Elijah preach the gospel. Later, many men joined together to lift the heavy wheelchair up onto the stage for the laying on of hands.

1.

A journey in search of the salesman sounds like a fool's errand. After all, this is America. One has only to wait for a little while, a few minutes, an hour at most, and a salesman will call. If the doorbell or the telephone does not ring to announce his arrival in person, he will appear on television or in the newspaper. The statisticians say that the average American is exposed to more than three thousand sales messages a day.

The problem with sitting still and waiting for the salesman to appear is that all the salesmen who come calling will have a message and a method derived from the situation in which they live; that is, they will be contingent upon this time and place. Any attempt to understand them, to gauge their worth, even to define their utility, let alone their necessity, will lead to examining their circumstances. What are the current economic conditions? How has technology affected the sales presentation? Do government regulatory agencies determine the ethical aspects of selling? And so on.

Without something to compare to the real estate hustler who telephoned during dinner or the insurance company representative who arrived just as dessert was served or the constant deluge of salesmen known as advertisements, thinking about the salesman becomes so mired in the moment that the archetype is lost. A human being, that muddy metaphor, possibly indicative of some aspect of the times, appears in his place. More than a single comparative will be necessary to isolate the salesman from contingency; all the qualities that describe a person in his time and place will have to be stripped away, otherwise we will have to begin in medias res, with our eyes focused on our desires and our hands on our wallets.

History provides several kinds of comparatives, but not all. It is based on recorded materials, still mainly written, and it is, by definition, chronological, the relation of incidents as they occurred in the order of time. Viewed historically, the salesman remains in his contingent role, and the change in that role over hundreds of years may reveal less about the salesman than about the society in which he operates. For example, mass-marketing techniques were a result of the improvement in the distribution of goods (railroads, packaging) and information (the web offset press) rather than a change in the aims or character of the salesman of the late nineteenth century. History will be important, of course, but it will not be the most direct path to the nature of selling and the salesman.

The comparative method favored by structural anthropologists depends largely on material that is either prehistorical or ahistorical, and it is based more on words, stories, and relationships than on facts. They devote much of their work to the study of myths and stories, comparing myths of one culture to those of another, moving outward from similar or related cultures to entirely separate cultures having no contact with each other and speaking mutually unintelligible languages.

By interpreting myths comparatively, the structural anthropologists hope to find something that applies to many cultures, abstract it, and arrive at a deeper meaning, perhaps a universal meaning, which can then be used to discover more about man.

By using some of the disciplines of this "science of myths" to think about the role of the salesman, it may be possible to discover a quality of selling that is common across time, distance, and cultural difference. A great journey will be necessary, however, for the examples lie beyond history, in the high desert of Arizona, the garden palaces between the Tigris and the Euphrates, the mountains of Mexico, the foothills of Olympus, the endless grasslands of unspoiled North America, and in Eden.

The goal of the journey is to discover those qualities of the salesman in one culture which can also be found in others, eventually to strip away all the influences of unique cultures and their histories so that the act of selling per se and the role of the salesman in society can be examined. The best place to begin is at the beginning. According to the people who coined the word, *paradise* denotes a garden or an orchard with a wall around it, making it easy to get a fix on someone there. And being paradise, it is a nice place to start.

There was a salesman in paradise. It does not matter whose paradise:

Eden, the Sumerian paradise of Gilgamesh, Quetzalcóatl's Tula, the Golden Age of Greece, or the American Southwest. Nor does it matter by what name the salesman is known—trickster, devil, courtesan, culture bearer, merchant, god. Human life always begins in paradise, and there is always a salesman involved in the conversion of the world from myth to historical reality. The salesman may be male or female, good or bad, human or animal, with or without godlike powers. There are many ambiguities in paradise, but there is always a salesman.

In paradise, salesmen have these qualities in common:

They speak.

They influence others to act, but do not themselves participate in the action.

They have the advantage of superior knowledge; that is, they know more about others than others know about them.

They know a great deal about the world of things.

They are privy, either through observation, interrogation, or intuition, to the deepest desires of others.

And they are always outsiders, floaters, wanderers, creatures without roots, more act than substance.

However, these early practitioners bear little resemblance, in their particulars, to the salesman who telephone during the dinner hour with a once-in-a-lifetime chance to own a retirement home in Florida. There was no winter in paradise. And no money, no concept of property, not even anything to barter: no cloth to exchange for food, no beads with which to buy an island. Even if there had been a concept of property, a market would have been impossible in paradise; since nothing material was lacking, there was no demand for goods. Paradise predates economics. Nevertheless, a salesman always worked the territory.

The salesman most familiar to the Western mind lived in Eden. This is who his customers were and how he worked, according to the Old Testament:

> The Lord God took the man and put him in the garden of Eden to till it and keep it. And the Lord God commanded the man, saying, "You may freely eat of every tree of the garden; but of the tree of the knowledge of good and evil you shall not eat, for in the day that you eat of it you shall die.". . .
>
> . . . the man and his wife were both naked, and were not ashamed.

Now the serpent was more subtle than any other wild creature the Lord God had made. He said to the woman, "Did God say, 'You shall not eat of any tree in the garden?' " And the woman said to the serpent, "We may eat of the fruit of the trees in the garden; but God said, 'You shall not eat of the fruit of the tree which is in the midst of the garden, neither shall you touch it, lest you die.' " But the serpent said to the woman, "You will not die. For God knows that when you eat of it your eyes will be opened, and you will be like God, knowing good from evil." So when the woman saw that the tree was good for food, and that it was a delight to the eyes, and that the tree was to be desired to make one wise, she took of its fruit and ate; and she also gave some to her husband, and he ate. Then the eyes of both were opened, and they knew that they were naked; and they sewed fig leaves together and made themselves aprons.

And they heard the sound of the Lord God Yahweh walking in the garden in the cool of the day, and the man and his wife hid themselves from the presence of the Lord God among the trees of the garden. But the Lord God called to the man, and said to him, "Where are you?" And he said, "I heard the sound of thee in the garden, and I was afraid because I was naked, and I hid myself." He said, "Who told you that you were naked? Have you eaten of the tree of which I commanded you not to eat?" The man said, "The woman whom thou gavest to be with me, she gave me fruit of the tree, and I ate." Then the Lord God said to the woman, "What is this that you have done?" The woman said, "The serpent beguiled me, and I ate." The Lord God said to the serpent,

> *"Because you have done this,*
> *cursed are you above all cattle,*
> *and above all wild animals;*
> *Upon your belly shall you go,*
> *and dust you shall eat*
> *all the days of your life."*

In verses 16–23 the authors of Genesis go on to tell of the punishments humans will have to endure: the pain of childbearing, the attraction of sex, a life of toil—exile from paradise.

Few passages in the Old Testament have engendered more exegesis

37

than the incident in Eden. In the more or less standard interpretation, the eating of the Tree of Knowledge is a fall from a state of grace. But there is another view, expressed by the twelfth-century physician and philosopher Moses Maimonides, a Jew whose readings of Aristotle had a great influence on the Scholastics. Maimonides understood knowledge as the connection between God and man. In such a decidedly Greek view of the temptation, the serpent becomes a culture bearer, more like Prometheus than like Satan.

No matter which interpretation of the incident obtains, the serpent plays the same structural role. *The Oxford Annotated Bible* says in its comment, "The temptation begins with the insinuation of doubt, increases as suspicion is cast upon God's motive, and becomes irresistible when the couple sense the possibilities of freedom."

In Eden, the salesman affected both the customer (Eve), by changing her perception of God's prohibition, and the product (knowledge), by describing its most desirable attribute: ". . . you will be like God. . . ." Without the action (in the form of speech) of the salesman, there would have been no connection between Eve and the prohibited fruit.

Did the serpent tell the truth? Yes and no. Eve did not die immediately after eating the fruit of the tree. That much was true. There was no lie of commission. On the other hand, the serpent did not tell her the cost of tasting the fruit: He said nothing about the life of an exile from paradise, made no mention of the pain of childbirth or the daily life of toil.

Was the serpent the possessor of superior information? Without question: Eve did not die on the day she ate the fruit of the tree. Did he know a great deal about her? The story gives us no indication that they knew each other prior to the temptation, yet the serpent understood enough about his customer's desires to tempt her into breaking the divine prohibition.

The verb traditionally used to describe the serpent's work is *beguile*, but *The Anchor Bible*,[1] which calls upon many sources and seeks accuracy before beauty in its translation, says that the serpent "tricked" Eve. Was it a trick or a sale? If the serpent intended to beguile, trick, or make a sale to Eve, why did he do it? No motive is attributed to the serpent by the authors of Genesis; he gained nothing and the only real punishment meted out to him was low status. The serpent, the salesman in paradise, affected others far more than he was affected. He was not the subject, nor was he the object. Nevertheless, he was and is vital. He was instrumental—the verb of civiliza-

[1] *Genesis,* ed. E. A. Speiser, 3d ed. (Garden City, N.Y.: Doubleday, 1980).

tion. Without the serpent/trickster/salesman, knowledge would have been withheld forever from the creatures God made in his image. Nothing could have changed in Eden or beyond without the salesman; he is the one who incites desire and enhances possibility—the ugly optimist in paradise.

2.

If Eden were the only paradise and the serpent the only trickster/salesman, it would be difficult to isolate him from the contingency of his author, but there were many Edens, and each one had its salesman. On the east, in the Sumerian Gilgamesh epic the wild man Enkidu is tempted into civilized life by a courtesan. The entire story of Eden, including a troublemaking serpent, appears in various parts of the epic, but the most revealing part is about Enkidu, a strange creature, who becomes civilized, dies, and then returns—a living man who has been dead.

In this last respect, he bears a strong resemblance to the tricksters of North America (coyote, raven, and crow), but to recognize the relationship it is necessary to peel the myths down to their structures.

Paul Radin and Claude Lévi-Strauss, among others, say that coyote and raven, all the tricksters, are mediators between life and death. Their thinking requires just a bit of an intellectual leap of faith, but it provides a fascinating way to look at a true commonplace of culture. Their conclusion is based on the role of these creatures in the real world, where they are scavengers, eaters of carrion. They do not kill, but they eat flesh. Coyote, raven, and their human and animal cousins exist in the world between the hunters and herbivores, between the killers and their prey, between life and death.

The trickster of the Middle East is the snake, a creature of many mediating attributes: It exists between the kingdoms of the oviparous and the viviparous and between the living and the dead. The snake lays eggs, but holds them inside its body until they hatch, and then gives birth to live offspring. At least once a year, snakes shed their skin, appearing to die and be reborn.

Greek and Aztec myths, which come later in the development of human societies, or as Rousseau would have it, further on in the journey from the youth of the world to its decrepitude, make use of gods rather than animals. The Aztec trickster, Tezcatlipoca (Smoking Mirror, also known as the Blue Hummingbird of the South), is the ultimate mediator; he is a creature of both nightmare and reality, a mediator between night and day, this world and the other. The Greek Prometheus is described in the *Oxford Classical Dictionary* as "the supreme trickster," but that is the early Prometheus, the one we read about in Hesiod. The later version, the one told by Aeschylus, presents the noble culture bearer who is made to suffer for bringing the gift of fire to man.

Every trickster is a mediator of one kind or another.[2] He lives "between," he makes things happen, he is a cause as well as a connection. In fact, mediation is the defining quality of the trickster. He, she, or it connects polarities, whatever they may be: life and death, day and night, innocence and knowledge, myth and reality, timelessness and history, speech and beastliness, god and man, good and evil, subject and object.

In myths and stories tricksters always know the desires of their subjects, but they cannot divine their responses, which may take the form of rage or even of countermeasures that prove disastrous to the trickster. No other insight is available to the trickster. The outcome of the trick, good or bad, is beyond his imagination.[3] Forethought (the meaning of Prometheus) is a matter of the trickster's planning one move ahead of his opponent, not of consideration of the ethical and social consequences of his actions. It is not by accident that neither Prometheus nor the serpent of Eden gets away with his trick. Tricksters can foresee nothing beyond the desires of their customers; they have no other advantage in the world; they are merely the oracles of desire.

In most myths the trickster connects desire directly to an object. It can be as simple as dinner or as encompassing as knowledge. Often the desirous

---

[2]   The idea that the trickster/salesman uses mediating techniques is not limited to the arcane world of structural anthroplogists; salesmen and felons also understand the practice. In testimony before a federal judge, Michael Milken described junk bonds as a " 'mediating force' that 'reduced the volatility of the marketplace.' " Quoted by James B. Stewart in the *New Yorker,* March 8, 1993.

[3]   This failure to anticipate the outcome of a trick (or sale) is not limited to the coyotes and ravens of myth. In 1993 the Maytag Corporation in England fired three of its top executives after they lost millions in two separate merchandise promotions. The first offered two round-trip tickets to Europe to purchasers of $150 (U.S.) of goods. Apparently unwilling to learn from experience, they then offered two round-trip tickets to New York or Orlando for purchases of $375 or more. The more they sold, the more money they lost.

The *New York Times* (March 31, 1993) estimated that one of every three hundred persons in Britain and Ireland tried to take advantage of the offer, which resulted in the company's having to take a $48.8 million charge against earnings.

---

one, the subject, has no object in mind, no dinner, no gem, no fact or idea. There is nothing but desire, the potential for action. It then falls to the trickster to understand the other person's desire so perfectly that he can choose the object, which may be new or old; a great cultural advance, like writing or fire; or a fall into taboo behavior, like incest. The intellectual burden upon the trickster is a dual one: He must know both desire and the world, for he must be able to choose the one object that can best satisfy desire.

When the object is as pleasant and familiar as a bunch of grapes or a good night's sleep, the trickster has only to present it, but he does not always have that luxury. The object is often new or dangerous (prohibited by the gods). Then the other quality of the trickster comes into play: language, the sine qua non of selling. The trickster must use language to influence either the object or the desirous creature or both in order to make the connection between them.

Although it might seem unlikely that words could influence an object, they do so indirectly by changing what is known about the object. For example, a person confronting a lobster for the first time might not be interested in eating the beast without some mediator to explain how anything that looks so bad could taste so good. Similarly, fire was to be feared only until Prometheus brought man the ability to control it, putting its powers to his own use.

When the trickster plays this role of culture bearer, either directly or indirectly, he serves as the link between the timeless "youth of the world" and history, like the hero twins of the Maya who mediate between the living and the dead, this world and the underworld, in the Popol Vuh. The eloquent, immortal salesman breaks the circle of paradise and sets in motion the endless series of changes known as progress or civilization.

Can that be the reason why tricksters are so often punished? Is there an ethics of mediation? A moral bias in favor of primitivism or the status quo? Or is the trickster punished for more ordinary transgressions, simply for being a trickster, one who beguiles others?

The answer lies in what Lévi-Strauss calls "the ambiguous character of the trickster." He may be good or bad, but he is always a mediator. Human thinking appears to require a mediating structure to enable the mind to deal with contradiction. No moral content is required or even implied. It is added—tacked on or wrapped around the structure—much later, if at all.

Ethics belongs in the realm of the contingent. The trickster, the instrument of mediation, exists at the level of necessity. Every act of the trickster is open to interpretation: The serpent brings about the fall from grace, *or* the serpent brings about civilization. But there must be a serpent, a mediator who causes the move from paradise to civilization.

After paradise, in the modern, economical world, the trickster becomes the salesman. But a trick is still a trick. The methods of the trickster/salesman pass virtually unchanged from one world to the next: neolithic to modern, primitive to civilized, paradise to property. Culture changes; the mind, which determines the nature of man, remains. The function of the trickster/salesman is a vital part of human society now, as it has been since the dawn of language.

To condemn the act of selling in all of its various forms would be tantamount to condemning human thinking and the society that springs from it. Without the function of the mediator/trickster/salesman, society would have been forced to develop along different, practically unimaginable lines, if society without the salesman's function were possible at all. There had to be a bridge, an active way to connect the contradictions of life, and no human activity is more closely allied to the building of bridges than a sale; it is the process that enables those without courage to make discoveries, the social miracle that makes alien perceptions into familiar faces. And to make a sale, there must be a salesman.

Since paradise the salesman has always been unlike all the other creatures of earth and imagination. He does not sow and he does not hunt; nevertheless, he eats. He is the creature who succeeds by guile, the trickster, the outside force who causes actions in which he has no stake.[4] He is neither subject nor object, a middle without substance, the place beyond gravity; neither the maker nor the consumer, pure communication, the cost of living a human life.

No one can judge the function of the salesman, as no one can judge nature; he is. But the quantity and the cost of selling can be considered: The most significant observation in this book is that a nation in which some salesmen necessarily live and work is not the same as a nation of salesmen.

---

[4] Aristotle, *Rhetoric,* bk. 1, chap. 2, defines rhetoric as "the faculty of observing in any given case the available means of persuasion," while "every other art can instruct or persuade about its own particular subject matter."

2

Masters of
Perception

*Let us . . . lay it down that there is no
single thing that is in and by itself.*

—PLATO

*They said, "You have a blue guitar,
You do not play things as they are."*

*The man replied, "Things as they are
Are changed upon the blue guitar."*

—WALLACE STEVENS

*A consumption economy . . . finds its
reality in appearances.*

—DANIEL BELL

The salesman was not unconscious. Out of the corner of one eye, he observed the young man. He had been watching him for days, since the young man first came into his room to disturb the tranquillity with his loud voice, his telephone, his incessant visitors, their laughter, their filthy exchanges of intimacies, and their cruel comments about the old man who lay so still and silent, his only signs of life the whine of his exhalations and the stenches that rose from his body, suffusing the room.

One evening, after the young man's friends had gone home for the night, leaving behind empty cups, cans, balls of crumpled paper, a string of ribbon for someone to trip on, crusts, crumbs, rinds, peels, seeds, and scraps, the old salesman lay still and stinking, studying his roommate. He was not even thirty years old, the salesman thought, a boy, a kid, an embryo. Yes, in terms of life, an embryo.

At ten o'clock, as always, the lights went out, but the glow from the corridor enabled the salesman to continue his observation. The young man also lay still, in the first depths of sleep. From a distance, the sounds of institutional routine came softly to the old salesman, clangs and squawks, incomprehensible voices, arias of laughter.

The voice of his visitor surprised the salesman. It came from behind him, somewhere in the darkness between the bed and the wall. The old salesman considered the effort it would take to turn onto his back and then turn his head to the side to enable him to see the person who spoke. It was more than he cared to undertake at the moment. He was left to imagine the visitor there beside his bed, a stealthy person or shy—perhaps a man, perhaps a woman; with some voices it is hard to tell.

"I know who you are," the salesman said or thought. Was it words or a variation in the whine of his breath?

"I hear you," the visitor said.

"Of course you do. And don't try to put one over on me. A salesman knows his customers."

"Very good," the visitor said, "then we can get on with our business."

"Sorry. I'm not interested."

"I can't take no for an answer."

"Listen to me: Nobody's easier to sell than a salesman, but a bully is never a closer. Take my word for it."

The visitor sighed. The salesman felt a chill. "I'm Death," the visitor said.

"I'm Leo."

"I've come for you."

The salesman spat out a sound, as if he had been punched in the gut. "I don't think so," he said. "You're a person of taste, refined; I can tell by the way you talk. Why would you settle for a miserable old man like me? Look over there, to my right. There's a prize! Go ahead, don't be shy. Walk over, take a look. It can't hurt, won't cost you a thing. Maybe you'll decide it's not for you. But listen to me: If you don't look, you'll always wonder, 'Did I do the right thing? Did I make the right choice?' "

The visitor made no response.

"I'm right, aren't I?" the salesman said. "Take a look; that's all I ask you to do. Compare! Comparison proves.

"Let me give you a for instance. Arms. What could be simpler than arms? Is this what you want, this flabby arm, this soft flesh, these bones without strength, these nerves—they don't feel, constricted arteries, exhausted veins? Or is it that other arm that pleases you? The smooth, muscular arm, the supple arm, the oiled joints, the fingers without a mark on them, the sensitive nerves, the exuberant blood."

"It is not a question of aesthetics," the visitor said.

"Of course not! Did I speak of aesthetics? Would I approach a practical person like you with foppish considerations? I know my customers, your worldliness, practicality, sound-as-a-Deutschmark sense of values. Which is why I point out these differences.

"Value! A person like you knows a good value. And I point to it, sleeping there, sleeping soundly there, breathing evenly, slowly, every cell a miracle, a perfect example of physiological integrity. And what a heart! Oh, what a heart! Great heart! Listen to it! Hear perfection; in the young the heart produces a melody.

"Or would you prefer a bag of gas, half a kidney, my misfiring heart? Put aside all questions of beauty, please. Examine the fluids of our bodies, compare us cell for cell. Do not be charitable; it's not called for here. Put yourself first; that's all I ask. Insist upon quality, never settle for anything less than the best. Follow that simple rule, and, believe me, you'll never go wrong."

The salesman lay quietly for a while, exhausted by the effort of his declamation. He opened his eyes and observed the young man again. In the faint light, he could see that the body of the young man twitched and turned, as if it were being examined.

It occurred to the old salesman that he had not heard from his visitor for some time. This was not good news, not to a man who knew how to close a sale. Leave a customer to think it over, and nine times out of ten the sale is lost.

Although the hour was late and he was very tired, the salesman knew what he had to do. He pushed and strained, he cranked up the ancient machine of his body, roiling his gut until the gases and fluids came pouring forth: gouts of bile, streams of feces, steaming sick urine, black mucus, gastric acids meant to devour flesh, even tears; and through it all the blurts and booms and whistlings of the gases of his belly and his rotted bowels. He floated in his own excretions, groaning and gurgling in the puddling muck that had come from the ruin of his body. And he was pleased, for he had made himself the unloveliest thing alive. He was still a closer.

1.

At the beginning of the 1990s, a series of strange, philosophical television commercials was broadcast in the eastern United States. All of the commercials concluded with the same statement:

Honda. The car that sells itself.

Of course, a commercial that sells the car that sells itself is a problem in logic or ethics. It is either self-contradictory or a lie. But the question raised by the illogical philosophers at Honda's advertising agency is not so easily dismissed. Can anything sell itself?

What would be required? And if not a Honda, then a pot, a knife, a spoon, a loaf of bread, a pinch of salt, water in a plastic jug! There must be something that can sell itself. Or do we live in a world we cannot ever hope to know? Does nothing speak to us? We have our senses, after all.

Or do we?

Listen to Montaigne. He begins by quoting Lucretius: "Our very life would fall, unless we dare to trust our senses. . . ." And then he goes on to argue,

> In case what the Epicureans say is true, to wit, that we have no knowledge if the appearances of the senses are false; and if what the Stoics say is also true, that the appearances of the senses are so false that they can produce no knowledge for us; we shall conclude, at the expense of these two great dogmatic sects, that there is no knowledge.
>
> As for the error and uncertainty of the operation of the senses, each man can furnish himself with as many examples as he pleases, so ordinary are the mistakes and deceptions that they offer us.

Montaigne is not so good a philosopher as the authors of the Honda commercial, for skeptics never seem to have the diligence to get to the bottom of things, but he does take the question one step closer to the raison d'être, as he might have said, of the salesman in the world of human commerce.

The salesman is a response, although not necessarily a solution, to the problem noted by Montaigne. Imagine! If Montaigne were wrong and the world were exactly as it appears to us, things could and would truly "sell themselves." In such a *known* world, no salesman could lie successfully, because every customer would know the truth about a product by its appearance. On the other hand, a salesman who told the truth would add nothing to the customer's knowledge of the product. The salesman would have no function.

A world without salesmen: The Honda commercial implies that it would be paradise. But even in paradise appearance and reality were not the same. The problem in Eden was that Eve did not know the reality of the fruit of the Tree of Knowledge by its appearance. God had to tell her something about it, then the serpent/salesman had to come along to help her get a fuller understanding. Appearance, Eve learned, was not the same as reality, nor was reality quite as advertised. Perhaps one of the intentions of the author of the myth of Eden was to advise the ancient Hebrews of that notion about appearance and reality expressed in our time as *caveat emptor*.

Since virtually everything about salesmen and selling grows out of the difference between appearance and reality, it is worth examining some other ideas on the subject. On the west side of Eden, the Greeks developed the tools of philosophy in large measure to examine the question of appearance and reality.[1] By the time Plato wrote the *Theaetetus* and the *Sophist*,[2] there was already a large and growing body of thought on the subject. Heraclitus, Parmenides, Protagoras, Democritus, and others wrestled with the reliability of the senses, the mind, and even the stability of the world itself. Heraclitus said that a person couldn't step into the same stream twice. Protagoras declared that "man is the measure of all things."

Plato agreed with Heraclitus that the world was constantly in flux. He also agreed with the skeptical view of perception that Protagoras and the Sophists preferred. This put him in an exceedingly difficult position: If the thing perceived was constantly changing and each perceiver brought something different to his perception,[3] what could be known? It was, as he said, a

---

[1]   "This sense of wonder is the mark of the philosopher. Philosophy indeed has no other origin, and he was a good genealogist who made Iris the daughter of Thaumas." Plato, *Theaetetus*. Iris (rainbow) is the messenger of the gods in Greek mythology. Thaumas is the goddess of wonder.

[2]   The late dialogues gathered, translated, and annotated by Francis M. Cornford under the title *Plato's Theory of Knowledge* (Indianapolis: Bobbs-Merrill, 1957).

[3]   The famous example of the different taste of the same wine on the palate of a sick man compared to one who is well.

world of shadows. Only the eternal forms, ideas extracted from the immortal soul, could solve the problem he posed.

Meanwhile, Plato's questions about appearance and reality suggest something interesting about the process of a sale. He had a curious notion about color: The eye sends out signals toward a thing, while the thing sends out signals about its color, with perception taking place somewhere in the meeting and mingling of the signals. It is a near perfect analogue for the dual origins of the sale and the twin tasks of the salesman, one of which has to do with the thing (the product) and the other with the viewer (the customer). The sale itself takes place somewhere in the middle, in what Plato called the mingling of the signals.

The trouble with Plato and Socrates, too, is that they were full-time philosophers instead of grocers or haberdashers who did a little philosophy on the side. They worried more about the price of goodness than the quality of olive oil. If only they had developed a commonsense approach to knowing things as they are rather than as they appear, Western civilization might have developed along a different track. During every human transaction, truths would have been out on the table, as plain as pumpkins. Dishonesty would have been difficult, if not impossible. This might have become an artless, uninteresting world, a mechanical world, but there would have been no salesmen and the definition of a sale would have been as simple as "this for that."

But they couldn't find the solution, not the shopper's solution. Nothing Socrates said about appearance and reality gave a consumer a hint of how to behave at K Mart or at Bergdorf Goodman. He just couldn't get his ideas to work out in this relative world, where no one can behold the real thing and the salesman makes his living by knowing a little more than the customer.

After Plato there was continuing consternation over the problem, but no practical understanding. The Romans certainly didn't offer much help. Montaigne ended up asking, in his usual way, "What do I know?" By the seventeenth century, Descartes was so annoyed by uncertainty over what was on the grocer's shelf that he came to doubt everything. For him, knowledge of the external world came from the mind, not the senses.

Kant took a new look at the subject-object relationship. He split the external world into the thing-in-itself and the thing as we perceive it. As far as he was concerned, "The thing-in-itself can never appear to us."

By the second half of the twentieth century, philosophers like A. J.

Ayer and Gilbert Ryle were becoming so exasperated by the endless bickering over appearance and reality that they spoke of commonsense solutions to the philosophical problem. Unfortunately, there was no commonsense solution to the practical problem. Just think of the supermarket: We do not know the reality of the apple that was picked from the tree, and we surely do not know the reality of the applesauce inside the metal can on the shelf. We have no more grasp of quotidian reality now than we did in Eden. In fact, less, for science and technology have complicated the world, making it even more difficult to distinguish appearance from reality now than ever before.

The earth, which appears to be flat, is not. Stars, which appear to be tiny dots of light in the heavens, are bigger than the world we live in. With each passing year, appearance seems to be a less useful clue to reality. Not just in the technological sphere but even at the dinner table. Fats, which make food taste good, turn out to be bad for our health. Peppers, which sting our mouths and bring tears to our eyes, are among the most healthful of seasonings. And the damned apple may have a worm in it!

Obviously, the senses cannot be trusted. "Our very life would fall," as Lucretius said, without some solution to the crisis. There must be a mediator between the senses and the world, some comforting way to know what is inside the package, to carry on a more or less rational existence in a world in which appearance and reality may have any relation from identical to opposite.

There is a logical answer to the marketplace problem of appearance and reality and a structural answer, and they are the same: the salesman.

He is the necessary adjunct of appearances; without a mediator, the commerce by which we move from moment to moment, act to act, in even the most ordinary aspects of our lives would be stymied. Having seen that the salesman is the mediator between opposites, now mainly appearance and reality, we have a starting point from which to explore a definition of the salesman and his work.

Curiously, even the most sophisticated and successful salesmen in America still use the old definition of a sale ("the exchange of a commodity for money or other valuable consideration," A.D. 1050). They know a great deal about market share and motivation, they are expert in pricing and packaging, yet even to them a sale is a sale is a sale.

But it is not.

2.

Once it is recognized that the thing-in-itself does not appear to the buyer (or to the seller, for that matter), the sale ceases to be "the exchange of a commodity for money or other valuable consideration." That exchange is not the sale but the result of the sale.

No exchange takes place in the sale. It is a mingling, as Plato imagined when speaking of vision and color. On one side lies the thing which sends out data by its appearance. But the data is either incomplete or unreliable or incomprehensible. A mediator must gather and organize the data into information and then organize the information into knowledge so that the prospective buyer can use it.

For example, data about piston displacement, consumption of fuel in the chamber, torque, and the like must be organized so that the prospective buyer can understand whether an engine is efficient or gluttonous, suited to a sports car or a sluggish economy sedan. Whether the product is a box of cereal or a supercomputer, information must be gathered and organized, there must be a mediator who knows more than appearance reveals, and that task has always fallen to the salesman.[4]

Mediation now occurs on a worldwide basis. In New York City, Eileen Bresnahan, an experienced and highly sophisticated agent for fabric mills, who sells their goods to garment manufacturers, described the process: "You know what it is they make, the category of garment they are known for in the marketplace, so you make the match in that way: Number one, the fabric to the garment. Or you think about the fact that the customer has production predominantly in a certain part of the world, so you think, I have a mill in Brazil; he does production in Brazil; it's a perfect match to have my fabric utilized by his factory."

Since reality, the thing-in-itself, does not appear to the prospective buyer, the salesman is theoretically free to present or withhold any information he has discovered or invented and to attribute it to the reality of the thing or product. There are practical limits, of course, ranging from common sense to governmental regulation. An apple cannot be successfully described as a horse. Within those limits, however, the information is as the

---

[4]   See Aristotle, *Rhetoric,* bk. 1, chap. 2, to compare his three kinds of persuasion to the salesman's influence on information and desire. Aristotle says that the first kind of persuasion depends on the personal character of the speaker. The character of the salesman will be examined in the final chapters of this book.

salesman presents it; the prospective buyer almost always lacks the information and the organizing capacity to challenge the salesman's depiction of reality.

Salesmen have always changed information to sell a product, although there were few records of their activities until advertising provided printed evidence. During the last quarter of the nineteenth century and the first quarter of the twentieth century, Sapolio was perhaps the most widely used soap product. Its early success resulted partly from the use of line drawings in advertising. The Sapolio ads showed happy customers using the product. As competing soap products took more and more of Sapolio's sales, the product remained the same, but the advertising changed to speak of Sapolio as an economical way to wash. The process has been used for hundreds of products, based on the knowledge that it is usually sufficient to change the signal from the product rather than the product itself. Claude Hopkins, who wrote the first major work on modern advertising, *Scientific Advertising* (1923), recognized the effect of information added by the salesman: "The product itself should be its own best salesman. *Not the product alone, but the product plus a mental impression, and atmosphere, which you place around it*" (italics added).

The signals that come from the other side, the buyer, are less changeable than those sent out by the product. They have traditionally been divided into two classes. Needs are biological, while wants are psychological; that is, one needs to eat enough to stay alive, but wants to eat caviar or Kentucky Fried Chicken. Some needs cannot be ignored. If it is cold enough, the need for warmth will cause a person to burn even the most wanted furniture. Members of the Donner party, near starvation, developed a new and previously unsuspected appetite.

Other needs are less urgent. Reproduction, for example, may be a powerful need, but one wonders whether there was a lot of fooling around during the last days of the Donner party. In other words, there is a hierarchy of need. At its peak, need becomes so overwhelming that discretion about things to be used or consumed disappears. At the other end of the scale, need can be put off or denied altogether. No one was ever sex-starved to death. And hardly anyone is obsessed with "Obsession by Calvin Klein."

Emily Dickinson described the vagaries of need in these eight lines written in 1862:

> *Undue significance a starving man attaches*
> *To food*

51

Far off, he sighs, and therefore hopeless,
And therefore good.
Partaken, it relieves indeed, but proves us
That spices fly
In the receipt. It was the distance
Was savory. [5]

The amount of information required to make the sale and the role of the mediator increase in direct proportion to the buyer's distance from desperation. But where needs decline to wants and whether needs can be psychological as well as physiological is difficult, perhaps impossible to know. Since the distinction has little practical purpose, it may be more useful to describe the will to possess a thing or service or quality as desire and then to consider desire as occurring along Dickinson's continuum, from starvation to satisfaction.

In his effort to promote the mingling of the two sets of signals, the mediator is required more to discover desire than to increase it. The wishes for safety and pleasure, for comfort and things, for ease and immortality, for more and more than . . . are nature's gifts to the salesman. Desire is the garden the salesman inherits. He nurtures the fruits of his garden, choosing those that are proper to the seasons of his ambition, but he can only cultivate the garden as it exists; he cannot invent the earth or extend the hours of the sun. The garden is.

Like the fruits and flowers of the garden, desire may be nourished, guided into the sun, pampered, pruned, put beside a pole to climb into fullest blossom. So the salesman must elicit the signals of desire from his customers. He is not a god; he came late to the earth; he must make do with what he found.

Does this mean that the salesman has no power in the realm of desire and therefore no responsibility? Not at all. The variety of gardens is infinite, and every garden, no matter how plain, bears the mark of the gardener.

Like the gardener who learns the soil, climate, seasons, pests, and varieties of plants that will grow under his administration, the salesman must discover the basic desires of his customers and how they can be fitted to his requirements. Like the gardener, he will not let desire go untended. Weeds

[5] *Collected Poems of Emily Dickinson,* ed. Mabel Loomis Todd and T. W. Higginson (New York: Avenel Books, 1982), p. 66.

are not his wont. The salesman will discover the desires most appropriate to his interest, and cultivate them. Although he cannot create it, he tries to manage desire so that the signal sent out from the customer fits exactly with the signal sent out from the product. The mingling then is his success, a sale, the wedding of information and desire.

Salesmen have been working both sides of the marriage for a long time. In 1899 the National Biscuit Company and its advertising agency, N. W. Ayer, published their awareness of the dual aspects of a sale. They had a brilliant new product: a soda biscuit packed in a "moisture proof" tin. Until then, people who wanted soda biscuits had to take their chances by picking them out of an old-fashioned cracker barrel. The advertisements described the virtues of the new package, which delivered biscuits to the customer "as crisp, tender and delicious as when fresh from the oven." There were no other manufacturers of packaged soda biscuits; National Biscuit had the market to itself. The only issue other than the package was desire. They named the product Uneeda Biscuit.

Although a sale does not take place until desire is wed to information, there can be a sale without a salesman. In less complex societies, those with little or no specialization, the hunter/gatherer is driven by original appetites and attracted to plants and animals by form, color, and availability. The sale that takes place at this level of social organization and technology requires no salesman. Only as societies become rich and choices begin to appear does the salesman have a role.

But what role? Is he an outside force, a mere externality? In one sense, that is correct, for the salesman is neither the buyer nor the product; the mediator does not participate in the action. Yet, no sale takes place except in the house a salesman invents. He bestirs the buyer and decorates the product; he manages the signals, bringing them to the mingling place; he is host to the sale, he creates the ambiance of the sale; he is not the parent of the bride or the groom, but the salesman gives the wedding.

There are many kinds of salesmen, but they fall into two distinct categories. The novelist Charles Simmons said that his father, who was a ribbon salesman, defined the categories as "the salesman who knows his line" and "the salesman who can sell anything." In other words, a salesman may concentrate on managing information or studying desire. But no matter which aspect he chooses, he can never ignore the other; the sale is always a wedding. To understand it otherwise would be tantamount to multiplying by zero.

Every salesman's strategy will always be to control both sets of signals. And every salesman's frustration will always be that he cannot invent either desire or the world of things; they exist. All of his battles, with his customers, his suppliers, and his competitors, will be for control of the signals. Some of his competitors will be salesmen for similar or substitutable products; other competitive forces will come from science, religion, the arts, journalism, government, and so on. Any information that relates to his product or a plausible substitute is the salesman's competition, as is any facet of health or culture that affects the desire of his customer. He works in a world that is, at once, hostile to his intentions and eager to enjoy the material, social, political, economic, or psychological wares in the salesman's portmanteau.

Great social and economic tides will force the salesman to switch his emphasis from time to time. The prominence of his work will rise and fall with the life cycle of nations. Over long stretches of time—more than decades, centuries perhaps—salesmen will evolve, accommodating their strategies of mediation to the patterns of history.

The cycle of civilization in which the salesman finds himself may not continue to change so radically as the eighteenth-century Neopolitan Giambattista Vico predicted, from the age of gods to that of heroes to the ascendance of the common people, the democratic age, and back to beastliness and heroes again. Perhaps Vico's fear of democracy was unjustified, and ordinary people will be able to rule themselves. But it may be that ages are bound to die, as Vico said, when there is a failure of conscience, an end to shame, the unchecked elevation of things, as in a nation of salesmen.

3

A Salesman's History of the World

Part 1: The Province of Man and the Province of God

Business is in itself an evil.

—SAINT AUGUSTINE

*. . . he is unfortunate whose mode of procedure
is opposed to the times.*

—MACHIAVELLI

If you build it, they will come.

—*Field of Dreams*

She was standing beside him at the window when the snow began to fall. She sighed. Nostalgia was carried on the slow-falling, occasional flakes, the introduction of the snow.

"You'll have to stop early," she said.

"I will," he lied.

The snow fell. He imagined the snow falling everywhere, in Aurora and Rockford and on into Iowa. He imagined the white roads, the winter fields, the fallen stalks covered by the snow.

He looked down at the DeSoto Airflow parked on the street. The snow had not yet begun to stick.

After a while he went into the bedroom and said good-bye to the baby, although he did not kiss the child, for fear of waking him. Then he put on his overcoat and picked up his valise and collection book and walked down four flights of stairs to the car.

He left Chicago with two packs of Camels in his coat pocket, enough to see him through the night. There was a blanket on the back seat, another in the trunk. If the heater went on the fritz again, he would stop, wrap himself in the blankets, and sleep until morning. He had done it before, always in Iowa. This was the third job that had begun in Iowa; the new territories, those known as opportunities, were always in Iowa.

North and west of the city, the snow had begun earlier. The roads were covered before he got to Skokie. After Elgin he drove in the ruts made by the trucks and cars that had preceded him. The moon was hidden in the snow-bearing clouds. He leaned forward, straining to see the tail lights of the car or truck that had to be somewhere ahead of him. There was nothing. The snow brought the darkness closer.

In the winter of '35 he had gone on the road with costume jewelry. In the summer of '35 he had gone on the road with rustproof fabric window screens. This winter the trunk of the car was empty; he had moved up to selling intangibles.

As the snow deepened, it disguised the world outside the car; the road blended with the fields, the snow covered the tire tracks, in drifts he lost all sense of the road. He drove a straight, imagined path, riding on geometry.

No cars came toward him in the diminished world of night and snow. He knew he would have to stop soon, long before Rockford. There was no hope of Iowa now.

He leaned forward, squinting into the night, searching for some sign: starlight, the moon, a house, a town, at least another car. He looked up, then to the left and the right, and when he looked back, he could no longer find the road. The snow lay smooth and white across all the rest of the world. It was not possible to go on. He let the car glide to a stop. Then he turned off the ignition and the lights, and sat in the darkness, with his hand upon the gear shift knob and his feet resting on the floor beside the pedals.

The car was very warm, but he knew the heat would soon dissipate. He got up on his knees and leaned over to get the thick blanket from the back seat. Although it was snowing heavily, it was not very cold, and he did not fear for his life. He put on his warm tweed overcoat, covered himself with the blanket, then spread newspapers over the top of the blanket to keep in the heat.

Time passed very slowly, and he did not seem to be able to sleep. He turned on the interior light for a moment, just long enough to open the collection book to the pages for Dubuque. First stop: Johnson. He knew the man by his street address and payment record. This was his talent, the mark of a born salesman.

The interior lights began to yellow. He turned off the switch. Then he put the collection book aside. In the darkness he saw that the Johnson house was small and poorly insulated. There was a slaughterhouse nearby. The neighborhood stank of death and bacon. Johnson opened the door. There was an old wood-burning stove behind him in the center of the room, and beyond it a couch that leaned on a broken leg.

Northern Life. Davidson call me Dave. Thanks for inviting me in. Understand, I'm not the collection man, I'm not threatening you or nothing like that. I'm reselling you, for your own good. Depression's been hard on your people, Mr. Johnson, men die. I don't know when death is due, Mr. Johnson, but I know that it comes for all of us. Some men die in their cars and some men die in their beds, some die by gas and some fall in the fire. Some die in pain and some have a smile at the very last. Men die, Mr. Johnson. You think the last word is a rattle, and that can be the truth unless there is a funeral to send a man off with Scripture and song. The weeping is the verse the widow writes, you know. I've been thinking about this all the time I'm in my DeSoto car, more in the winter than in the summer because death is cold. Cold, Mr. Johnson, cold like a ghost who leaves his widow without a penny and no way to earn, cold as a baby without what to eat, cold as a widow without a place to rest, cold. They say death is darkness, death is black, but I say death is the color of snow, Mr. Johnson, white as a sheet, white as a ghost. Death is nothing, death is when everything is forgotten, no family, no funeral, no food, nothing. Death is in two steps, like a dance, Mr. Johnson, the first step is the snow and the second step is after the snow melts. What is there when the snow is gone, Mr. Johnson? Nothing. No funeral, no weeping, no widow's words, nothing. What happened to the snow that you could hold in your hand and roll up into a ball? I'm talking insurance, Mr. Johnson, it's insurance or nothing. Insurance or ghosts. Insurance or death. We call it life insurance, Mr. Johnson, twenty-pay-life. This quarter of a dollar I'm talking about, Mr. Johnson, this twenty-five cents that stands between you and death, we call it life. What do you say, Mr. Johnson? What do you call it? Who do you love? Who loves you? Kiss that baby, Mr. Johnson, hold that baby in your arms. Keep the ghost away. The snow is going to melt, Mr. Johnson, I promise you, the snow is going to melt, and when the snow has melted there is nothing, only the ghosts, nothing but the ghosts, I promise you on my Certified Life Underwriter's oath. And I thank you, Mr. Johnson, and I feel happy for you, Mrs. Johnson, knowing that you sleep in peace, without fear of the melting snow.

1.

Before there were economies, there were salesmen. They went by different names in ancient empires: tradesman, merchant, usurer. To a large extent they were the cause of cities, the carriers of culture; they were the alternative to theocracy, the spur of production; God's competitors. No one loved them.

In the myths of the Middle East, recalled and written as early as 2500 B.C., the salesman appears mainly in the role of trickster. But a little more than thirteen hundred years later, the ancient Hebrews begin to reveal the attitudes of an agricultural people toward the mercantile world. The salesman gets no direct mention in the Ten Commandments, but he did not escape notice in the books of Moses, in his role either as usurer or as profit maker:

> If you lend money to any of my people with you who is poor, you shall not be to him as a creditor, and you shall not exact interest from him. If ever you take your neighbor's garment in pledge, you shall restore it to him before the sun goes down; for that is his only covering, it is his mantle for his body; in what else shall he sleep? (Exodus 22:25–27)

> You shall do no wrong in judgment, in measure of length or weight or quantity. You shall have just balances, just weights, a just ephah and, a just hin. . . .[1] (Leviticus 19:35)

Confucius, writing early in the fifth century B.C., has his philosopher Tsang examine himself daily on three points, one of which has to do with faithfulness "in transacting business for others." Also in *The Analects*, the

[1] Dry and liquid measures: about a bushel and a gallon and a half, respectively.

Master says, "He who acts with a constant view to his advantage will be much murmured against."

At the same time, ancient Greece was entering the height of its economic and intellectual development, and the salesman was no more appreciated there. Plato spoke of those who sold goods or ideas, combining his distastes in the *Protagoras*:

"Surely, I (Socrates) said, knowledge is the food of the soul; and we must take care, my friend, that the Sophist does not deceive us when he praises what he sells, like the dealers wholesale or retail who sell the food of the body; for they praise indiscriminately all their goods, without knowing what are really beneficial or hurtful; neither do their customers know. . . ."

When Plato wrote *The Laws,* the sour, pessimistic book of his waning years, his hostility to salesman was remarkable, perhaps because he had come to the conclusion that the purpose of trade should be the redistribution of goods, not the maximization of profit. Not only did he set down the rule that the seller "must not push anything he has for sale," meaning that he is prohibited from behaving like a salesman; Plato termed "adulteration" one of the crimes of commerce, calling it "essentially the same sort of thing as lying and deceit." He complained of swindlers and the salesman who named "two prices for his goods," detailing the proper punishments for them.

The evidence of the poor reputation of salesmen in Plato's time is not entirely indirect, however. After setting out the rules of behavior for salesmen and the punishments for breaking those rules, he asked, "Why then is trading thought to be such a low and disreputable occupation? Why has it come to be so abused?"

Aristophanes, the master of abuse, offered his view of salesmen in *The Knights,* a play in large part about a sausage seller. He describes one tradesman as "a filthier scoundrel" than another. His salesmen, who are always cheats and rogues, "repulse honest folks."

By the time Jesus began preaching to his people, during the Roman occupation of Palestine, there was greater interdependence among the parts of the Roman Empire, but still not a true market economy, according to M. I. Finley in *The Ancient Economy.* Prices were relatively stable, shortage and abundance resulted from the vagaries of nature or war rather than from the competition for markets, cities arose because of their convenience to commodities rather because than manufacturing, and money was not amassed or borrowed for the purpose of increasing productive forces.

Jesus could not yet have been preaching about capitalism or economics in the modern sense; his target was the rich, especially the salesmen. He said in his Sermon on the Mount, "And forgive us our debts, as we also have forgiven our debtors," and, only a few lines later,

> No one can serve two masters; for either he will hate the one and love the other, or he will be devoted to the one and despise the other. You cannot serve God and mammon. (Matthew 6:24)

And gave his view of merchants and people engaged in foreign exchange (the money changers converted currencies) a few chapters after that. The unforgettable last phrase of the quotation below equates the salesman's profit with theft.

> And Jesus entered the temple of God and drove out all who sold and bought in the temple, and he overturned the tables of the money changers and the seats of those who sold pigeons. He said to them, "It is written, 'My house shall be called a house of prayer'; but you make it a den of robbers." (Matthew 21:12)

Although the New Testament shifted the emphasis of ethics further from the temporal world to that of the spirit, making clear in the Beatitudes who was blessed and who was not, the world did not disappear. Seven hundred years after Jesus, the Moslem collectors of the Forty-two Traditions of An-Nawawi wrote an ethics of the desert kingdoms: "Do not be envious of each other; and do not outbid each other; and do not hate each other; do not oppose each other; and do not undersell each other; and be, O slaves of Allah, as brothers."

It was a recognition of the role of the salesman that Jesus would not have countenanced, but it was realistic. Heaven was not going to come to earth, at least not anytime soon. For more than three thousand years after Moses and two thousand years after Jesus, the salesman was destined to exist in the hypocritical interplay of business and religion, life and (life after) death: He was to become a growing power in the lives of nations, fitting himself to the theologies of the times, while the theologians tinkered with the rules of admission to heaven, eventually accommodating every aspect of the salesman's work. This tortuous journey to predominance would leave indelible scars upon salesmen and nations, especially the United States.

The third-century Roman emperor Gratian was among the first to make a sinner of the salesman: "Whosoever buys a thing, not that he may sell it whole and unchanged, but that it may be material for fashioning something, he is no merchant. But the man who buys it in order that he may gain by selling it again unchanged and as he bought it, that man is of the buyers and sellers who are cast forth from God's Temple."

A century later, Diocletian's edict on prices was aimed at putting "a stop to the dishonest practices of merchants who were forcing up unduly the price of provisions and other commodities thereby doing serious harm to the entire country. . . ."[2]

By the ninth century, Charlemagne's Capitulary of Nijmegen produced a broad new list of economic misdeeds including:

> Clause 15. Those who by various manoeuvres dishonestly plan to amass goods of all kinds with the express aim of making money are acquiring ill-gotten gains.
>
> Clause 17. All persons who at harvest time or when the grapes are gathered acquire corn or wine which they do not need, but get simply through an underlying motive of greed, for instance buying a hogshead for two deniers and keeping it until they can sell it again for six deniers or even more, are guilty of what we call dishonest gain. If on the other hand they buy it because they need it, so as to keep it for themselves or give it away to others, that is a business transaction *(negocium).*[3]

Condemnation of the salesman was the ethical chorus of the Dark Ages. One could quote Saint Augustine: "Business is in itself an evil." Or Saint Jerome: "A man who is a merchant can seldom if ever please God." Yet commerce continued. According to Barbara Tuchman, "Merchants regularly paid fines for breaking every law that concerned their business, and went on as before." Like everyone who studies the Middle Ages, she questions whether the bankers and merchants of the period were at all anguished

[2]   Quoted in Robert Latouche, *The Birth of Western Economy: Economic Aspects of the Dark Ages,* trans. from the French by E. M. Wilkinson (London: Methuen, 1961), p. 16.
[3]   Ibid., p. 156.

by breaking the religious prohibitions against usury in its many forms, and finds an amusing answer in the attitude of Francisco Datini, the merchant of Prato: "He was evidently able to reconcile Christianity and business, for the motto on his ledger was, 'In the name of God and of profit.' "[4]

In the Middle Ages the salesman's profit (still often described as usury) was considered sinful because it involved making money by using time, which belonged to God.[5] It takes a medieval mind to comprehend the casuistry: Interest is paid for the use of money over time, and time belongs to God. Profit on the sale of goods follows the same rule: The merchant bought the goods, held them for a time, and sold them at a profit; since he did nothing but hold the goods, he must be selling time; what else?

These convoluted arguments against profiting through the use of God's time didn't even get through the Dark Ages unscathed. Saint Thomas Aquinas drew a distinction between labor and time, making life a little easier for the merchant. Aquinas accepted the idea of profit, although not as an end; he said that profit was acceptable if it was actually the wage for the seller's labor. This "just price" theory did not allow much latitude for the salesman, but it opened the door. As R. H. Tawney wrote, with obvious amusement, the true inheritor of Aquinas's ideas was Marx's labor theory of value.

Nevertheless, the problem for the salesman continued to depend on what was and was not regarded as usury. He could be condemned for almost any activity that fell into the expandable category. As a member of the English Parliament said, "It standeth doubtful what usury is; we have no true definition of it."

Beginning in the sixteenth century, the medieval mixture of piety and avarice, which made of the salesman a kind of indispensable outlaw, was to be stood on its ear by two powerful forces: Cities and towns, many of which had grown up around the markets where the salesmen worked, were becoming more populous and influential than rural areas; the urbanization of Europe had begun; the business of selling would provide the economic

---

4   *A Distant Mirror* (New York: Knopf, 1978), p. 38.

5   During much of the Middle Ages in Europe, only Jews were allowed openly to lend money at interest, following the exception provided in Deuteronomy 23:20, which allowed the Hebrews to collect interest from strangers. However, moneylending in various forms (mortgages, etc.) was widely practiced during the entire period by many people, including the Catholic church itself. A reversal of this prohibition was to occur in the British colonies in America, where the only gentlemanly business was the employment of wealth for profit.

underpinnings of the Renaissance. The other force came from the moral suffering of a young theologian and teacher in Wittenberg. Tortured by questions of "the righteousness of God," enraged by what he saw as hypocrisy, Martin Luther came to a radical new understanding of the relation of each *individual* man to his God, and thought, "At this I felt myself to have been born again, and to have entered through open gates into paradise itself."[6]

2. The First Transformation

Luther cautioned the inhabitants of the new, urban civilization, "A man should not say, 'I will sell my wares as dear as I can or please,' but 'I will sell my wares as is right and proper.' " Calvin finally gave the salesman some comfort: His "elect of God" had to prove that they were elect by doing well in the world. The salesman—the haggling, sweating, market stall and countinghouse mediator, whose business necessitated the cities in which Western civilization was to have its great Renaissance—was no longer despised and damned by the arbiters of morality.

The church had been the ultimate authority on moral issues all through the Middle Ages, but in the sixteenth century the church became handmaiden to the needs of the secular, increasingly commercial world. The Calvinist church not only recognized economic values; it applauded them. An urban, commercial society required continuing expansion merely to maintain stability, and who but the salesman/entrepreneur could be counted on to deliver?

Puritanism became a handy helpmate to those who wished to expand the economy. John Bunyan may have railed against "hucksters,"[7] and ostentatious displays of wealth may have been frowned upon, but the salesman had secured a place in the moral code during the sixteenth century. Getting rich was doing God's work. Preachers who found the idea incompatible with their readings of the Bible were likely to find themselves without congregations.

In summing up the new alliance of religion and economic necessity,

---

[6] From the autobiographical section of the complete works, 1545.

[7] As did virtually every major figure in the history of the English-speaking world, from before Sir Thomas More to long after Jonathan Swift.

Tawney wrote, "After all, it appears, a man can serve two masters, for—so happily is the world disposed—he may be paid by one, while he works for the other. Between the old-fashioned denunciation of uncharitable covetousness and the new-fashioned applause of economic enterprise, a bridge is thrown by the argument which urges that enterprise itself is the discharge of a duty imposed by God."

Max Weber had a somewhat harsher but not fundamentally different view of the effects of Calvinism: "In the place of the humble sinners to whom Luther promises grace if they trust themselves to God in penitent faith are bred those self-confident saints whom we can rediscover in the hard Puritan merchants of the heroic age of capitalism. . . ."

The basic tenet of the new ethics in the United States was first discussed by Richard Baxter, then immortalized by Benjamin Franklin: "Time is money." Instead of being condemned for taking advantage of time, which belonged to God, men were chastised for wasting time, which belonged to God. Sloth, rather than covetousness, became the greatest economic sin.

The Great Awakening, in early-eighteenth-century America, converted many of the colonists to Calvinist teachings, but Calvinism did not capture everyone's heart, nor did it determine everyone's behavior in colonial America. Gentlemen were not to engage in trade, especially at the retail level. It was the duty of gentlemen, who often made their money by lending money, to consume, if only to give employment to the rest of the population.

Other people, the great puritanical majority, were left with the Calvinist view of ostentation: They frowned upon pleasure in worldly things, even though they were urged to work hard and get rich. The distinction between the life of a tradesman and that of a gentleman was borne out in the career of Benjamin Franklin: The Philadelphia tradesman who filled books with aphoristic writings about hard work and thrift abandoned business as soon as he was financially able, and took up the ways of a gentleman. One can hardly blame Franklin for his lack of consistency: Of the two roads to heaven, it was more fun to take the one that demanded a high level of consumption.

Franklin's wish to separate himself from hoi polloi was clear by 1730 when he produced an essay on "lying shopkeepers," advising them to get rich by telling the truth. "There are a great many Retailers," he wrote, "who falsely imagine that being *Historical* (the modern Phrase for *Lying*) is much for their Advantage; and some of them have a Saying, *That 'tis a Pity*

Lying is a Sin, it is so useful in Trade. . . ." He knew that the salesman had been transformed from evil to necessary evil, but evil nonetheless; it was in the interest of the ambitious printer to side with honest folks against the salesman.[8]

3. The Second Transformation

The American Revolution began the Second Transformation of the Role of the Salesman. A profound change in the status of merchants, tradesmen, shopkeepers, and Yankee peddlers was hardly the aim of the elite founders of the United States, but there was nothing they could do to hold it back. Everything was changing. The political revolution of 1776 was to become a social revolution as well. Individualism, begun with Martin Luther and nourished by the Enlightenment, had linked up with self-interest in the fledgling democracy to produce a new kind of citizen in a new kind of nation.

A new philosopher, Adam Smith, introduced a systematic view of "political economy" that excited the economic thinkers of the newly formed nation. "Without the disposition to truck, barter and exchange," Smith said, men would have been consigned to life at a level below that of a tribe of hunters or shepherds, for even they knew enough to exchange such simple things as a bow and arrow for meat or clothing. He said this business of exchange gave rise to the division of labor, a form of political economy in which the retailer was as necessary as any other component.

Smith had another, even more powerful argument on behalf of the salesman or anyone who sold his goods at more than the natural price: self-interest. If everyone just took care of his self-interest, according to Adam Smith, an "invisible hand" (presumably that of God) would come along and guarantee an efficient political economy.

The economic freedom offered by Smith's economics fit the political and social ideas popular in the new nation. A new vision of man himself was emerging, seemingly not by any conscious design, but as if designed by an "invisible hand." The new man was an individual, but also part of the

---

[8]   Richard Baxter preached a similar lesson from his pulpit at Kiddermaster: "In no case may a man doctor his wares in order to get for them a higher price than they are really worth and in no case may he conceal any defects of quality. . . ."

general population, a statistic (the word first came into popular use during this period), mass man, less personal in his commercial relationships, no longer a bartender or storekeeper for a few of the more important families in his vicinity. He could do business with anybody. The salesman was on his own now, frightened perhaps to have lost the comfortable old relationships, but independent, and proud of it. The ideal American quality, as Emerson said, was self-reliance.

Paper money made business increasingly abstract, befitting a nation of statistics. Any American could do business with any other American. The salesman, once mainly a supplier to those landowning gentlefolk who did their duty by consuming, now sold to other salesmen, who in turn sold to him. It was the division of labor, efficient, just as Adam Smith had explained. Moreover, a seller who was also a customer was the equal of any other customer or seller. In addition to the political democracy promised by the Constitution, a nation in which everyone sold to everyone else was an economic democracy.[9] There were still rich and poor, but a vast middle made of landless middlemen and tradesmen was taking over the character and the culture of the land. The new commercial class had little use for the fancy ways of the gentry. Education was important to the self-made man, but only as a means to improve one's ability to do business.

The advent of a commercial class brought about an unprecedented change in the reason for most purchases. Customers were no longer mired in poverty, driven by desperate need to buy food, clothing, and shelter merely to stay alive. They developed a new and more malleable kind of need; the common man in America now had a sense of luxury. It was a salesman's dream come true: the birth of the American consumer.

By the early 1800s America had become the most commercial nation on earth; everyone was involved in the business of selling. It was only a few years later that a new title emerged in the lexicon of American occupations: businessman.[10] As power shifted from government to industry, the businessman replaced the legislator as the representative of the community and its wishes.

[9]   See Gordon S. Wood, *The Radicalism of the American Revolution* (New York: Knopf, 1992).

[10]   The single word *businessman* is not recognized by the *Oxford English Dictionary*. *Man of business,* according to the *OED,* originally meant one "engaged in public affairs," as David Hume used the term to describe Pericles. By the end of the eighteenth century in England, the phrase *man of business* had come to mean a commercial traveler or an attorney. Only in the United States was the occupational title a sign of esteem.

Alexis de Tocqueville, arriving in America in 1831, observed, "In democracies, nothing is more great or more brilliant than commerce: it attracts the attention of the public, and fills the imagination of the multitude; all energetic passions are directed toward it." He noted that there was little capital available in a nation with only a few small fortunes, but he added, "Yet no people in the world have made such rapid progress in trade and manufactures as the Americans. . . ."

No one could deny that political and economic democracy had vulgarized the American people, at least in comparison to the elite landowners who had set the cultural standards of the colonies. Tocqueville, himself an aristocrat, perhaps with the excesses of the French Revolution in mind, was interested in the power of the many in a democracy and the possibilities for the abuse of power in the demand for conformity, the love of material things, the overweening self-interest.

Tocqueville envisioned no great individuals in the United States, no great literature, no great art, nothing but mass man, taking strength from his clubs and organizations, filled with postrevolutionary ambition, grasping for wealth, displaying his success through the purchase of mass culture. It is sometimes said that Tocqueville erred in his failure to recognize the individual genius of Emerson and the transcendentalists, but it can be argued on the Frenchman's behalf that late in life even Ralph Waldo Emerson came to question the individualism of Americans in comparison to the power of the group and public opinion. Everybody was an American and America was everybody! The only question was how to move the mass of common people, how to send them west, sell the products of their factories, mills, presses, bakeries, forests, ranches, and farms. A new science, one step more complex than the political economy of Adam Smith, was coming into being. It was called economics, and it differed from previous ideas by one vital factor: demand.

Selling had achieved a new importance. The salesman was now responsible for supplying people to fill the empty farmlands and towns of the westward expansion and customers to buy the machine-made, mass-produced goods coming out of the northern factories and mills. In a country as large and populous as the United States, it was no longer possible to make every sale in person. An impersonal form of selling was necessary, a way to call on more customers and at the same time to call on them in distant places. Advertisements had been used in local newspapers since the first newspapers were printed, but something more was required—national advertising to assist in the growth of demand on a national scale. In 1848, fifty million advertisements were published in U.S. magazines.[11]

Technological development and expansion returned the salesman/mediator to his ancient role as culture bearer. He was the Prometheus of the machine age, the hero of the age of expansion. Store-bought clothing had needed him, but the steam engine, cotton gin, sewing machine, plate glass, telegraph, photograph, and Otis elevator needed him even more. Before the end of the century, salesmen would have to bring dozens of basic new ideas to the American public: automobiles, packaged foods, typewriters, streetcars, mass media, department stores, and the vast production of Thomas Alva Edison's "invention factory."

The salesman also had to sell new versions of himself to the public: the printed word, the shop window, and then the department store. Richard Sears and Montgomery Ward used catalogs to sell goods to Americans on farms and in small towns across the country. No salesman but the catalog ever came to call. The advent of rolled plate glass enabled shopkeepers to have large windows, which they filled with merchandise and signs expected to begin, if not to close, the sale. In New York, Philadelphia, and Chicago, the great department stores—Macy's, Wanamaker's, Marshall Field's—which the historian Daniel J. Boorstin called "Palaces of Consumption," invited customers to walk through floor after floor of enticingly displayed merchandise. The department store display was even more effective than the store window, because the customer could touch the merchandise, hold it up for size, even try it on; the salesman became the arranger of merchandise, the window dresser of information.

The individual customer disappeared, became truly an atom in the mass of customers, when the seller had to deal with tens of thousands of unknown people in areas of the country he had never seen. At first, mass marketing was intuitive; the salesman applied his own situation to that of a multitude. But intuition soon lost its luster. Nineteenth-century businessmen as well as scientists sought repeatable and reproducible results. In 1879 the N. W. Ayer & Son advertising agency did the first market research study. It was crude, and probably no more useful than the manufacturer's

[11] That is, the number of advertisements in each magazine times the number of copies printed came to a total of 50 million. By comparison, the average American is now exposed to more than 3,500 advertisements a day, according to the *New York Times,* January 17, 1993.

The statistics for 1848 are probably more reliable than those for 1993, but no great credence should be given to either set of numbers except as indicators of very broad patterns.

sales records or the analysis of coupons sent in by magazine readers, but it was a start—a scientific method had been applied to the understanding of desire.

The quality of information also underwent a change in the nineteenth century. Boosterism produced a new, more "imaginative" presentation of reality. Every new town had a booster newspaper or two or three, and every one served the same function: It sold the town, not as it was, but as it was going to be. Booster newspapers were true not to reality but to dreams. Some of them wrote the praises of towns that did not yet exist; others spoke of a cluster of houses and a general store as a metropolis to rival Philadelphia or Chicago. Although newspapers in America had always been as much an advertising medium as a means of disseminating news, the booster newspapers were different in that their goal was to create an illusion; the editor was a salesman, and the entire newspaper was an advertisement.

The booster who described a cabin, a horse corral, and a well as one of the fastest-growing towns west of St. Louis was certain that people would come to his imaginary town and make it into the fastest-growing town west of St. Louis. Moreover, he knew that those who came first would enjoy the greatest opportunity. Boosters were believers, not cheats. They did not think of themselves as dishonest; in America hope was not a form of lying. George Bancroft's ten-volume *History of the United States* was a booster history of love and expectations for his country, not a book of lies.

By blurring the distinction between hyperbole and deceit, boosterism defined the character of American selling. It gave respectability to a greater discrepancy between appearance and reality. Boosterism fit comfortably into the culture of a nation just beginning to enjoy the benefits of mass production, for it was mainly a quantitative notion. America was a *big* country, with *tall* trees and *high* mountains and *great* plains. Boosters seldom spoke of art or craftsmanship. They were aggressive, competitive. Big wasn't good enough for a booster; bigger was better. The tone of the American salesman, quantitative and comparative—bigger, better, longer, higher, wider, newer, cleaner than clean, whiter than white—belongs to the booster. Best was important to the booster mentality, but in a quantified world, dependent upon public opinion more than upon individualism, best-seller was the true superlative.

Although boosterism affected his method, the salesman's function was still largely that of culture bearer. Without a salesman to serve as mediator between the old and the new, technological change was slow and difficult.

Had it not been for a salesman, the sewing machine might have languished for decades before coming into wide use. At the end of the eighteenth century and all through the early years of the nineteenth, inventors were exhibiting machines that could sew. Most were crude, but one, developed by Elias Howe and patented in 1846, sewed several times faster and with greater uniformity than the best seamstress.

Howe didn't know how to sell his invention, but Isaac M. Singer, a former actor and theater manager as well as an inventor, knew enough about promotion and advertising to popularize the sewing machine. Within a few years the machine that Singer said would end the drudgery of the seamstress was selling very well.

Isaac Merrit Singer, whose success proved the Promethean function of the salesman, was apparently not satisfied with the role of salesman. He turned over the commercial part of the business to Edward Clark in 1851, and from then until he retired to England, Singer supervised manufacturing and the "experimental department, where he continued to improve the design of the machine." Something about selling did not satisfy the salesman. Was it the memory of ancient prohibitions, or was Prometheus put off by the part in which he was cast?

The social standing of the salesman/promoter changed toward the end of the century. Great fortunes, like that of Singer, purchased membership in a new class of gentry. Unlike the elegant landowners of the eighteenth century, this new class was rough, crude, and ostentatious. Even though it began in the grip of Puritan ethics, and passed through a period of Jacksonian populism, the nineteenth century closed with rude displays of wealth in emulation of long-dead French kings. It was not consumption but a particularly rude kind of consumption that came to dominate the taste of the country.

Thorstein Veblen did not speak of salesmen in *The Theory of the Leisure Class,* but the forty-two-year-old University of Chicago professor understood that a new form of desire had entered the mind of the American consumer. Veblen wrote about surplus and its use in the ostentatious display of wealth, exactly the kind of display the Calvinists of an earlier time had found contrary to the will of God. He named the manner of spending this wealth "conspicuous consumption" and the method of getting it "predation."

Predators, according to Veblen, were those who "reap what they do not strew." Since predators did not work, but lived off "a margin worth fighting for, above the subsistence of those engaged in getting a living," Veblen found them guilty of turpitude, harking back to Saint Thomas's view of those who profited beyond the value of their labor. In a complex analogy of mortal combat to sports to social character, Veblen said, "[T]he prevalence in the community of that predatory temperament which inclines men to sports connotes a prevalence of sharp practice and callous disregard of the interests of others, individually and collectively."

According to Veblen, it was the upper class that fit the role of predator, but he went on, "It appears . . . that there is no wide difference in temperament between the upper and the lower classes . . . in good part due to the prescriptive example of the leisure class and to the popular acceptance of those broad principles of conspicuous waste and pecuniary emulation on which the institution of a leisure class rests." The salesman entering the twentieth century was able to feel comfortable as a predator in dealing with customers. Fraud, which Veblen linked to the sporting temperament, had become acceptable under the rules of predation. Decisions would henceforth be made according to the rules of efficiency, at least until governments imposed a legal code of ethics upon the business world.

Adding to the comfort of the predator was his distance from the customer, which increased during the first third of the new century. The most common salesman was now an advertisement, a catalog, or a department store display.[12] The insurance agent, the automobile dealer, the Fuller Brush man, and the real estate salesman still dealt with the customer face-to-face, but the advent of competition among marketers of mass-produced, low-priced goods, from foodstuffs to paper products, clothing, hardware, soap, cigarettes—everything refillable, renewable, returnable, consumable, or disposable—made it necessary to reduce the cost of selling. Compared to putting a salesman on every doorstep or at every food counter, the cost of an advertisement was minuscule. Media salesmen used cost per thousand (CPM) to describe the efficiency of their product, but also to compare it to the cost of a personal salesman.

More and more effort was devoted to understanding the desires of the distant consumer. The Russell Sage Foundation underwrote the first "scientific" study of public opinion in the United States in 1907. N. W.

[12]   Claude Hopkins wrote in 1923, "Advertising is salesmanship. Its principles are the principles of salesmanship. Success and failure in both lines are due to like causes. Thus every advertising question should be answered by the salesman's standards."

Ayer and other advertising agencies had been claiming a "scientific" approach to their business for a quarter of a century when Cyrus H. K. Curtis, publisher of the *Saturday Evening Post* and the *Ladies' Home Journal*, commissioned a market research study in 1911.

Advertising of the period devoted much of its effort to changing the desires of the customer rather than to presenting information that satisfied existing desires. Some cultural critics believe these efforts were highly successful; for example, they credit advertising with teaching habits of cleanliness to the masses.[13] "Cleanliness is next to godliness" did become a popular phrase of the day, but it is difficult to believe that advertisements alone were powerful enough to make an urchin brush his teeth or a slattern wash her face.

The salesman-as-hygienist theory results from a confusion of ends and motives. Salesmen had to cast their ethical lot with Adam Smith rather than with Jesus: It was the salesman's job to sell as much as he could to whomever he could, without regard to the effect upon the individual or the nation, for there was an "invisible hand" arranging all the efforts of all the salesmen into an efficient economy. Rather than wanting to improve the hygiene of the masses, it is more likely that advertising copywriters found a cultural trend early, and profited by dramatizing and intensifying it.

When the Great Depression came, the salesman was put to a test: Production had outstripped consumption. Stockpiles of unsold goods caused factories to close. Unemployed workers could not buy the goods they had produced. The country was near collapse. Say's Law, which said that consumption would rise to meet production, had proved to be less accurate than Karl Marx's prediction that capitalism would crash under the weight of its own greed and overproduction: The salesman could not create desire.

During the Depression the large advertising agencies turned from selling goods and services to writing inspirational copy, urging people who were desperate to find any kind of job to "go to work." When inspirational copy from the people who had told their clients they could manipulate public sentiment failed to work, another kind of advertising appeared: crude, often deceptive, cheap by any standard. A nation unhappy with the failure of business turned on the salesmen. Books and articles attacking

[13]   Roland Marchand took this position in *Advertising the American Dream* (Berkeley: University of California Press, 1985).

salesmen and advertising appeared everywhere. All selling came to be considered "high pressure selling." Criticism of deceptive practices led Congress to give the Federal Trade Commission control over advertising in 1938.

Many people blamed salesmen for the Depression, and stock brokers, the ultimate salesmen in the public view, were not the only villains. Installment buying had been invented by salesmen to fuel the Republican mirage of limitless prosperity, and installment buying had led to overproduction, stockpiling, and so on down into the abyss of economic depression. It was the salesmen who had stimulated the national appetite for goods people could not afford. It was the salesmen who had brought about the bankruptcies of farmers and factory workers all across the country. Those Americans who proudly told the world, "I can sell anything," spoke softly during the Depression; many of them were out of work, too.

A generation bankrupted by salesmen never forgave them. Less than a month before the start of World War II, the situation of the salesman, especially the one who worked through advertising, became desperate. The Association of National Advertisers (the clients) and the American Association of Advertising Agencies met to discuss the problem. Fifty years later, the results of that meeting still affected the advertising industry. Sidney R. Bernstein, former editor of *Advertising Age,* recalled the central event of "the most important meeting he had ever attended." In a column published in 1991, he wrote, ". . . James Webb Young, one of advertising's all-time greats, suggested prophetically that 'a greater use of advertising for social, political and philanthropic purposes will help immeasurably to remove the distaste for advertising which now exists among many influential people.' " The Advertising Council was formed a few months later to promote war causes, and it has followed Young's profoundly cynical strategy for more than fifty years, producing thousands of print and broadcast advertisements to fill the time and space no advertiser would buy.

After the war the nation had little need of salesmen. Americans had waited half a dozen years for new cars, refrigerators, washing machines, radios, stoves, all the goods that had gone to war. There was a baby boom, a surge in housing and highway construction. America's productive capacity, which had expanded during the war, continued to grow.

The pipeline began filling up during the 1950s. America's productive capacity needed customers. The Cold War used up some of the capacity through military procurement, but there was more and more being built, and even more being planned. With memories of the Great Depression in mind, American industry could not take Say's Law seriously; production was no guarantee of consumption. The medieval villain, stern success of the Enlightenment, hero of the nineteenth-century expansion, goat of the Great Depression, was called upon once more; the salesman was to undergo yet another transformation.

4

A Salesman's History of the World
Part 2: War, Peace, and TV

Whether or not the dealers are moving them, the cars keep coming off the assembly lines and you've got to do something about it. You learn to scramble and move quickly. You learn to produce, or you get into trouble—fast!

> —LEE IACOCCA,
> on his early years
> selling Ford automobiles

Their situation was hopeless. The Japanese had pushed them out of the fine china business; they were going under. The chairman had no more to say; now it was his turn to listen. He abandoned himself to the beauty of the voice, like a concertgoer immersed in the sound of romantic music. For the first time in more than a week, the chairman did not feel the pain in the back of his head; he had to fight to keep his eyes open.

The sound of the sales manager filled the room. He was a huge man, larger by far than anyone else in the company, white, and swollen soft with food and lassitude. His front teeth were long and protruding, yellow now in middle age. He had an old rodent's fixed smile.

Success had come late to the sales manager. He had been a failure as a child, a situation that had to do mainly with his appearance. He reminded people of fairy-tale creatures, rabbits that wore bridles and saddles and carried little girls on their backs or giant mice with long whiskers and sad eyes. When he was in the first grade, a teacher said that he had the look of a creature who wished to be human. Children were not so kind. They called him Pink Eye, Elephant, MousieMousie, and Big Bunny, but after his mother enrolled him in dancing school, he was forever more known as Prancer.

The one thing about Prancer that everyone admired, the feature his mother referred to as his saving grace, was his voice. Puberty had put a public address system in his throat. He could talk.

It was his voice that had erased the failures of Prancer's childhood. He used it to escape from the circle of boys who owned soldering irons and masturbation rags and wore clip-on flip-up sunglasses. His voice was, he often said, a God-given gift; it had rescued him from loneliness, brought the light of society and opportunity into his life, and rid him once and for all of the hideously ironic nickname of his childhood. When he thought of his voice, he bowed his head and closed his eyes for an instant. Above and behind and around the great teeth, his lips formed the word *Jesus*.

He clapped the chairman on the shoulder. "Even you can't win them all," the sales manager said.

The chairman smiled, but the marketing director, a man in his forties, with three children considering colleges, bowed his head and covered his eyes with his hands. It was not the clichés the marketing director found unendurable, it was, he often said, the "goddamned goodness." Once, during better days, he had screamed at his sales manager, "Shit happens!" And the sales manager had replied with a smile, "Yes, but there is light at the end of the tunnel."

Now there was no light to be seen. The chairman had told them there would be only one more paycheck before they closed the doors, and there was no money for parachutes. Even the medical plan was shaky.

The sales manager continued speaking. The chairman smiled. He heard every sound, but not a single word. It was as if he were a boy again, sitting in church, attendant upon the music of the Word and oblivious to its meaning.

After the meeting the sales manager went to his office and gathered up some of his personal things; over the years he had been presented with a great many plaques, photographs, scrolls, trophies, gavels, paperweights, clocks, and desk sets, and he had kept them all. They filled four large cardboard boxes furnished by the shipping department.

He also kept a bottle of Canadian Club in his desk and another in the credenza behind the desk. He screwed the caps down tightly and packed both bottles.

That evening, following a large, bland, home-cooked meal of pot roast, mashed potatoes, green beans, and almond cake with white frosting, the vice president of sales sat down in the living room in his recliner, which had been a fortieth-birthday present to himself, and read the Bible. After his wife had cleared the table and put the dishes in the machine, she joined him. They sat very far apart, for each of them favored a different part of the room. His wife, who was as wide as he, but not nearly so tall, and whose teeth were not at all unusual, concentrated on her work, sitting very upright in the circle of light thrown by an old bridge lamp. She embroidered.

Sometimes they did not speak for most of an evening. At other times he rattled on aimlessly, as if practicing the use of his God-given gift. During his college years he had picked up the subtleties of public speaking from his only extracurricular activity—debate. He learned to whisper astonishments and shout commonplaces into profundity. He spoke quickly when he wanted to stall for time, and put long spaces between the words he wanted his listeners to remember; he learned to make sorrowful drawls and many kinds of laughs: guffaws, snickers, giggles, chuckles, howls, roars, the ironic hah! and the disbelieving ho! What he lacked in logic he made up for in volume and timbre.

The debating team coach had cautioned him about his proclivity toward clichés, which was good advice to a college debater, but the sales manager had learned later that, in life, clichés worked.

He closed the Bible and looked over at his wife. "The business is going under," he said. "The mighty Japanese economic machine has cleaned our clock. Sayonara."

She did not respond. He glanced over at her. The light of the bridge lamp was reflected in her eyeglasses. She did not look up from her embroidery.

He cleared his throat. "The fates have not looked kindly on us," he said. "Which brings my career to a fork in the road. If I tell you that every cloud has a silver lining, however, will you think ill of me?"

Her mother and grandmother had also been interested in embroidery. Every tablecloth, napkin, handkerchief, pillowcase, bed sheet, and guest towel in the house that had not been the work of one had been the work of the other. She was careful not to compete with ghosts; she made little dresses, bibs, and other practical items for the children of the little mountain village in Guatemala that was supported by their church. "Thirty-one years," was all she said.

"Would that it were so!"

She nodded.

"First, we ate the seed corn," he said. "Then we used up everything we had set aside for a rainy day." He spoke carefully, for he was aware of his reputation: He was known as a meditative man. People could tell by the sound of his voice that he was never impulsive, never foolish. He was a good-humored man, high-spirited, some people said, a fellow who liked to take a drink or two now and then, but not a drunkard, not a wastrel. Soothing was what people said of him, deep; it was there in his voice. And he said, not only to his salesmen, but even to his customers, "Every sales call is a homily."

"Well," she said. Although she was a New England woman, with roots in Maine as well as New Hampshire, she had not always been taciturn. There had been a great joy about her as a young woman. She had liked to go barefoot, and she wore summer dresses and bows in her hair well into autumn. Even after they were married, at least for the first few years, she had been open, almost garrulous, in a girlish way. Only in the progression of marriage had the sound of his voice expanded into her consciousness, crowding out the morphemes that had been her announcement to the world.

He picked up the Bible, opened it to the place he had marked with the ribbon, and read aloud:

> *Some put their trust in chariots and some in horses,*
> *but we will call upon the Name of the Lord our God.*
> *They collapse and fall down,*
> *but we will arise and stand upright.*

He closed the book with a flourish of care. She looked up from her embroidery, lifting her face out of the circle of light cast by the bridge lamp. The work lay in her lap, white cloth, pastel thread; a stork scissors, the glint of the needle outshining the steel bands that held tension in the cloth. She wore thimbles on her forefingers.

"Psalms," he said. "Twenty. Verses seven and eight." He leaned back in his chair until the footrest rose, then he closed his eyes and brought the Bible up from his lap and held it against his heart. If he were to put God's gift to God's work. . . . He imagined the color of his flesh become rosy in contrast to the stark white of the clerical collar. A man his size in priestly robes would seem like a monument. He had been born to stand before congregations, multitudes, to read from the King James Version, to proclaim the gospel.

The sales manager opened his eyes and turned his head slowly until his cheek lay flat against the back of the recliner and he could see, with both eyes, his wife, the lamplight, and above and beyond her, in darkness, a promise as of heaven in the here and now: a true calling, work without end. He let out a gasp of life, sound without sense, but full of meaning, the rumbling ineffable.

If she heard, she gave no sign. Inside the lighted circle her hands were still. The thimbles rested, the cloth stayed exactly as it had been. Her face remained hidden in the contrast of light and shade, a secret of the inequality. A long time later, after he had turned his head away, when his eyes were closed again and he was perhaps dreaming once more of the white collar and the roses of the flesh, she leaned forward into the light and said, in a voice both soft and plain, all that she knew of him after nearly thirty years, the sum of her beliefs: "Prancer."

1.

Shortly after Richard Nixon surprised the world by opening relations with China, a group of advertising executives went to Beijing to investigate the business possibilities. They knew very little about the country, except that it was the home of more than a billion potential customers. The Chinese, for their part, knew very little about Americans, except that they were rich and that their riches were kept in hard currency. It was a meeting of dreamers: Madison Avenue and Mao. Although they did not know it, the Americans were about to travel into their own past, to encounter the congruencies of post–World War II big business and socialist planning.

The journey began with painful inoculations, followed a few weeks later by a very long flight from New York. Almost immediately after their arrival in China, one of the advertising executives fell, suffered a severe head injury, and had to be flown home for treatment. The food in Beijing, sumptuous by Maoist standards, was sickening to men who had lived for many years in the magical nexus of business, taxes, and pleasure, where everything was fantastically expensive and absolutely free. And there was nothing in *The Little Red Book* of Chairman Mao about bimbos.

The Maoists took the offensive, making proposals to sell to the American market. In one meeting, reported by N. W. Ayer's emissary to the deeps of socialist planning, the Chinese said they were prepared to deliver five million wrenches to be sold in the United States. They explained that China had great reserves of coal and iron, many forges, and a vast supply of labor—everything needed to make the wrenches.

When they displayed some samples, it was immediately apparent that the wrenches were crudely made, more or less to the requirements of the metric system, and of cast iron rather than steel. Although none of the Americans was familiar with the hardware business, they knew from having toyed with a faucet in Greenwich or visited a Sears store in Westchester that the wrenches were not properly sized for the American market of the time, and worse, they were of such poor quality that few Americans would buy them—at any price.

Five million, the Chinese repeated proudly, five million for America.

Advertising executives have many flaws, but tactlessness is not one of them. In response to the Chinese proposition, the Americans did not criticize the wrenches; they delivered a brief lecture on marketing. Before you make something, they explained, you must be certain that someone will buy it.

The Chinese were puzzled. They had developed the capacity to produce five million wrenches. It was a triumph of socialism. What was wrong with the Americans? Perhaps they were not sincere. It was the end of the visit. The Americans packed their Lomotil and went home.

Later, long after the disgrace of the president who had opened relations with China, a trade fair was arranged. The Chinese were to bring examples of their goods to the United States to see if they could sell everything from heavy machinery to tiny umbrellas made of rice paper and matchsticks. To advertise the trade fair a free-standing insert approximately the size of a Sunday newspaper rotogravure section was to be designed by N. W. Ayer and produced and distributed by the *New York Times*.

In the course of this tedious, bureaucratized, and profitless activity, an English-speaking man and woman from the trade mission were escorted to my office one afternoon. By that time industrialists from Beijing no longer wore gray Mao jackets and little caps decorated with red stars. They dressed in Western clothes. The man wore a dark blue double-breasted suitcoat and brown trousers. The woman wore a brown double-breasted suitcoat and a dark blue skirt. When I first looked up and saw them, in their dour harlequinade, I thought of Maoist playing cards: a colorless queen and her bespectacled knave.

We greeted each other formally; then I invited them to join me at the conference table so that we might talk for a while. They sat stiffly, hands folded on the table. I offered them tea; they declined. I smiled; they stared. Once, I saw him sneak a look at the view of Manhattan from the windows of the fortieth-floor office.

There was a moment when the trade representatives of the People's Republic and I almost conversed. I had tried talking about *Quotations from Chairman Mao,* telling them I was glad to see our two countries engaged in acts of trade rather than imperialism. They listened, but not with interest; my American liberal politics must have seemed puny to them. Then the woman, who appeared to be in charge of the mission, leaned forward, her face suddenly animated, transformed into an operatic mask of curiosity. She said, "Tell us about your work, please. What is demand, and how is it found?"

2.

For the Chinese trade representatives centuries of deprivation followed by the social and economic turmoil of the revolution had produced a vision of the market as a great, insatiable maw into which they pushed anything they could produce. Although the standards of living were not comparable, the Chinese were in a situation like that of the United States following World War II: Production was the central problem, in fact, the only problem.

American sales problems of the postwar period were rooted in the Great Depression, when the unemployment rate rose to 25 percent while the per capita gross national product fell by 33 percent from 1929 to 1933. Nothing like the centuries of utter poverty, especially in the rural areas of China, had come to America during the Depression, but the fall from prosperity was precipitous. For those who held on to some capital, economics became a matter of conservation. For those who lost their jobs and virtually all of their earthly goods, hunger ruled; economics became a matter of want.

If the salesmen of the time had been able to interrupt the cycle of deprivation and anxiety, the Depression might not have been so deep or lasted so long, but they were not up to the task. The salesmen chose to concentrate on desire, and they failed: The customer's uncontrollable economic anxiety did not respond to sermons from Batten Barton Durstine & Osborne. Nor did the owners of businesses heed the homilies offered by Madison Avenue. The manufacturers who paid for the advertisements urging people to have faith and spend cut their own investment spending by 84 percent.

Washington was not much help, either. Government purchases were only 54 percent higher in 1939 than they had been a decade earlier. But the war changed everything. In 1945 government spending was five times what it had been in 1939. Even private investment was triple what it had been at the depths of the Depression. Enormous production capacity was being built up while civilian consumption remained low.

By the end of the war, America had become a Chinese market. For six years goods had been unavailable at any price, and for ten years before that people had lacked either the money or the will to buy what they desired. The problem in postwar America was like the problem in postrevolutionary China: Production! Demand, which existed somewhere out there at the end of the empty pipeline, appeared to have no limit. Salesmen had no function. As Roger B. Smith, former chairman of General Motors, told me, "They didn't sell; they took orders."

In fact, the desire for goods was so great that it allowed the salesmen to go beyond mere order taking. A Cadillac dealer in a small town outside Chicago solicited bribes from people who had made large profits during the war and wanted to display their wealth in four-door fashion. He was not unique. The practice was so common it merited a euphemism: In the economy of scarcity, extortion was called "selling over list price."

To deal with the production problem, the investment pattern of the war economy was almost exactly reversed. From 1945 to 1950 annual government spending fell by two-thirds while private investment tripled, and held at that level. But filling the pipeline was not an overnight task. Real GNP per capita almost doubled from 1939 to 1945, then fell after the war, and did not again reach the 1945 level until 1962.

As if the postwar boom was not sufficient, the Eisenhower administration, urged on by automobile manufacturers, truckers, and oil companies, poured money into the interstate highway system. New, high-speed highways were instrumental in extending the area of suburbs around America's major cities, making it possible to put up more single-family houses, all of which needed refrigerators, stoves, furniture, and so on.

Although no one seemed concerned at the time, the suburbanization of America was reversing one of the miracles of civilization, the city. Since the growth of markets in the Middle Ages, cities had been the hearthstone of culture and society. The punishment of the poor had been existence at the farthest extremes of the city. America had followed the same pattern until the end of World War II. By 1960, however, the number of people living in suburbs was equal to the number living in cities. The redistribution of the population put more of the affluent out of the reach of the personal salesman, even as it increased the internal market for America's goods.

Without a revolutionary technological change in the salesman's methods, the nation might not have been able to survive the potentially ruinous overproduction of its farms, mines, ranches, and factories. The useless salesman of the Chinese phase of the post-Depression/postwar economy was to undergo one more transformation, propelled by four ineluctable forces in the new version of the business cycle: (1) shortages and (2) innovations (war research and development applied to civilian needs), followed by (3) increased capacity and (4) population redistribution, leading to arcane markets and glut.

3. The Third Transformation

The industrial age in America, which had peaked during the war, continued for more than a third of a century afterward. The first sign of the success of the productive side of American industry came in the 1957–58 recession. GNP fell. Unemployment in 1958 was 50 percent higher than it had been a year before. The pipeline was filling up, the Chinese market had come to an end, but American industry refused to recognize the change. For the first time in American economic history, prices did not fall during a recession. Big business, which had become gigantic business during World War II, loved the profits of capitalism, but thought more like a push than a pull economy.

Although the 1957–58 recession was serious, no shrinking of productive capacity was contemplated by the leaders of the group Dwight David Eisenhower was later to describe as "the military-industrial complex." The burden of maintaining a syncretic push/pull[1] economy fell on the one economic activity capable of maintaining the market at the end of the pipe-line—sales. Capital would be pumped into the economy by government to pay for war or welfare expenditures, but the responsibility for keeping capital in play in a nation that already had the highest standard of living in the history of the world was given to the salesmen.

During this period the owners of industry and the powerful managers who actually ran the companies separated themselves from the salesmen, reviving a class system that had not been much in evidence since the spread of paper money and the democratizing of the nation after the end of the Revolutionary War. The chief means of distinguishing the owners and managers from the salesmen were the wholesaler, franchise, and agent relationships that had become increasingly common since early in the century. Franchisees, especially automobile dealers, were permitted by the manufacturers to grow rich, but only as long as they obeyed the commands of the men from the company. The burden of selling was passed from the owners and managers down to the dealers, wholesalers, and agents who were required to sell a certain number of cars or donuts or gallons of gasoline in order to maintain the franchise.[2]

Chrysler, Ford, General Motors, Studebaker, Nash, Hudson, and Kaiser built cars according to the always overly optimistic forecasts of their executives, then pushed them onto the dealers who had to pay for the cars, bearing the finance charges until they were able to move the cars out of their showrooms. The dealer was kept in a constant state of fear by the manufacturer. If he didn't meet quotas, the dealer was likely to get less desirable models and colors to sell the next year, and if he continued to fall behind, he was in danger of losing his dealership or, even worse, having the company franchise another dealership in his market area.

The pressure to meet the quotas forced upon the dealers by the manufacturers resulted in business practices that ranged from high pressure to fraud. Automobile and other hard goods dealers appeared on television

[1]   John Kenneth Galbraith has dealt often with this curious aspect of the modern industrial state, wherein the industrialists want the certainties of push (or, at the very least, planned) economies and the profits of the high-risk pull economies.

[2]   By 1990, franchises accounted for more than a third of all retail sales in the United States.

wearing outlandish clothes and screaming at their viewers about bargains, one-day sales, "free gifts." They were known as Madman, Crazy, Wildman, Crackpot, Looney, The Clown, Jester, Joker, and Wheeler-Dealer, and they were never undersold, always willing to bargain, to allow the customer to name his own price, and to give trade-ins that were fantastic, crazy, way over book value. They did handstands, spoke in exclamation points, wrote the arithmetic of haggling on floors, ceilings, windshields, skies, streets, walls, even on their own hands and faces. And no one trusted them.

Through the franchise system the managers and owners had pushed these automobile, appliance, furniture, clothing, building materials, insurance, and real estate salesmen down into the ethical depths they had endured in the Middle Ages. The salesman was once again despised, but this time on practical grounds: The inconstant interpretation of the will of God had been replaced by the iron rule of self-interest. Everyone had winked at sinners, but no one wanted to be the victim of a crook. The salesman was forced to become a seller of himself. A new elite was created in the world of commerce. Salesmen who wanted to have clean hands practiced a different trade: marketing. Those who could not climb into the ranks of marketing dressed themselves in lesser titles: representative, executive, counselor, agent. It was more than mere euphemism. In a world of beleaguered consumers, the one who called himself salesman was cast out of respectability into the slough of hagglers and cheats.

Having the dealer/agent/franchisee system to protect them from the rough dealings of the marketplace, the industrialists were able, for a time, to avoid thinking about the necessary balance between supply and demand. When demand declined, they increased pressure on the dealers. If sales declined, despite such pressures, they raised prices to make up for the loss of revenue. The dealers served as a buffer for the manufacturers, smoothing their schedules for production and profit.

Two other forces were employed by the manufacturers to maintain and steadily increase sales volume, which they called growth: research and development laboratories and advertising agencies. Basic research came out of universities and such commercial organizations as Bell Laboratories, RCA, Hughes, Xerox, Polaroid, and General Electric. Still in the flush of success following the defeat of Germany and Japan, U.S. companies allowed much of their research to be developed and exploited by foreign competitors.

The transistor, a Bell Laboratories discovery, was licensed to the Japanese for a few thousand dollars. Not many years later RCA gave its engineering to the Japanese, who built television sets at low cost and high quality for sale under the RCA brand name as well as their own. Hughes invented the laser, but apparently could not maintain patent protection. The copying machine, which was most important in Japan because the number of characters used by the Japanese made hand lettering and xerography a more efficient method than typing, was invented in the United States, but the market eventually came to be dominated by Japanese manufacturers.

Advertising and sales, however, moved in the opposite direction. U.S. advertising agencies expanded their overseas operations after the war. At first they sold the products made by U.S. multinationals, but slowly began to take on European clients as well. Only in Japan did the U.S. agencies fail. While the Japanese moved into U.S. markets by employing American salesmen, they kept their own market by developing an entirely different structure for advertising agencies. Dentsu, a Japanese agency, accepted clients who were direct competitors, such as two automobile manufacturers. Without the limitation of noncompetitive agreements, Dentsu quickly became one of the largest agencies in the world. Unlike the banking and manufacturing arms of the cartels, the Japanese advertising and sales groups could not establish a beachhead in the United States: While a mediator could move with relative ease from one Western society to another, it was very difficult, almost impossible, for the mediator to cross over from Western to Eastern culture or vice versa; the mediator is, after all, a structural element in society, not an adjunct.[3]

Although the burden on the salesman/mediator was increased by the added inventory exported to the United States from Europe and Japan, a technological advance in the mediation process enabled the salesmen to meet the needs of the producers. James Burke, former CEO of Johnson and Johnson, observed, "I sincerely believe that television saved us after the second world war. Without television, we'd have gone back into the Depression."[4]

Television pictures had been transmitted successfully before the war, but it was not until the 1950s that the medium moved from experiment to

[3]   A homologue does not necessarily translate easily. When the structuralists leap from European fairy tales to myths of the Amazon, they must discover a common triadic structure as an intermediate step. The work is analytical, but not creative.

[4]   Quoted in Martin Mayer, *Whatever Happened to Madison Avenue?* (Boston: Little, Brown, 1991), p. 114.

curiosity. Programming was thin in the early years. There were few choices, the quality of the black-and-white picture was poor, the major movie studios had not yet released their films for television, and the only alternative to live transmission of programs was a film process with almost no gray scale called kinescope. Nevertheless, sporting events, old burlesque hall comedy sketches, and a rebirth of "kitchen sink" drama joined with the genuine comic innovations of Ernie Kovacs, Sid Caesar, and others to deliver an audience to the salesmen.

As the number of households with television sets grew, the number of sales calls also grew. In a period still rich with the innovations that came out of war research, no innovation was better suited to the Promethean role of the salesman than television. Like no other medium, including a live human being, television was able to demonstrate new products and new technologies. Everything came out perfectly. Frozen dinners were always delicious, ice cream never melted, soups were as thick as stew, copy paper never got stuck in the Xerox machine, Polaroid photographs showed only celebrities, and every car ran flawlessly forever on the black-and-white electronic highways of the television screens. The mass producer's dream, which was to send a salesman to every household in America at a cost of only a few cents per sales call, had come true.

On live television a talk show host was able to photograph one of his guests with a Polaroid camera, wait for a minute while the picture developed, then present his guest with a photograph which the guest then held up for the camera to complete the demonstration to the audience. In any other medium the sale would have been much more difficult. Even a home demonstration would have been less effective, for it would have not have come with the endorsement of the talk show host and his famous guest.

Xerography was equally well suited to the television demonstration. Although a demonstration could have been done in a store, the early versions of the machine were too heavy to bring to a potential customer's home or office. Only television could bring the demonstration of the new technology to the customer.

New kinds of refrigerators, new styles in automobiles, high-performance engines, improved washing machines for dishes and clothing, frozen foods, every innovation that came out of the war and the boom years of converting war technology to civilian use was demonstrable on television. Even television sets themselves sold best when sold on television.

But television was not merely an economic asset. Among the effects of television on American culture was the placement of a mediating process between people and reality. Instead of touching a thing, one viewed it on television; instead of looking out the window at the rain, one saw rain in a picture made by the television camera on the roof of the television station. Reality did not cease to exist, of course, but much of what people understood as reality, including virtually all of the commercial world, was mediated by television. It was as if a salesman had been placed between Americans and life.

Before television, the salesman, who mediated between desire and information, was able to affect only a part of life. He worked at what is now usually called the point of sale. His effect was largely limited to manipulating information in the brief encounter. Television operated differently, moving back from the point of sale into the processes of imagination and desire. As television mediated between Americans and more and more of reality, it had a greater opportunity to affect the customer, to change desire, than any previous salesman, including the trickster in Eden.

Television emulated the activities of the trickster/salesman by mediating between dream and truth, reproduction and actuality, the dimensional and the flat, the natural and the willed. Even the word that came to denote all indirect communication, *media,* locates the middle place of the trickster as well as the television transmission.[5] Television behaved like a salesman even when it was not employed as a selling tool. It thrust mediation into the lives of Americans in virtually every activity, replacing reality with appearance, not in the manner of art, stimulating the mind to new imaginings and understandings, but in a limiting way, controlling the imagination and the tendency to inquiry, as salesmen wish to do.

In Plato's version, perception was a meeting place between the eye and the object. With television, the meeting was no longer merely that of the observer and the thing; a third force, a mediator, was introduced into every perception. As the observer had once brought himself to the observation, television now brought camera operators, editors, writers, directors, producers, artists, and lighting technicians. The mediator, following the imperative of technology, sought to control the information about the thing and the desires of the observer.

[5] The first use of the word to denote means of communication is put by the *Oxford English Dictionary* in 1929; it did not come into wide use in the United States, however, until the popularization of television.

Television was perfectly suited to selling, because it could not only change the perception of the thing-in-itself by providing information about it; television could change the thing-in-itself. The perceiver encountered the thing-as-televised rather than the thing-in-itself. Television limited freedom by controlling the world available to one's perception. Through television, America became comfortable with a mediated life, one in which an interpreter came between a person and the world, changing the world according to the interests of the interpreter, as the salesman interprets the product to the customer. There was no essential difference between the sales messages and the news and entertainment programs on television: All were mediated. The customer now lived in a limited world or, more accurately, a world of limited information.

The widespread use of television marked the most profound cultural change since the invention of writing. As writing vastly enlarged the world available to human thought by permitting the accumulation of knowledge, television reduced the world available to direct human experience. Americans were imprisoned in a vast amusement park in which all the rides and all the games, even the hot dogs and cotton candy, were mediated by a machine. No matter how many networks, stations, cable channels, or tapes they were able to choose from, they could not escape from the picture-perfect park in which the barkers and the moon were formally indistinguishable.

Television was also capable of controlling desire, channeling it into areas where desire had not existed; it could affect the precepts or tastes that one brought to perceiving the world. Before television, tastes changed slowly, but once life could itself be mediated every morning, noon, and night—three, five, seven hours a day—desire was more available to change. The continuum on which desire existed remained bounded by need and disinterest; only the variety and the intensity were affected. A new world was thrust into American life. Nothing in this new world was original—that is, direct. Everything was heightened, abbreviated, and pleasurable. And every new aspect of desire wore out quickly, for it was satiated by the experience of the indirect world. Speed increased constantly, leading to faster and faster changes in the aspects of desire. The salesman had his magic machine in television, if he could control it.

Through the mediation of television, things gained in importance. Neither ideas nor relationships could move quickly enough for the speed of television; only things could be matched with the new vagaries of desire. It was a long journey from the *Texaco Star Theater*—with its old vaudevillian, Milton Berle, smoking a cigar while wearing a scullery maid's costume and a bosom made of balloons—to a boy in California killing another over a pair of sneakers, but the direction was set with the introduction of the technology.

4.

Like nothing else, scarcity had taught the American people to treasure consumption. When there was little butter, people developed a taste for butterfat; when there was less than a tankful of gasoline available, people developed a yearning for automobile travel. Goods became the forbidden fruit to people who had the money but couldn't spend it. The speed of television combined with this appetite for material goods to produce a further change in America. A powerful sign of the new society of things came in 1965. It was not the first manifestation; aspects of a society based on consumption had been appearing regularly since the last years of the previous decade, but this was a deep change, for it involved not only the wants of the people; it went to the heart of their political lives. America, now firmly in the hands of the salesmen, had learned to understand political relations as the interaction between people and things rather than simply between people.

A young lawyer published a book about the Chevrolet Corvair, a small car powered by an air-cooled, rear-mounted engine. Ralph Nader said the Corvair was "unsafe at any speed." His book would have caused little comment had not General Motors executives, believing that Nader was employed by Ford to discredit their new design, hired detectives to follow him. The scandal resulted in a public apology by the president of General Motors, the demise of the car, and the beginning of the consumerist movement in America.

Ralph Nader had discovered the change wrought by television and the salesmen. The Depression was finally over. American radicals were no longer socialists or communists; in a nation herded into buying everything it could afford—and more—the dragon slayer took his sword to burned-out toasters and innovative little cars, refrigerators that didn't stay cold, screen doors that rusted in the rain, washing machines that didn't wash, and dryers that didn't dry. With the appearance of Nader and the consumerists, the

value of ordinary material goods was raised to a height beyond the salesman's most glorious dreams. While the hippies, America's bourgeois rebels,
lolled in the streets of San Francisco and the East Village, the consumerists,
working in a loveless and inadvertent alliance with the salesmen, had accomplished the apotheosis of things.

The transformation of the salesman was complete. He had changed his
name to marketer, representative, account executive, creative director—the
ludicrous semanticist and U.S. senator S. I. Hayakawa had even called him
poet. The salesman had moved from the point of sale to the point of
conception. In the wedding of information and desire, the salesman, so long
limited to the control of information, had now entered the realm of desire,
not accidentally, no longer as an adjunct to the greater forces of history but,
thanks to television, as one of the forces that determined the world. Prometheus was no longer sufficient; less than a dozen years after the end of the
Second World War, the ascent of the salesman was in full gallop. The
wretched peddler of God's kingdom had become a titan.

5

A Salesman's History of the World

Part 3: *The Death of Prometheus*

> *. . . the greater share of the fiscal burden passed from the wealthier sector of the population to the poorer, with an accompanying depression in the status of the latter. None of this was completed overnight . . . but in the third century* A.D. *it had visibly happened. Meantime the possibilities of further external solutions . . . gradually came to an end. . . . The ancient world was hastened to its end by its social and political structure, its deeply embedded and institutionalized value system, and, underpinning the whole, the organization and exploitation of its productive forces. There, if one wishes, is an economic explanation of the end of the ancient world.*
>
> M. I. FINLEY

After the Korean War, when Eisenhower was president and young women still wore hats and shivered at the taste of martinis, she went to New York to be a success. All the way across the country, from San Francisco to the change of trains and stations in Chicago, to the last, breathless night aboard the 20th Century Limited, she thought of adjectives and adjectival phrases. She had chosen a career in fashion, but not in design, not directly in design; her field was merchandising. It was artistic, too. Hadn't she won a competition in which more than three hundred graduating seniors from some of the best colleges in America described three pieces from the new Coco Chanel collection?

The Store (the name hadn't been revealed to the contestants, but anyone who knew anything about fashion merchandising knew who was meant by The Store) had promised a one-year training program, five hundred dollars toward a wardrobe, and a ticket to New York from anywhere in the forty-eight states. And she had been chosen!

She recalled now how she had walked the length of the train to the lounge car, thanking the porters or the gentlemen who pulled the heavy doors open on either side of the vestibule as she passed. The smell of perfume, cigarette smoke, and old plush fabric hung in the Pullman cars. They were going south and then east, now traveling through Indiana. She saw sidings, railroad crossings, lights through the reflections in the windows beyond the seats. It was nearly dark when she arrived in the lounge car. She found an empty chair and sat down. A waiter in a white mess jacket put a tiny napkin and a bowl of salted nuts on the small table in front of her. "Sherry," she said. "Please."

The grace and bearing of the waiter interested her. She thought of adjectives to describe him: the color of his skin, the way his hair was turning gray, the crease of his mess jacket in the crook of his arm. She remembered thinking that he was a man, not a manikin, and should not be the mere object of her description; she ought to do something for him. There was plenty of money in the family, insurance, the proceeds from her father's business; even though she was not yet working, she could afford to leave a big tip, and she did.

Her welcome by The Store was beyond their promises and her expectations. They put her up at the Barbizon for a week while she looked for an apartment, and on her first day in New York City she went to lunch at the Algonquin and sat within sight of the fabled round table. As a *New Yorker* reader, she told the head of the advertising department and the head buyer from hosiery and lingerie, she knew quite a lot about Dorothy Parker and her crowd.

The next day, two fashion writers and an advertising person from the *Herald-Tribune* took her to lunch, and the day after that she and an editor from *Mademoiselle,* just the two of them, had drinks in Peacock Alley. She and her mother had been to New York several times, but she had never been inside the Waldorf, with its sense of worldwide commerce. There was a very handsome man at the next table wearing a turban! The editor from *Mademoiselle* had leaned across or rather around the little table and asked in a whisper if she could imagine what it would be like to be alone with him. And she had! She had brought the memory of him home to the Barbizon, where it lay with her all night, like a fire in summer. She went wearily to work the next day.

A young artist on the advertising staff asked if she wanted to share her apartment. "The rent is killing me," she said. That evening they went to the apartment together. It was small, just off Third in the Fifties, but clean. It had been passed down from one newcomer at The Store to the next. There was a rule: the newest girl slept in the living room, but paid only 40 percent of the rent.

It was an almost perfect year at The Store. She made friends and learned the business. There were a few dates. She could still recall the Yale boys, the way they seemed to think they could have her, not just sexually, but emotionally, intellectually, politically, any way they could imagine. It made her smile now to think of their surprise when she disputed their wishes or their wisdom.

There was a Wall Street boy near the end of the year. His name escaped her now. After a few dates, he had pulled her aside at a party, taken her hands in his, and told her she was the wittiest woman he had ever known. "You must be a virgin," she had said so everyone could hear. "My God, there's a virgin in New York City, and I've got him." Of course, he hadn't phoned again after that, but the moment had been worth it; she remembered how everyone at the party had laughed.

She was still a virgin then, and she was to remain in that state for several more years. The only physical change that had taken place in her during that first year in New York was the need to begin using a real girdle instead of the panty girdle that had seen her through college. She liked to eat, and she had found several drinks that interested her more than sherry; gimlets were her favorite.

At the end of her training period, the merchandising department, which included advertising, hired her. "You'll stay on with us," Miss Robbins had said, without ceremony. "Do something with those damned sheaths on four; I'm leaving it up to you." The no-nonsense acceptance, especially in the hard voice of the woman who had changed the language and look of department store advertising, was what she had hoped for. Blessed by a smoker's hack, baptized with a martini straight up; it was New York! Dreamy, schemey New York, she called it, Fashion City, Paris with an erection.

She had proved early on in her training that she could sell. She had a way, her bosses said, of packaging anything to make it appealing. She had style, panache; she knew how to give things pizzazz.

Her middle filled out more the second year. She didn't get fat; she just got a middle. The first time she had a man, she did it in the dark, because she didn't want him to see her middle. "You were a virgin," he said.

"Don't kid yourself, sweetie; you caught me at the very beginning of my period."

"I should have known."

They went out for drinks. It was nearly midnight. She felt giddy. The next morning, she threw up. She was sure she was pregnant.

It wasn't a bad idea, she thought now. Pregnancy. If there had been a child, a little boy, she would have dressed him in short pants; she liked little boys best in short pants with suspenders of the same cloth. Dark blue. A soft wool. Softer. Something that wouldn't irritate those little legs. A cashmere blend. Navy. Cuffed and belted. No, not cuffed. It might irritate him. Hemmed.

In her second year on the job, she named two collections, practically every sale, got rid of the word *gorgeous* once and for all in The Store's copy, and started the trend for using the language of food and art in fashion: *Delectable* was one of her favorites. She once described a fabric as positively pointillist. But she was even more interested in perspectives and palettes, symmetries and surfaces. Anything given into her hands became original, beautiful, desirable. At the end of her third year at the store, the management did something that shocked the industry: They split advertising off from merchandising and put a twenty-three-year-old girl from California in charge of the new department.

As she imagined New York, the city gave her dreams in return. She lived a round of excitement: Lunch at the Ritz, drinks at the Monkey Bar, late-night excursions into the Village, to the White Horse Tavern, and even to dangerous places, where she could observe people breaking the rules of the night as she broke the rules of the day.

On her vacations she went to Paris, not to see the collections (that was business now) but to study cooking with Cordon Bleu chefs. She confused everyone in merchandising as well as advertising when she came back from lunch one day wearing severe, rimless eyeglasses. "Why hide your face with plastic?" she replied to her roommate, who said she looked like she had borrowed the glasses from her maiden aunt. "And do something about your hair!" her roommate said.

"For my own good."

"It's not my head, dearie."

"I cause fashion," she said. "I am not a slave to it."

"You enslave others . . ."

They had never had an unpleasant exchange before, and they vowed never to do it again. To seal their friendship they took on a freelance project: the design of a small boutique on Madison Avenue in the low Sixties. They worked on everything, from merchandise display to the size and color of the type on the register receipts. A week before the store opened, the new *Herald Tribune Sunday Magazine* sent a reporter and a photographer to do a story about the designers.

For the session, the art director chose to dye her hair jet black, put Japanese rice powder on her face, and rouge her lips like a prewar tart. She answered no questions; she posed, as if she had designed herself to fit best into one spot in the corner of the boutique.

It was the writer, the girl with rimless eyeglasses and the granny roll in her hair, who spoke the boutique into existence. She described the clientele as if the store had been open for years. She filled the racks and dressed the naked mannequins with the merchandise of her mind. The new *New York* magazine gave them six pages. The store was a success, but they were famous.

She gave up drinking "for the duration" to devote herself and every extra cent she could get her hands on to the election of John Fitzgerald Kennedy, whom she described as "the Boston squeeze." A week after his election, she surprised The Store by announcing that she had taken a job in San Francisco. She and her roommate had accepted a challenge: Could they do for a moldering chain of California department stores what they had done for a Madison Avenue boutique?

It was an indelible moment. She had been inspired by the new president. Perhaps it was then that her walk had changed, her stance had become more open, assertive? She couldn't recall now. But the exhilaration of the moment! Yes, she could recall that. And the sound of Miss Robbins coughing. What had she said? What had she said? *Renouncing,* that was the word. Renouncing! Miss Robbins had coughed her out of the church.

At the farewell party, held right there in the department, with booze out of people's desk drawers and canapés from the restaurant on eight, she had raised her glass of vodka to the world, and said, "My fellow Americans, we have, uh, got to move forward. We're taking fashion to the moon and beyond: to California!"

They spent six months on high salaries thinking about the California chain before they went to the office of the president with a few splashes of color on a piece of canvas board and her favorite word in very large orange and pink letters: *Pizzazz!*

"Pizzazz?" he said.

"Everywhere," she said.

"We'll start by painting the exterior walls orange and pink. You don't sell clothes; you sell dreams, beauty, fashion, pizzazz."

The business was, as he put it, in the toilet. He shrugged. He painted.

She pinched his cheek as if he were a child. "You stink of cigars."

He called her gorgeous.

The excitement she felt during the transformation of the stores was unlike anything she had ever known; she could feel it, even now, like the flush that comes of eating hot peppers.

National magazines covered the opening. She had telephoned them herself, but she told everyone the publicity had come out of the blue. Most of the stories described her as a genius. One woman reporter said she was ursine.

When her roommate married, she gave her a professional gas range with six burners and two ovens for a gift. "But you're the Cordon Bleu cook," the bride said.

The empty bedroom had looked to her like a coffin. She held a hanky to her nose to keep out the smell of loss. Swept clean, swept clean! Still the odor of dust. Particles floating. She saw them in the morning light, unsettled memories on the air. Nothing had ever been quite so difficult as grinding the coffee beans.

She did not go to the office. She baked meringues and filled them with ice cream, then poured hot chocolate sauce over them, and ate.

The opera was her date during the season. In late spring she went to the ballet. For summers she bought a house in a distant place, in the country, far from fog. She could still smell the handyman. He had beer on his breath. She unbuttoned his pants. "For Christ's sake! You're not wearing shorts!" It still made her laugh. He had been angered by her laughter, but her perfume, the silk of her underwear, had been enough to bring him back.

She dressed him. One of the suits still hung in the closet. She cut his hair and manicured his fingernails. After a few months, he went to Reno for the weekend, and never came back. She prayed for his soul, for she knew he had died. When enough time had gone by, she invited a few of her most intimate friends to a memorial service held in the garden he had made of her country house.

Jack had been killed. Then Martin. And Bobby. She had been watching television the night Bobby was killed—murdered, like her man in the country.

Now she wondered whether he was really dead at all. He hadn't left much behind.

Wagner. Nights of Wagner.

And fog.

A line of merchandise made in Hong Kong precipitated the first problem. It was "kicky," her new favorite word, "colorful and quick." She put on one of the blouses and wore it home. That evening, she undressed in the bathroom, as usual. She saw it first in the mirror, as if in a nightmare. The blouse had printed its pattern on her arms, her shoulders, and every part of her chest and back that was not covered by her slip.

It felt alive to her. Her skin crawled. She reached around and touched herself, even now, years later, feeling the color seeping into her blood. Science fiction, she had said. And laughed. But something had happened to her, perhaps a poison contained in the dyes had really entered her bloodstream. She couldn't think of a thing to say about the new knock-off coat line they were bringing in. Instead of giving it pizzazz, making it kicky, she used the manufacturer's copy.

No one noticed. The coats sold, but they did not sell big. It was not terrific.

"I am no longer terrific," she told the art director, who had moved far from the city to a house in the darkness of the shadows of redwoods. "I have lost my pizzazz."

Although the art director disagreed, she did not disagree vehemently. The friendship cooled; they blamed it on the distance.

In the third year of President Ronald Reagan's second term, the man who smoked cigars and never called her anything but gorgeous had a slight stroke. When he had recovered enough to be sent home from the hospital, he summoned her to his house beside the bay. They sat out on the lawn together near the water, having a light lunch, enjoying the midday sun. To complete the lunch they had big slices of watermelon.

"They took away my cigars," he said, "but I have a new vice." He spat a watermelon seed out over the edge of the breakwater into the sea. "You see how far they go?"

She filled her mouth with watermelon, sorted out the seeds with her teeth and tongue, and spat. The seed fell on the grass in front of her.

"If a young, healthy woman can't spit better than an old man with a stroke, one of two things must be happening," he said. "Either she's not so young or she's selling him something. So tell me, gorgeous, what are you selling?"

"I'm not so young," she said.

"Aha!" he cried, "memories."

She smiled. He smiled in return. His mouth was slightly crooked, marred by the stroke. They sat together in the sun, with their eyes closed, occasionally rousing themselves to spit seeds toward the beginning of the sea. He would not ever be going back to work, and soon neither would she. All around them the department stores were closing, dragged down by the discounters and the shopping malls. The world was changing. Across the blue water of the bay, the city had grown tall and steely. Subterranean trains ran silently under the streets, under the Bay. There were too many cars, too many dresses, too many sweaters, too many pearls, too many. The city had grown tired by the effort of building itself so tall and steely. She spat more seeds toward the Bay, but they fell short of the beginning of the sea. It was the end of the century. There was no more pizzazz.

1.

When I was a boy, before I was old enough to go to kindergarten, when the Depression still withheld the comforts of hope from my family, my grandfather used to lift me up onto his knee to tell me about General Motors. He spoke of stock and margin calls and the stroke that nearly killed him that afternoon in the little park near the stock exchange when he was not yet forty years old. If he had held on to General Motors instead of buying the woolen mill. . . . I did not know what he meant. I had just begun to read, to know the patrician promise in FDR's voice, when he told me of the other pillar of American life, the pillar without a face or even a voice, the lost dream of my grandfather's life.

Thirty-five years later, I witnessed the shock that destroyed the dominion of General Motors, the largest privately owned manufacturing organization in the history of the world. The shock did not come from Japan, as we are prone to think now, forgetting that history does not follow obvious paths; it came from the Middle East. Suddenly, there was no gasoline; the

Arabs had shut off the lifeblood of the automobile industry.

On the fourteenth floor of the General Motors Building in Detroit, where the receptionist looked like the actress Greer Garson and spoke with the same British accent, middle-aged men in dark gray suits and white shirts, an army as neat as numbers, stepped out of the private elevator and passed through the heavy glass doors to the corridors of unmarked offices, where they worked in a mad burlesque of serenity. An unimaginable catastrophe had befallen the American automobile market. Sales had dropped below the replacement level, and stayed there.

The Chinese market that developed after World War II had taught American business that the replacement level was a perfectly dependable minimum upon which to build, rock bottom. There were variations, of course, dips, blips, shortages, strikes, but there was nothing to fear, for the replacement level was always there; the automobile business stood on solid ground. And then the ground gave way.

It was a sales problem, said the men on the fourteenth floor. What was needed was advertising, pricing, dealer incentives, sales contests, a change in the product mix to feature more of the smaller cars, the uncomfortable cars, the little ones, like those pieces of tin that rusted out on the way over from Japan, that junk the Japanese sold to college professors and other politically and socially unreliable people, mainly on the two coasts.

In one of the offices a soft-spoken man in a dark suit, buttoned into his vest, leaned forward to look more closely at a sheet of slick white paper covered with black type. He had been an executive for more than two decades. Although he was not an arrogant man, he had become accustomed to the comforts of those who exert hegemony over world markets. He preferred gray Beluga caviar to the black. He sent a company jet to Germany to have his color slides processed, because he thought the German laboratories did better work. "What are we going to do?" he asked. He looked down at the paper again. There was something plaintive in the message he and his fellow executives had written. Within days the words on the page would be translated and published in Japan as a sign of the vulnerability of the U.S. auto industry.

On the slick white page, the last pillar of American invincibility, the only untied, undefeated contender now that FDR was so long dead and so nearly forgotten, asked people to buy cars, American cars. Do not be afraid, General Motors advised; be loyal. Buy cars, big cars; big cars are better.

"What are we going to do?" the soft-spoken man in the dark suit asked again. He recognized the arrival of obdurate reality, but it was too late: Selling had become the religion of the company. The task of an executive was not to bow before reality; this was General Motors, America; the executive was honor bound to produce a corporate theodicy, justifying the corporation's business error as if he were a theologian vindicating God's act of permitting evil in the world. "This oil crisis is confusing the public," he said. "People aren't buying the cars that are best for them."

My grandfather came to visit that evening. He sat beside me on an airplane. We looked out the window together as the plane passed over New York City, east of the Statue of Liberty and up the East River toward La Guardia Airport. He spoke at length of the fall of General Motors. For him it had never ceased to be America, the twentieth century, upward mobility, the defeat of the Nazis, equality, business as usual, safe home.

He had not noticed the filling of the pipeline, the reliance upon selling, the acceptance of the replacement level as the God-given right of American industry. Although he had invested in the Tucker automobile and lost, he had not lived long enough to see a Japanese car. He remembered gasoline price wars, not imported oil. Expansion was the way of the world to him, the true spoils of war. Nobody ever had to sell him anything; he bought a new Cadillac every three years. He was the replacement level. And he was dead.

A few years later, after the Japanese had used the oil crisis to intrude into the U.S. market, Alex Maier, the General Motors vice president in charge of invention, sat in a small office, a borrowed room, and told the history of what had happened. He was a maverick by then, a man who argued that the best way to reduce cost was to improve quality. He had no voice inside the organization; he spoke to vendors, underlings; he avoided only the press.

Maier had no style, not even the arithmetical demeanor the corporation preferred in its executives. He said that he came from a blue-collar family, that his brother worked on an assembly line. Feisty, wiry, a Scotsman who walked as if he were on the way to clan war, he was past sixty by then, entering the age of angry chronicles. He spoke in a dialect contrary to his profession, an anti-engineering language: words without numbers, ideas, colors, visitations from the statistically unconfirmed world of aesthetics and the soft sciences. For Alex, the fall of American industry had come after the war, but it was not the postwar glut alone that caused the problem; it was culture. Something had changed. Culture, culture. He used the word again and again. He touched the finely made old walnut desk that sat between us. He ran his hand along the edge; he caressed it, speaking reverentially not of the thing, or even of the craftsman who made it, but of the culture that produced such care.

The Japanese still had such a culture, he said. That was the difference between Honda and an American manufacturer. But memory would not allow him to stay with such a simple explanation. He recalled the years before the war, the beautiful things that had been made by American culture, the famous Cord automobiles, the beautiful Cord automobiles. And then he came to the years after the war, the years of production and more production, the production that could not cease, the factories that had to be kept running, the products that had to be sold.

It was the culture, he said. He was expert in the culture of the making of things. He could explain through the example of the careful making of a Honda piston versus the crude production of an American-made piston why Honda automobiles could be smaller, lighter, quicker, more comfortable, and more efficient, all at lower cost. Culture, he said. He spoke as man the maker, the brother of a man who still lived by selling his labor. There had been a change in America, he thought, the rage for quantity had produced a cultural fall from grace. The world had been taken out of his hands.

Perhaps what Maier had seen but could not describe was not a change of culture but something more like Géricault or David painting the tragedy of twentieth-century America: *The Death of Prometheus at the Hands of the Salesmen.*

The situation was the same almost everywhere, not just in the automobile business. Products, forms, methods, varied as the salesmen exercised their power over the culture. In San Francisco the Folger family sold the West Coast remnant of its coffee business to Procter & Gamble. Folger's had been a coffee taster's company, a buyer and roaster of expensive beans. Its advertising and wholesaling had been lackadaisical. The company had the flavor of beans grown at high altitude in volcanic soil to attract customers.

When Procter & Gamble took over the company, a group of humorless men was sent from P&G's Cincinnati headquarters to take charge of the marketing of Folger's coffee in the West. These were the Jesuits of marketing, rigorous thinkers, examiners, cold men, driven by the rules of marketing logic to question every aspect of the business.

They put the business to the rack, the thumb screw, and the boot of the salesman's religion. Every morning they began the inquisition early, continuing it into the afternoon, the evening. The room in which they conducted the inquisition took on the odor of the fear sweat that runs in the body's most hidden creases. No one could resist them. They had the power, they were on the side of the lord of business, they were the marketers.

Before long, they began the testing of new ways to sell the coffee. They peered, as best they could, into the minds of coffee drinkers, and then they changed the information about Folger's coffee. The beans became invested with magical powers to save marriages, foment love and affection. A woman with a Swedish name, Mrs. Olsen, emerged as the shaman of coffee. The advertising budget increased, the sales promotion budget increased. Sales of Folger's coffee in the western states were greater than ever before.

One change they did not advertise, however, was the effect of P&G's policies on the market for high-quality green (unroasted) coffee beans at the port of San Francisco. Ernest Kahl, a coffee broker, told me that prices had fallen sharply. The drop coincided with Procter & Gamble's takeover of Folger's. The decision was obvious to everyone in the business: P&G had chosen to put its money into selling coffee instead of buying it. Obviously, the marginal return on a dollar spent for sales and advertising was greater than the marginal return on high-quality beans. In a world in which information could be changed to match the known desires of the buyer, the ratcheting downward of the quality and character of the product was not only possible; it was profitable. The marketers had only to avoid the Promethean risk of introducing something new; they had only to limit themselves to variations on a cautious theme.

Arthur Miller described the caution of the salesman in the interplay between Willy and Ben in *Death of a Salesman*. Ben was the dreamer, the entrepreneur—a man utterly unlike the salesman, the timid, jealous, mean-spirited man who sought the comforts of the bar car and the call girl. A salesman may live on commissions, but he demands a draw, something to smooth his way, security.

2.

Marketing, which slowly replaced the entrepreneurial spirit in the postwar years, is the capitalist's draw. The purpose of it is not Promethean; marketing seeks to avoid errors. The marketer's dream is the successful repetition of a successful repetition: the line extension, the cloned product put out to fracture the market, taking more of the total sales in the category. For any marketer the greatest problem is innovation. How can the marriage of information and desire be predicted when the information is new and the desire is untried? The newer the product, the greater the risk.[1]

By the middle of the 1980s, advertising and marketing experts were telling prospective customers that the cost of selling had itself become a barrier to entry; it would take more than ten million dollars to introduce a new product. And that was just the cost of selling the product after it was produced and put on the supermarket shelf. Be careful! the marketing experts warned; most new products fail, even when they are introduced by huge corporations with enormous resources; what can a small entrepreneur expect?

The salesmen, led by the advertising industry, studied the views of economists and journalists, producing answers for every question. With the advertising industry in the lead, the salesman sold themselves as the saviors of the republic. Among their chief antagonists was Robert Reich, who argued for innovation, improved quality, and productivity. Reich said that the nation would have to shift to the production of higher-valued goods in order to maintain its standard of living. In response, the American Association of Advertising Agencies (AAAA) produced a brilliant, if specious, argument.

The basis of the argument was the definition of productivity sold by C. Jackson Grayson, Jr., chairman of the American Productivity Center:[2] "Pro-

---

[1]   In *The New Industrial State,* 2d ed. (Boston: Houghton Mifflin, 1971), p. 198, John Kenneth Galbraith began his series of three chapters on demand with a quotation from a 1967 *Fortune* article explaining how Bristol-Myers does not develop products in its labs and then try to market them, but does extensive consumer testing to find a market opportunity, "then turn to the labs for products that might meet these specifications."

Recent events lead to some thoughts about a modification of Galbraith's notion of a "revised sequence" and other certainties about the salesman's ability to manage demand. These are discussed in chapter 11.

[2]   Mr. Grayson sought to understand white-collar as well as blue-collar productivity, at one time intending to open a White Collar Productivity Center. Toward that end he gathered a group of wise men and women in the boardroom of the Bristol-Myers Company. Among those attending the day-long meeting were a fellow from the Yale Management School, the productivity manager of Manufacturer's Hanover Bank, various consultants, academics, scientists, business executives, and me, perhaps because of work I had done for AT&T, which did not want to spend a day of one of its own at the meeting.

Using his definition of productivity, I asked Mr. Grayson how he would figure the productivity for the day, the week, the month, the year, or even the decade for the white-collar workers who invented the transistor. I was prepared to ask about Einstein's productiv-

ductivity is nothing more than a mathematical ratio. It's output over input, that simple." The AAAA argued that it was a mistake to think of productivity as "simply a matter of cost reduction." This erroneous notion, the AAAA said, had caused all the problems of layoffs, and the like. The answer to the productivity problem was added value. For a moment it seemed as if the salesmen's salesmen had accepted the Reich argument, but it was not to be. The AAAA went on,

> *Added value* enters into the equation, as a full and equal partner of reduced cost. Increasing the "output" of product value can improve productivity every bit as much as decreasing the "input" of cost!
>
> Most important, America and other advanced Western economies can deal with the concept of added value. Price realization is a far more comfortable area of competitive endeavor for American business than cost reduction. . . . Competitors do not have the same unconquerable advantages, growing from their lower levels of industrial wages and consumer expectations. The playing field is suddenly more level—or at least more to our liking.

The conclusion of the AAAA argument was inevitable: ". . . *all* roads to profit (including growth in market share and the ability to command a higher price) lead through the gateway of perceived product quality."

Although the booklet in which the argument appeared created little interest in the business community, the attempt to change the commonly used distinction between appearance and reality was a daring move. Since Plato, perception had been a meeting place between the person and the thing. Kant had enlarged the role of the person in perception, but he had not denied the existence of the world. Now, with extraordinary boldness, the American Association of Advertising Agencies said consumer perceptions "are a fundamental part of *manufacturing the product*—as much as size, shape, color, flavor, design, or raw materials."[3] Information, the salesman's only contribution, was no longer merely about the thing; it had become part of the thing itself.

---

ity or even that of Mr. Grayson, but it was not necessary; the transistor seemed to have made the point. If there were further meetings of the group, I was not invited.

[3] The AAAA quotations are from *The Value Side of Productivity,* published by the AAAA in 1989.

Was it possible? Had the salesman moved from being mediator to being maker? Or was it merely an exaggeration of the mediator's role in the sale? The booklet described a desperate case: Reality, as the AAAA judged it, was for the foreseeable future to be on the side of the Western world's competitors. Only the salesmen could save the American economy.

The AAAA's case grew out of the most discouraging development of the half century after the end of the war: the absence of a Promethean revolution. With no great social change, like the one that followed the beginning of the industrial age or the geographical expansion of America or the compression of time and distance that came with the automobile and instantaneous electronic communication, there was nothing but the salesman to keep the country in motion.

As the relentlessly unimaginative years went by, the Promethean salesman, the optimist, with his classic liberal view of the perfectibility of practically everything, gave way to the pessimism of the conservative. Change, as the authors of the AAAA booklet knew, was not coming soon. Innovation in America was likely to be no more than marginal: Cola would change from brown to clear; it would not be replaced by a tablet, a satisfying inhalation, or a thought. The pessimists despaired of perfection or even change; they accepted the world as it was, and described it differently.

At first there had been a certain discomfort among intellectuals about the course of postwar America. In the thoughtful final chapter of his trilogy, *The Americans,* Daniel Boorstin found that the great force at work in America was technology. He wisely separated science from technology, tipped his hat to the increase of knowledge, then went on to voice his concern about the mindless growth of technology.

Writing at the end of the 1960s, Boorstin held that progress toward the consumer society of the period was steady. He characterized the developers of America as "go-getters," and he named inventors, boosters, lawyers, and advertising men among his pantheon of go-getters. Boorstin was not without admiration for the ingenuity of many of his go-getters, but he was also not without concern for the kind of society they created. His massive research had led him to the end of the national expansion; his salesman was still the Promethean actor in the development of America. Boorstin closed his books just before the beginning of the fall in what may yet become the American tragedy.

3.

There was a liberal dream in postwar America, a great expectation: An Age of Information, an economy based on knowledge, was coming. The dream had two major soothsayers, one corporate and one intellectual—AT&T and Daniel Bell.[4] In *The Coming of Post-Industrial Society*, Bell said, "[A] post-industrial society is characterized not by a labor theory but by a knowledge theory of value. It is the codification of knowledge that becomes directive of innovation."

AT&T's view was related to Bell's, but based more in the hard sciences.[5] At the heart of the AT&T view (we did not have the daring to name the entire society, just the communication and computing aspect of it) was the hierarchy of information. Data were at the bottom. Data were known or observed facts, but not in any order. The Nobel laureate Arno Penzias explained the concept to neophytes with a joke. "If I see some brown, sweet, gelatinous stuff on your tie, it's dirt. But if I put that same stuff in a dish, it's chocolate pudding. Data is like dirt, but once you put it in its proper place, in order, it becomes information."

Information, arranged in order, became knowledge. Wisdom was another category entirely. Our view was that AT&T was in the "knowledge business"; that is, by combining computing and communication, AT&T could use machines to aid in the production of knowledge. By extension, we were able to describe a worldwide knowledge system, in which virtually all information could be instantaneously available to any person in any language anywhere on earth or its environs. There were some technical problems to be overcome, of course: the hierarchy of searches, the apportionment of costs, and the danger of making knowledge accessible only to the rich. Nevertheless, AT&T was for a time willing to describe itself as "The

---

[4] As an institution, AT&T (prior to divestiture) was generally managed by political conservatives, but operated as a liberal institution, favoring such things as "social pricing," the use of profits from long-distance service (used by the more affluent) to subsidize local service, and so on.

Daniel Bell was a classic political left/liberal early in his career, but had moved away from many of those views by the 1970s. Nevertheless, *The Coming of Post-Industrial Society* must be counted among the paradigms of liberal thinking in postwar social forecasting.

[5] AT&T's concept was the work of many scientists, planners, and executives, perhaps too many. Although I was responsible for synthesizing some of the ideas and making an orderly exposition of them, the thinking came out of Bell Laboratories.

Knowledge Business." Urged by Edward M. Block, a member of the Office of the Chairman and one of the more thoughtful businessmen of the time, Charles Brown, CEO, and Randall Tobias, vice chairman, began speaking to large audiences about the future as imagined by AT&T.

Meanwhile, Daniel Bell went on to describe what he imagined as the eleven dimensions of postindustrial society. Although it has been two decades since Bell put forward his version of this society, and he lacked Bell Labs' and AT&T's appreciation of many of the technical, economic, and resulting political and social problems, his stately optimism remains of historical importance.

Bell said that the creation and use of knowledge would dominate the future, producing a new class of knowledge workers as the economy shifted from goods to services. There would, he said, be a change in the character of work:

> In a pre-industrial world, life is a game against nature . . . . In an industrial society, work is a game against fabricated nature, in which men become dwarfed by machines as they turn out goods and things. But in a post-industrial world, work is primarily a "game between persons" (between bureaucrat and client, doctor and patient, teacher and student, or within research groups, office groups, service groups.) Thus in the experience of work and daily routine . . . persons have to learn how to live with one another. In the history of human society, this is a completely new and unparalleled state of affairs.

He foresaw a change in the role of women in this world, a more powerful place for science, and a change in the way politics operated, with situses, by which he meant the places where intangible things meet or are located, as political units. "There are four *functional* situses," he said,

> scientific, technological (i.e. applied skills: engineering, economics, medicine), administrative and cultural—and five *institutional* situses—economic enterprises, government bureaus, universities and research complexes, social complexes (e.g. hospitals, social-service centers), and military. My argument is that the major interest conflicts will be between situs groups and that the attachments to these situses might be sufficiently strong to prevent the organization of the new professional groups into a coherent class in society.

He saw nothing but good effects: meritocracy, a time of plenty, and a new economics of information. By the end of his book, however, Bell had second thoughts, reining in his vision in the concluding chapter.

AT&T's expectations were, it seemed, vestiges of the old, highly regulated monopoly. After the Justice Department forced the breakup of the company, everything was changed. Instead of one company serving as the communications link among all the telephones in America, it shrank to its long-distance network, and then the long-distance network began to shrink as MCI and other companies made inroads under the protection of the federal court's mandated "umbrella pricing."[6] The company's venture into the computer business was managed by Arch McGill, a former IBM executive who was touted by Tom Peters as one of the shining examples of modern American business management.[7] In fact, McGill produced one of the most expensive debacles in the history of American business. His brief reign cost AT&T billions and kept the company out of the computer business for more than a decade.

Meanwhile, AT&T's onetime rival IBM, described by Daniel Bell as the paradigmatic business venture of the last third of the twentieth century (General Motors held that honored place, in Bell's view, during the preceding third), was falling apart. IBM was built as a marketing organization rather than an innovative producer. It suffered from the salesman's conservatism, a useful way to do business when the cost of entry for competitors is prohibitive, but a liability when experimentation and even some manufacturing can be done after hours in a basement or garage workshop.[8]

---

[6]   To keep AT&T from using predatory pricing to drive competitors out of business, the government required the company to maintain its prices at a relatively high level, permitting competitors to get a start in business by pricing their services under the umbrella of AT&T prices.

[7]   Peters, the author of several enormously popular books on management, is one of the most successful salesmen of the last quarter of a century. His theories, based in large measure on what he learned from Arch McGill and the management of People's Express, a defunct airline, were not worth much, but Peters sold them in book and lecture form as if they were magical.

The chairman of the board of a small corporation that served both the telephone and the airline industries paid thousands of dollars for the rights to play a Peters videotape at a sales meeting. But the chairman had a problem: His employees knew the facts of the McGill and People's Express cases. If he played the complete tape, including those two examples, his employees would think both the chairman and Peters were fools. He took his cue from Peters, and behaved like a salesman. Prior to the meeting, he had the AT&T and People's Express sections edited out of the tape.

[8]   A Small Business Administration study published in 1982 confirmed that small busi-

Its early arrogance; the promotion of systems network architecture (SNA),[9] a closed architecture that forced customers to choose between IBM and other suppliers rather than putting together networks of equipment from various suppliers; neglect of the software side of the business; and blind dependence upon mainframe computers when smaller, linked computers could provide similar power at much lower cost—all these put IBM in an untenable position.

By 1990 the company was an obvious anachronism. Daniel Bell had apparently missed the real course of the century by a fraction. History showed that the paradigmatic business of the first quarter was U.S. Steel, the paradigm of the second quarter was General Motors. The third quarter belonged to IBM. The last twenty-five years of the century belonged not to a single corporation but to many. It was, indeed, the Age of Information, but information was not the precursor of knowledge; it was the tool of salesmen.[10] The last quarter of the century was dominated by pessimism and conservatism.

William J. Clinton, a conservative Democrat, became president of the United States in 1993. He made much of being born in a town called Hope, but he surely had little faith, for he immediately embarked upon a program to cut the federal deficit by raising taxes and reducing federal spending. Expansion, which had been the synonym for hope during the first two

---

nesses (those employing fewer than 500 people) produced 16.8 percent more innovations per million employees than large businesses, even though 96 percent of the spending on research and development was by large companies.

The flaw in the study is in the definition of innovation: AT&T provided the transistor and the feedback amplifier. Hughes Aircraft or AT&T (there is some dispute) produced the laser. UNIVAC, by some definitions the first electronic computer, was built at General Electric. Can those innovations from large companies properly be compared to the work of one individual, Lazlo Biro, a Hungarian journalist, who invented the ballpoint pen?

Much of the cause of the American decline can be attributed to the failure of America to invent and embrace a new idea powerful enough to transform and energize society. It is unlikely, although not impossible, that a tinkerer, working in a basement workshop, will produce such a basic change. Thus, the choice of American industry to devote increasing amounts of money to marketing and sales rather than to research and development must lead to stagnation.

[9] IBM people actually pronounced the acronym as a single syllable, Sna. To voice the acronym in full and proper IBM fashion requires a curled upper lip, as in a snarl.

[10] A case can also be made for an Age of Services. At the beginning of the twentieth century, nearly three-fourths of all workers were employed in agricultural or blue-collar work. By the end of the century, according to most estimates, nearly 80 percent of all employment will be in service industries.

---

hundred years of the republic, was not the key to his plan. The last liberals, Kennedy and Johnson, had spoken of a New Frontier and a Great Society; Clinton spoke of a lower deficit. *Newsweek* described him in its March 1, 1993, issue as "The First Salesman."

4.

In every tragedy, according to Aristotle, there is a peripety, "the change . . . from one state of things within the play to its opposite . . . in the probable or necessary sequence of events." The American peripety occurred at some time during the last quarter of the century. Lester Thurow placed it in the middle of the 1970s. Kevin Phillips puts it a decade later. Both men are correct, for the size and inertia of a drama so great as America produces such momentum that change takes place over decades.

In *The Zero Sum Society*, Thurow wrote, "In the period from 1972 to 1978, industrial productivity rose 1 percent per year in the United States, almost 4 percent in West Germany, and over 5 percent in Japan. These countries were introducing new products and improving the process of making old products faster than we were. Major American firms were reduced to marketing new consumer goods such as video recorders, which were made exclusively by the Japanese."[11]

Thurow described the fall in income of the lowest 60 percent of the population, and how it was made up by income transfer payments. He predicted further problems with transfer payments in the 1980s, and he was correct. Income was redistributed in the 1980s through a diminution of transfer payments, except payments to the elderly and accumulations of money by the wealthy. The eventual result of this was to be the inability of the salesmen to maintain the continuous rightward shift of the demand curve.[12]

While the rich can hardly ever be oversold, exhausting their resources, the poorer a person is, the more quickly that person can be oversold. As the numbers of the rich in relation to the poor and middle class shifted, that part

[11]   (New York: Basic Books, 1980), p. 5.

[12]   On the classic economists' charts, increases in demand are shown on the horizontal axis; increases in price, on the vertical axis. If a factor other than price, such as a change in consumer attitudes, a demographic change, greater availability of credit, and so on, increases demand, the entire curve moves rightward; that is, at any given price, demand is higher.

111

of the population which was oversold increased dramatically. The economic problem Thurow foresaw as a zero sum game, an accurate abstract description of a stagnant nation, was in fact worse than that.

Kevin Phillips, with the advantage of another ten years of history, placed the peripety in the 1980s, when the share of the national wealth held by the top 1 percent of Americans increased from 27 percent in the 1970s to 36 percent at the beginning of the 1990s, according to the *New York Times*. During that same period the share of income of the top 1 percent nearly doubled.

In *The Politics of Rich and Poor,* Phillips noted that "median family incomes had started to sag in the 1970s, yet the gap between the top 1 percent and the people in the middle got steadily bigger under Reagan— and government tax policy, deregulation, budget shifts, tight money and high interest rates all played a role."[13]

Phillips began the first chapter of his book, "As the Reagan years ended, the uncertain future hung like a temperature inversion over America's substantial prosperity. The economy was enjoying the century's longest peacetime recovery cycle. But economic power and riches were realigning around the world, and the two most striking economic groups of 1989 represented a stark contradiction: billionaires—and the homeless."

The facts of the peripety were unavoidable: median after-tax family income fell, housing ownership for people under forty-five years old began to fall; however, between 1975 and 1989 the price of Impressionist paintings, according to Sotheby's index, increased 1,500 percent. During the same period, the decrease in the percentage of children living in poverty (an accomplishment of the Great Society programs) turned around and began to climb rapidly.

Between 1965 and 1989 the pay of corporate CEOs rose almost twice as fast as that of workers. The divergence reached three-quarters of a million dollars a year in 1988: $773,000 to $21,735.

Phillips noted the change in family income by decile, with the first eight losing income in constant dollars between 1977 and 1988 and the ninth and tenth deciles gaining. The loss of the first decile (14.8 percent) was nearly equal to the gain of the tenth decile (16.5 percent). No doubt the peripety would have become apparent sooner, perhaps as early as the end of the 1960s, had it not been for the advent of selling via television and

[13] (New York: Harper Perennial, 1991), p. xi.

Lyndon Johnson's Keynesian distortions toward equilibrium.

The growth rate of the gross national product, which had averaged 4.6 percent during the first half of the 1960s, surpassed that level only once in the next thirty years: in 1984 it was 6.8 percent. From 1966 to 1970 it fell to an average of 3.0 percent; and from 1971 to 1983 it averaged less than 2.5 percent. The official recession came at the end of 1989, but the peripety had begun long before. Among the many signs was the foreign debt. During the first six years of the 1980s, the United States went from being the world's largest creditor nation to being the world's largest debtor.

Americans could still sell, especially to each other, but the making of goods for sale was often done better and at lower cost by foreign competitors. The Japanese became the world's largest creditors, largely by using American salesmen to push their products.

During the 1980s, when the peripety was taking place, the financial markets in the United States boomed, reflecting not the economy, or even the value of the companies whose stocks and bonds were bought and sold, but the value of selling itself. Michael Metz, chief investment strategist at Oppenheimer & Company, told the secret to *Fortune*:[14] "There is nothing like higher prices to attract more buyers. In department stores you mark merchandise down to move it. On Wall Street, you mark it up."

In department stores one also offers installment credit to move merchandise, for it momentarily lowers the price to zero, changing the psychological and economic character of the transaction. Given its power to alter the mind of the consumer, the acceptance of installment debt was probably the most important sale made in the United States in the twentieth century. And one of the most difficult. A nation founded by people with an Old Testament aversion to usury, with centuries of Protestant preaching against debt in its cultural memory, and the lesson of the harsh life of indentured servitude not quite buried in the past of many families, did not come easily to installment buying. The 1920s, however, were an ideal time to present a new morality in America. The war was over, the Allies had won, the world was safe, the Federal Reserve System was sure to put an end to financial panics; optimism overcame the old taboos about debt. Between the early twenties and the crash, personal debt increased by 50 percent.

The experiences of the Depression, when homes and cars were repossessed, wiping out the assets of entire families, must have been fresh in the

[14] April 5, 1993.

minds of the people asked to take on new debt in the postwar era. Yet, the salesmen were able to persuade Americans to go into debt again, and to a greater extent than ever before. The Securities and Exchange Commission set limits on margin buying in the stock market, but no government agency set limits on installment credit or interest rates.

In 1950 total consumer credit was $23 billion. By 1990 it had increased over 3,400 percent, to $794 billion. Installment credit alone rose from $15 billion to $738 billion over the same period, an increase of 4,900 percent. Credit was the salesman's indispensable ally; in his effort to promote the wedding of information and desire, he had at last found the key to unleashing consumer demand.

The availability of credit had two powerful effects on American society. People without ready cash could raise their standard of living through credit, narrowing the apparent gap between rich and poor. A similar leveling effect had come about when paper money enabled the early-nineteenth-century tradesman to separate himself from the social bondage of barter and alliances with wealthy families. Credit produced a different, although equally quiet, social revolution. It was also egalitarian, a democratizing force. Installment credit allowed people to acquire material goods, but at tremendous cost. As the salesmen used the lure of credit and the pleasures of possessions to break down the old Protestant inhibition of desire, there was an increase in spending and a decrease in saving, which left less affluent Americans with negative capital.

More money flowed to the lenders as the annual rate of interest on installment loans passed 20 percent. The price of a television set at 20 or even 22 percent annual interest paid over five years was double the ticketed price. By selling installment credit the salesmen were able to keep the factories and stores operating, avoiding the economic debacle of overproduction, but the cost to middle- and working-class Americans was disproportionately high. They paid twice as much as the rich for the same goods. Interest costs ate into their ability to buy real goods. Unless they could borrow an infinite amount of money, the fall of their standard of living was inevitable.

The burden of installment debt contributed to the divergence between rich and poor during the Reagan and Bush presidencies. Yet, the salesmen could not have succeeded without it. Along with the power of television, installment credit held off the second Depression of the century.

The other effect of weakening the inhibition of desire was not so salubrious. It changed the character of the people who spent their money and then their credit in pursuit of an equality of things. They could no longer bear the pain of falling behind in the quest. Credit taught Americans that they did not have to wait; under the salesman's tutelage, pleasure displaced hope. The game, as everyone knew, is to the swift.

Consumption had been a contest since Thorstein Veblen wrote about it at the turn of the century, but this agonistic[15] aspect was then limited to a few distasteful people—the rich, who carried out a more or less civilized reproduction of the predator's games of the playing field. Credit brought the agonistic habits of the rich to the lives of the poor, but it could not bring the wherewithal to satisfy the uninhibited desire for things. Inevitably, the poor, the working class, and the middle class were defeated in the contest to achieve an ever higher standard of waste; their desire was disappointed, and it became yearning. They suffered anguish, as if for the lost or the dead. For some the anguish was unbearable. At the extreme a child killed another over a pair of athletic shoes; a gang member in East Los Angeles described the tragedy of ghetto life: "Sure I got a bicycle, but I didn't get a bicycle when I wanted a bicycle." The sale had been made. There was no way to turn off the wellspring of desire, but there was no more credit, no more expansion; the salesmen had left the customers at an unbearable impasse.

In a zero-sum economy, the salesmen could find no new customers; there was nothing left for them but to turn on each other in a struggle to increase their share of a stable or diminishing market. By the end of the 1980s, *Fortune* put its imprimatur on the new character of the salesman, advising its readers to "think murderous."[16] The grammar was a bit dicey and the advice less than original, but nothing revealed the new role of the American salesman so well as the brutally stated imperative from the editors of *Fortune*. The culture bearer had become a killer.

Advertising, the public sales call, reflected the change early on. During the first sixty years of the century, the role of advertising had been to introduce new products, creating new markets and expanding existing markets. Many people still recall AT&T's famous campaign to increase long-distance telephone usage: "Reach out and touch someone." The auto industry put its efforts behind creating the two-car and then the three-car

---

[15] Veblen chose this word rather than *competitive,* the more common word, because *agonistic* carries the news of its origins, which were in the Greek athletic contests as well as in the struggles between characters in drama and debate.

[16] October 5, 1990.

family. Tobacco companies sought to expand their market to include more women and children. Public disparagement of competitive products, known in the industry as "ash canning," was frowned upon; gentle persons did not even mention their competitors in public.

The first major break in the etiquette of public selling came when Chrysler Corporation published an advertisement inviting readers to "compare all three," meaning Ford, General Motors, and Chrysler products at the same price.[17] Some eyebrows were raised, but most people saw it as a good strategy for the industry laggard; common thinking at the time was that only market leaders were rewarded for expanding the market.

A quarter of a century later, Louis T. Hagopian, who had managed advertising at Chrysler, complained of the change that had taken place in the character of competition. "It's no longer a matter of taking business from a competitor," he said. "Now people are out to kill the other guy." And it was true. After deregulation, airlines forced each other out of business. Electronics companies cut each other's prices with no intention other than forcing the competition out of business. Retailers discounted themselves into bankruptcy while trying to ruin their competitors. Large businesses suffered, and small businesses suffered even more. The federal government lent Chrysler more than a billion dollars to keep the company from going out of business, but the corner grocer and the small electronics manufacturer or the auto parts maker had no allies. By 1990 the number of business failures was five times as high as it had been at the beginning of the decade.

Geico, an insurance company, proudly told the press how it looks for markets in which its competitors are having problems, then increases advertising expenditures and cuts prices in those markets. The AAAA produced a pamphlet called *Advertising in a Recession* to urge advertisers to increase their budgets instead of cutting back as sales fell. The thesis of the booklet was that by increasing advertising budgets during a recession, a company was likely to take market share away from its competitors. The booklet offered many examples, concluding a chapter on the history of advertising during recessions with a case study of the beer business:

> . . . Miller versus Schlitz in 1976, Schlitz's major media expenditures
> were $30 million, to Miller's $28 million. But in the recession years,

---

[17] In the competitive lexicon of the auto industry, a car that won sales away from a competitor was known as a "conquest vehicle."

Miller boosted advertising, rising to $32 million in 1977, $50 million in '78, and $59 million in '79. When Schlitz finally went to $44 million in 1979, it was spending about 25 percent less than Miller. The rest is history.

No tale of the salesman as killer could be more exemplary. There had been many successful breweries in the United States until Anheuser-Busch and Philip Morris, which owned Miller, determined to kill the competition. Using huge advertising expenditures, as well as some of the harsher practices of distributing beer learned during Prohibition, the two companies killed Schlitz and their other major competitors. Wine distributors followed similar practices. Every company that sold through supermarkets adopted the same strategy.

Nice people said the work had to do with strengthening brands, increasing share of market, but the truth was that Vico's cycle, in which the age of men led back into the age of beasts, seemed to have more validity as the expansion begun in Eden came to a stop. The salesman, although still principally a mediator, invaded every aspect of life. *Business Week* described the ideal head of a corporation as "salesman-in-chief." Books began as marketing ideas, films were defined by their box office results, the sequel was more to be treasured than the original, the president of the United States relied upon the salesmen who had run his political campaign to guide the conduct of his office.

There was no end to selling. The best of newspapers and magazines vied with the worst to see which could sell themselves most effectively. Surgeons wooed referrals from internists with cases of wine and yachting vacations. Marketing dragged the lowest common denominator down toward bestial appetites. The separation between appearance and reality was widened for the sake of power and then for the sake of survival. Genius was confused with persuasion. Whoever did not sell languished.

A crisis of recognition occurred, for it was not to the advantage of the nation to be known as an agglomeration of salesmen. It had been a long and extremely parlous journey from the first mediations in Eden or the youth of the world, and there was more than a little danger that, in America, the salesman had come to his destination.

PART
2

Deception

is always meant

to please.

6

Tolerance,
Indifference,
and Democracy

> . . . right *consists in* liberty *to do or to forbear, whereas* law *determines and binds to one of them, so that* law *and* right *differ as much as* obligation *and* liberty, *which in one and the same matter are inconsistent.*
>
> —THOMAS HOBBES

Some people who sell advertising are still known as time or space salesmen, but most of them are called media representatives now, which gets shortened to media reps, or just reps, and there are a few who are known as reptiles. He was a reptile.

Everyone said he looked the part, which was not true. He bore no resemblance to a snake or a Gila monster or the other scaly things that lived in the area covered by the station's signal, but it was not easy to look at him. He had a strangely naked head, like a rubber doll, and something had wounded him, probably at birth, leaving a deep depression on the right side of his face, distorting his cheek and his right ear and causing a bulge in his forehead.

The wound would have evoked pity or at least sympathy had it not been for the rubbery, ductile appearance of his head, which made it seem likely that at any moment the deformation would pop back into place, returning him to normal, in fact banal, unattractiveness. As a result, his wound was presumed to be a deception, a salesman's trick executed with the complicity of nature, just the kind of thing a reptile would do.

No one could understand why the station hired such a strange, unpleasant man. The old hands blamed it on absentee ownership, wealth inherited by children who didn't care about the business. A reptile was out of character for the station, they said. It was the "quality sound in town," the first station in that part of the country, the most reliable place for news, the only local station that would broadcast the Metropolitan Opera on Saturday afternoon, the one that still refused to play rock and roll. When President Kennedy was assassinated, they had refused to broadcast commercial announcements for a full week, even deleting them from the network feeds.

From the moment he arrived, everyone at the station disliked the reptile. There were no exceptions. He was a negative man, the kind who never let up. If you said you loved America, he would speak of the beauty and culture of France. If you said you loved France, he would argue that it didn't compare to Italy. But with his customers. . . . Oh! how different he was with his customers! He fought for the best places on the log, he tried to sneak in extra spots, he knew how to work a rate card; there was no question about it, he was willing to screw the station to help his customers!

He did favors for his advertisers, even the little ones, especially the little ones; he stayed up nights working on their copy; he urged the disc jockeys to plug their merchandise, promote their sales. Although he never took anything away from his colleagues on the sales staff, he was known around town as a thief, the kind of guy who took spots, whole schedules, away from other stations.

The reptile didn't waste much time in small talk, except to amuse himself by demeaning people, but every week after the sales meeting, he and the rest of the staff went over to Matilda's Lunch for coffee and donuts, and the reptile held court. He never permitted anyone else to speak while he told them his secret over and over again, pounding the point home in his tough Brooklyn Irish accent: "Think! Think, for crissake! What do your customers want? You find out what they want, and then you give it to 'em. Service. Your customer wants his ass kissed, get him a blow job. He wants a blow job, get him a whole fuckin' orgy. That's service! And service is money in your pocket, boys. Mark my word."

When the reptile was adamant—and he was almost always adamant about something—the bulge in his forehead pulsed. The chief engineer said it made him look like science fiction. The disc jockeys averted their eyes. The other salesmen seemed not to notice; sometimes they stayed with him at Matilda's through the lunch hour.

Notice of the reptile's promotion to sales manager came in a letter from the owners, who lived in Bermuda. The man he replaced was a fixture in the community, a former city councilman, one of those tall, upright, leathery men who belonged to the legendary West, a white-haired gentleman in Tony Lama boots. Everyone at the station complained about the loss of class, the degradation. There was an incident between the reptile and the program director.

"I don't like the way you do business," the program director said. "Your interference with the logs may actually be illegal, and your methods are cheap."

The bulge in the reptile's forehead pulsed. "Oh, you make me sick with your cockamamie culture. You tell us you're a gentleman, but you have a cracker soul, you son of a bitch. You tell us now that when you worked in Oxford, Mississippi, you knew William Faulkner. But you're so fuckin' dumb you didn't know you knew Faulkner until I told you so. You thought he was the town drunk, didn't you, you feeble-minded fuck. You're nothing but a redneck asshole. A fart, man, a phony fart—you don't even have any stink to you. Even so, you make me sick!"

The program director closed his hand into a fist, and drew his arm back, but when he saw the reptile do a dancing step and waggle his rubbery head, the program director changed his mind, and ended the confrontation with a sneer.

No one approved of the elevation of the reptile, but no one quit. Within a few months, he had transformed the sales staff into a nest of reptiles. The number of accounts on the air increased by a third over the previous year. Revenues, however, went up less, because reptiles took small accounts and knew how to work the rate card.

At the end of the year, the reptile wrote to the owners in Bermuda, telling them he wanted to add another salesman to the staff. With the growth in the number of accounts nearing 50 percent, he explained, he was afraid that the staff would not be able to service their customers properly.

Moreover, getting business was no longer easy; there were now two rock and roll stations in town, and they were improving their ratings every month, hurting everyone, even the shitkickers.

Agreement from the owners came by return mail.

The reptile advertised the job, and personally interviewed every person who responded to the ad. He asked many of the candidates to come back for a second or a third or even a fourth interview before he made up his mind. Then he hired a Mexican.

In the forty years since the founding of the station, there had never been a Mexican in a white-collar job, not a salesman or a bookkeeper or a secretary, not even a receptionist or a telephone operator. The other reps greeted the Mexican with a shrug. A new man made very little difference to them; he always got a couple of house accounts to keep him from starving to death and a list of dogs to try his mettle. As they saw it, the worst part of joining the staff now was the training; the Mexican would be spending a lot of time in the company of the sales manager.

The training was more intense than they had imagined. The reptile kept the new man with him all day, every day. They ate together, went on sales calls together, examined the next day's log together, complained to the national account reps in New York together; some people said they even went to the toilet together.

For the first few weeks the Mexican had a difficult time. He was a shy fellow, with a fat face and a high-pitched voice. Although he dressed well, always in brown suits with a slightly western flair in the stitching, he had trouble holding the attention of customers. They spoke over his head, they looked around him, through him, as if he weren't there. They wanted to deal with the reptile. He was their man, they said; he knew how to work the rate card.

Most people at the station thought the Mexican would not survive. They avoided him, they made the world into a desert around him, they left him to die. If he smiled, they nodded. If he asked a question, they grunted. If he offered a stick of gum, they folded their arms and turned away. The rumors started after the third week. The reptile was going to fire him. It was inevitable.

But the Mexican caught on. His voice came down an octave and the slowing of his breath allowed his cheeks to deflate, giving some definition to his face. He stopped sweating and blinking. As if by a miracle, he suddenly looked like a man who knew how to work the rate card. And the sales came.

He could talk to the salesmen who owned the clothing stores and auto repair shops. One small account after another gave its business to him.

When the reptile asked the Mexican if he knew the secret of his sudden success, he answered, "Yes. I can hear them now. I can hear between the words, as you said. I get the message."

"You're still a shit-for-brains, like all the rest," the reptile said, "but you'll make a living."

Long after his training was complete, the Mexican and the reptile continued to work together, the first to get to the office in the morning, the last to leave at night, two men who never let up. Their demise came about slowly. One contract after another went sour. The accounts they lost were the big ones, the solid ones, the Establishment: four banks and all three utilities, two of the town's leading car dealers, a department store. They were the old accounts, house accounts, the bread and butter of the station.

Most of the cancellations came by letter, a few by telephone. There were no explanations, no promises. The accounts just dried up and blew away, things on the wind, flowers at the end of their season. The Mexican lost the octave of confidence he had won from his voice, but the reptile did not falter, not for a long time, not until all the days of his work were empty, not until he too heard the old cowboy song.

1.

Salesmen do not stay long in other people's lives. Someone buys a car, a pair of shoes, watches a television commercial, or glances at an ad; the purchase lingers, the salesman moves on. The encounter reveals nothing about the character of the salesman; it is not to his advantage to let his customers know what he thinks, especially what he thinks of them.

He does not announce the way his gut responds to the color of the customer's skin, or his politics, or the smell of the food cooking on the stove. He keeps his feelings secret. If the salesman lets his customers find out that he considers them strangers, unappealing, people who must be tolerated, he won't make many sales.

For that reason tolerance, which enables the salesman to expand his business beyond his "natural market," to sell to people unrelated to him, unlike him, has always been the unspoken aspect of his work, the one that does not appear in sales manuals or autobiographies. A salesman is, above all, a practical man. He keeps the secret of his virtue, because he knows that if it were made public, he could not do his business. Some customers would find his tolerance an explicit insult; every customer would be suspicious of his handshake and his smile. Who would trust the sincerity of a person who found it necessary to tolerate him? The salesman's virtue would be understood as patronizing, a polite form of holding his nose.

The salesman also keeps his tolerance a secret from himself. He wants pleasures, not comforts; great victories, not a little cache of virtue. He prefers to be one of Veblen's predators, an agonistic man, not one who suppresses distaste. Yet, tolerance guides him, defines him, permits him to trudge through the encounters of his daily work.

If I had not been a salesman, I might still have imagined this, but I would not have known it, and if I were still a salesman, I would not admit to it.

Tolerance, the virtue in the salesman's life, is both a secret and a lie. In other words, it is a false virtue: The salesman tolerates, but he is not tolerant, which may seem contradictory now, but will become clear later in this chapter. But first, I think it will be useful to give a few examples of tolerance in the world of salesmen.

2. Four Variations on Tolerance

It was long after the end of the Vietnam War when I made a trip overseas in the company of two General Motors executives. One of the GM[1] men on the flight, John W. McNulty, was then assistant to the chairman of the board. Before joining the company, McNulty had worked as a fund-raiser, a publicist for John D. Rockefeller, and then as a speechwriter for President Lyndon B. Johnson. Although we knew each other by reputation, McNulty and I had never met.

Since it was an evening flight, dinner was served shortly after the plane finished its steep climb into the sky over the Atlantic Ocean. McNulty and the other GM man ate quickly and headed up into the small lounge in the hump of the 747 to play gin rummy. While they played, they drank. It was

---

[1] Spelling is one of the few areas in which General Motors has consistently been more efficient than the Japanese. Company style spells GM without the usual periods and employe without the second *e*. Although I have never seen the figures, I feel certain that an employe on the GM financial staff has calculated the time, ink, and paper saved by these efficiencies on an annual basis, broken out by division and staff.

long after midnight when they abandoned the gin game, and came down to the main cabin. McNulty sat down beside me. He was tired and a little drunk. We began to talk about the car business. Suddenly, the weariness disappeared from his face; he turned to me, and said, "You think selling Chevrolets is important? What difference does it make if we sell a Chevrolet or a Pontiac? When I worked for President Johnson, we had to sell the Vietnam War."

We talked about his work in the White House, the Johnson social programs, the Voting Rights Act. He had worked with Bill Moyers and Peter Benchley. It had been a good time, except for the war. After a while, I thought it best to clarify our positions. I said, "While you were working for Johnson, I was writing pieces for *Ramparts* and a lot of other antiwar newspapers and magazines. Jack, we kicked your ass."

He laughed, I laughed, and we had a drink. Although neither of us ever changed his position on the Vietnam War, McNulty and I worked together for more than ten years. After a long time we became friends, but in the beginning we tolerated each other, as salesmen do.

Every sale requires tolerance; some require too much. I knew a man who was, in his own life, perfectly decent. As a salesman, he was required to service a customer who demanded food, drink, and sadomasochistic whoring as inducements. The sale was a very large one, tens of millions of dollars, so the salesman let others, his minions, provide the whores and the leather goods, while he oversaw the business.

After a few years the customer got fed up with the salesman who did not drink with him or participate in his whoring. Since he was the customer, he did not have to be tolerant. One day he telephoned the salesman's boss, and said, "I don't want any Boy Scouts on my business. Get rid of him."

When the boss fired him off the account, the salesman was surprised. He thought he had been tolerant. He told the boss he had done all that he could and was sorry if it had not been enough. The boss was very understanding, but he never again assigned the man to a very large account. The boss told me later that the man had disappointed him: He was not a good salesman.

Now and then, the transfer of the tolerance of selling to the realm of politics required no metaphors. When I worked in San Francisco, Peter Dailey and I used to excuse ourselves from meetings in the late afternoon to attend to other business. He went off to Sacramento to ride in the next morning's Reagan ranch breakfast, and I went down the street to work on *Scanlan's,* an antiwar magazine. Pete knew where I was going, and I knew where he was going.

A few years later, after I had moved to New York, I read in the newspapers that Pete had been named to head the November Group, which had as its sole mission the reelection of Richard Nixon. I was disappointed. I had always thought Pete went to the Reagan ranch breakfasts to look for new business. It made no sense to me then. Pete's lawyer was one of the leading antiwar attorneys in Los Angeles. I had worked in his San Francisco office. But there he was! Peter Dailey, a man so open in business dealings that I had wondered whether he was naive, was managing the campaign to reelect the president.[2]

Not more than a week later, Pete telephoned me in New York. We chatted for a few seconds; he invested a flattering sentence or two, then said, "I'm forming a group to do the advertising for President Nixon's reelection campaign. I'd like you to give us the advantage of your thinking."

I was astonished. He knew me and my work. He must have known that I had recently met with the leaders of the Provisional Revolutionary Government (Viet Cong) in Paris, and yet he was inviting me to work for Richard Nixon. How was it possible? I wondered. The piece I had published about my conversations with the Viet Cong contained their rebuttal to Nixon's argument that a Communist victory in Vietnam would result in a bloodbath.

I declined with laughter: "Pete, have you got the wrong guy!"

He seemed surprised. He said something about "coming around," and then he laughed, too.

Pete was a true salesman; he took me for such a salesman too. In his world there were many products; I think he could not understand why there were so few in mine. He really did go to the Reagan ranch breakfasts to find new business for his company, even if the business he found was ideology. His interest was not in the product but in the sale. The irony of his situation was that at the core he was neither a Democrat nor a Republican, he was a democrat; it was the competition that pleased him, he had no interest in the beauty of the rules.

---

[2] Dailey also managed the advertising campaign for Ronald Reagan in 1980.

The speed of business makes it almost impossible to think. There is barely time enough to scheme, plot, plan, let alone contemplate the meaning of ordinary acts. No salesman ever explained his tolerance to me. Pete Dailey described it, but he did not or could not explain. On the other hand, salesmen constantly advised me not to discuss my politics with engineers, financial executives, professional managers, or owners. And on the few occasions when I tested their advice, it proved correct. The manager of a business threatened to have me fired for writing an article unfavorable to S. I. Hayakawa, who was then a U.S. senator from California. The editors of *Human Events,* perhaps the most right-wing magazine published in America, with the help of Ronald Reagan, attempted to ruin N. W. Ayer and me because we bought space in magazines they did not agree with.

It happened this way: Spurred by an editorial he had read in *Human Events,* then former governor of California, but not yet president of the United States, Reagan twice used his weekly radio broadcast to attack N. W. Ayer and its clients General Motors and AT&T, for placing advertisements in politically liberal/left magazines, arguing that these corporations were aiding people who preached the violent overthrow of the government. He did not mention that the same advertisements ran in politically conservative/right magazines.

The rightists singled out the placement of an ad in the *Progressive,* which had been added to the schedule at the suggestion of Anthony G. DeLorenzo, the legendary vice president of public relations at General Motors. DeLorenzo had attended the University of Wisconsin with the publisher of the magazine. There was no political connection, for DeLorenzo was a staunch Republican, but he admired the quality of his friend's magazine and believed that its readers should know more about General Motors.

From the salesman's point of view, it made more sense to compete with the ideas in the *Progressive* than to agree with the ideas in some other magazine. Reagan did not understand the world that way, for he had never been a salesman; he had been a spokesman, a tool of salesmen, but never a salesman.

For the most part, the tolerance of salesmen does not involve the morality of the Vietnam War or the dealings of great corporations. It takes place in retail stores and living rooms, in affluent suburbs and ghetto neighborhoods. The difference between the tolerance of the salesman and that of the customer in the ghettos of New York City and Los Angeles demonstrates the point: In both cities, Asians, mainly Koreans, have opened small retail stores in black neighborhoods. The Asians, who often arrive in the neighborhood speaking little English and knowing almost nothing about black culture, learn the language, the diet, the style of preparing food of the blacks; they do business, they instigate business contacts, they sell. On the other side, the customers often demand that the Asian store owners move out and turn their businesses over to blacks. In ordinary times the customers organize boycotts of the stores; when there is a major disturbance in the neighborhood, the stores owned by foreigners are the first to be looted and burned.

Whether these businesses in culturally foreign neighborhoods exploit the residents or bring necessary services to them is an important question, but it is not the question here. What matters is that the sellers may not like the buyers, they may find them strange, unappealing, or whatever, but they tolerate them.

It is no different when a black electronics salesman encounters an Asian or a white customer. The salesman may be put off by the sound of the Asian language or the smell of a white man's breath. He may hate whites. A cross may have been burned on his front lawn when he was a child, but he tolerates his customer.

3. Capitalists and Salesmen

If there were some sort of quantitative study of the souls of salesmen, this would be the ideal place to present it, but there is none that I know of. The anecdotes I've told here will have to do as the direct evidence of the tolerance of salesmen, providing an entrance to the politics of the mediator's life.

At the core every salesman is a practical person who understands himself as a creation of competition. And here a distinction must be drawn between capitalism and competition. The salesman is not usually a capitalist; he is a mediator between those who have goods and those who have money or credit to spend. Capitalists live on one side of the business, consumers on the other, with the salesman in the center, like a sign in logic describing the relation of one proposition to another.

Viewed from the capitalist's perspective, competition drives prices down, interferes with profit margins, brings an element of risk into the business, and so on; tolerance is not to his advantage, he would prefer to be a monopolist. From the salesman's perspective, competition is the very reason for his existence; he not only tolerates competition, he embraces it, for the greater the competition, the greater the value of the salesman. In this, the salesman and the capitalist are at odds.

4. Practical Tolerance, Moral Tolerance, and Indifference

The behavior of the salesman sometimes appears to be a result of indifference rather than tolerance, especially in the political world, but the salesman has no experience with indifference, either historically or in the practice of his business. Historically, the salesman was never more than tolerated; that is, he was disliked, even condemned, like most dissenters or heretics, but he was permitted to operate in the world because he was necessary or useful.

In this respect, salesmen, blacks, Jews, and Asians share a similar history. Never more than tolerated, the Jews became tolerant, liberal. When Jews achieved power, as in Israel, and were no longer merely suffered, they showed less tolerance. It is the same with blacks and Asians: Liberal when poor, blacks in power show much less tolerance, as in the case of a black woman member of a New York City district school board who opposed teaching about homosexual rights. The achievement of power apparently causes a form of deracination.

The effect shows up in salesmen who move into management or ownership positions. They change, and it is not as if they were indifferent to political and social diversity when they were salesmen, and suddenly became engaged. Indifference is not a precursor either of tolerance or of intolerance (as in the famous case of Thomas Hobbes, who had no interest in religion, but opposed religious tolerance), for indifference denotes no feeling, no contest, no connection, neither approval or disapproval. It is not an experience but a refusal of experience. Indifference has no place in the salesman's world; his work precludes it.

In his economic way the salesman is the most engaged of creatures. He competes within a product category or for a share of disposable income or for what marketers sometimes call "share of mind," by which they mean salience in the pandemonium of signs, symbols, and sentences that pester the sanity of modern man. Most often, the salesman must engage simultaneously in all of those competitions, any one of which could interfere with his task of wedding information to desire. As a result, he cannot afford to be indifferent to anything. Nor can he afford to be intolerant, because he never knows whom he is going to be working for next: He may sell bread today and books tomorrow, but he does not own the books or the bread; he is the mediator, matchmaker, hired hand, an ecumenicist in a partisan world.

So the salesman gains the habit of tolerance, not out of indifference, but because tolerance is in his immediate self-interest: He tolerates those who are necessary to him, his customers. His attitude is practical, not moral or political.

If it were political, he would tolerate people who may offend him and are not immediately useful to him. He would tolerate these people because they belong to the same polity; that is, as citizens he and they have a common interest (which may differ from the salesman's immediate self-interest). Furthermore, his tolerance would be based on the rules of the polity rather than the rules of the marketplace. He would tolerate equals, not objects, expecting tolerance, not profits, in return.

If his attitude were moral, it would not be tolerance but acceptance.[3] This last is the difference between Jesus, who washed the feet of sinners, and the shoe salesman who sells to a man with dirty socks. Or in a more secular comparison, between Walt Whitman, who said that nothing human disgusted him, and the stockbroker who does business with criminals.

Salesmen tolerate the poor as well as the rich, everyone equally, whoever is useful, all customers. It seems counterintuitive, but the salesman may have even greater love for the poor and the middle class than for the rich. He lives in the real world, where the poor and the middle class vastly outnumber the rich. The numerically great classes eat more breakfast cereal and buy more cars, storm windows, vacuum cleaners, shoes, shirts, candy bars, wristwatches, laundry soap, and diamond rings.

5. Two Freedoms

Compared to the buying power of the poor and the middle class, the rich fade toward insignificance. Selling to the rich has been a precarious way to make a living in the United States since colonial tradesmen lived like serfs at the edges of the lives of gentlefolk. At the first opportunity, which came with paper money and the equality of anonymity, the salesman became an egalitarian.

[3]   The moral life of the salesman is the subject of chapter 12.

To survive in the world of his business, the salesman depends upon freedom as toleration, the form of freedom beloved of John Stuart Mill.[4] Like Mill, who wanted to extend toleration from politics to morals and manners, the salesman also wants to extend toleration or negative freedom—liberty. The more tolerance, the more competition; the more competition, the greater the role of the salesmen.

Salesmen are now engaged in two major contests over positive versus negative freedom in the United States, where the terms have come to mean telling people what to do versus doing whatever an individual wants to do. Practically every trade organization involved in sales demands full First Amendment rights for commercial speech. Advertisers and other salesmen argue that restrictions on their ability to sell anything in virtually any way they choose violate the First Amendment. They believe that complete freedom to say whatever they like is their right. Consumer organizations favor the use of positive freedom to limit advertising of cigarettes and alcohol and force full disclosure of such things as finance charges, delivery charges, limitations of guarantees, and so on.

In the growing dispute over the right to privacy, many consumers and government officials favor the use of positive freedom to protect consumers from efforts by salesmen to learn their telephone numbers, buying habits, names of their relatives and friends, and so on. Salesmen insist that these are not invasions of privacy, that the liberties required to sell goods and services efficiently will ultimately redound to the benefit of the consumer.

Since the salesman wants the largest possible market, he likes a dollop of positive freedom; he finds profit in laws promoting social justice (transfer payments, for example), as long as they expand the market for goods and services rather than provide necessities directly through government-controlled or -regulated nonprofit distribution systems.

Tocqueville's understanding of American democracy in the first half of the nineteenth century promised an irresistible wave of positive freedom, conformity so powerful a salesman would be left with nothing to sell but vulgar commodities. Of course, Tocqueville was not quite correct; vulgarity became more differentiated in America than in any other country in history.

---

[4]   Isaiah Berlin has written several essays using the terms "positive liberty" and "negative liberty." Some people prefer to speak of "freedom to" and "freedom from." Hobbes preferred the terms "right" and "law." As the distinction moves from thinking to political action, the terminology becomes more and more confusing: statism and classic liberalism or late-twentieth-century liberalism and conservatism.

Despite the heavy influence of conformity, a kaleidoscope of desires flour-
ished, and no one gave it a greater boost than the salesman, who made the
celebration of the nuances of differentiation, advertising, an American institution.

All forms of differentiation are acceptable to the salesman. He takes on
whatever he is offered to sell, for he is comfortable with the concept of
limitless variety, which he sees in nature as well as in society. The only
barrier he cannot overcome is the customer's lack of desire. He cannot sell
ice cream that tastes of salt or pass off manure for tobacco. He operates
within the limits of human taste, and the more common the taste for his
product or service, the more likely he is to make a success of his business.
Arcana, from the music of John Cage to the jewels fashioned for the nose,
present the same problem as products aimed at the rich: The market for
them is small, often difficult to locate, and quick to change.

6. Homelessness

Equality and equal distribution are more to the salesman's advantage. He
favors egalitarian politics out of greed and anxiety, just as he practices
tolerance out of necessity. Equality is also an easy path, as natural as symmetry; it needs no justification. One has only to look in a mirror or examine the
sides of a leaf to learn how nature loves symmetry. The law of the distribution of gases exemplifies nature's love of equality. In the salesman's view the
mass market is God's own doing.

From the beginning of the nineteenth century, everything fit nicely for
the American salesman: Equality provided him with the largest possible
market for his products. Variety and tolerance provided him with a reason
for existence. As a mediator, he was pure function, process; he had no
loyalties. His work put him in the middle, he existed in the between of the
world, but he was not truly of the middle, not of the middle class.

Because a process has no place, every mediator is homeless. The notion seems like a trick of language, but it is not. The lack of place, of home,
has always been the mediator's fate. The mediator lives alone. The snake had
no mate in Eden. Coyote had no companion. Raven alighted by himself. No
mate came to rescue Prometheus from his chains. Quetzalcóatl went off
alone in his paper boat, set himself afire, and rose into the sky a single
beautiful bird. The mediator lives between life and death in the mythical

world, and he is neither here nor there in the real world as well.

Most salesmen belong to the economic middle class, but they do not live in that class or any other. The nature of the mediator precludes commitment. While the salesman, like everyone else, wants to be rich and secure, he cannot find a place for his economic loyalties. In voting, for example, the salesman works for the owner, the capitalist, who calls on his loyalty, but the salesman's customers are much more often employees, people who sell their labor, rather than owners. If the government does not tilt toward the customer, how can the salesman succeed? If the government does not tilt toward the owner, who will hire him? The mediator, as one would expect, lives in a classic double bind; he truly has no vested interest but himself, no guide but his own anxieties.

Hannah Arendt said that the atomized person is the bourgeois isolated from his class. Could there be a more fitting description of the salesman? He is not the small businessman, the artisan, the one who plays the property taxes and takes home the profits, who passes the assets of a business life onto his children: The salesman works in the small businessman's shop. He neither makes nor owns the goods. Then what is he? Is a person who works on commission a seller of labor or an entrepreneur? What does the salesman own?

The salesman lives in the middle, isolated not only from his class but from any class, atomized. To be so isolated from a class affects a person in many ways, most of which will come up in later chapters. The question here is how his atomized state affects the salesman's politics.[5]

7. Democracy

As an atomized person the salesman has no true connection to his country (used here in the sense of the polis, that is, the political rather than the geographical country). He lives in the polis,[6] but he is not truly a part of it. The salesman sees his country as a mass of customers, objects, cases, storehouses of profit; he examines them, learns them, affects them, but in his role

[5] I do not mean party politics, but politics as a means for living among other human beings.

[6] I use the Greek word *polis* (city-state, usually now in its idealized form) here for clarity, and to avoid questions of the salesman in the state, nation, nation-state, society, and so on.

as salesman is not one of them. Unlike the maker or the laborer, the salesman does not increase the wealth of the country by his work; he adds nothing, he has no product.

The salesman lives as if he were in exile, among strangers. Loyalty for him is the love of negative freedom; he appreciates the country as long as it is indifferent to him or even tolerant of him. He may be willing to defend the country, if the liberty by which he survives is threatened. He may be willing to engage in politics, if he feels threatened by some advance of positive freedom, either in the form of increased state power or some consensus that begins to approach a general will, with all the dangers of unlimited power the development of a general will may portend. But the salesman as salesman fights for himself, not for love of country.

Salesmen and the country act on each other according to the rules of indifference and tolerance, but disinterest is not the stuff of citizenship. To be a citizen requires a willingness to take sides, to hold an opinion, to be part of something, within, at risk. A mediator finds nothing but limitations in the role of citizen. Isolation and disconnection serve him best, because the salesmen works the levers of life, and the longer the lever, the more distant the object, the more power the salesman exerts.

Since he must follow a rule of nearly absolute tolerance (which customer will he not sell?), the salesman finds it efficient to live without adhering to a theory of political or social justice. He believes only that all men are entitled to the right of desire. That is what he serves and all that he serves: desire. He tolerates desire, almost without limit, which is how the salesman becomes an appearance of democracy, a false expression of citizenship.

History tells us that democracy is not a creation of salesmen. The ancient Athenians did not learn democracy from the marketplace; it was not a function of the economy. According to M. I. Finley, there was not even anything in ancient Greece resembling what we call an economy.[7] Democracy arose as a magnificent compromise between order and liberty; the genius of fifth-century Athens was the discovery that men could make the rules they live by. Plato, who was no democrat, made facetious reference to the salesman of political ideas and marketplace goods, but he did not attribute democracy to the marketplace.

In a democracy, as we know it, men make the rules they live by.

---

[7] *The Ancient Economy,* 2d ed. (Berkeley and Los Angeles: University of California Press, 1985).

Political democracy has no other meaning. There are many intermediaries—senators, representatives, executives, judges—in a democracy, but no mediators, because there is no division into we and they; as the Constitution says so clearly at the outset, "We, the people . . ." In a democracy the relation of we to they is confined to the market. It is true that partisan politics harbor the agonists we and they, and that there is a place for salesmen in partisan political campaigns, but political campaigns are not democracy; they are a tool of democracy, one of the means the people use to make the rules they live by.

The two kinds of democracy can be distinguished by the ends they seek: Political democracy is a relation among human beings who control themselves. Market democracy is a competition in which people try to control each other. The people who do the controlling in a market democracy are called salesmen. They are rewarded according to their ability to use information to influence people to do one thing instead of another, an act they celebrate as the workings of the free market.

Since the end of the eighteenth century, salesmen and their apologists have insisted that there can be no democracy without a free market, and there is some merit in their arguments, for the two forms of organization known as democracy coexist comfortably. Nevertheless, the forms are not interchangeable, and one is a misnomer, for the control of one human being by another, no matter how subtle the means, is no democracy.

7

Constant Mind, Constant Method

The handicraftsmen of democratic ages . . . strive to give to all their commodities attractive qualities which they do not in reality possess.

—ALEXIS DE TOCQUEVILLE

She began every sales call the same way, leaning forward from the hips, speaking in her toodle-oo voice, with a big smile, a broad smile, a twenty-tooth and more-than-a-little-gum smile. "Hi, there. It's the perfume lady."

Customers were charmed, especially the more sophisticated customers, who were like the people at the network, where she was employed during the day. The 1930s voice and delivery were completely out of keeping with her ethnic New York good looks and her street-smart makeup and clothes. The combination made them laugh. It wasn't exactly camp, people said, but it was close. It would have been camp, if there hadn't been so much hunger in her eyes.

"You can't bring camp down from The Bronx or up from Brooklyn," the associate producer of the network's hot new afternoon talk show said. "Camp can come in from Davenport or Sioux Falls, or it can get born right here in Manhattan, but it doesn't change boroughs. What can I tell you? From Queens it breaks your heart, you know what I mean. Like AIDS from a transfusion."

The perfume lady needed money. And she didn't mind saying so. "A research assistant at this network doesn't get paid shit, oh, my goodness, I'm sorry . . . spit," was her explanation to everyone but those people she considered her friends. For them she had a fuller explanation: a younger sister, a father who had run out on the family when the perfume lady was only five years old, a mother who lay dying in a nursing home in Florida.

"Hi, there. It's the perfume lady," she said, showing her white teeth, her pink gums.

She licked her lips, she painted her eyebrows, she wore eyeshadow and eyeliner, lip gloss, blusher, base, pancake, conditioner. When her front teeth, which were slightly too large, dried in the air of laughter and conversation, she brought her upper lip down over her teeth or wet them with her tongue.

"Hi, there. It's the perfume lady," she said, accompanying her greeting with a delicate wave of her hand, the kind of wave a princess might bestow on commoners, if the princess were four years old and blessed with chubby thighs and dimpled knees.

When she was interviewed by the cosmetics company recruiter, she confessed that she was not interested in sales; what had appealed to her was the free sample kit and the discount on makeup and especially perfume. The recruiter told her that many of their most successful salesladies had been drawn to a career in personal selling by the same offer.

In the third through the sixth training sessions, she learned sales techniques, all of which ended with closing the sale. The training instructor praised her technique in asking for the order, but the future perfume lady never lost her conviction that it was the beginning rather than the end of the sales call that had the most effect. "Hi, there. It's the perfume lady," she said over and over, singing the first word a little more, lowering the pitch of her voice on the word *perfume,* testing substitutes for *lady—woman, girl, kid, person—*to see if she could find any combination of words more appealing than the six words she practiced.

The seventh and final training session was about natural markets. The instructor said that the most successful people in the company sales force were those with large families and many friends, acquaintances, and co-workers. She greeted the news with a sigh. Her family was small. The objects of her life were men. She dressed for men, she laughed for men, she wore bustiers and garters and perfume for men. Her natural market was not promising. Women did not interest her. She had only a few friends.

Her co-workers at the office became her best customers for perfume. She looked up names in the company directory and called them on the telephone: "Hi, there. It's the perfume lady. I think we met last month in the cafeteria. Anyways, I'd like to give you a sample of a new scent that just came out. There's no obligation. Can I come by?"

The perfume lady developed a technique for visiting people at home rather than in the office. She was advised by the company bulletin to develop relationships with her customers. Repeat business, the bulletin promised, was the most profitable kind.

"Hi, there. It's the perfume lady; remember me?" she said.

The bulletin told her to notice photographs, furniture; not to be nosy, but friendly; not intimate exactly, but cozy. Every issue of the bulletin used the word *relationship*.

She was pleased when her telephone presentation brought an invitation to a director's apartment to show the line. Until then her clientele had been limited to secretaries, telephone operators, assistants of one kind or another; she needed people with more disposable income, affluent customers who could raise her revenue per call.

The director bought a "B" starter package for herself and ordered three smaller packages to be sent as gifts. It was the largest sale the perfume lady had ever made. She was careful to express her gratitude and to notice the velvet sectional and the portrait of a woman in an old-fashioned dress, which turned out to be a family heirloom. As the perfume lady was preparing to leave, the director asked whether she had a moment more to give her, time enough for a demonstration.

"Of course, I do. I will. I'd be glad to."

It occurred to the perfume lady that in her excitement she had forgotten to ask for payment. She decided to put it off until after the demonstration.

A towel was necessary to cover the director's blouse during the application of the eye and face makeup. The perfume lady admired the color of the blouse and said it looked like the best-quality silk. She licked her teeth and promised to be careful, but the director said she had a better solution, for the blouse was very, very expensive silk; she would simply take it off.

The perfume lady shrugged. Perhaps it was best. She stood beside the director, who fingered the tiny glass buttons of her blouse, methodically working them loose, moving down from the neck. The director was not quite as tall as the perfume lady, and she was made of straight, clean lines; there was nothing of the southern, the eastern European compliance in her figure. When she smiled, she used the corners of her mouth, for her lips were thin and quick.

After she had removed her blouse, the director stood for a moment without moving. Her blue gaze was lifted to meet the perfume lady's eyes. "Rouge my nipples," the director said. She spoke in the doubtless voice, the flat, commanding voice of the control room.

A pain, more fire than hurt, like the first sensation after the shock of a deep wound, came into the perfume lady's body. It entered just below the ribs and spread up and out, confusing the rules of her belly so that a warning of nausea rose in her gullet.

She stayed for a long time in the director's apartment. When she left, she did not forget to ask for the check, nor did she fail to compliment her customer on the velvet of her couch or the elegance of her ancestor.

1.

In the city of Jerusalem, in the age of kings, it was said by Solomon himself that "the best wine . . . goes down smoothly, gliding over lips and teeth." So, too, an unremembered merchant standing in the shadow of the partly constructed temple, may have whispered to a customer that his wine was the best, that it went down smoothly, meshing perfectly with the requirements of the palate, for the fruit of the vine was both sweet and tart, mild and heady. Three thousand years later, two oafs appeared on television to tell their customers that Bartles & Jaymes wine coolers went down smoothly, meshing perfectly with the requirements of the palate, for the drink was both fruit and wine, sweet and tart, mild and heady. From the age of Solomon to the age of Gallo, there has been no essential change in the method of selling.

Like philosophy, selling does not become outdated. If dogs or turtles participated in these activities, the methods of investigation and persuasion might be different, but the human mind determines the way one can speak to it, then and now, here and there, without exception. The problem of other men's minds raised in Plato's *Theaetetus* was no less a problem for Ludwig Wittgenstein in the twentieth century; similarly, the discovery of another person's desires is no less a question for the stockbrokers of Merrill Lynch than it was for the merchants of Cathay.

Ptolemy, Avogadro, Mendel, all the old scientists, are reduced to quaintness now, their understanding of the world long ago superseded. Not so the philosophers, not so the salesmen. If the thinkers and the mediators have something in common other than venerability, it is their concern with men's minds, their interest in questions of appearance and reality, the problems of how to live, what to value. What separates the philosopher forever from the salesman is not means but motives. The tools, as every philosopher, from Plato to Kant to Wittgenstein, took pains to tell, may be employed in many ways.

On occasion the wisdom of ancient philosophers and the techniques of contemporary salesmen connect across the centuries, making the relation of the disciplines astonishingly clear. One such occasion occurred in San Francisco. It was a unique city in America: There were ragamuffins filled with certainties on every street corner and leftover philosophers in every coffee-house, but it was sometimes necessary to import salesmen, as in the case of the marketing and selling of a new toy, a dollhouse whose occupants responded to a magic wand.

The problem for the owners of this triumph of American ingenuity—a magnet glued on to the end of the wand attracted a piece of iron in the base of the doll—was that few people in San Francisco understood the toy market, including the first and perhaps most important step, how to package the product. After a long and thoughtful meeting of the inventors and owners of the magical magnetic dollhouse and their advertising agency, it was decided that a consultant would have to be imported from New York. Several weeks later, with the annual New York toy show rapidly approaching and some major decisions still to be made, an elderly gentleman, Mr. Solomon from New York, arrived in San Francisco to attend a day-long meeting with the toy makers and marketers in the conference room of their advertising agency.

Mr. Solomon was treated with great deference by his clients. Bagels and cream cheese were ordered for his midmorning snack. For lunch, he said, he required a deli sandwich, corned beef, but lean. Such a sandwich, on rye, along with a half sour dill pickle and a cream soda, was brought from one of the city's two kosher delicatessens.

For Mr. Solomon's benefit a prototype of the magical magnetic doll-house was set up on the conference table. Tiny couches, tables, lamps, chairs, and beds were placed in the proper rooms. Then each member of the resident family was introduced and moved into place by means of the magnetic wand. When the family dog was placed inside the house, a fifty-year-old advertising executive, dressed in a three-piece suit, performed his part in the sales presentation.

"Woof, woof," the executive said.

"Bark, Dexter, bark," the others said.

"Woof, woof," the executive said.

Mr. Solomon said nothing.

All day an argument raged over the design of the box. On one side were those who believed the box should depict the dollhouse. The others favored a picture of a delighted girl using the wand to move one of the tiny dolls. Product information or the satisfaction of desire? Which would please the parents? Which would please the children? Was the primary market parents or children? Which would sell the most dollhouses?

Mr. Solomon, who sat in the position of honor or power or both at the head of the conference table, listened to the discussion. He did not comment. Not a word came from him while he ate his bagels or sipped his coffee. He did not speak during the eating of delicatessen sandwiches and pickles. Mr. Solomon listened. He studied the sketches, the mock-ups. Near the end of the afternoon, when the light turned gray in the financial district and the overhead lamps brought a yellow weariness into the conference room, Mr. Solomon looked at his watch. He had been promised a fee for one day of consulting and one day only. Soon he would have to be driven to the airport.

The owner of the toy-manufacturing venture saw Mr. Solomon's gesture, and took the hint. He reminded everyone in the room that the toy show was in August and that a choice had to be made between the delighted child and the beauty shot of the product. Then he turned to Mr. Solomon. "You've heard our arguments; which shall it be?"

For one last moment Mr. Solomon pondered the question. He seemed to be reviewing the evidence presented by the proponents of each option, comparing it to his vast experience, like some great computer sorting information. Then the venerable mediator raised his right arm, extending it straight up from the shoulder. His eyes were clear, his jaw was firm, his nose a prow of intelligence cutting into the windstorm of disputation. It was, in the parlance of San Francisco, a zen moment. Mr. Solomon lowered his arm toward the table, his fingertips describing a great arc. As his arm descended, he spoke at last: "Divide the box in half."[1]

2. Antilogic

Over a period only somewhat shorter than that from Solomon the king to Solomon the consultant, the methods of Euthydemus, who was Plato's chief target in the dialogue lampooning specious reasoning, are repeated in the training of insurance agents in New York City. "If I go see someone," the teacher of insurance agents says, "and they reject me, they're not rejecting me; they're rejecting themselves."

The ancient method called antilogic—starting with the opponent's position *(logos)* and arguing to an opposite position—appears as chapter 25 of J. T. Auer's *The Joy of Selling:* "Use the Prospect's Objections to Close the Sale."[2] Here is one of Auer's examples. The customer says, " 'I had one of your earlier models and was never satisfied with it.' " Auer advises the salesman, "Avoid talking about the past. Focus on the present! Say, 'Am I to understand, Mr. ———, that if I could prove to you that our newest model meets your specifications, and that it has been improved tremendously, you would give me your order today?' " As in antilogic, the opponent must either abandon his position or accept both positions as true.[3]

Ross Perot, a computer services salesman who turned his experience to politics in 1992, demonstrated the salesman's use of antilogic in a television interview with Charlie Rose.[4] The subject was the possible use of American military force to halt the policy of "ethnic cleansing" in Bosnia. At the time of the interview, the Clinton administration, which had apparently committed itself to stopping the systematic destruction of the Muslim population by the Serbs, was waffling. Rose put the question to Perot, who apparently

[1]   Although I have changed some details and the name of the barking executive, the story is not apocryphal. The consultant's name was Solomon and his advice was to divide the box in half. John van der Zee, the novelist and author of *The Gate,* the standard work on the building of the Golden Gate Bridge, was a witness.

[2]   (Toronto: Stoddard Publishing, 1989).

[3]   Unlike characters in a Platonic dialogue, modern practitioners skip steps in the argument. Here the salesman is toying with the values of better and worse, but he doesn't go through all the steps of showing that the product can't be both better and worse.

[4]   May 12, 1993, Public Broadcasting System.

opposed U.S. military involvement, in moral terms.

Perot replied that there were many places in the world in which people, including children, were being killed. He pointed out the Middle East as a prime example, then reminded Rose that black children, Asian children, Arab children, should all be saved; it was a matter of principle. However, Perot concluded, if the United States followed the principle, it would have to intervene in every place in which innocents were being killed; was Mr. Rose suggesting that the United States send troops to stop all such conflicts everywhere in the world?

Rose was left no choice but to join Perot or abandon his own position. He could not abandon his own, well-known position that black, Asian, and Arab children were the equal of white children, nor could he accept the idea of U.S. intervention in thirty or forty ongoing conflicts. He was forced either to abandon his own moral position or to agree with Perot. Unlike a character in a Platonic dialogue, however, he did not declare himself, choosing instead the tacit concession of silence.

Napoleon and Benjamin Franklin, two salesmen of more recent vintage than the Song of Songs or Euthydemus, also figure in modern sales methods. Napoleon and Franklin share the "T" in selling. Auer uses the Napoleonic "T," a method for arriving at decisions in which a line is drawn down the center of a sheet of paper and arguments for and against are listed on either side. The customer is asked to write the many advantages down as the salesman dictates them. Then the salesman asks him to list the disadvantages on the other side, but gives the customer no help. At the end, after the unprepared customer has listed only a few negatives opposite the salesman's long list, the salesman finishes the argument by counting the number of pros and cons aloud. Auer writes, "Think of the psychological effect of this closing method. . . ."

An insurance salesman at the Equitable Life Assurance Society uses what he calls the "Franklin T Close," a method based upon the strategy of Benjamin Franklin, who founded the first fire insurance company on this continent, in Philadelphia in 1752. In the Franklin T Close, the two sides of the T are headed "Your Obligation" and "Our Obligation." Under "Your Obligation" the agent writes $234 deposit. Under "Our Obligation" he writes a long, long list: "Immediate money, Liquidate all debts, Emergency funds, Debt-free house, Child care, Education funds, Retirement funds, Dignity!"

Every salesman uses ancient methods of argument. The method that served the snake in Eden works on a used-car lot. Eristic,[5] the attitude toward reasoning championed by some of the late Sophists, who went from town to town teaching this art of persuasion through false reasoning, is exposed by U.S. Senator David Pryor's Committee on Aging in the sales scripts used by people who prey on the elderly.

As the owner of the Henderson Insurance Agency in New York City told a group of trainees, "All your sales points have been logical, and when you get down to the end, the customer has no place to go." The form of the argument has not changed; Aristotle would make a fine consumer watchdog, for the mind still wishes to travel what seems like a rational path.

3. Trust Me

Perhaps the most important moment in every sale is the beginning, when the salesman sells himself. Every book and video on sales techniques deals with the opening, from the way the salesman dresses to the way he or she shakes hands, to the establishment of the salesman's character and his knowledge of the subject.

Donald Trump, a real estate salesman, began his first book, "I don't do it for the money. I've got enough, much more than I'll ever need."[6] That was in 1987, before certain financial reverses made it clear that Mr. Trump didn't have quite enough. Nevertheless, it remains a good, if tasteless, example of the salesman's opening.

Lee Iacocca, a man of similar modesty, began his autobiography, "You're about to read the story of a man who's had more than his share of success."[7]

In the opening to his *Confessions of an Advertising Man,* David Ogilvy tells the reader, "My boyhood hero had been Lloyd George, and I had expected to become Prime Minister when I grew up. Instead, I finally became an advertising agent on Madison Avenue; the revenues of my nine-

---

[5] Eristic was not strictly a method, but a point of view about truth. Eristic is often described as contentiousness. The word comes from Eris, the goddess of strife. Plato, always seeking ways to attack the Sophists, accuses them of relying upon eristic. It is likely that some Sophists used eristic, and earned a good living from teaching others how to argue with no other aim than to win. It is not true, however, that all Sophists practiced eristic and surely not at all times.

[6] *The Art of the Deal* (New York: Random House, 1987).

[7] *Iacocca: An Autobiography* (New York: Bantam, 1984).

teen clients are now greater than the revenue of Her Majesty's Government."[8]

The authors of more straightforward manuals on selling are not quite so disingenuous. Robert L. Shook can write, "If it sounds like I'm tooting my own horn, I am, but only to emphasize an important point." This, after saying, "For the record, I write about my subject with authority." Mr. Shook just can't stop introducing himself. He speaks of his "strong track record in sales," his "unique background," and his "close contacts . . . with sales leaders, a phenomenal resource virtually untapped by other writers."[9]

A brilliant young cardiologist in New York City, David Blumenthal, recognizes a similar technique in doctor/patient relations.[10] When a new patient comes for consultation, the physician, already recommended by another person, usually another doctor, has a receptionist seat the patient in a chair facing a wall of framed certificates of excellence: college and medical school degrees, board certifications, and so on. For Dr. Blumenthal selling (he accepts the word, but prefers to speak of persuasion) is often a matter of saving the patient's life. If he cannot sell the patient on giving up cigarettes or losing weight or simply taking the prescribed medicine, the patient may die.

Beginning with Socrates, or perhaps even earlier, the teacher, philosopher, or salesman introduced himself to his audience by displaying his moral virtues. How else would they know whether it was worth their while to listen to him?[11] A generation later, Aristotle said, "It is not true, as some writers assume in their treatises on rhetoric, that the personal goodness revealed by the speaker contributes nothing to his power of persuasion; on the contrary, his character may almost be called the most effective means of persuasion he possesses."

All of these, including the physicians and philosophers, are good salesmen, but none so good as the Navaho practitioner of the Apache Way ceremony, who sells magic even more esoteric than that of the heart. He comes down from the northeast to a hogan in the shadow of Black Moun-

---

[8]   (New York: Atheneum, 1983).

[9]   *Hardball Selling* (New York: Morrow, 1991).

[10]   Excerpts from a long interview with Dr. Blumenthal on various aspects of selling in the practice of medicine will appear later, in chapter 13.

[11]   A step in the use of rhetoric, protreptic was used to introduce the teacher or philosopher to his audience. *Protreptic* is usually translated as "exhortation," but its meaning is more complex, for the protreptic let the audience know the moral character of the speaker, assuring everyone of the value of his presentation.

147

tain, a man of startling visage: strong, perfectly clear-cut features, eyes that seem to see through and beyond anything in the room, a commanding nose. His patient is a tubby man, bespectacled, with a pimple or two.

The medicine man defines himself before he begins the ceremony. He tells the tubby patient, the one whose face is confused into a permanent grimace, that he, the medicine man from the northeast, the patchwork land, was riding on his white horse one day, when he saw an eagle above him. He lassoed the eagle, brought it down with the rope, and plucked out one of its tailfeathers. Then, with a dramatic gesture, he shows the feather.

The salesman has sold himself, the Apache Way ceremony can begin.

4. The Study of Desire

In the ritualized sale of Apache Way, the salesman knows the desire of the customer (or patient), because the patient tells him so. Knowing the desires of the customer is still the salesman's best tool. Here is Roger B. Smith, former chairman of the board of the General Motors Corporation, describing his method of selling.[12] In this case, Smith wanted to sell Eiji Toyoda on starting a joint venture with General Motors to build small, fuel-efficient cars at GM's Fremont, California, plant.

Talking with Roger Smith is a little like listening to Willie Nelson paraphrase the *Harvard Business Review*. "We knew Japanese methods, because we already owned a big chunk of Isuzu," Smith said, speaking in his characteristic mixture of country expressions, dropped final *g*'s, contractions, run-on sentences, and business jargon. "We wanted to find out if Japanese methods would work in the United States. And we wanted the product. We needed it. We didn't have a car down in that price class and that fuel economy. We were desperate for it. We were gettin' all we could from Isuzu, but we needed Nova.[13] It turned out, that still today is a helluva car."

The meeting between Roger Smith and Eiji Toyoda took place over

---

[12] Part of a long interview with Roger Smith. Other parts will appear in later chapters. The interview was done after Smith retired from his position as chairman, but before he left the GM board of directors. It should be noted that the interview was friendly. I have known Roger Smith for more than ten years, although not at all well and always as a "vendor."

[13] A car using Toyota Corolla components and engineering, as well as U.S.-made components, and assembled in Fremont, California. The nameplate was later changed to Geo Prizm, in part because the large Spanish-speaking community in California understood Nova as *no va*, or "won't go."

dinner at the Links Club, a private club in Manhattan. Smith had learned his customer's desires before he arrived at the club. "You've got to study," he said, "you've got to know. The salesman has got to know where the buyer's button is. You sit down and say, 'Eiji. I appreciate your coming here. I knew you were in California, but I wanted to talk to you. I wanted to tell you that I think that this situation between Japan and the United States has reached epidemic proportions and our two countries, they aren't gonna go to war, but we're gonna have one of the biggest messes you've ever seen. This thing has grown to a problem of dimensions that I just . . .'

" 'I can't tell you how the anti-Japanese feeling in this country is just going like wildfire and we're not gonna be able to stop it and I just want to tell you that I'm sorry about it and I apologize for it, but it's just gonna be terrible. I wish there was something that we could do. You're a leading guy in Japan and certainly the most visible here in the United States. You and Akio Morita. And his name isn't really associated with his company. And I know Toyoda and Toyota are very different. You know everybody associates and zeroes in on you and that's unfortunate and it really shouldn't be allowed to go that way.'

"The soup goes over there. I've got the raspberry soufflé.

"Then, 'Well, as I was saying, you people build a good product. We don't really want to see this thing get into the situation it is now. We had one item that we were thinking about where if you put General Motors and Toyota's forces to work on solving this Japanese/American problem maybe something might happen where we could get this . . . to show our two countries can work together and two people, business leaders, could come out and do something, you know, a joint venture or something like that. And what I was thinking about, I don't know, we got a plant out in California now that we've closed and it's right near the port. Maybe we could get together with you and build a Corvair or some model that you've got some extra capacity on that you'd like to sell here. I guess it might be something we might want to explore, you know, to show people that, yeah, Americans and Japanese can work together in harmony and there's no big bogeyman in this thing. That you are a genuine world citizen, you know, that understands all these things and we brought out some old charts here.'

"And when he got in his limo, I told Jack,[14] 'Pack your bags.' "

---

[14] John F. Smith, no relation to Roger Smith. After the board of directors forced Robert Stempel (Roger Smith's successor) to resign his position as chairman of the corporation in 1992, John F. Smith was named chief executive officer, but not chairman of the board.

Smith summed up the evening: "I was selling Toyoda. There's no question about that. I got him to come to New York, we went up here to the Links Club, sat down and we laid a deal on him that I thought would be good for him and good for us. He had no idea what I wanted when he came in there. When he left that night, you know what I said to myself, 'I got him. I got him.' I could tell by the look on his face. You know, they're so impassive and all of that stuff, but man, he was eating it like chop suey, really. I knew in my heart. He was saying he had to think it over and all that kind of stuff and he'd be in touch.

"I had Jack Smith with me at that time. I said, 'Jack, go home and pack your bag, you're going to Japan.'

"He says, 'The hell I am.'

"I said, 'Jack, I know it. We got that guy. He wants to do this. I know he does.'

"It was all over and done right there at that dinner. When Jack went to Japan, he said, 'What if they don't. . . .'

"I said, 'Listen, you ride what you think is fair. They're not gonna turn it down. They want to do this deal. All you got to do is make it fair to us; don't give the store away.' A couple of times Jack would call me and say, 'We're stuck on this or that,' and I would say, 'Jack, tell them what you've got is fair and if they don't want to do the deal, you'll come home. Don't you worry, you're not gonna leave. They won't let you leave. They want to do that deal.' "

Toyota entered into the joint venture with General Motors in Fremont. Roger Smith had understood the desires of his customer: one man, a Japanese industrialist.

Marketing grew out of the need to find the desirous among the millions. As America grew, and by dint of mere numbers began to develop some of the aspects of a mass society, the sellers had to seek out the potential buyers. It was no longer the physician, the wine merchant, or the shaman looking into the customer's eyes to discern his desires. Nor was every person a potential customer or every customer the same. Tocqueville had apparently overstated the dangers of a democracy: There was pressure to conform at the end of the nineteenth century, but democracy had not produced a monolithic culture. Economic necessity alone dictated a variety of occupations, a division of interest and enterprise as well as a division of labor.

By 1879 the N. W. Ayer advertising agency was faced with the problem of finding out where to advertise farm equipment: Which newspapers were read by farmers who were likely to buy the manufacturer's products? The agency was promised the manufacturer's business, if it could answer the question satisfactorily. The problem produced one of the first marketing studies. N. W. Ayer used federal and state government agricultural records to find out where corn, wheat, and other grains were produced. From there it was easy enough to determine which newspapers covered those areas. The method by which the salesman worked had not changed, but the quantities of the village and the town required one kind of technology in the search for customers, and the quantities of a great nation required another.

When N. W. Ayer first studied the national market, advertising agencies still made their commissions by selling space for newspapers and magazines. They were agents for the media, not for the advertisers. Today the situation is reversed: The agencies are generally paid by their clients. However, the burden of locating the market still falls almost entirely on the media. Every print and broadcast medium uses survey techniques to study its audience. It measures the size of the audience, then the demographics (with emphasis on income and spending habits), and finally the tastes. Since all media are direct or indirect competitors, they constantly challenge each other's statistics.

The broadcast media claim that print statistics are unreliable, because no one can say for certain which pages or portions of pages are actually read. The print media argue that there is no reliable way to find out who is watching or listening to any station at any given time. The data and challenges ultimately end up in the hands of media salesmen, who conform the information to the desires of the advertising agency time and space buyers. No one says much about the fallacy of induction, which proves that statistical samples are subject to error; the research methods are compared to each other, not to reality.

Even so, the basic information provided by the media rarely fails to pass the test of reason; that is, the readers of *Harper's* are better educated than the readers of *People,* and although there are fewer readers of *Harper's* they have more money than the readers of *People.* Locating the market becomes a bit more difficult when comparing *Time* to *Newsweek* or *Reader's Digest* to prime-time television.

Yet more difficult questions had to be answered: Who, if anyone, has desires that can be satisfied by the product? Should there even be such a product? What sales volume can be expected, at what price? The colonial

American craftsman or the ancient Chinese cloth merchant answered these questions out of experience and common sense, but the modern marketer is far removed from his market. There is an old, perhaps apocryphal tale about Harvey Firestone (of the tire company), who told his advertising agency not to schedule television commercials on Sunday afternoons, because everyone is at the polo matches. The distance between the seller and his customer has closed somewhat since then, but the cultural and economic gap still requires the seller to deal with his market as if the seller had recently arrived from the moon. He must meet his customers abstractly, in test markets, which use one or more small cities to represent the entire nation. The marketer scales down every aspect of the national selling effort—advertising, merchandising, shelf space, couponing, and so on—to the size of the test market.

The problem with test markets comes in isolating the various factors in the sale: the product, advertising, shelf space, and exogenous factors, from war to weather. However, test markets have the great advantage of enabling the seller to measure the repurchase rate of a product. If sales are poor from the outset, the marketer can relate the problem to a lack of desire or an ineffective presentation of the product. If sales fall precipitously after the first wave, and do not recover, the marketer can usually locate the failure in the product itself.[15]

Other studies of desire deliver less reliable results, for they require potential buyers to think imaginatively. Worse, all the data requires analysis by market researchers, multiplying the opportunity for error.

Since salesmen discovered long ago that changing tastes or desires is very expensive and often impossible (Claude Hopkins refused even to consider the idea, saying that it was just too expensive), market research about the buyer has been devoted almost entirely to discovering the tastes, trends, interests, desires of the market and the way in which appearances appeal to them. If there are any market research firms that purport to know how to change desire, I doubt they could stay in business for long. Salesmen like to be sold, but they don't like to appear foolish.

---

[15] Products with poor repurchase rates are either reformulated or withdrawn. Advertising is usually tested before being put into a test market. In fact, everything is tested with small samples before a product is placed in test market. The failure of so many products in test markets attests either to the inability of small samples to predict success in real situations or to the incompetence of the people who set up the test markets and analyze their results.

5. The Fallacy of Reason

How to present the product to desire elicits the most inventive thinking from the salesman. Although it was always part of the personal salesman's method, "reason why" selling did not become respectable in the public world of advertising until the early part of this century, when it achieved the status of scripture under the tutelage of Claude Hopkins. Before that, most "reason why" advertising was done by retailers of patent medicines. Drs. Starkey & Palen of Philadelphia, proprietors of the "COMPOUND OXYGEN" treatment "for the cure of chronic diseases by a true process of re-vitalization" went so far as to offer "FREE! A Treatise [200 pages] on COMPOUND OXYGEN, with many testimonials to most remarkable cures." Two hundred pages is a lot of reasoning.

"Reason why" selling is related not to dialectic or even to reason but to argument, as Hopkins made clear when he wrote, "People recognize a certain license in selling talk as they do in poetry." He was out to win, not to stimulate thinking or find out the truth. It is worth listening to Hopkins on what Plato would have identified as eristic.

> In the old days all beers were advertised as "Pure." The claim made no impression. The bigger the type used, the bigger the folly. After millions had been spent to impress a platitude, one brewer pictured a plate glass room where beer was cooled in filtered air. He pictured a filter of white wood pulp through which every drop was cleared. He told how bottles were washed four times by machinery. How he went down 4,000 feet for pure water. How 1,018 experiments had been made to attain a yeast to give beer that matchless flavor. And how all the yeast was forever made from that adopted mother cell.[16]

The character of the argument admired by Hopkins comes clear in his next sentence: "All the claims were such as any brewer might have made." He lauds deception, which is the intent of the argument: to create a false distinction, to trick the reader into believing that only one beer is made by those processes. According to the standards of a teacher of eristic and the twentieth-century salesman, a brilliant ambiguity.

[16] *Scientific Advertising* (1923; reprint, New York: Chelsea House, 1980).

In 1993, with mutual funds taking over the investment role once held by bank savings accounts, money market funds, and certificates of deposit, eristic found a new role in selling.

> DOUBLE-DIGIT TOTAL RETURN
> THROUGH THREE PRESIDENTS,
> TWO RECESSIONS AND ONE WAR.

The sales pitch goes on to say, "Some investments seek capital growth but carry considerable risk to principal," assuring the reader that this fund carries no risk to principal. Only in "mice type" across the bottom of the advertisement did the bank reprint the standard disclaimer: "Past performance is not a guarantee of . . ."

Claude Hopkins would have been pleased. Citibank said nothing dishonest. Neither did it say that the fifteen-year history to which it refers came during the presidencies of Ronald Reagan and George Bush, when it was so easy to make money by investing in stocks and bonds that many other mutual funds could produce similar or even better statistics.

The "reason why" approach enables the salesman to use information to alter reality, as in the case of beers or mutual funds. It works best, of course, when the salesman has also determined the customer's desire. The beer ad in which the bottles were washed four times was written nearly three-quarters of a century ago, when hygiene was not quite so carefully monitored. Beer drinkers wanted to get drunk, but not sick. The bank ad, published in 1993, was aimed at investors who wanted to get rich without risk. In both instances the salesman had to alter reality so that his product—and his product alone—matched the desires of the market.

6. A Substitute for Reason

"Reason why" selling, which translates into demonstrations on television, works best with innovative products. But the conformist imperative of post–World War II marketing has vastly reduced the number and the quality of innovative ideas: One soap powder spawns another, one flavor reproduces the next—to distinguish between Diet-Coke, Diet-Pepsi, and Diet-RC Cola demands the palate of a French vintner. Reason cannot distinguish among commodity products, except to choose the one with the lowest price. The marketer, having driven the producer into a coward's corner, endeavors to stave off disaster with one of the oldest rhetorical devices, selling emotion instead of reason, the speaker instead of the speech, the salesman instead of the thing to be sold.

Appearance has never strayed so far from reality in the selling of tangible goods. To differentiate one commodity product from another, the marketer reifies the salesman. The advertising industry, in the business of making phrases, has made one for itself to describe the process; in fact, it has made several phrases, because agencies seek to separate their commodity products, too: branding, brand character, brand personality.

Although the American Association of Advertising Agencies (AAAA) has been arguing the case for branding more vehemently every year, the response from some of America's largest marketers has been to cut prices and reduce the number of brands they sell. In 1993, tobacco companies countered the inroads of generic brands by reducing the prices of Marlboro cigarettes and other heavily advertised names. Proctor & Gamble, which had once led the industry in "fracturing the market,"[17] announced that it would drop White Cloud toilet paper to concentrate on Charmin.

With one brand virtually indistinguishable from another and sales of the most famous brands declining after decades of growth, the stability of the mass marketers was threatened. For half a century the achievement of the first rank in any product category had all but guaranteed the maintenance of that position. Brands, while lacking "character" or "personality," had generally proved reliable. Poor people and new immigrants had shown great loyalty to these "best" and most expensive items in every category— beer, scotch, basketball shoes, women's wear, rice, to name a few—for the brands had worn the economic imprimatur of the promised land.[18]

If nothing else, branding had made the categories orderly; it had made the markets reliable. A producer could plan against such markets. Brands served as the forms of business; they made the rules. Without brand recognition, the product could not get much shelf space, if any, in the supermarkets. On the other hand, the advertising used to make brands known funded newspapers, magazines, radio, and television; in a sense, they made

[17] P&G and other large marketers attempted to increase share of market by putting more products into a category, each of which was expected to take some sales from its own brands, but more importantly from those of its competitors, thus raising P&G's aggregate share in the category.

[18] Market surveys now show brand loyalty to be highest among Latinos.

the marketplace. To preserve this orderly market in a stagnant time, at the end of the century, in the chaos of repetitions, the producers have three alternatives: cut prices and profits, embrace invention, or remake the world in the image of the salesman. They have cut prices and chosen the salesman, too. Advertising is less and less about the product, and more about its surrounding celebrities, music, children's faces, love, any sign of emotion. In short, the shoeshine and the smile have been transferred to the product; they are part of its *personal*ity.

7. Service

The face-to-face salesman of the ancient marketplace often knew his customers; the modern salesman deals almost entirely with strangers, forcing him to use various ploys to get to know his customers. One of the most common practices is to present the sale as a service: The salesman masquerades as a counselor in order to find out the customer's desires. Stockbrokers and insurance agents do it all the time.

Service, of course, is yet another ambiguity. The salesman really wants to learn "what buttons to push" when the time comes to close the sale. He may truly serve the customer by selling him insurance or stock warrants or water filtration or aluminum siding, but the aim of the interview has nothing to do with service; the salesman wants to find out the precise point at which the prospect will take the salesman's pen and sign the contract.

All personal selling requires the salesman to understand the customer, but intangibles demand the most of the salesman. For that reason, elaborate schemes have been devised. One brokerage firm offers computerized analysis of financial situations, another promises a retirement review, and so on. In each case the firm wants to find out the most powerful desire in the customer's life. Then a salesman on a personal visit or a telephone call has a map, a way through the swamp of defenses into the customer's mind.

Any information he can get about the customer, any lead ploy, reduces the risk of a sales call. Most salesmen require some kind of lead, usually the name of a person who has responded to a coupon in an advertisement. If he can't have a coupon, the salesman wants a mailing list that indicates desire for a similar product or service. He wants somehow to be assured of the existence of desire before he begins the mediation. The completely cold call, the one in which the salesman knows absolutely nothing about the person at the other end of the telephone, has a very low success rate. The rejection suffered by a salesman in cold calling drives many people out of the business. An insurance salesman told me that by the end of a day of cold calling, he would be smashing the telephone against the wall. A stockbroker said he beat his head on the desk after hours of cold calling randomly selected prospects; the rejection was intolerable.

For a salesman, working alone, to attempt to do the basic job of marketing, to locate the desirous in a nation of 250 million people, is virtually impossible. Without leads, without the customer's history, some affinity, something more than a zip code and a telephone number, the salesman can only rely on luck or his natural market. Even a crook, a person selling worthless stocks out of a motel room in a swampy Florida town, wants something more than randomness, a list, anything, even a magazine subscription list to go with the script prepared by his crew leader:

"Good afternoon, Ms. Lee. As a reader of *Graceful Aging* magazine you are entitled to a free financial analysis and consultation. Now, if you'll just go over this information with me to be sure we don't have one of those computer errors. . . . My goodness, we wouldn't want to risk having an error in *your* analysis!

"That's Lee, Roberta E. Area code 305-555-1234. Is that right? Well, I see we're off to a good start. Now, let's see which group of investors you belong to.

"You don't invest! Well, I hope you've got a son or a daughter or someone who loves you looking out for your interests. You are protected from the ravages of inflation, aren't you?"

And then he waits. What will she say? If the woman had been an investor, he would have followed another path on the script. He waits. What if she tells him she has no money? What if she tells him she's dying? What if she tells him to go to hell?

Every mediation begins with a discovery about the customer. For a talented salesman, it may take no more than a cough, a glance, a hesitation to uncover another human being's desires. What more did Eiji Toyoda offer to Roger Smith?

The personal sale cannot take place with a stranger. The salesman must take the encounter out of the modern, massified world before he can serve as a mediator. Personal selling requires the salesman to accept the existence of an authentic person, a human being with desires based on history, character, and intelligence not shared with any other creature on earth. There is no need for the salesman to love or like his customer—he may even despise his customer—but he must concede the customer's humanity, or he will never know who it is he has to sell.

8. Conforming to Desire

In the United States after the Second World War, marketing went through a great reversal. Instead of locating customers for products, it was used to find out what people wanted so that products could be designed and manufactured to conform to their desires. For the first time since the end of the Neolithic age, something limited creativity. A world that believes nothing will change, a circular world, and a world based upon conformance to existing desire both oppose invention; in the former it is the gods and in the latter the mass of consumers who dictate what may be imagined. Both the primitive gods and the modern market are abstract, insistent, and largely inexorable. The irony is unmistakable: The most modern communications, computing, and sampling techniques drive the world back toward stasis.

Instead of examining the entrails of a chicken to divine the will of the gods, the modern manufacturer employs market researchers to divine the will of the market. Modern sampling techniques are used to derive statistically valid information and psychologists conduct interviews with groups and individuals, all in an effort to divine the will of the buying public.

The logical problem of this pernicious aspect of marketing is never discussed: How can the market choose what it wants from what it does not know or does not yet exist? The customer can speak only of the past. Moreover, market research or polling has an unavoidable tendency to encourage conformity by conflating desires and opinions, because the research always seeks the largest possible market, the broadest pattern of behavior or belief that can be defined and used.

Market research, like the primitive man's gods, keeps telling the producer to do it again, just the way he did it before. If it seems a silly way to do business, the salesman's worst mistake, it is. From an economic viewpoint, the conformity of the market-driven organization inhibits innovation. From a broader viewpoint, it can make Tocqueville's fears about the abuse of power and other political and cultural dangers of a mass democracy begin to come true.

Only in the short run does this circularity offer benefits, but those benefits are important enough to keep the market researchers in business for many years to come, because they reduce risk. The market researchers tell the producer to make an automobile just like the successful automobile made by his competitor. So one automobile looks more and more like another. Market research works on movies and television programs and books, too. Not only do the stories in genre novels resemble each other; many of them even have the same male model on the cover.

Market research may be applied to anything, from electoral politics to dishwashing detergent to pantyhose. It is the most timid work the salesman can do, and the most certain to produce results. In many ways it is the most satisfying work, for it gives the salesman a great sense of power. As the interpreter of the desires of the market, the salesman tells the inventors what to invent and the designers what to design. He speaks with great authority, like one who has divined the will of the gods.

8

Democracy
without Politics

*. . . the first negative advertising to hit the screen predated television by
several years, and the creator was not an ad director but a Hollywood
producer: the revered Irving Thalberg. In fact, Thalberg might be called
the Father of the Attack Ad.*

*The year was 1934, and Upton Sinclair . . . a lifelong socialist, was
running for Governor of California. . . . To defeat him, the state's
Republicans virtually invented the modern political campaign, introducing advertising and public-relations techniques that later came to
dominate the election process.*

GREG MITCHELL[1]

*My favorite show is the C-Span. That's what I watch: C-Span 1 and
C-Span 2. When I'm not watching CNN.*

BARBRA STREISAND,
adviser to President William J. Clinton

The first time a man puts on lipstick is never easy. The thickness of it
surprises him. His tongue tells him that it should be licked away, scraped off
by his teeth if need be, then scrubbed with saliva until no trace remains,
until his mouth is manly again, as unsullied as the mouth of a pure gray
granite man astride a horse in a park in Iowa.

He felt this physical discomfort, but not the embarrassment he had
expected, perhaps because the lipstick was applied by another man and

---

[1] *New York Times*, April 19, 1992. Mitchell is the author of *The Campaign of the
Century: Upton Sinclair's Race for Governor of California and the Birth of Media Politics*
(New York: Random House, 1992).

because the man was quick. Even so, he kept his eyes closed, for he did not want to see the transformation of himself into this other creature, this thing he had so long avoided, so long despised.

A third man watched. He stood to the side, with his arms folded across his chest, seeing everything inverted in a mirror. He controlled the transformation, which had been his idea, his insistence, his demand.

The man who now wore lipstick felt a threat of nausea in his throat, for he knew that the lipstick was merely the beginning. It would be followed by the application of makeup to his forehead, cheeks, and eyes. He had shaved closely, very carefully, but even the adumbration of his beard would have to be disguised.

It was like theater, the third man had said, performance, trompe l'oeil, sleight of hand, the creation of a persona, magic. He had spoken of the act with delight, he had been near to dancing because of his pleasure at the thought of it; yet, he issued a warning, a rule of theater: An actor must prepare, a performer must be the part.

In the chair, placed before the mirror, the one undergoing the transformation noted each touch of the makeup applicator, the cool sponge, the pad of tiny wet pores, as it stroked his face, covering over the marks of the history of a man. Confrontations occurred between the makeup and the flesh, not truly confrontations, but bursts of memory, as in the coruscations of distant dying stars.

The cut at the hairline, healed into a ragged berm, contested the stroke of the sponge, producing the glitter of memory: the conk sounded within his skull, the face of the policeman hidden behind the dark green plastic shield, horses, the sweat of horses, the long brown batons, conk, the conk of the baton, the conk of the stone street, conk, conk. And then the blood.

At the corner of his right eye a hole in the flesh, an ancient imperfection, refused the makeup once, and again. The third stroke of the sponge filled the depth of the hole; the cold color gathered in a tiny pool, overflowed, and lay drying on his skin like an immutable tear. The hole did not get filled. The hole remained; it was the recalcitrance of the man written on his face, like a tattoo.

On the cheek below the eye, eight stitch marks had nearly disappeared, but the line between them, the memory of the waiting, the long time until morning, the odor of earth and beans on the hands of the striker who first washed the wound, the sign, remained, a red line, as if the skin had not lost the anger of the night.

He coughed.

The man jerked the sponge away.

The third man made a sound of reassurance, like humming; he said the name of the man whose lips wore a thick, unnatural glaze of red.

After a moment the makeup applicator touched his face again, cold once more, resupplied. It would soon be time. The man who wore lipstick felt sweat under his arms, in his crotch. He dared not speak, he dared not move; his eyes remained closed. The sponge came to the torn place, the ragged patch, where the skin had gathered in a crimp of flesh, as if to protest the mismatch of the sides of the chin. A boy had sewed him up, a boy younger than he, a medical student wearing an improvised Red Cross armband. He saw again the eyes of the boy who threaded the curved needle. The boy had asked him, please, to look away, not to watch, while he sewed human flesh on the sidewalk beside a park in Chicago.

Under the makeup the skin of the man lacked all signs of vigor. The skin spoke of libraries and meeting rooms, of nights and waiting, courtrooms; it looked to be the skin of a man of argument, not of action. The skin was yellowgray; it did not have the elasticity of afternoons.

After the cloth that had protected his shirt collar and tie from the makeup was removed and the back of the chair was raised to vertical, the man opened his eyes and saw himself in the mirror. He thanked the man who had applied the makeup and lipstick, and apologized to him for what he was about to say. Then he turned to the third man, the one who was pleased, and said that he did not like the face he saw in the mirror.

"It is not my face," he said.

"Oh, do you like your face so much?" the third man asked.

"It's my face."

"Don't be old-fashioned."

The made-up man moved closer to the mirror. He could not see himself; he could see only what he had become. Although he had lived a long time and fought many battles on behalf of those people whom he loved and also cared for, he had been a stern man, a pillar of resolve. He seldom laughed; no one had ever known him to weep. The problem, his consultant had said, was that he showed no emotion; he was a machine of compassion, a business of goodness. It took a mellower man to get elected.

Now, with the band playing and the crowd clapping, the made-up man stood before the mirror and wept.

1.

In retrospect, the convention seems like madness, the nomination of John Wilkes Booth instead of Abraham Lincoln. Perhaps it was inevitable. I should have known. California politics should have prepared me. George Murphy, a tap dancer, had been elected to the U.S. Senate from California. Ronald Reagan, an actor and television pitchman, had been elected governor of the state. Shirley Temple, she of the Good Ship Lollipop, had also won the votes of her fellow Californians. Even so, the convention retained something of the quality of a nightmare or a very bad movie.[2]

Halfway through the convention, it became clear that two changes were taking place. I had anticipated one of them, the takeover by the right wing of the party, and chose to sit with the Virginia delegation, perhaps the most radical rightist delegation in the hall. But the other change surprised me. Not only was Ronald Reagan going to be the nominee of the Republican Party; he was still an actor, still in the role of an actor. The very men who were handling his campaign were willing to say obliquely or to imply or to say off the record that they thought he was an ideologue, and not very bright: He could win only if they controlled what he said, if they kept him from "putting his foot in his mouth."

"It's morning in America," the sales pitch for Ronald Reagan said. The film came out of the mind of a copywriter from BBDO, a New York advertising agency. It was like a movie, but it was also very different from a movie; there were no ideas, there was no content, there was no story. The screen was filled with photographs of mountains, fields of grain, blue-eyed children laughing, and the simple notion that this land belongs to those who can afford it.

All day and into the night, I listened to the orations of the right wing of the party, exuberant, in lubricious love with itself, like a film star; I crouched in the aisle beside Jacob Javits while the party booed him, booed Rockefeller, hooted down the broken moderate wing of the party; but I did not understand that the dogged arguments of interests had been superseded by the mirrors of marketing. Pete Dailey, Peter Hannaford, and Phil Jouanou told me, the constant references to Richard Wirthlin's polling data told

---

[2] *Harper's Magazine* had sent me to the 1980 Republican convention to write one of those essayistic pieces that appear in monthly magazines long after the event.

me, but I had known some of these people, all of their methods, for too many years; I misunderstood when they implied that control of the party had been given to new people; I thought they meant politics.

Even when one of the old men of Reagan's informal California cabinet, the rough-edged, self-made men who financed him right from the start, explained to me, "Ron isn't going to run the government like a politician; he's going to run it like a businessman, chairman of the board," I did not grasp the import of his words; I thought he meant economics.

What they implied, what I could not hear, was that the Republican Party, now in the grip of the Reagan forces, had abandoned the reality of the retail world in which politics had always been done; they had put emotion to work in the service of ideology. The politics of the nation had been given into the hands of the salesmen, and it was certain that the salesmen would win, for they had learned the secret of modern politics, which is that no one can refute the arguments of the heart.

2. Jefferson, Lincoln, Clinton & Brown

Politics and fishmongering do not have the same ends, but the methods of the marketplace of goods and the marketplace of ideas are similar. In fact, while a customer can look at a fish or scrutinize it with his nose and make a decision based on his observations, a citizen always has to be persuaded to pay more taxes or risk his life in war, making the methods of persuasion even more important to politics than to fishmongering. But selling and politics have never been identical. Politics did not arise from the marketplace; the fish did not legislate for the fish.

The chief distinctions between selling and the political process rest with the role of the persuader. In political persuasion, the speaker argues on behalf of ideas about himself and those like him; in selling, the speaker acts as a mediator between a product and the potential customer. In politics, the persuader participates; in selling, the salesman stands outside the sale. From its inception, politics was practiced by the participants in the polis; there were always speakers and listeners, but there was never a distinction between those citizens who belonged and those who did not.[3] In the Athenian

---

[3] The obligatory disclaimer about Periclean Athens: The Athenians did not permit women or slaves to participate in the government of the polis, which we now understand as unethical behavior. However, M. I. Finley's admonition must be remembered: The application of modern morality to fifth-century Athens is an anachronism. And any sense of moral

version of a legislature, the members were chosen by lot, not by election, denoting that every citizen was capable of making and applying laws. Politics was an argument among participating equals; the salesman's role, that of a mediator, an outsider, was the antithesis of politics.

One has only to compare Machiavelli's ideas in *The Prince* to those of *The Discourses* to see that historically democracy and tyranny have used different methods of persuasion. He advises his Prince, ". . . men must either be caressed or else annihilated. . . ." At times, Machiavelli could be running a sales meeting for a pack of shady storm-door or used-car salesmen: ". . . it is necessary . . . to be a great feigner and dissembler; and men are so simple and so ready to obey present necessities, that one who deceives will always find those who allow themselves to be deceived." And finally, the famous sentence: ". . . in the actions of men, and especially of princes, *from which there is no appeal,* the end justifies the means."

In *The Discourses,* where Machiavelli speaks of a republic as the best form of government, he writes, "And though, as Tully remarks, the populace may be ignorant, it is capable of grasping the truth and readily yields when a man, worthy of confidence, lays the truth before it." The tyrant sells, the republican does politics.[4]

Jumping forward to the early history of the United States, one finds that the distinction between selling and politics continues unchanged. All of the documents defining the new nation, from the revolutionary tracts to the Declaration of Independence and the Constitution, were written by participants. No one mediated the American Revolution; it was the idea of participants and the war of participants. The political discourse leading to the definition of the new nation was influenced by Locke, Rousseau, and other outside thinkers, but it was entirely a discourse among citizens (to be).

Every man spoke for himself, but no man worked entirely alone; no man was above his fellows in the realm of ideas. Even the Declaration of Independence, largely written by Thomas Jefferson, was edited by others and signed by many. The Constitutional Convention was attended by representatives of every state, and the document produced by the convention had

---

superiority we moderns may harbor should be tempered by the history of universal suffrage in the United States, not to mention the willingness of many Americans to fight a war over the issue of slavery.

4   Whether Machiavelli preferred the methods of *The Prince* or *The Discourses* remains in dispute. At long last, however, the simplistic position, based on a reading of *The Prince* alone, has been replaced by the more sophisticated views of Sir Isaiah Berlin and Felix Gilbert.

---

to be ratified by all the states. Had it been a salesman's document, the work of a mediator, it would have begun with the second-person plural pronoun of the salesman's repertoire, but it was a purely political document, and it spoke as such, from the outset: "We, the people . . ."

American political figures produced most of their own articles and speeches, without the help of salesmen, until the election of 1840, when William Henry Harrison, the old general who had won the battle of Tippecanoe, was chosen by the Whigs to run against Martin Van Buren. In what may have been the forerunner of modern political campaigning, the Whigs built Harrison's persona out of songs, a log cabin/hard cider image, and some telling exaggerations of President Van Buren's tastes for French cologne, gold spoons, and British carriages. The campaign was notable for its lack of content. There were no political aspects, nothing but parades, log cabin badges, and songs. The hero of Tippecanoe had nothing to say.

Harrison barely won the popular vote, but he had a 4-to-1 margin in the electoral college. When it came time for him finally to speak some serious thoughts at his inauguration, Daniel Webster had the temerity to present Harrison with the text. True to the American political tradition, the old general refused Webster's offer. Instead, he labored and produced an endless, boring speech based on faded memories of ancient history. Webster edited the speech, joking that he had "killed seventeen Roman proconsuls as dead as smelts." But Webster had still left too many Romans standing. Harrison delivered the truncated version on March 4, 1841, the coldest inauguration day in history. It took an hour and forty minutes. Standing there without a coat, he caught a cold, which developed into pneumonia. A month later the first beneficiary of a pure "image campaign" was dead.

Selling moved more deeply into politics in 1852, when Nathaniel Hawthorne volunteered to write a political biography of Franklin Pierce. Hawthorne was not at all timid about selling his candidate. He argued that the alternative to electing Pierce was "to retard the steps of human progress." After the election, Pierce paid the sales fee by naming Hawthorne U.S. consul in Liverpool, the best job the novelist ever held.

Lincoln followed the pattern set by Washington, Jefferson, Madison, and Harrison, writing his own speeches and other materials. He employed no campaign biographer, but he did demonstrate a deep understanding of persuasion and politics. Although he was a corporate lawyer, with some very large railroads among his clients, Lincoln portrayed himself as a man of the people, born in a log cabin. Perhaps the log cabin story was cynical, pure salesmanship, but the story of the rail splitter's humble origins also served to make Lincoln "of the people"; it kept him in the middle of the crowd, where he could do politics.

He was not, like Andrew Jackson, a general who encouraged egalitarianism from the saddle of his riding horse; the public Lincoln eschewed his business connections entirely, preferring the log cabin. In his first presidential campaign, Lincoln supporters marched down the streets of American cities displaying pieces of split rails. Even so, the election of 1860 turned upon issues of slavery, states' rights, and sectionalism. Lincoln won the election with a million fewer votes than his combined opponents; apparently, the candidate's mythicized origins failed to carry the day with most voters.

The national political conventions of the major parties began as political debates, but moved in the direction of sales meetings in 1828 when the popular vote first became a factor in presidential elections. Harrison and Tyler, of "Tippecanoe and Tyler, too," were not chosen for reasons having much to do with policy; Harrison figured to beat the snooty former diplomat Van Buren on the strength of Harrison's log cabin image and his willingness to say little or nothing of substance.

National political conventions took on a new role: to pick the candidate likely to win the most votes, then to stir up enthusiasm for the candidate among the sales representatives who were sent out from headquarters (centrally located, Chicago was the most common site for conventions) to persuade the electorate to vote for the candidate. Since there was always competition, the campaigns had a powerful agonistic aspect, which was as stirring as the politics: Who had the best parade? the biggest Fourth of July picnic? the grandest posters? the most campaign workers? and finally, the most votes?

By the 1912 Republican National Convention, *sell* had suddenly become a fresh word in the American language, and everybody was doing it, according to the historian Ralph G. Martin.[5] It was a convention of powerful sentiment, a turning point in the history of American political parties; the demonstrations were raucous, and one of them was astonishing. It was about such conventions that William Jennings Bryan wrote, "A convention feels about demonstrations somewhat like the big man who had a small wife who was in the habit of beating him. When asked why he permitted it, he replied that it seemed to please her and did not hurt him."

The politics of the 1912 convention were exceedingly contentious.

[5] *Ballots and Bandwagons* (New York: Rand McNally, 1964).

Teddy Roosevelt had recently discovered something called "social justice," and with his characteristic enthusiasm he turned it into a grand campaign for "the Square Deal." By 1910, he was arguing that "fair play under the present rules of the game" was insufficient. He wanted more "equality of opportunity and of reward for equally good service." His ideas differed less and less from those of another candidate, Robert La Follette, the progressive from the Midwest. All through the campaign, Roosevelt became more radical; he argued that democracy was not merely a political idea but an economic idea as well. The third candidate, the conservative and the favorite of the party bosses was Big Bill Taft, the jolly three-hundred-pound incumbent.

At one point in the convention, a woman in a pale, almost white dress, holding a bouquet of sweetpeas in her hand and bearing a Roosevelt poster, nearly turned the tide for Teddy. She stood at her place in the gallery, waving the huge Roosevelt poster in time to the music. Then, as Martin describes it, the woman "started a speech in pantomime aimed in a kind of mute appeal to the Taft men on the platform as if asking them to be fair to her hero, and soon her mood changed again and she was throwing kisses to the Roosevelt delegates. The whole convention was now with her, staring at her, cheering her."

During the cheering, she let the poster float down from the gallery into the crowd, which responded by picking up the poster, carrying it to her, then carrying her to the platform, where she said nothing, emitting only one tiny, high-pitched cry, a sound that set the convention into motion in a grand spontaneous demonstration. But for whom? No one ever figured out whether the demonstrators on the floor of the convention agreed with the woman or opposed her. Perhaps Bryan, certainly among history's best salesmen, was right about demonstrations. In any case, the conservative Taft was nominated to run for another term, Roosevelt broke away from the Republican Party to start his own Bull Moose Party, and Woodrow Wilson, a Democrat, won the 1912 election.

The Republican National Sales Meeting of 1912 had been a political convention with great and lasting effect. After that, conventions became more and more sales meetings, until 1956, when television changed the sales meeting into something else. There were 400 people from NBC and 335 from CBS at the 1956 Democratic National Convention. CBS had thirty cameras in operation. The history of the party was told in a film produced by Dore Schary of Hollywood, who said that he chose John F.

Kennedy to narrate the film because Kennedy had written *Profiles in Courage*, a best-seller.[6]

What had been a political meeting of the party faithful, the salesmen of the party who were expected to win the election in the front porch and barbershop discussions of American politics, was becoming something else. The concept of a political convention, the nature of political persuasion, was being changed by technological developments.

A significant change had taken place when candidates stopped writing their own speeches. Woodrow Wilson, the professor from Princeton, was among the last *writers* to hold the office of president. After Wilson, communication, which had been direct on the stump and through the printed word, was mediated. A speechwriter, the Nathaniel Hawthorne or Daniel Webster of an earlier time, was employed at every opportunity. FDR, like Franklin Pierce, employed very good writers, among them the playwright Robert Sherwood, but writers, mediators nevertheless. By the time FDR went to Chicago to accept his first Democratic nomination for president, his speech was not only written by Samuel I. Rosenman and rewritten by Louis Howe and Raymond Moley; it was subjected to comments from one of the nation's most famous salesmen, Jesse Strauss, chairman of Macy's.[7]

Along with the change in the conventions, television brought mediators into every aspect of politics. Hollywood had used Irving Thalberg to produce little films against the leftist Upton Sinclair in the 1934 California gubernatorial campaign, and then Hollywood had provided film again in 1936 for Alf Landon's presidential bid, but it was only after the war, when the actor/director/producer Robert Montgomery was hired to direct Dwight D. Eisenhower's television commercials and appearances, that the role of the mediator began to overwhelm that of the candidate. Eisenhower's speeches were written by one group and his appearances were directed by another. Roosevelt had said that Howe and Moley were the most important people in his presidential campaign, but in Eisenhower's case, Robert Montgomery, the cameramen and soundmen, and the speechwriters *were* the campaign. General Eisenhower was, in many respects, a replay of General William Henry Harrison, with modern technological aids. Both men were old when they ran, neither was political, and both were primarily images created by salesmen.

---

6   Kennedy's authorship has now come into question.
7   Ted Morgan, *FDR* (New York: Simon and Schuster, 1985).

The change in the use and character of political conventions speeded up rapidly in the 1980s and 1990s as the parties adjusted to the selection of candidates through primary elections and the influence of television. Anthony Shorris,[8] who was responsible for operations on the podium for the Office of the Secretary at the 1980 through 1992 Democratic National Conventions, described what may have been the turning point:

"In the 1988 convention Dukakis was going to be the nominee, but there was some discussion about how Jesse Jackson was going to be treated, what level of deference was going to be accorded him. The convention was viewed as a symbol of how Dukakis was going to deal with the base of the party as opposed to trying to broaden the base. Jackson was at the heart of the base and the last remaining candidate and critic from the left.

"Overlaying that tension was a different tension, which was between the television aspect of the convention, especially that designed for the consumer and that designed for the red meat crowd in the hall.

"We met every morning to do our planning. The meetings were sort of jointly run by the DNC [Democratic National Committee] hierarchy and a group whose influence rose and rose as we got closer to the convention; not as you would expect, the Dukakis group, but the really important people at the convention, who were Gary Smith and Dwight Hemion, the television production team. Gary Smith was the director of the show. He believed in Mike Dukakis, no doubt about that, but Gary is a television producer and this was a television show. Gary understood what that meant. It's got to get good ratings; it's got to appeal to the sort of mass viewership. It's not supposed to get entangled in little party niceties that would be understood only by the party faithful, and it's got to be, most of all, fun, fun to watch, good television.

"The best example of this was the dispute over who would sing, first, the national anthem, then the closing song. The Jackson people had some interest in a gospel singer, who would appeal to the base, the party faithful, and the Dukakis campaign wanted a country music star to sing, because that would appeal to exactly who they were looking for, the consumers that

---

[8]   Anthony Shorris is my older son. He prepared for a career in public service at Harvard and the Woodrow Wilson School, and has put some of his ideas into practice as a commissioner of the City of New York and first deputy executive director of the New York–New Jersey Port Authority. In 1993 he was a member of the Clinton transition team. We have been known to disagree on some political questions. I have a tape recording of his comments.

they're trying to sell the product to. The debate went on for days. Gary [Smith] said, 'I can work with Mahalia Jackson or the country-and-western star. You guys decide, but I have to know; I have to put the show together.' Meanwhile, the debate went on, country-and-western or gospel singer. And the time got closer and closer. So after much dispute the Dukakis and Jackson campaigns finally locked themselves in a room to resolve this important symbolic issue, and out they came with a compromise, and we went to the meeting so Gary could hear the compromise. The compromise was that the gospel singer and the country-and-western star were going to sing together.

"Gary held his head, 'Are you kidding? What kind of music am I gonna play? This will never work, forget it.' And back they went to work out another compromise, but a compromise that met the test of the really important person in the room, the person that ran the television show."

He saw less of that in 1980 and 1984, when the conventions were still in the hands of the convention managers. By 1992 each of the candidates had a personal Hollywood producer who handled every aspect of his appearance: Harry and Linda Thomason worked for Governor Clinton. Sidney Pollack handled Senator Bradley. Oliver Stone occupied a special place in the Jerry Brown campaign; he even seconded the nomination.

From his seat on the podium, Tony Shorris believed he saw the future of political campaigns in Brown's use of technology: "He understood the idea of going direct to the consumer, not through the media. The 800 number was an example of Jerry trying to connect people on a mass basis directly with the campaign. That got extended with the Perot campaign; they did even more of that. Historically, there was always a difference between representative democracy and direct democracy. In the next campaign, the voter may have a different connection with the candidate."

3. Nixon's Beard and the Advent of Mob Politics

Salesmen had nothing to do with the defining moment in modern media politics, which came during the tight presidential race of 1960. Richard Nixon and John Kennedy met in the first nationally televised debate between presidential candidates. Nixon came to the studio with all of the advantages: He had served as vice president in a very popular administration. His opponent was young, with a less than distinguished record in the

Congress, and Kennedy was a Roman Catholic. Yet, Nixon left the studio that day doomed to defeat. In the black-and-white eye of the television camera the vice president of the United States looked like a shifty-eyed, unshaven B-movie villain.

What many still consider the first direct communication ever between candidates for the highest office and all the citizens of a large constitutional democracy had been something quite different. The occasion had been mediated by the directors, cameramen, set designers, lighting technicians, makeup people, and the technology itself.

Sophisticated political handlers and salesmen guessed what had happened in the Nixon-Kennedy debates. A technology more powerful than anything they had heretofore imagined had become available to politics. Elections would, from here on, be about images placed on a screen; the opportunities for mediation were unlimited. The genius of one New York advertising commercial producer, Tony Schwartz, was to realize that the most effective way to reach an unsophisticated audience was not through argument, as in the old politics, but through allegory.

Johan Huizinga had described the appeal of allegory to audiences of simple folk in medieval times, but his classic work, *The Waning of the Middle Ages*, was not widely known among political operatives and television producers. For Schwartz and other salesmen allegory had to seem like new ground, and they used it with the brilliance, enthusiasm, and lack of limits common to pioneers. In Schwartz's famous daisy commercial, produced only four years after the Nixon debacle, a small girl pulled the petals from a flower, counting down from ten. At zero, the film cut to a nuclear explosion. It was all that had to be said about Barry Goldwater's campaign. The power of the allegory was so great that the commercial had only to run once to be instrumental in delivering one of history's greatest landslides to Lyndon Johnson.

A generation later, the Republicans used allegory to bolster Reagan's policies. While the commercial was not quite so powerful as Schwartz's hydrogen bomb, Hal Riney's use of a bear in the allegory of America and the threat from the "evil empire" helped to sell the nation on Ronald Reagan's vast expenditures for defense, including the Star Wars program.

The use of allegory by the salesmen who stand at the edges of politics, acting like levers upon the political mind of the citizenry, demonstrates one of the major distinctions between politics and selling. Politics can never be separated from the great moral issues of the time, while selling can never be bound by them. The methods of Schwartz and Riney are indistinguishable; the anti-Goldwater allegory and the pro-Reagan allegory turn on the same issue: nuclear war. Both commercials sought to rise above partisanship to matters of life and death, matters proper to allegory, and both were enormously successful. Both commercials sought to reach the mass of voters, not merely the partisans, by going around the discourse of representative democracy to the deepest instincts of human beings, and both were enormously successful.

Instead of representative democracy standing between power and the mob, the salesman had taken that role. The inevitable next step was the use of propositions, a form of plebiscite, to determine the actions of government. A proposition, placed on the ballot, and voted up or down by the citizens, is the form of democracy that gave nightmares to Aristotle, the raw majority, which he characterized as mob rule. In a sense, the use of propositions is apolitical, for no dialogue can be permitted, no compromise can be reached; the proposition must be approved or discarded as it stands, word for word. But it may be that no one ever votes for the proposition, because it always gives way to the power of the salesman, who shapes it for the public mind.

One of the most effective salesmen of propositions works out of a modest second-floor office in San Francisco. Hal Larson doesn't think of himself as a salesman; he doesn't like the stereotype. Larson certainly doesn't look like a stereotypical salesman, and he doesn't sound like one in conversation, which may be part of the reason for his long and very successful career. Now nearing seventy, he looks fifty, forty-five from across the room, a man physically out of joint with the time, as if he were the young father of Hal Larson, the boy from Oregon who "drove airplanes" during World War II. In the advertising community Larson still holds down three jobs: mentor, hero, and peerless copywriter.

"The key to winning an initiative," he said, "is to define the issue in your terms instead of the other guy's terms. If you let the other guy define you, you lose. In issue advertising, the advertising is the candidate. If you're doing advertising for a person, you can define him to a certain extent, but he, his presence, defines him; he's so tall, he sounds like something, he may cat around, and you can't redefine that. If he does that, it's part of his persona. But an issue is precisely what you say it is, neither more nor less. If we do our job properly, the people are voting for the issue as we define it. Or said differently, for or against the advertising."

The distance between the salesman and the political concept does not remain constant for Larson, as he explained, "We did a campaign two years ago [1990] for the booze business here, for Ernie Gallo and all his friends, all the alcohol people. There was a tax proposal, probably not an unreasonable tax, to be fair. They paid me to stop the tax.

"When we went into it, the issue was framed: Booze is bad and booze should be taxed; we need the money, and that's a good place to get it.

"We defined the issue as one that is misrepresenting what it is, because in fact, they did misrepresent it. The money wouldn't go into the good works that everybody thought at first that it would; it would go importantly into the pockets of the people who prepared the initiative. So we pointed out that it was other than they represented it, and put the focus on the people who prepared the initiative.

"Then, I was also part of a consortium that thereafter prepared a voluntary tax that they imposed on themselves. So it's the yin and yang a little bit.

"I turn down as many as I accept. I'm not snow white about it. In the case that I just told you about, it was a mixed bag, and I didn't have any trouble opposing it, even though it was on a public enemy, booze. I've defended tobacco. I've also defended the gays for no money on an initiative that would have been outrageously punitive."

Larson has worked on twenty issues. His success rate is uncanny. "In every one I've ever worked on, people in the beginning opposed me [that is, the position he was hired to sell]; if I'm for it, they're against it, and if I'm against it, they're for it. Every one I've ever worked on, and in very large numbers frequently. And by the time the thing is over, they agree with me in sufficient numbers. So, something happened between A and Z. Did I create a want? I don't know. But I helped define something so they see in a new light . . . that they already opposed it and didn't know it. That sounds obscure. Or already wanted it and didn't know it." He paused for a long time. His feet were up on his desk. It was a warm day for San Francisco. He wore whites, a style learned in a vacation house in Mexico. "You've changed their behavior," he said, as if conceding a point, "but you haven't changed their basic attitudes and beliefs."

He is the best of salesmen, he knows the tools and the limits of his trade, but he is not political. He worked for Ronald Reagan, for the Republican National Committee, but his own beliefs are gentle; he feels comfortable in the role of defender. Yet, salesmen do not decide such political things; in the game of politics the mediators do not play, they stand at the side of the world and work the levers. Larson maintains his distance; he knows the weakness inherent in passion.

4. The Playmaker

Democracy in the United States, which chooses leaders by ballot rather than by lot, now demands a salesman for every campaign. Even small children who run for office in junior high schools appoint campaign managers, attempting to market themselves to the electorate. By the time the electorate reaches the numbers required to elect someone to the U.S. House of Representatives, the money and media coverage available to the candidate enables the campaign manager to use all of the salesman's tools.

The effectiveness of the sales tools often determines the result of the election, but not always. Some people are simply unelectable, some ideas are simply unacceptable. As in any sale, the customer's desires determine the limits of the salesman's success. One can see how the limits are stretched by looking at the history of totalitarian regimes; these perversions of democracy arise when the population suffers in some extreme way—war, severe economic depression, or some other form of hopelessness—that causes the limits on desire to break down.

In a more or less comfortable democratic society, the salesman who runs the campaign can avoid the ethical questions associated with politics by stating his belief in the wisdom of the electorate; it is the moral comfort of the "invisible hand" brought to politics.

The distance between selling and politics varies from campaign to campaign. When a consultant works for a Republican one year and a Democrat the next, the distance approaches the realm of objectivity; the salesman could have come from another planet. At other times, however, the salesman holds views similar to those of the candidate and has an intimate connection to the electorate, he feels himself a part of it. Then the gulf between selling and politics narrows, and a citizen/salesman, the modern man of politics, emerges.

John Cooper, of the Shelbyville, Tennessee, Coopers, stands on such syncretic ground. He has a Harvard education and Tennessee holler vowels, an M.B.A. and a passion for politics that has carried him to Washington and Louisiana and always home again to Tennessee. The son of Governor Prentice Cooper of Tennessee knows mergers and acquisitions and the best moonshiners in the Cumberland Gap. He carries within him the here and there of modern politics, the delicate balance between the citizen and the mediator.

"The two [U.S. congressional] races where I was absolutely in charge," he said, "[Buddy] Rohmer in '80 and my brother [James] in '82, the candidate took on a modern sense of being an actor on a stage. Not that they're not very important, but just time and the effort involved means they can't really run the campaign. Because if you're really gonna be efficient about it, you give them the schedule, you get 'em out of bed at five o'clock in the morning, you run 'em until ten o'clock at night, you get the information about what they're supposed to say where they are."

He stops for a moment, as if to argue with himself. The picture he has begun to draw of the candidate does not please him. "Product is too definite a word for the candidate. A candidate is an idea. He's a feeling. The candidate is comfortable in saying who they are and what their biography is. It requires an interpreter. It requires a Moses in a way. Not to be too blasphemous about it. It requires a Judge David Douglas for Abraham Lincoln to create sort of the touchstones, the myth, because all politics is about myth really. But you can't ever lie in this political stuff. No myth can ever be completely made up. Abe Lincoln did grow up in an unfinished log cabin and he did split rails, but he became more than that.

"It's the playmaker, the manager, the consultant, who's able to take the politican who's a modern-day actor and cast him in a play and write the script of the play. The play, though, only has about three or four lines in it. That's about all that you can get across to five hundred thousand people in a congressional race. It's just the three or four things about the person that makes the play work."

He turned to his brother's congressional race against Cissy Baker, the daughter of former U.S. Senator Howard Baker, the race John Cooper had managed down to the last detail. "So in Jim's case, he'd gone to Groton, he'd been a Rhodes scholar at Oxford, he'd gone to Harvard Law School. He practiced law for six months in Nashville, which is not in the district.

"And the first line about Jim that worked, he came up with. His slogan was 'The hard-work candidate.' And once we took the slogan, we went and bought a little Chevrolet automobile and we put him in the automobile and we just put him driving on the road. And every time the odometer hit another milestone, we took his picture in some godforsaken part of the district, which is five hundred miles long, and sent that picture out to the newspapers and they'd all print it. As the months went by, Jim Cooper, the hard-work candidate for congress, crossed thirty thousand miles in the district, campaigning virtually nonstop.

"By doing that people said, 'Well, by golly, if you were in Lawrenceville last night and Pulaski this morning and you're in Fayetteville today, you sure work hard.' But the only way that could work is if you had a command post back there, in effect running the guy up around the gauntlet and sort of making everything else happen in the campaign.

"The other thing that the playmaker, the consultant, the manager, has to decide about a campaign is, What is the question? Every election asks and answers a question. And everybody who's running tries to make it their question, the election about the question that could be answered in no other way but that it would be favorable to yourself. We want control of the idea and of the question. In our case it was 'What are you for? Are you for the rich man's daughter, or are you for the hard-work candidate?' " he said, giving a textbook example of the ancient method of argument.

The extent to which his theory of political campaigning employs the philosophy of selling comes clear in his understanding of how the candidate affects the electorate. "I don't think there are many winning campaigns where you actually persuaded anybody of anything," he said. "What happens is you do cater to their world view, and you define your boy or girl in a way that fits into their world view.

"You can only give 'em what they want," he said, as if democracy were beyond the reach of the salesman. Then he put the electorate back in the salesman's hands: "You can make them think that what they want is what you're giving them."

If he were cynical, an ironic man, the last statement would be the stuff of deception, but John Cooper is a southerner, a defender of the moral character of the South. He says that a candidate must learn to "love the district" before he can be elected to Congress, and he knows, for it would be difficult to love the district more than John Cooper loves his part of Tennessee. He speaks of people in the district "at the highest and the lowest levels of society" who are "stand-up people, prudent, fair, honest," who he says "are so great they make you cry, and that's what the country's all about."

Only then does one finally come to the mixture in the man, to the defender of the people, who is transparently, politically, defending himself, the playmaker who knows that he belongs in the play.

---

5. Market Leader

We, the people
—U.S. Constitution

Our forefathers
—LINCOLN

My friends
—FDR

My fellow Americans
—LBJ

The American people
—PEROT

In the middle of the 1980s, a political low point for national Democratic Party politics, a group of highly paid New York advertising and public relations executives offered its services to the Democratic National Committee.[9] The offer could not have come at a more opportune time, or so it seemed to the New York group. The "Reagan revolution" was under way, most of the programs put in place by Democrats during the preceding quarter of a century were being terminated or gutted. The use of marketing and sales techniques by Michael Deaver, David Gergen, and the rest of the White House staff had made it clear to most people in American politics that there had been a fundamental change in technique.

The Reagan administration had embraced fully, without qualification, the idea that the president was the chief executive officer of a giant sales organization. Hal Larson, who executed some of those sales campaigns for the White House, said of the president, "Sure, he was a salesman . . . ; it goes with the territory."

[9] I was one of the members of the group, along with senior officers from some of the largest advertising agencies in the world, including Grey; Doyle Dane Bernbach; Ayer; McCann-Erickson; and Ogilvy & Mather. The group expertise comprised marketing, research, media, public relations, and the production of print and broadcast materials.

Before the group disbanded, it had reached out to Chicago, Los Angeles, and San Francisco.

Whether Ronald Reagan was truly a salesman or perhaps only a president who used sales and marketing techniques is a point to be discussed later. In the eighties the question was academic. Ronald Reagan was changing the country, and the Democrats not only couldn't stop him, they couldn't even slow him down.

On the way down to Washington to meet with Paul Kirk and the staff of the Democratic National Committee (DNC), Edward M. Block of AT&T, widely reputed to be the best, most ethical public relations executive in the United States, and I discussed the difference in the marketing of the two parties. The Democrats, we concluded, were expert at retail, while the Republicans did better at wholesale or national selling. The distinction may seem like a commonplace to people unfamiliar with the methods of selling, but it was, or could have been, useful to the Democratic Party, for the two forms of marketing require entirely different approaches, from the concept of the audience to the level of detail.[10]

We made this point to the DNC, explaining to the executive staff that we would be willing and able to convert the policies of the Democratic Party into a national campaign, if the DNC would give us an outline of its political ideas. The New York contingent made it clear, however, that the political ideas would have to come from the DNC, because we believed it was unethical for advertising and public relations practitioners, using market research and marketing techniques, to set policy for a national political party.

[10] By hewing to retail techniques, the Democrats have not had a major victory since Lyndon Johnson defeated Barry Goldwater in 1964. Jimmy Carter's election for one term following Watergate was a repudiation of Nixon, not a victory for Democratic policies, and Clinton, of course, was not elected by a majority.

In politics at the city level, the Democrats do not sell at all, they do business, as Colonel Jacob Arvey explained to me after the 1968 Chicago Democratic Convention. The loyalty of the people to Mayor Richard Daley and to the party Daley represented, he said, was genuine. He reminded me of stories my father had told about the use of food baskets and jobs to politicize the Chicago electorate during the Depression. In Chicago, as in most big cities, politics was a family business.

Block and I brought this notion to the Democrats. The Republicans were salesmen, the Democrats were more like employers; they made government into a rich, but hard-nosed uncle who bartered jobs for loyalty. The national problem for the Democrats was that they confused their success at family business with selling.

Franklin Delano Roosevelt, of course, had expanded the retail concept of political barter to the national level. The Democrats who followed him, with the exception of Lyndon Johnson, could not comprehend the idea. They could neither sell nor do business.

Whether the Kennedys were running a family business or selling is difficult to say; their peculiar combination of thugs and snobs is difficult to categorize.

One commercial was written by the group. The actor Martin Sheen produced and recorded it, paying all the costs himself. Nothing else was ever done. The DNC and the New York group reached an impasse over the question of who was to decide the policies of the party.

It was a minor incident in American politics, hardly worth noting except that it came just as a study group within the Democratic Party, led by the governor of Arkansas and others, was beginning to make its presence felt at the DNC. These conservative politicians, although still Democrats, showed more interest in power than in ideas; they led the party away from politics and toward marketing, which they expected to supply the winning formula.

No one could have known it then, but the expectations of the Democratic Party, in the midst of the Reagan revolution, were about to produce the first market-driven presidency. Bill Clinton, one of the likely contenders for the Democratic nomination in 1992, had been preparing to run for the office of president since he was a boy. People who knew him personally said that Clinton was so interested in the campaign process that he sounded, in private conversation, "more like a political consultant than a political candidate."

The undistinguished governor of an undistinguished state entered the only kind of race he could have won; he took on an incumbent, the kind of candidate whose ability to sell is so precisely determined by reality that he will either breeze into a second term in good times or be forced to turn his entire campaign to attacking his opponent in bad times.

From the Democratic National Convention until the election, Clinton had little to do but avoid suicidal acts, for George Bush had fallen from grace. The American economy was in recession, and Americans traditionally put their pocketbooks first. Given the situation, Clinton ran a poor campaign, allowing Ross Perot, a man with the charm and good looks of a locust, to carry 19 percent of the vote, while George Bush needed help from Pat Buchanan and the Quayles to give away enough of the centrist vote to lose the election.

If the American electorate found one aspect of Clinton most unpalatable, it was the suspicion that the Democratic candidate was a salesman, "Slick Willie." Apparently; they could live with the rest of his foibles: his subtle resistance to the draft during the Vietnam War, his reputed philandering, and so on. But they didn't want a salesman in the White House. George Bush and his handlers knew that was Clinton's weakness as a candidate, but the Bush campaign was completely disorganized; it couldn't choose between opposing affirmative action and abortion and defeating Clinton. Bush tried. In the debates, he accused Clinton of "waffling," but he couldn't crystallize the accusation into a defining idea.

More interesting than the Bush failure, however, was that the voters demonstrated their ability to distinguish between Ronald Reagan, who had worked as a salesman for General Electric and then put his campaign into the hands of the salesmen, and Bill Clinton, who was a salesman. Apparently, they recognized the signs of politics and the signs of selling. Reagan, softly speaking, handsome, a corrupt Will Rogers, never strayed from his ruthlessly conservative politics. Even in 1980, when George Bush characterized his tax policies as "voodoo economics," Reagan smiled, and moved ahead. He was a part of the electorate, party to his politics. Although he appeared disengaged, drowsing through the presidency, he never abandoned his crude social and economic goals, he never stepped outside where he could use the salesman's lever. Ronald Reagan stood with his supporters, he was one of them; he employed salesmen, but he practiced politics. In the office of president, he led the nation. He was not a market-driven president; he did not change his political views or even the issues that concerned him because the market demanded it. If he did not truly lead the public, at least he waited for the public to come around to his system of beliefs.

The Clinton campaign, a product of the expectations of a party long out of power, was not driven by politics. Bill Clinton behaved according to the rules of selling. He let the market choose his campaign. A survey conducted on November 3, 1992, by Voter Research & Surveys, a consortium of ABC News, CBS News, CNN, and NBC News, reported the importance of issues in determining how people voted. The pollsters had been correct from the outset: The economy was first at 42 percent, followed by the federal deficit at 21 percent and health care at 20 percent. If there was any doubt about how Clinton chose his issues and conducted his campaign, the steadiness of the polls should have put it to rest. The battle cry of his campaign, "It's the economy, stupid," was based on market studies. He changed no one's mind, brought no new ideas to the public debate; Bill Clinton studiously avoided the great domestic questions of our time. He kept Jesse Jackson in the background and never spoke the words *social* and *justice* in that order. Even the less dangerous issues did not hold an important place in the campaign. Education, for example, did not get Clinton's attention then, and it has not gotten his attention since.

On most issues put before him during the campaign and in the early part of his presidency, Clinton has shown no stomach for politics or principle. For example, when the House of Representatives made changes in his economic program, Clinton praised their wisdom instead of attempting to protect his principles. When some people reacted badly to his choice of a black-Jewish woman as assistant attorney general for civil rights, which is an enforcement but not a policy-making position, he said he hadn't known her work—even though she was a personal friend who had written extensively in law journals on the subject of voting rights—and withdrew her name from nomination. The woman, Lani Guinier, responded with an astonishing display of generosity; she told the press that she wished she had been given the opportunity to explain her views before the Senate Judiciary Committee, but that she still supported Bill Clinton.

On one issue after another—homosexual rights in the miliary, nominations to high office, taxes, entitlements, the war in Bosnia, and so on—the president showed himself outside politics, not party to any principle, a salesman. A little more than four months into his term, Clinton confirmed the public view that he was a salesman, not merely an employer of salesmen, by naming David Gergen to stand at "the intersection of policy and politics and communication."

In a profile of Gergen the *New York Times* called him a "master salesman," and quoted the following from the former Reagan White House communications director: "It is clear now, in contrast to how Clinton presented himself during the campaign, that the Democrats' true agenda is to reverse the direction set by Ronald Reagan. And the irony is that they are attempting to do this by using the same techniques Reagan used."[11]

An accompanying editorial in the *Times* said of the appointment, "It points up a deterioration of political values . . . ," and went on to remind readers of Gergen's past works: "He was an artful promoter of politics that coarsened the quality of social compassion, spread suffering among the most undefended citizens and pulled back the Justice Department from its mission of civil rights."[12]

---

[11] Gergen's statement wasn't quite the same as the reality. For example, Reagan nominated Judge Robert Bork to the U.S. Supreme Court, and refused to withdraw the nomination even though Bork's extensive writings in law journals made his confirmation virtually impossible. Following Clinton's withdrawal of the Lani Guinier nomination, Bork reminded the public of that difference between Reagan and Clinton.

Since Clinton behaves like a salesman, how much of Reagan's revolution will be undone depends entirely upon the market for justice.

[12] On October 31, 1993, in the first issue of its new, more market-driven format, the

No one doubts that David Gergen works as a salesman rather than a man of politics, although he made his living for many years by working with the followers of Adam Smith and Herbert Spencer. By hiring Gergen as his chief salesman—that is, by giving him the power to define reality according to the rules learned beside Richard Nixon during Watergate and Ronald Reagan during his days of revolution—Bill Clinton declared himself, finally and irrevocably, a salesman. Politics, the process that resolves the tension between liberty and order in self-government, no longer engaged him; selling, the conforming of the appearance of the product to the desires of the market, was foremost in his mind.

6. With a Foot in Both Camps

The fact of the matter is that because they have a foot in both camps, they fail in both of the respective purposes for which philosophy and statesmanship are worthwhile: they actually come in third, but want to be thought first!

—PLATO, *Euthydemus*

With the election of Bill Clinton, the market-driven presidency had arrived; the end of politics was possible. Or was it? If true salesmen, men and women without politics, were elected, they would be irrelevant, unwilling and unable to govern, for they would respond exactly to the will of the majority. In theory, a government of salesmen would be a continuous plebiscite, a town meeting without the restraints of law, history, or custom. If such a government were to come to power in the United States, it would

---

New York Times Magazine gave its cover to a long piece about David Gergen written by a *Times* staff reporter, Michael Kelly. It was an interesting, nicely written piece, with "lots of good reporting" (as they like to say at the *Times*), but either Kelly and his editors at the magazine failed to understand the relative roles of Gergen and Clinton or they chose to limit the piece to reporting on political advisers and media, without giving consideration to the meaning of Clinton's appointment of David Gergen.

The profile and criticism of David Gergen in the *Times* would have changed, I believe, if the writer and the magazine had chosen to investigate the nature of salesmen and politics. The distinction they would have found between tolerance and democracy would surely have led them to place greater emphasis on Clinton's decision to hire Gergen and to evince less surprise at Gergen's decision to accept the job.

However, along with John R. MacArthur's book *Second Front* (New York: Hill and Wang, 1992), on the behavior of the press during the Persian Gulf War, the *Times Magazine* piece contributes to a new understanding of the character of the press in the 1990s.

---

be limited, at least in its early days, by the Constitution, but the Constitution would come under pressure from the majority almost immediately. The salesmen who had been elected to govern would, according to the rules of the market, amend the Constitution to meet the desires of the market. A republic governed by salesmen could not survive; it would become a mob.

While the methods and morals of selling have often been applied to government, especially to campaigning, in the United States, no salesman has ever won the presidency, and I doubt that a true salesman has ever managed even to capture a governorship or a seat in the Congress. Selling requires the objectivity of a lever, tolerance born either of indifference or of arrogance (the sense of being so unlike the customers that one belongs to another category, as kings and tyrants differ from commoners), and politics in a society that still retains some semblance of democracy—as democracy was understood by its philosophers, from Pericles to Lincoln—is always engaged, for politics is a passion practiced by those who despise loneliness.

So there will be no salesmen in public office, or there will be no public office as we know it; neither Willy Loman nor Donald Trump nor David Gergen can govern in a democracy. Even Lee Iacocca, the flag-draped salesman invented by his advertising agency and his ghostwriter, dares not seek engagement with the American commonwealth, for he has always lived as a stranger, a salesman, a man outside. Strangers may not govern in America; when public office serves as no more than a lever for the officeholder, the citizens deem the officeholder corrupt. Loman, Iacocca, Gergen, and Trump have no passion for engagement in the public world; they cannot practice politics; they have chosen the life of lonely conviviality; they sell.

Bill Clinton, for all that he tries to be a man without motives, a nowhere man, cannot make himself a fishmonger, for in reality no one can reduce the republic to a fish. The assumptions of a democracy will not permit his inclinations; he must do politics, even if passion goes against his nature, even if a life based on motives frightens him, even if it pleases him to stink of salmon and the guts of perch. The problem lies not in the possibility of accession but in the complexity of the market. The grand, simple notion Rousseau named "the general will" does not exist in America; the reality is that the salesman in government, pure and true to his calling, can never find out exactly what his customers want. He is sentenced to some measure of autonomy, condemned to beginnings.

Yet, the new president differs from his predecessors in that he does not merely employ salesmen; he is a salesmen. Bill Clinton does not sell in order to govern; he governs in order to sell. Selling dominates the thinking of his administration, but the complexity and changing character of the nation make it impossible to follow completely the rules of selling; in other words, the president often wastes the authority of government on selling and still doesn't produce policies that please the market, as in his seemingly endless debacle over homosexuals in the military.[13]

The president's nemesis Ross Perot is a faux salesman. At some time in his life, he may have had a salesman's tolerance for others, but no more. He must still dress himself in the trappings of a salesman, as if selling were democracy, because that is what his followers expect of him, but he tramples the market instead of acceding to it. Perot is a mirror image of Clinton: one wishes to sell, but cannot avoid governing; while the other wishes to govern, but cannot avoid selling.

With the salesman forced to do politics and the tyrant in the wings having to sell, the nation suffers two men who live with a foot in both camps. Plato's argument applies: They are neither the best salesmen nor the best men of politics. Such men can govern, but they cannot govern well.

[13] The debate over the North American Free Trade Agreement, a product of the Bush administration adopted by Clinton, showed Clinton more interested in passage of the agreement than in its contents. His stand-ins argued that failure to pass the agreement would damage Clinton's presidency. Interest was centered on the question of whether Clinton could sell the NAFTA rather than on the agreement. A debate between Vice President Albert Gore and Ross Perot became a contest of salesmanship. Following the debate, the media lamented the lack of substance and returned to concentrating on the contest rather than the political character of the agreement. The Clinton-Gergen White House sales organization, with the willing participation of the media and Ross Perot, made the sale the end rather than the means.

9

A Recipe
for Hotcakes

To bring the case closer to home, consider the proposal you have before you. You will buy it or reject it not so much for its merits as for the number of books it might sell. Thus, I sold it to (my literary agent) Roberta Pryor knowing that she would sell it to you by pointing out that you will sell many copies to booksellers, who will buy them on the expectation of selling them to the public, many of whom will buy the book because they think it will help them to sell goods or services. In other words, we are selling sales.

If this proposal was utterly foolish and the writer was barely literate and not at all conversant either with ideas of culture or the scope and mechanics of selling in the United States, but you thought the book would sell three hundred thousand copies in hard cover, would you buy it? I am not asking you to examine your soul, just to consider the value you place on selling compared to the value you place on the work.

You are not alone.

—From the proposal to publish this book[1]

Some people have a sense of the market and some people don't. Steven Spielberg has it . . . Judith Krantz in her way. Woody Allen has it, for the audience he cares about reaching, and so does Sylvester Stallone, at the other end of the spectrum.

I like to think I have that instinct.

—TRUMP, *The Art of the Deal*

Ethics and aesthetics are one.

WITTGENSTEIN, *Notebooks, 1914–1916*

He preferred to work in luncheonettes and coffee shops. The din, he said, gave rhythm to his prose, and when he sought new voices, inflections, the

---

[1] Book proposals are generally not addressed to a specific publisher, although they may be submitted to one or many houses. Since this proposal was submitted only to W. W. Norton, the question was academic, perhaps even a subtle flattery . . . selling.

raw data of ordinary life, he had only to put down his ballpoint pen for a moment and wait for the world to come to him. He was never disappointed by his storefront world: If the customers did not provide the enraged seminar of New York life, then the cooks and waiters satisfied him with the crash and clatter, the cries and curses of the luncheonette itself. In the long, narrow room, full of steam and the mist of fat frying, he was privy to the language of immigration and ambition, bitterness, business, and what he called the transient glories of city life. The luncheonette offered him everything but the words and silences of love, for which he had to rely upon imagination.

His friends said that he was a good writer and a serious man, an artist, for he had never published. He followed the rules of artists very carefully, which was the secret of social life in this last wretched part of Manhattan available to artists. He had very little money, he washed in the basin beside the door to his room, his fingernails were dirty, and all the clothing he owned was stained, torn, tattered, or patched. He observed the etiquette of earrings, tattoos, black cotton, work boots, and pallor. He sent out stamped, self-addressed envelopes and laid his rejection slips on the floor of his room in natural disarray, like leaves, like God's own leaves. His hair had been cut in a display window while tourists and newcomers to the East Village watched. When he needed money, which was often, he worked as a messenger, riding a bicycle as thin as a cigarette through the maddening traffic of lower Manhattan. Now and then, he worked nights in the back office of a brokerage firm keying transactions into a computer, but intimations of repetitive stress syndrome frightened him. He feared the city traffic less than the slow destruction of whatever was said to be connected to his fingers through a carpal tunnel.

In his room he lay on a futon or squatted on the floor. He had no furniture, not even a chair. Because the room had been built without closets, he kept everything he owned piled on shelves affixed with screws and nails to the old plaster walls. Sometimes the plaster gave way, and the shelves and all their contents fell onto the floor. After two bad experiences he learned to protect himself by keeping his futon in the center of the room, out of reach of the falling objects.

The artist's life was not lonely, nor was it uninteresting. He met poets and criminals, the former this and the ex-that. Many women were available to him. But he feared AIDS. Wherever he went, he saw people who suffered or could be suffering with the disease. He did not know who had it, who could transmit it, or how. Whenever a woman asked him to use a condom, he was pleased. When the woman did not ask, he could not make the suggestion, for it seemed cowardly, outside the rules of daring by which artists had to live. He lay awake nights on the futon in the center of his room with the uncertain shelves all around him, and he thought about the possibility that some woman had transmitted the virus to him. Although he was an artist, he could not imagine the life cycle of a virus; he was limited to empathy for sentient things.

On occasion he received money from his mother, who still lived and worked in Ohio. She had never been to New York City, but she said she had read about it often, in the works of Henry James and John Cheever, and in many, many articles and stories in the *New Yorker*. Once in a while, she sent fifty dollars to him; more often fifteen or ten. For social and political reasons the bank had made her a vice president, but she still sat at the same unadorned desk and she still opened new accounts and directed customers who had important business to the real officers of the bank. She believed in art; she had majored in world literature at the branch of the state university.

His father did not send him money or encouragement; he did not even send Christmas or birthday presents. Whenever the question of money came up, his father said exactly the same thing: "A man of thirty-(two, three, four, five, six, seven, [and now] eight) years should be able to take care of himself, goddammit!" Even when his son was hospitalized with pneumonia, the father refused to help him: "Let the Feds do it; that's what I pay taxes for, goddammit!"

Whenever he wrote about people like his father, he ended all of their sentences with exclamation points, because that was how they talked. There were no exceptions.

Whenever he wrote about people like his mother, he tried to make the words sound like lamentations, but he could not do it; he could not make the time of day or the temperature of the bath contain the same tragic sense that was always in his mother's voice. It seemed to him one of his failings as an artist.

His father called himself an entrepreneur or a venture capitalist, but he was really a salesman, he persuaded people to buy stock in companies that had, in truth, very little chance for success. When the value of the stock reached a level that produced a nice profit for the founders of the company, his father dumped it, leaving the new investors to catch the proverbial falling knife. It was not the kind of business calculated to appeal to a son with the temperament of an artist; it did not even appeal to a woman who worked in a bank. The banker divorced herself from the venture capitalist when their son was in the first grade.

Once, the father had asked his son what he wrote. "I want to know what you're doing, goddammit!"

"I am a chronicler of the farts and whines of existence, what used to be called facticity. But I do this not in what you would consider a cogent fashion, for life itself is not cogent. I am not a bricklayer, piling one fact upon another, as if life were a simpleton's structure, like a wall. I write the fullness of things. A bead of sweat is round. Come is not a flat surface. Love has odors. And nothing I write is exactly as it seems to me, but as it seems to you. Words are multiples, possibilities are endless. It is all a starting point. I begin knowing that I am the mute speaking in words you must shred in order to comprehend."

"Goddammit," the father said, "goddammit to hell!"

Now the writer sitting in the luncheonette, the white pad on the formica table, the lines of tiny writing falling toward the lower right-hand corner, the smudge marks of his sweated palm rendering the color of the ink uneven, thought of his father. "If the old man had been an artist . . ." But the old man could not have been an artist, because the old man understood the world as if it were a carefully laid wall of brick and mortar. His son said that the old man had a one-sided brain, and added for rueful emphasis, the wrong side.

While giving a reading in a makeshift auditorium located between two large vats in the basement of a dry-cleaning establishment, he was approached by a man who bore a very strong resemblance to his father. The man wore business attire, including a flowered tie. "I am an agent," the man said, "and I would like to manage your career."

"My work is not what it seems to me, you know; only what it seems to you. How do you know it will seem to others as it seems to you?"

"Marketing," the man in business attire said.

"If you sell what seems to you, it may no longer seem the same to me."

"There are compensations," the man in business attire said.

"Money is not what it seems."

"It is better." The man in business attire smiled. He reached into the inside breast pocket of his dark blue jacket and withdrew a thin leather case. "This is my card," he said, taking a white card from the case; "if you are interested, phone me."

A silence came between them. They stood beside a vat, amidst the odors of cleaning fluid and soiled clothing, but apart from the colloquy of artists who came into the basement auditorium to live in the presence of seeming, to act upon literature as it acted upon them. The writer who worked in luncheonettes thought for a very long time about the card that lay in his hand. The card had meaning; it was to him unlike the way it was to anyone else in the world. Was it the contrast between what was written on the bleached paper and the way God had decorated the flesh of his palm? He had to know what he saw, he had to interpret the sign; the interpretation of the sign was the revelation of himself.

He stuffed the card into his mouth, and chewed it into a pasteboard wad, repeating again and again, in muffled song, the newfound mantra of his literary life: "Goddammit!"

1.

It may be an error, a confusion of categories, to consider the selling of culture aside from the general subject of this book, which is the culture of selling. After all, the best definitions of culture are generally the most inclusive. It might be better just to speak of the selling of art, which would have been a good idea in an earlier time, but at the end of the twentieth century it brings up the difficult question an old friend once posed to me. "What is art?" he asked, speaking of literature. "Is art ever like hotcakes, made especially for you?"

What about painters? one might respond. Great portraits come to mind. And musicians serving at court? Mozart perhaps. There is always an audience, a consumer for art—citizens of Athens, Aztec nobles, whole dynasties of Chinese, merchant princes of the Renaissance, Elizabethan playgoers, certain members of the French middle class, you and me. In a simpleminded way art is always like hotcakes.

But it isn't.

The question of culture to be considered here has nothing to do with courting rituals, kinship structures, or the position assumed during the birthing of children. It is not even about which hand one puts into the communal pot. By culture I mean to corral all those acts belonging to the extended family of art: If Emily Dickinson is at the center, journalism belongs with the most distant cousins; if Aeschylus is the patriarch, television series must still be accorded the rights of bastards.

Neither is this the place to argue current critical writing about art: the Hegelian notions of Arthur Danto, the complaints of Robert Hughes, John Updike at his best, George Steiner at his worst, the deconstruction of paragraphs that should never have been put together in the first place. The question here is where the influence of selling enters the world of culture. If, as in times past, the marketing of cultural objects comes after their production, if marketing is no more than a means of dissemination, culture continues along its ancient, crooked, much divided path. On the other hand, if marketing, with its scientific determination of the desires of the buyer, has reached back into the process of imagination, to the very soul of the maker, then marketing has begun to determine the course of human society, in a limiting, perhaps profoundly conservative way.

When the market works as a driver of culture, it includes an extra step between the creator and the audience, not unlike the step required by allegory. The Dutch historian Johan Huizinga described both the process and the effect of allegory in *The Waning of the Middle Ages:*

> Having attributed a real existence to an idea, the mind wants to see
> this idea alive, and can only effect this by personifying it. In this way
> allegory is born. It is not the same thing as symbolism. Symbolism
> expresses a mysterious connection between two ideas, allegory gives
> a visible form to the conception of such a connection. Symbolism is
> a very profound function of the mind, allegory is a superficial one.
> . . . [A]llegory in itself implies from the outset normalizing. . . .
> [T]he use of it supplied a very earnest craving of the medieval mind.

The density of his prose cries out for examples, which Huizinga found in the *Roman de la Rose:*

> Let us recall . . . the allegorical personages. . . . To us it requires
> an effort to picture to ourselves Bel-Accueil, Doulce Mercy, Hum-
> ble Requeste. To the men of the Middle Ages, on the other hand,
> these figures had a very vivid aesthetic and sentimental value, which
> put them almost on a level with those divinities which the Romans
> conceived out of abstractions, like Pavor and Pallor, Concordia, etc.
> To the minds of the declining Middle Ages, Doux Penser, Honte,
> Souvenirs, and the rest were endowed with a quasi-divine existence.
> Otherwise the *Roman de la Rose* would have been unreadable.

Allegory, in all its superficiality, appears frequently now in popular fiction, from comic books to Stephen King novels, which would otherwise be unreadable. Unlike fables, which are morality tales, allegories may have a moral, an amoral, or even an immoral outcome, as long as the meaning on the level of abstraction determines the action and characterization. Sidney Sheldon writes morality plays dressed in underwear from Victoria's Secret. Judith Krantz writes allegories in which the personifications of greed, avarice, lust, and others of Ms. Krantz's menu of virtues triumph.

Did Dante also produce an allegorical tale? Of course, but to think that the terza rima of Dante and the mashed potato prose of Sidney Sheldon belong to the same category is absurd; we do not read Dante for the allegory, and we do not read Sidney Sheldon for the poetry.

Science fiction, whether invented by Ray Bradbury, Tom Clancy, or the authors of *Star Trek,* deals almost entirely in allegorical characters and actions. The characters in *Star Trek,* for example, represent abstractions of race and ethnicity rather than Doux Penser or Doulce Mercy. Stephen King's *Christine* is an allegory about the hubris of technology, in which man's things, in this case an old car, turn against him. The same allegory occurs in the *Popul Vuh* of the Maya, in which the pots and other things of the manikin people turn on them.

The extra step allegory adds to the process of making and explaining fictions has an analogue in modern market-driven culture: research, the scientific examination of the audience, produces an abstract description of the desires of the prospective audience. As in ancient allegory, the abstraction is then personified: a role is created for Arnold Schwarzenegger or Madonna or Candice Bergen or Christine. No more than a single word is required to define the personifications, including the car: *violence, sex, feminism, technology.*

In the Middle Ages and for a long time afterward, the abstractions used in allegory were provided by religion rather than by the market. The modern world has a different driver. The users of culture determine the objects of culture. But an abstraction also comes into the process. Only this time it is an abstraction of the desires of the audience. The process moves within a rigidly constructed circle. Market-driven culture leaves no place for the nooks and pinnacles of genius or morality; the audience gets what it wants and wants what it gets. The craft of the producers of market-driven culture is limited to staying within the lines, like a child obeying the printed cartoon in a coloring book.

The likely result, that the American democracy would produce no great art or literature, because of the demand for conformity from its citizens, was predicted by Tocqueville, who foresaw a new kind of tyranny in the rule of the majority, a tyranny more cultural than political. For over a century it appeared that Tocqueville had been wrong in this prediction of dire normality for the United States. Whether Americans produced great art or merely interesting and innovative painting is the subject for a debate, but the deviance from normality in the work of some American painters cannot be disputed. American literature has the quirky miracle of Emily Dickinson at its high point, with Melville, Twain, Wallace Stevens, Stein, one of the James brothers, and so on nearby, but the years since World War II have been lean. The war did not produce a single major work, indicating that the American voice may finally have been lowered to a whisper, or even stilled.

Although he predicted what would happen to American culture, Tocqueville could not have known the process that would push the nation in that direction. The tools to carry out the tyranny of the majority were not yet available. Statistics was a new branch of political science at the beginning of the nineteenth century; the 1797 edition of the *Encyclopaedia Britannica* described it as "a word lately introduced to express a view or survey of any kingdom, county or parish." Before long, however, *statisticks* crossed the Atlantic to the United States, where it came to mean the collection of facts on any subject, eventually including public opinion.[2]

Three more conditions were required to produce a market-driven culture. The first of them, the development of scientific marketing, was a simple process of applying statistical thinking to demand. By the end of the nineteenth century, American companies routinely used statistics to discover and measure the markets for their products.

The other side of marketing, the discovery of desire, was a post–World War II development. Although pollsters still made gross errors, such as predicting Dewey's victory over Truman, their influence over manufacturers

---

[2] Modern statistics grew out of William Petty's *Political Arithmetic,* rather than the mere collection of data.

   Gordon S. Wood, in *The Radicalism of the American Revolution* (New York: Knopf, 1992), pp. 360–69, argues for the virtues that result from this obsession with facts, pointing out its role in the creation of true political and social equality, vast productivity, the greatness of the United States, while not neglecting, in the closing lines of the book, the other face of democracy: "its vulgarity, its materialism, its rootlessness, its anti-intellectualism." He was wise to conclude on the demurrer, given the role statistics has come to play in American political and cultural life.

continued to grow, for a statistical being could be understood and manipulated far more efficiently than a human being. But the final, and most vital, aspect of market-driven culture developed slowly, beginning in the nineteenth century with the growth in revenues for publishers of newspapers, magazines, books, and sheet music, as well as plays and musical revues.

With the advent of movies, something happened to culture that had eluded artists, writers, and composers for thousands of years: It became important. In ancient times, cultural advances (still excluding such things as fire, farming, and putting the proper hand into the pot) had been a non-profit endeavor. Mythmaking, representational art, phonetic writing, religion, philosophy, mathematics, and revolutions like the one caused by Copernicus defined human thinking and behavior, but there was very little money to be made from culture. As culture was a business—a pot here, a play there, a painting for the prince—it was unsophisticated, not much beyond the level of barter. Technological advances, primarily movable type, made only a small difference, at first. By the late seventeenth century it was possible to earn a living from the sale of printed materials. A hundred years later, a writer could be comfortable on his earnings, although many books still depended upon subscription publishing.[3]

Shakespeare did extremely well financially, making investments, buying properties, all with his earnings from the theater. Nineteenth-century writers were able to earn small fortunes from their work, but for all the shrewdness of Benjamin Franklin, the vast popularity of Victor Hugo, the charm of Mark Twain, and so on, culture remained a nickel-and-dime business. Only at the end of the nineteenth century did newspapers and magazines begin to develop into large, powerful companies. But the marketing of these materials came after they were produced.

William Randolph Hearst didn't discover the market for sensationalism, jingoistic politics, and half-truths through a public opinion poll or a study of the psychology of newspaper readers; yellow journalism was a crude expression of his own view of the world. The arrogant, opinionated founder of the Hearst empire would not have been comfortable running the Newhouse newspaper chain, which a member of the Newhouse family told me bases its editorial views on the politics of its readers, Republican among

---

[3]   Prepublication sale of a book, often by the author, to friends and acquaintances. When sufficient sales were made, the book was printed. Subscription publishing was most common in the eighteenth and nineteenth centuries.

Republicans, Democratic among Democrats, and so on, changing its political and moral stance to fit the fashion of the neighborhood.

For the Newhouse family, among the richest on earth, culture serves as a product, nothing less, but nothing more; they have made a business of it. No distinguished newspaper has ever been published by the company, and as it moves into other aspects of publishing, it has engaged in a systematic substitution of market considerations for aesthetic tastes. However, the financial worth of the family, revealed during its public dispute with the Internal Revenue Service, continues to grow, confirming the importance of culture as a product.

There is nothing unusual about the Newhouses' understanding of the importance of culture. They have simply been more disciplined about their work, not allowing social, political, or aesthetic considerations to interfere with business. They are, in a sense, pure in heart, the perfect conduits for Tocqueville's tyrannical democracy.

Like the Newhouse properties, virtually all producers of culture on an important scale are now market-driven organizations. They examine the tastes of the market, subject their findings to statistical analysis to produce a theoretical map of desire, then create objects of culture accordingly.[4] Any

---

[4]   One afternoon, over lunch in the cheerless basement cafeteria at *TV Guide* headquarters, in King of Prussia, Pennsylvania, I asked Walter Annenberg how he had come upon the idea of a TV guide. He told me that it happened in Havana in the early 1950s. He saw a line of people waiting in front of a newsstand, and asked what they were waiting for. The *Racing Form*, he was told, the only publication that carried all the information about all the races. It was then, he said, that he came upon the concept of "essentiality." The *Racing Form* had that quality.

When he returned to the United States, Annenberg applied his newfound concept of "essentiality" to television: Without the *Racing Form* people did not know which horses were running; without a guide, people did not know which programs were showing. He said that he discussed the concept with several other publishers, all of whom had told him to save his money. Annenberg listened carefully to their advice, and went ahead with his plan, buying up all of the guides to television programming that had sprung up in local markets, including one called *TV Guide*.

With no competition, *TV Guide* became one of the great successes of American publishing, eventually reaching annual sales of more than a billion copies and more than covering its costs from newsstand and subscription sales. As newspapers began publishing comprehensive weekly guides to television programming, Annenberg's gold mine became less profitable, and he sold it.

During his reign—and he was that kind of owner, micromanaging the organization, driving his people to produce ever greater profits—at *TV Guide*, Annenberg attempted to start several other magazines: a more sophisticated version of *TV Guide*, a magazine about food, perhaps others that I didn't know about. Both the food and the sophisticated television magazines failed. They were dull, irrelevant, timid ventures. Annenberg apparently had no

product that doesn't fit the map is rejected. It is a closed system, but the owners of the system have proved that it is efficient; newspapers, magazines, books, films, television programs, T-shirts, musical compositions, fashions, and architecture all prosper inside the system.

The insidious nature of the process enables the market researcher's abstraction to penetrate the imagination of the artist. What may appear as innovation has already been subjected to the constraints of the theoretical construction of desire; the artist comes to the corporate producer with a market-driven invention. To seal the circle against intrusions, the final products are subjected to market testing. If they don't satisfy the audience, they are changed or discarded. Everything is, in effect, sold by subscription, the eighteenth-century publishing system for which the "proposal" was invented. Nothing can be left to chance; the goal of all market-driven activity, including market-driven culture, is certainty. The closed system offers the same virtue advertised to cynical travelers by a Holiday Inn: no surprises.

2.

Since even market-driven products must be sold, culture has its hucksters, and they are the comedians as well as the villains of the affair. The comedy comes from the need of culture's salesmen to dress themselves in the skin of artists, to be public persons, even famous, sometimes outrageous, while living by the narrow rules of the market. The villainy grows out of the same set of circumstances. When art and the market share the same bed, one of them is going to get squeezed.

The style of the squeeze depends on the category. Practically everyone knows a story about a movie mogul who destroyed a work of art or an artist, usually a writer, for the sake of the market. William Faulkner, F. Scott Fitzgerald, and a dozens lesser artists come to mind. Tales about Louis B. Mayer weeping, cajoling, threatening actors, directors, writers, and producers constitute an entire genre of complaint or literature. The book publishing business, as practiced by most of the big commercial houses, has the makings of a new class of villains. Television suffers from a shortage of pretensions, but the decline of television news may yet rescue the medium from the obscurity of mere business.

---

idea of how to put that kind of magazine together; *TV Guide* had been a market-driven product rather than a magazine from its inception. As Prometheus, Annenberg was a flop.

All the stories are good ones. Nothing is easier than to make the producer or the publisher appear greedy or foolish; any artist worth his or her salt can sell circles around a salesman. The problem is that the artist may also be a salesman. In which case the tragedy of the artist becomes a farce, comedy inside the structure of a greater tragedy.

Having made, bought, sold, and consumed culture of various kinds, I am more inclined to laughter than tears, for I know the pratfalls of unremarkable defeats, the scarcity of people who, like Bartleby the Scrivener, would really prefer not to. There might be more such artists, but marketing is an insidious, almost irresistibly easy way of dealing with the world, and the findings of marketers published in books and newspapers, sometimes in the form of research, more often as lists of best-selling movies, records, books, television programs, newspapers, and magazines—enter the consciousness of the producers of culture, just as they invade the minds of the builders of automobiles and manufacturers of laundry detergents. Once that happens, the debate, still framed as a contest between an artist and a salesman, becomes a contest between peddlers, and that is the stuff of which comedy is made.

A Bust

One such contest took place a few years ago in a Manhattan restaurant. The antagonists were a hungry writer and a feisty publisher. The judge was William H. Ryan, then an editor at *Esquire* magazine, formerly the publisher of *Contact,* a West Coast version of the famous literary magazine of the 1920s, formerly this and formerly that. Ryan had bad lungs and a clear head, when he wasn't drinking. He was—the bad lungs and an irrepressibly romantic view of life eventually caught up with him—among the beloved of writers. During his tenure as publisher of *Contact,* he made a deal with a local radio station to trade advertisements: unseen pages for unheard moments. But when it came time to prepare the radio commercial, he was at a loss. Several of his friends volunteered to produce a commercial. The recording took place in my apartment. The commercial opened with the voice of a professional announcer.

ANNOUNCER: Ladies and gentlemen, we are privileged to present Mr. William H. Ryan, publisher of *Contact* magazine, reading a selection from his own works. Mr. Ryan . . .

RYAN: Unsolicited manuscripts must be accompanied by a self-addressed stamped envelope . . .

A few years in New York had changed Ryan's outlook, however. A job at Random House, a stint hustling people at an employment agency, and now the "editorial gig" at *Esquire* had given him a salesman's sense of the market.

When he telephoned to invite me to a "free lunch," I said, "I don't need a free lunch. I have a job."

"No, this is on a publisher; you gotta go."

Since he had made it a point of honor, I agreed. Our host was to be Donald I. Fine, then the publisher or editor in chief or both of Arbor House, a small, more or less independent book publisher. The party was to be completed by Philip Nobile, a fellow who had written a book about the *New York Review of Books*.

When I arrived at the restaurant, Mr. Fine was standing outside. He was a small, neatly dressed man with a large bandage on his thumb. He was in extremely good humor. He had, as he explained, just had a terrible argument with the headwaiter. With that bit of repartee completed, having nothing else to say, I asked about his thumb. "Aah!" he said, holding up the bandaged digit, "my wife. This morning, I had a fight with my wife, and she bit me."

Just then Ryan arrived, and we went inside, where Mr. Fine and the headwaiter glowered at each other and Ryan treated his emphysema to a cigarette and a drink. Nobile arrived last, a young man with a cheery face and a loud tie.

Nobile quickly got to business. He had an idea for a book, and he wanted to tell it to Fine, to make a verbal proposal, right there at lunch. Nobile began at the beginning. His presentation was so ordered, so perfectly articulate, I thought he must have rehearsed it. "The brassiere," he said, "there has never been a book about the brassiere."

"You're certain of that," Fine said, leaning forward in his chair, suddenly focused.

"I'm sure of my research."

"Your scholarship," Fine said, editing.

Nobile spoke for fifteen, perhaps twenty minutes, pausing only to allow Ryan's fits of coughing to pass. He started with the history of the breast itself, the development of the fatty tissue in the upright female creature, the only one that faced the male during sex. From there he moved on to the introduction of clothing, to questions of shame, modesty, the full bosom and the flat bosom, décolletage and binding.

Fine was transfixed. Without a vulgar word or a lascivious allusion, as delicate and deceitful as a Victorian dressmaker, Nobile was creating a lecherous tale. He turned to the business of the brassiere, to style, the pointed brassiere, the padded brassiere, large brassieres and small. He spoke of cantilevering and cup sizes.

Fine asked if he had talked to the manufacturers.

Nobile mentioned that one manufacturer was going to open its archives to him.

Fine threw out a name.

Bigger, Nobile replied. He told the name. Fine was awed. His mouth fell open. It was the biggest manufacturer of all.

Nobile confirmed the name with a nod. He said they would show him everything. Then he began his summation: physiology, anthropology, sociology, psychology, fashion, finance. He paused. Lana Turner, Jane Russell, Marilyn Monroe. He paused again. Anita Ekberg. Sophia Loren! With every sentence, every name, the value of Nobile's work increased; he changed from a kid with one whining book under his belt to Ariès, Braudel, Durkheim reborn.

Nobile had described the market for his book without ever mentioning it; not only women would care about such a book, but every mother's son. Fine was glowing, but placidly. A suckling's delight shone in his vaguely focused eyes. The offer of a contract was in his throat, heading for the tip of his tongue. For confirmation he turned to the man from *Esquire*. "What do you think, Bill?"

Ryan laughed. "I don't know," he said. "I've always been a garter belt man myself."

Fine was startled. He thought about Ryan's comment for a moment, then he said, "Yes, me, too."

Nobile was done for. The project was over, failed in its first test, dead. The marketer had lost out to marketing.

Publishing decisions are made less often at the lunch table now. Marketing is a sober business; the kind of science that sours the wine. Only when the stakes are very high, as in the autobiographies of presidents and movie stars, does marketing give way to the culture salesman's wish to wear the artist's fame. Then it becomes worth an extra million of a conglomerate's money to get your name in the papers. But the day-to-day business belongs to marketing.

The two largest publishers of general-interest books in America are run by men with no apparent interest in literature. Alberto Vitale, the chief executive of Random House, who has often said that he doesn't have time to read books, even those he publishes, came from the Wharton Business School. Jack Hoeft, who heads Bantam Doubleday Dell, was a marketing executive at Pepsico before entering the publishing business. According to the *New York Times,* Hoeft "has a reputation as a highly effective sales-man." The *Times* went on to comment that his appointment to the job "reflects how publishing companies are looking increasingly to people with marketing expertise, rather than to scholars of literature, with a love of books, to lead their enterprises."[5]

Simon and Schuster, another of the largest publishers, and a house with a battered reputation in the literary community, is headed by Richard E. Snyder, who came into his position with more expertise in sales than in literature. There is, of course, nothing wrong with the head of a publishing house coming from the sales department. Bennett Cerf, the founder of Random House, had a keen interest in selling books. Alfred Knopf made his most remembered comments about sales, rather than literature. Donald Lamm, who heads W. W. Norton, came into the business on the sales side.

Among contemporary publishers, Hoeft and Vitale speak of "prod-uct," while Roger Straus of Farrar, Straus and Giroux, Lamm, and a few others still deal in books. The distinction comes not at the point of sale but at the moment of creation. The writer who deals with the Hoeft/Vitale/Snyder school of publishing must begin with the market in mind.[6]

Although good books can be written that way, the market seems always to take its toll. One of the best writers I know, the winner of several prestigious prizes, begins with the market, agonizes over the market, writes the book, then devotes a year or more to promoting the finished work, guiding it through prepublication excerpts, appearing on radio and televi-sion programs with every new edition, and so on. Between books, the writer devotes a great deal of time to self-promotion, which causes the period between books to grow longer and longer. How long the writer will be able

---

[5]   June 25, 1991.

[6]   See the Response, below, for Kant's idea of the role of self-incurred tutelage and the use of critique in his definition of enlightenment.

to produce books of the first rank depends on luck now, and the enormous skills developed during years of attention to craft. When will the subject that passes the test of the mass market prove too thin? When will the subject be so forced that the writer cannot summon the craft to attend to it? This writer, like most, works alone now, without an editor's help, for editors have other tasks; the market does not spare them either.

The place at which the market enters the life of the book determines the life of the editor, as well as of the writer. Those editors who concern themselves with the market become "acquiring editors." They have very little interest in books. They may not even read the books they acquire, preferring to give them to junior editors, or not to bother with editing at all. Acquiring editors are like product managers in any other business, separate from both manufacturing and research and development, concerned almost entirely with the marketing of the product.

These acquiring editors must be loyal to marketing rather than to culture, a change from an earlier view of the editor's role that can best be seen in the Random House group of publishers, including Knopf and Pantheon. When Bennett Cerf guided Random House, he chose to take up the cause of James Joyce's novel *Ulysses,* which had been banned on grounds of obscenity. Cerf and Random House carried on a long and costly court battle that resulted in 1933 in the famous decision permitting the book to be published in the United States. Sonny Mehta, who inherited the mantle of Alfred A. Knopf, also figured in a question of taste and literature. When *American Psycho,* a novel by Bret Easton Ellis, was judged so tasteless, offensive to women, and without literary worth that even Simon and Schuster abandoned its plans to publish it, Mehta bought the rights from Simon and Schuster, and published the book under the Knopf name. The question of censorship was never raised; the house of Knopf had made a marketing decision.

Every such public defeat of the canons of taste by the canons of marketing serves as a lesson to the mind of the artist. Mehta's exemplary vulgarity wounds the quality of books yet unborn. His teachings add to those of Steven Schragis, who brags that his Carol Publishing Group makes money through the promotion and selling of *dreck*. Schragis has more publicists than editors on his payroll, which he considers a triumph of marketing, one that compares favorably to the organization of a house like Simon and Schuster, where the numbers of publicists and editors are merely equal.

These lessons to artists generally come through newspapers and magazines. A young writer who finds out through an article in the *New York Times* that Viking Press has spent $200,000 to promote the work of Eileen Goudge, in hope that she will become another brand name author, like Danielle Steel, cannot fail to compare the rewards of literature to the rewards of marketing. With publishers coming out of business schools and the marketing departments of soft drink and potato chip companies, the search for brand name cultural products has become an obsession.[7] F. Scott Fitzgerald and Ernest Hemingway had their good sales and bad, but Danielle Steel never misses. Philip Roth has a best-seller now and then, but Michael Crichton always makes the top of the list.

Once artistic values can be eliminated from the object of culture and replaced by a product produced according to the desires of the market, all the tools of selling can be applied, and in amounts sufficient to affect profits. The question is whether the same tools can and should be used to sell cultural objects that are not market-driven products but works of greater intrinsic value. For example, knowing that most people who enter a bookstore leave without buying a book, publishers could devote more effort to point-of-sale materials, beginning with package design (book jackets). Inexpensive test marketing techniques could easily be applied to the package design.

An attractive package does no harm to art or literature, but something else happens when publishers of books, magazines, and newspapers begin to cross-promote, following the principles established by companies like Pepsico, which can use the power of its Pepsi-Cola brand to introduce a new product from its Frito-Lay Division. Pepsi's endorsement of a new kind of potato chip has little economic or cultural importance, since competition among potato chip makers is intense and the effect of snack food on the culture and health of the United States has long ago been discounted. It is another matter when an excerpt from a book published by Knopf appears in *Vanity Fair* and *Vogue,* and the book is reviewed in the *New Yorker,* all magazines controlled by S. I. Newhouse, who also rules over the Random

---

[7] Price plays an unusual and complex role in the selling of books, records, and periodicals. There are no generic brands, house brands, or even discount brands in the market. Since the demand curve for every book is different, plotting the point where price and demand generally intersect is extremely difficult. The only efficiencies book publishers can seek are textbook adoptions of general-interest books and brand name authors.

House/Pantheon/Knopf/etc. complex of book publishers. The cross-promotion may not be an illegal restraint of trade, but given the limited amount of information about books published in those magazines, it is surely a restraint of culture.

In the forms of cross-promotion used by Advance (the Newhouse company), Time-Warner, News Corporation, and other media conglomerates, the topical publications fall prey to the demands of marketing. Perhaps neither *Time* nor *Entertainment Weekly* will ever consciously stoop to using its review sections for purely promotional purposes, but they have become suspect; every writer worries, every editor wonders. Advance has been the most blatant, routinely using its magazines to promote its books, reaching back into the minds of its editors to teach them that not only the market but the cross-market must drive the imagination, that culture can only be measured quantitatively and soon, for the market predictably has its fill of one course and turns to the next.

The opinionated journals, which often represent themselves as the most virtuous of periodicals, live within an equally closed circle, as Norman Podhoretz, editor of *Commentary,* explained to Jack Howland, then head of advertising for AT&T. According to Howland, Podhoretz said that readers and writers of "intellectual publications" were not going to change their opinions on the basis of what they read in advertisements. Since Howland was using Podhoretz's statement as a reason to drop *Harper's, Atlantic,* and the *New Yorker,* as well as the opinionated journals—the *New Republic,* the *Nation, National Review, Commentary,* and so on—from his media list, I replied that Podhoretz was only projecting when he argued that an intellectual is a person with a closed mind.

In fact, Podhoretz was correct about some of the magazines, but not about the readers, as a *neo*-conservative should have known. No market is more clearly defined, ferociously abstracted, and demanding of those who serve it than the market of the opinionated. Whoever writes for opinionated journals must obey the market absolutely, the only alternatives being silence or a change of venue. As a result, the opinionated journals follow the rules of selling to perfection: The writers use information to define the universe and all its nooks and crannies exactly as their customers wish it to be.

Another category, the journal of opinion, reads its market differently. The most interesting of such journals, the op-ed page of the *New York Times,* not including its columnists, and for longer pieces, *Harper's* and the

Atlantic frequently infuriate large parts of their readership by printing the partisan views of all the parties to a serious debate.[8] While journals of opinion have, like the big slicks, sought to find out who they are by learning what the market wants to hear, the demands of the audience for a publication like the *New York Review of Books* are not for repetitions but for new thought or, if not new thought, at least for thought.

Unfortunately, periodicals have not one market to please, like books or movies, but two: readers and advertisers. And the market of advertisers is also split, made up of creatures who behave like viruses or golems. The golems, like the semihuman beings of folklore, have no minds at all; they merely reinforce the demands of the market of readers. Some of the golems have been replaced by computers, which match market demographics between target markets for products and the readership of magazines. If ever the editors of magazines stray from the demands of the market of readers, the golems of advertising bash the heads of the editors.

The golems are big and have very heavy hands, but an editor can outwit a golem now and then. The viruses present a different kind of problem, for they possess both a genius for opportunism and the amorality of insentient creatures. While the golems can only feed or kill a magazine or television network, the viruses know how to enter it, attaching themselves to a piece here and there, causing changes inside the living organisms. Among the works of the viruses in the print media have been the following:

- sponsorship of complete issues of magazines (*American Heritage*)
- sponsorship of articles within a magazine (*Esquire*)
- enticing a magazine into lending its editorial format to advertising (Absolut vodka in *Harper's*)
- producing entire sections of a magazine or newspaper (a common practice)
- asking for editorial space to complement an advertising campaign (clothing designers in fashion magazines, *Vanity Fair,* many others; home builders and car dealers in local newspapers)
- punishing the media for negative editorial (General Motors withdrew

[8] And even their old friends and contributing editors. I have often disagreed with the editors of two of those journals, Mitchel Levitas and Lewis H. Lapham, over the publication of opinions which differed from mine. In retrospect, I cannot think of a single instance in which their commitment to fair and open debate was not correct and my illiberal complaint was not wrong.

its advertising from *Time, Fortune,* and the American Broadcasting Company to punish them for, respectively, a negative review of the design of a new Buick, unfavorable treatment of Chairman Roger B. Smith, and reports of brake failures in the Chevrolet Citation and other models built on the same platform; similar treatment by GM and other manufacturers of the car buff magazines is routine)

implied threats of withdrawal of advertising (prior to divestiture, the Bell System, then a monopoly regulated at the state and federal levels, ran heavy advertising schedules in local newspapers and magazines to remind the publishers that editorial opposition to rate increases could result in a loss of revenue). One entire category of newspaper reporting has been pushed beyond the pale by the implied threat of major advertisers: Investigative reporting of overpricing or unsanitary conditions in a large food chain that advertises heavily in the Wednesday or Thursday "best food day" editions of newspapers is virtually unknown, as are negative stories about large department stores.[9]

None of these exerts as much influence as the mindless, unwitting alliance of golems, which advises the publications constantly of the need to lower the cost per thousand and to move the readership into the demographic group most desirable to advertisers. The punishment for failing to produce an audience of 18- to 24- or 18-to-49-year-old affluent readers is the execution of the editor and his or her staff. When the death of the editor does not accomplish the goals of the golems, they kill the publication.

Newspapers also depend on dual markets, although it was possible until the last third or even the last fourth of the twentieth century for a newspaper to be so valuable to its readers that it could stand above the demands of the market of advertisers. Among the last newspapers to become market driven was the *New York Times.* It survived the threat of losing the market of readers to television, but no newspaper has been able to defend itself against the demands of the golems and the viruses. In the 1970s, in what now appears to have been a last-ditch effort to satisfy the viruses without harming the news sections of the paper, the *Times* added the "C sections"—Sports, Science, Home, Living, and Entertainment.

[9]   The Center for the Study of Commercialism, in Washington, D.C., collects and disseminates information on this subject. A booklet, *Dictating Content: How Advertising Pressure Can Corrupt a Free Press,* was published by the Center in 1992.

The extra sections had no apparent purpose other than to mollify the viruses, who insist that "the editorial environment" be compatible with their products. Like other metropolitan newspapers, the *Times* had few alternatives; they realized that broadcast media, suburban papers, and even shoppers were eating into the advertising revenues they had gained when many urban newspapers went out of business shortly after the advent of television. Moreover, they saw the decline of the department stores, traditionally heavy newspaper advertisers.

It was clear to outsiders that the new sections were merely the beginning of the capitulation of one of the last great newspapers to the dictates of marketing, with its lust for affluent 18-to-49-year-old readers. The resources of the paper had to be shared between covering the news and fighting the viruses; the organism would have to change to survive. After the extra sections were added, the next step was to change the tone of the editorial coverage. Amusing stories and cute writing came into the paper.[10] By the early 1990s the *Times* had begun telling job applicants that it was interested only in reporters who had experience on tabloids. There was no alternative for the *Times* or any of the other metropolitan dailies. Either they changed from newspapers to entertainment vehicles containing some news, or they would not survive. *USA Today,* a version of television in print, set the pattern for market-driven journalism, and everyone followed.

Although it remained one of the best newspapers in the world, the circle of marketing and culture was closing at the *Times.* A Sunday Style section was added. An insert devoted to services to the consumer, from movie times to the location of potholes to the description of neighborhood events, was added. In keeping with other stylistic changes at the paper, Alessandra Stanley, who had brought the hiss of sorority sister gossip to the main news section, was named a Moscow correspondent of the *New York Times;* apparently, one defeat by the forces of the market deserved another.

[10]   The *New York Times* serves here as the best example because of its great prestige. Given the history of the *San Francisco Chronicle,* for example, it would be difficult to show how that paper deteriorated. The industry has, in general, determined to let the falling literacy level in the United States drag down the level of newspapers. The "literacy" committee of the American Society of Newspaper Editors commissioned a study to find out how to attract younger, less literate readers. The results, couched in euphemisms, suggested that newspapers become less literate to match the market. (*New York Times,* April 2, 1993.)

Newspapers are only now catching up to the advice against "fine writing" given to advertising writers by Claude Hopkins half a century ago. Hopkins also argued that higher education was a handicap to salesmen.

The Resurrection,
according to General Motors

If the chairman of the board of General Motors hadn't been a religious man, it might never have happened, and the effect on a television production of its many markets might not have been so clear. The time was the 1970s. As his reign neared its end, the chairman must have realized something about rich men and the eye of a needle, for he agreed to pay, out of the pockets of the stockholders, the entire production and broadcast costs for a television production of *The Life of Jesus.*

The mini-series was to grease the needle's eye for another businessman as well. Lord Lou Grade, the British music hall performer become film and television producer, had another conversion in his background: He was an English Jew turned Roman Catholic. Lord Low Grade, as he was known to some of his admirers, displayed the convert's passion for his new religion. He hired the prolific novelist and critic Anthony Burgess to write the script for *The Life of Jesus,* based on an original story by Matthew, Mark, Luke, and John, then had the script translated into Italian to be vetted by the Vatican. Various ecclesiastical emendations were made, after which the script was translated back into English, and given to the operatic director Franco Zeffirelli to bring to the small screen.

When Protestant Fundamentalists in the United States got wind of the Vatican's veto power over the script, they began a national campaign against the mini-series. Thousands of letters were sent to General Motors promising never again to buy their products, if the corporation went ahead with the "papist" project. It fell to Waldo E. McNaught to deal with the Protestant protest. After one particularly difficult day, he telephoned me to complain. "The things I do for this goddamned corporation," he began. "Today, I was down on my knees praying."

Ever the vendor, taking the role of straight man, I asked, "What's wrong with that?"

And he said, in a voice made tremulous by outrage, "With a Protestant!"

Propelled by fears for the future of American industry, McNaught, the chairman's assistant John McNulty, and I went to London to have a look at the film, which was by then in the form of a rough cut, still lacking some opticals, music, and so on, but with all the voice tracks laid in.

We checked in at our hotel, then went to the offices of Lord Low Grade, where we met with Grade, two people from NBC, which was to broadcast the mini-series, Zeffirelli, and several of Grade's minions. Grade's office was decorated with dollars; that is, framed U.S. one-dollar bills, each of them autographed by a famous actor (Grade pointed out Richard Burton's bill), were hung on the walls. The woman from NBC[11] greeted me as if we were friends. She said loudly, so that Grade and the man from NBC would hear, that she had read the series of critical essays I had been publishing in *Harper's*. Grade, an effusive man, who looked like an egg with thick lips, sucked on a Churchillian cigar, silent in his displeasure. From that moment on he avoided speaking to me or even looking in my direction. The worst had happened! A novelist, a writer of literary criticism no less, had entered the camp of a producer who decorated his walls with money.

The woman from NBC looked at me and winked.

For the next two days we were to watch the rough cut in Grade's screening room, in the company of the egg-shaped lord, the operatic director, many minions, and the man chosen to write the musical score, Maurice Jarré.

While the film rolled, we all watched. Now and then, I took out a notebook and wrote in it. After the first morning's screening, I saw that every time I wrote in the notebook, the egg-shaped lord winced, as if someone had driven a bamboo sliver under his pink, manicured fingernail. I wrote a lot.

From time to time Grade and Zeffirelli spoke to the tiny audience in the screening room. Grade always spoke from his seat in the back. Zeffirelli, dressed in suedes that draped like silk, carrying a leather purse, stood at the front. During each presentation Grade and Zeffirelli had a brief salesman's exchange. One was so extraordinary that I put it in my notes:

GRADE (in cockney English): And this part, right here, where the infant Jesus is born to Mary, right here, is where we have the choral music. Through my connections with His Holiness, I have every confidence that I will be able to secure the services of the Sistine Chapel Boys Choir.

[11] Neither her name nor that of the other NBC executive would add anything to the scene.

ZEFFIRELLI (in Italian English): No, no; he is just wanting to use the name. This singers from the Sistine Chapel is not good enough to be in my film. Costs more, but we are spending the money to get professional singers.

GRADE: Whatever you want, Franco; the best! the best is none too good. If the Sistine Chapel Boys Choir isn't up to your standards, then you get a choir that is. That's what I told 'im. And I won't bill General Motors another penny. It's my gift.

ZEFFIRELLI: You see! He gives me everything. It's a miracle!

No one laughed

The next day at lunch I was split off from McNaught and McNulty. Our host was Jarré, the composer. A long table in a nearby restaurant had been arranged so that he was seated next to my wife, who had come to London with me. Jarré, recent winner of an Academy Award for the score of *Dr. Zhivago,* looked like a movie star. Handsome, a White Russian in his forties, speaking English with a strong French accent, the composer was a ladykiller. He was also a salesman, for the task of the composer in the movies is to sell the picture to the audience. This time, however, the salesman had been sent to sell the picture to my wife, who had joined us for lunch. Between the appetizer and the soup, I looked at the head of the table, where Monsieur Jarré, holding the hand of the woman seated on his right, my wife, gazed into her eyes, and said, "I see by zee green color of zee eyes zat you are Spanish." To which my wife, who had spent many years in the movie business, replied, "They're hazel."

When the last hour of the mini-series had at last been viewed, the egg-shaped lord spoke again to his market of three, after which the market—McNulty, McNaught, and Shorris—were driven to their hotel, where they planned to gather in the suite shared by the two men from GM to discuss the mini-series.

It was July, and it was hot in London, hotter than Riyadh, hotter than Jidda, hotter than it had been in years. Our hotel, the Dorchester, was not only without air-conditioning; its new owners, a group from the Arabian peninsula, apparently did not think it necessary to turn off the steam that coursed through the towel racks in the bathrooms. By the time I got to the McNaught/McNulty suite, the gentlemen from General Motors had stripped to the waist, and were drinking bottles of cold beer. It was not a pretty sight.

Within moments, the telephone rang. McNaught picked it up in his bedroom. "Shorris," he shouted, "it's for you. It's that dame from NBC."

I answered the phone in the other room. The woman from NBC asked, "How did you like the film?"

"Well . . . ," I said, dragging out the word, not wanting to offer a comment until McNaught, McNulty, and I had been able to compare notes, ". . . I just got here. We were going to talk."

"It's a piece of shit," the woman from NBC said.

"You think so?"

"Sure, it's a piece of shit, but it'll get great reviews. No critic is going to attack *The Life of Jesus.*"

"You know more about that than I do."

"Well, I just wanted you to know. We're going back to New York tonight. I'll see you there."

"Sure."

McNaught had been listening on the other phone. He came in to the parlor wearing his Alice-in-Wonderland smile. "It's so good to hear from our benefactors at NBC. And what is your opinion, Mr. Shorris?"

I had made notes about more than a few scenes; the most memorable of them had to do with the scourging of Jesus. Rod Steiger in the role of Pontius Pilate looks at the actor (since forgotten) who plays Jesus, and says of this bedraggled blue-eyed blond young Englishman, "Ecce homo!" then turns to the camera and explains, "Behold the man." The woman from NBC had been correct about the quality of the film. But that had been clear from the beginning. What I had noted during the screening was a series of anti-Semitic statements, all of them gratuitous.

I made my case to the men from General Motors, saying as I recall, in a good-humored way, that if the film were to be presented without deleting or modifying those scenes, I would never again work for General Motors, nor would I even speak to anyone, meaning them, who worked for the corporation. McNaught raised his eyebrows and pursed his lips, mocking my earnestness. McNulty merely nodded. He is a tall man, fair, and with a rather large nose for a leprechaun. "Did cha see anything else wrong?" he asked, Saint Thomas Aquinas speaking in the accents of Ireland and the farthest reaches of the borough of Brooklyn.

"No. I don't think so."

"Did cha see anything wrong with the ending?"

"No. Was there something wrong?"

"Yeah," he said in several syllables, "they didn't resurrect 'im."

"Oh, my God!"

He paused for a moment, and then said for the only time in the twenty years that I've known him, "Ahem."

The error, which had gone unnoticed by Anthony Burgess, Franco Zeffirelli, the Vatican, NBC, and even the egg-shaped lord himself, had been spotted by Jack McNulty. At his insistence, the producers reassembled the necessary members of the cast on location in North Africa and filmed a new ending, leaving no doubt that Jesus had been resurrected.

The egg-shaped lord and the operatic director had demonstrated once again that unlike other salesmen, those who run the film and television industries are not only willing but able to move heaven and earth to satisfy the desires of their customers.

Nothing satisfied the Fundamentalists, however. They mounted a great campaign of letters and postal cards. Along with the opinions of the woman from NBC and other critics, the Fundamentalists finally won out. A few days before the program was to be broadcast, Roger B. Smith, heir apparent to the chairman's job, totaled up the amount of money GM spent on NBC. Then he called the network. The ironclad contract evaporated, NBC sold the show to Procter & Gamble at distress sale prices, and *The Life of Jesus* went on the air as scheduled, with some emendations and a new, happier ending.

If the clients seem venal in the case of *The Life of Jesus*, it should be noted that during the years when I worked with General Motors and AT&T I saw the clients and their advertising agency attempt, again and again, to move the networks away from utter trash toward better-quality programming, offering to pay for both airtime and production costs, only to be told by the networks that it was impossible, because it would hurt their lead-in and lead-out shows and lower their overall ratings. The clients turned to PBS, where General Motors underwrote the production and sponsored the broadcast of Ken Burns's *The Civil War*, which cost only a few million to make, delivered ratings that would have been acceptable on the commercial networks, but could not ever have been broadcast on commercial television, which is the most tightly encapsulated market-driven system in American culture.

Television entertainment programming grew out of the film business, which in turn, grew out of a mercantile rather than an artistic tradition. The studio heads and exhibitors moved from the retail business with no real goal other than to sell products to customers: A ticket was the same as several pairs of gloves to the movie marketer. If the gloves could be made to marry the desires of the customer by creating a thumb of words, a palm of promises, the movies could be "exploited" with trailers and posters and gossip columns and movie magazines and newspaper advertising made of fraudulent praise and alluring drawings that sometimes had little to do with the films they sold.

Stars could be created, the products of wishes, the stuff of dreams. By the 1930s, in the middle of the Great Depression, the movies had learned, like the editors of opinionated magazines, to reinvent the world according to the desires of the customer. It should be no surprise that the movie business became a haven for ideologues, since the movies presented an even better opportunity than the opinionated journals to use information in the service of sales. In the 1980s Japanese business invested heavily in Hollywood, understanding the industry not as an art form but as the salable product intended by its original owners. These investors admired the salesmanship of Americans, and here was a business in which the salesmen controlled the world. In a movie like *Jurassic Park,* nature itself could be transformed into a multimedia sales pitch, and married into every mind in every city and town in the nation:

At the edge of the continental divide, west of Laramie, in the roadside town of Rawlins, Wyoming, in a great shed converted into a movie theater, the blushing boys and girls behind the candy counter had been dressed in caveman costumes to complete the sale of the dinosaurs of their dreams. Inside the cavernous theater, with its widely spaced rows of ancient rocking-chair seats, children giggled with anticipation, asking who was most likely to scream, who could possibly faint. Then the movie began, gigantic and loud, a pastiche of monstrous reflections from the far end of the hall, but no one screamed, no one fainted, no one seemed to care. The chairs rocked, asynchronous and irritating. People got up to buy more popcorn and soft drinks. Outside, in the rutted streets of Wyoming, on the very lands where the dinosaurs had walked, on the dried-up sloughs where the stegosaurs wallowed, on the hunting grounds of the tyrannosaurs, nature resisted the movies. These Americans, descendants of Germans, Mexicans, Irish, and Cheyenne, walked out into the starbright Wyoming night holding their McDonald's mugs and plastic brontosauruses, having failed to faint, disappointed at the absence of screaming from big sisters and small, and set their jaws, and went about their business, knowing they had been advertised, cross-promoted, publicized, sold something that never existed, except in their innocent dreams of a thoughtless, cold-blooded Eden.

What would they say to their friends? They had no choice but to sell what they had been sold. The market for popular culture works like a pyramid scheme. It has as many elements of fraud as of selling. No real product gets in the way of the information. The one who has bought the best-selling film or book or record must sell it to someone else or risk being taken for a fool. Once the information about the object of culture is converted into the appearance of the will of the majority, the customer cannot spurn the cultural object without seceding from the culture. Of course, some individuals do spurn films like *Jurassic Park,* but the salesmen of culture don't mind, for they have calculated the risk/return ratios of consensus versus the great majority, and learned to settle for the lion's share.

In the case of a film like *Jurassic Park,* the endorsement of McDonald's in the cross-promotion means much more than the cover stories in magazines and the film clips shown on television, because McDonald's has the cultural authority of being the greatest best-seller of them all. It represents the majority. By using all of the available means to create information, *Jurassic Park,* a film so badly conceived, so ill-written, and so lackadaisically directed that it could not hold the attention of an eight-year-old child in Rawlins, Wyoming, was sold and resold and sold again to millions of people. The film itself was of no importance; an icon made of information had been created in its place. On the morning after the disappointment of actually seeing the movie, the patrons of the barnlike theater in Rawlins, gathered now in a coffee shop beside the interstate, were heard to remark on the thrills of watching one of the best movies they had ever seen.

3.

Of all the many roles accorded to culture, none has more importance than its creation of a barrier between civil society and the mob. Philosophers have long feared the ruin of the barrier, the end of that moment of hesitation we call the civilized life. Having learned as much, tyrants burn books before churches and make sure to tear down libraries before resorting to chains. Fortunately, the suppression of culture has always been difficult and incomplete. We have the examples of Jews in exile, Christians in Rome, poets despite Stalin, and so on.

Under totalitarian regimes, like Nazi Germany, the suppression of culture precedes the decline of civil society. People become massified, the crowded, indistinguishable, unthinking members of a mob. So far, this process has always grown out of democratic rather than autocratic rule, but not democratic as in Periclean democracy, with its powerful sense of autonomy. The democracy of totalitarian regimes lies much closer to market democracy, in which the mass determines all, because its will is expressed through methods which cannot take into account less common notions.

As market democracy drives culture to an ever-increasing extent, the principles of civil society fall victim to the economic and political power of the market. Canons of taste collapse first: The simplicity of violence replaces the complexity of social life, sex loses its connection to love or exultation, poetry deteriorates into mindless rhyme, music descends from the sound of the mind to the rumblings of the gut, beauty goes unrecognized.

When the market takes command of culture, the ethical question changes from "How shall we live?" to "What do we want?" The explicit difference is in the loss of the sense of limits, the hesitation between the will and the act which can last forever in a society built on principle.

Tocqueville's fears, learned from Aristotle, can be expressed as fears for the safety of culture and its quirky love of principle, its growth out of the peaceful, aesthetic engagement of one human being with others, with even one other. The market knows no peace; it cannot contemplate, it can only demand. When the market heeds the authority of culture, civil society proceeds at its ungainly, stuttering pace, but when the market, in its beastly abstraction, commands culture, the glories of civilization are pushed to the farthest margin, and ethics has no place in the world. In such circumstances, hope lies in samizdat and the whispers of malcontents.

10

A Lie
Is Not Poetry

... the primary function of language is to state what is true or false.

—A. J. AYER,
The Central Questions of Philosophy

In 1962, Tony Shorris, who was then five years old, was invited to partici-
pate in a research project at the San Francisco office of the Fletcher,
Richards, Calkins and Holden advertising agency. He was asked only
one question:
  "Do you believe what they say in television commercials?"
  "No," he said, "it's not chocolate."

My daddy was a sweet man, in and out of prison all his life until he was in his forties, when they discovered that he was schizophrenic or manic-depressive or some kind of sickness that could never be cured, but just slowed down into remission now and then. Hell, I loved him anyway. He was always good to us kids. Didn't do shit for us, because he couldn't, but good to us. When he was out of prison or out of the hospital, he would bring us toys, me and my brother, and be so good to us all, mostly to Momma, who he treated like a queen the way he talked to her.

He was the most extravagant-talking man in Atlanta when we lived there and in Washington, D.C., when we lived there and all over Virginia when we were moving every day, it seems like. I didn't have shit when I was little. Black kids used to take pity on me. I was little and I wore glasses and I didn't have shit, and if somebody said my daddy was a nut case, I'd go after them like a banshee, no matter how big or small they were.

That got old after while. That's not exactly true. It got old pretty fast after a couple of boys who were a lot bigger than I didn't take pity on my size or my eyeglasses, and just whaled the shit out of me. Oh, man, I could tell you stories about lumps and bruises that would make your hair stand on end.

When I was in my third year in high school, my daddy got cured. Just like that. He ate a pill every morning that made him as normal as salt. I'd say he turned into a routine man, except he talked a lot, and fast, and very smooth. We lived in a project among a lot of black folks, who said my daddy was the sweetest-talking white man they had ever seen. Everyone predicted the same future for him: sales.

You can imagine how pleased my momma and us boys were at the thought of the old man pulling himself up by the bootstraps from recidivist to nut case to sales. First thing he did was get himself a job in a big discount camera and electronics store. If I asked him once, I asked him a hundred times how a man with his past got hired on the first job interview he went to, knowing as I did that he had not worked at real employment since before I was born. (To tell you the truth, I was conceived during one of his furloughs. I figured that out by counting backwards when I was only nine years old.)

Next thing you know, I turned sixteen and dropped out of school to work with my daddy in the camera department. He was a lens man. Didn't care much for backs or bodies. Strobes, meters, filters, turned his eyes to stone. But lenses! Hot damn! that man could talk lenses.

I saw him one time, not more than a week after they put me on at the store; he had this rube leaning over the counter, looking into the case at lenses. Oh, man, you never saw such a rube: He was forty-five if he was a day, and still fighting zits like a jerk-off kid. Well, my daddy, he said to this rube, talking like in a whisper, "I got the lens, I got the lens for you. Wide, brother, wide. Open wide. I know what you want to do with this lens, I wasn't born yesterday, I can tell when a man of the world stands here at my counter. You're a pussy shooter, sure enough. I can see it in your face, the way you look at those lenses. Don't tell me; I don't want to be the possessor of your innermost secrets, my man, but I know. I been places where men tell, I been places where there's nothing left to hide. So let's look here at the widest of the wide, the point seven. Point seven! And fast! Think of it, my man, you get a little light, like a pinlight, and you can get in there so close with this lens you'll feel like you're on the inside looking out. That's what I say, that's what I mean, my man. This is the lens for your—shall we say— needs. And don't quibble about price; I won't hear of it. We didn't know you were coming, so we discounted it, discounted it down, down, down to where a damn pinhead could afford it, and you get it for just that little. I'll wrap it up, I'll pack it in cotton, and put a little pink around it just to get it in the mood."

That rube paid three hundred dollars for a lens so fucked up it had a shimmy in it like a busted steering column. Daddy was so pleased he couldn't stop talking. He started in telling me how this rube didn't have any sense at all, how he was nothing but a damn fool pimple-faced pinhead jerk-off who didn't know shit about lenses.

The rube was over at the cashier paying for the lens while Daddy was bragging on what he sold him. I knew Daddy was talking too loud, but you don't tell your daddy to hush when you're sixteen and he just sold a lens that's about as clear as pond water in August. It wasn't certain how much the rube heard of Daddy's words, but it was enough. He turned right around from the cashier's and back he came. His face was so red and swollen up with anger, it made his pimples pop.

"I heard what you said," was what he said, and he was mad.

Daddy was littler than the rube, but he looked him straight in the eye, and he said, "Well, I'm glad, because for a man who don't know shit about lenses, you sure took us good. Why, if you hadn't of made your move, I would have switched you over to the one point two at the same price, and made myself one hell of a commission. Damn! I could of stayed home for the week."

"You bullshitting me?" the rube asked.

Daddy didn't stop talking. "You can always switch to the one point two. I can handle the paperwork for you lickety-split, lickety-split, hah, hah, lickety-split."

The rube just burst. He still had the lens in his hand. He put it right in his palm, flat against his palm, and he grabbed Daddy by the back of the head and pulled him across the counter, and shoved that lens in his mouth, and commenced pushing and shoving like he wanted to force it clear down his throat. All the time Daddy was still talking, not trying to get loose or anything, still talking. Blood was coming out of his mouth and he was still talking. I saw his teeth break from that rube pushing the lens into his mouth, and Daddy never gave up talking.

Everybody in the store grabbed the rube. I stuck a mechanical pencil into him, right into his flesh, like you stick a fork into a pork butt when you're about to carve on it. He howled and took a swing at me, but he let go of Daddy's head, and the lens came out onto the counter, with all of Daddy's blood and teeth spilling on out after it. And I heard Daddy talking, telling the rube how he couldn't do anything to a lens so fine, so absolute quality that it could withstand a salesman's teeth.

1.

Salesmen and philosphers use the same tool—language. They are equally interested in the tool, although they profess different motives and different ends. For both salesmen and philosophers language includes words, pictures, numbers, and other signs, such as music, odors, and the weather.[1] Words remain the most common form of language, although there are studies that claim words are only a small part of communication. Since these studies are usually published in books or magazines, it is sometimes difficult to take them at their word.

Many salesmen have spoken about language, although they are not so careful as philosophers to distinguish language from argument. In the realm of words, scripture came from the pen of Claude Hopkins, the preacher's son who turned to writing advertising copy; most of the manuals on selling have to do with argument rather than with language.

Virtually all philosphers have had something to say on the subject of language. Plato distrusted language, and said so. He was forever nagging people to define their terms. Aristotle had relatively little to say on the subject, but what he said about grammar still holds. It really wasn't until the twentieth century that philosophers started looking to their tools as a means to understanding their own business.

In 1933, when he was teaching at Cambridge, Ludwig Wittgenstein dictated his thoughts on language to his students. Later he had the notes duplicated and put inside a blue wrapper, which gave them their name, *The*

---

[1]   It is not my intention to reinvent semiotics here, only to point out in a plainspoken way that the language of selling is not limited to words.

Blue Book. Never a man to begin slowly, Wittgenstein opened the class with the question that was to dominate his thinking: "What is the meaning of a word?" It is one of those questions, he said, that "produce in us a mental cramp."

Perhaps because he taught in England, where the great dictionary puts all its store in usage, Wittgenstein decided that words have the meaning we give them. He had other thoughts on the subject, but for the purpose of thinking about the language of selling, which will later extend to pictures, numbers, and sounds, as well as words, usage should make it possible to know when salesmen are lying, as opposed to changing the meaning of a word, and when they are describing the world as somebody thinks it is Somebody. But who?

There can be no question about the power of language in the market-place. It has been proved, time and again, to be able to overcome the experience of the senses. Cigarette makers and breakfast cereal purveyors, soap manufacturers and coffee roasters, have all tested their products with and without accompanying words. In blind taste tests, words invariably change the way people perceive what they put in their mouths. Identical cigarettes or cereals taste better when accompanied by words that say they taste better. Are people simply credulous? Are the higher faculties more powerful than mere sensation? I leave those questions to the scientists. The issue here is language, beginning with words, what they mean, what they picture.

2. Words

Usage differs appreciably from the pulpit to the market-place; the latter, as might be expected, admits the use of relatively new and effective words and turns of expression, even by fastidious persons.

—THORSTEIN VEBLEN

Which world deserves to be the real world? The one seen by the salesman or the one seen by the customer? And how is it that the chief salesman for Benneton, a seller of clothing, mainly sweaters, advertises by showing a world of AIDS patients dying, innocents drowning on the Indian subcontinent, the horror of fires, explosions, and the like? Is that a picture of the word *sweater*? Or is it an adjective? What does *dead* mean? What does *drowned* mean? If we believe Benneton the salesman, agreeing that a person in the instant of dying of AIDS is a picture of the word *sweater*, we are indeed on the way to "a mental cramp."

Not all such cramps come from traditional salesmen. On April 12, 1993, New York City's commissioner of consumer affairs, Mark Green, announced his candidacy for the newly created office of public advocate, saying that he wished to make the office a "democracy czar."

While one might expect the commissioner of consumer affairs to be an anti-salesman of sorts, a defender of Alfred Ayer's notion of the function of language as a statement of truth, the opposite holds true here. Is the intent of the commissioner of consumer affairs to speak nonsense, to create yet another unintended oxymoron in the English language? Or to deceive? Does the candidate wish to appeal both to those who favor democracy and to those who favor autocracy? No cramp so pains the mind as an oxymoron; it cannot be salved by reason, because it cannot be solved by reason. Nevertheless, oxymorons seem to sell, as if the suffering mind seeks a resolution in the transaction. As far back as 1910, advertisements for Salada tea claimed that it was both "a stimulant" and "a sedative."

The cramp grew worse as the language of selling became more public through the growing use of advertising. Whispered lies became public lies; clandestine nonsense became the language of billboards and full-page advertisements. During the Great Depression E. B. White of the *New Yorker*, apparently suffering from a severe cramp, attacked the question of "truth in advertising." In a "Talk of the Town" piece that was part parody, part reportage, part editorial, and all scornful, White took for his text a discussion of truth during the twenty-fifth-anniversary celebration of the advertising industry. It was a masterful bit of tightrope walking by White, sharp enough to please his readers, yet not so sharp that it would drive advertisers away; in other words, it was both a stimulant and a sedative, the literary equivalent of Salada tea:

> Advertisers are the interpreters of our dreams—Joseph interpreting for Pharaoh. Like the movies, they infect the routine futility of our days with purposeful adventure. Their weapons are our weaknesses: fear, ambition, illness, pride, selfishness, desire, ignorance. And these weapons must be kept bright as a sword. We rise to eat a breakfast cereal which will give us strength for the tasks of the day; we vanquish the excesses of the night with an alkaline fizz; we

cleanse our gums, stifle our bad odors, adorn our diseased bodies, and go forth to conquer—cheered on with a thousand slogans, devices, lucubrations. What folly for our leaders to meet in Boston in quest of an unwonted truth! We live by fiction. By fiction alone can Man get through the day.[2]

What is the meaning of a word anyway? If we hear White correctly, you and I, or our counterparts in 1936, are fearful, ambitious, sickly, proud, selfish, avaricious, and ignorant; in addition to which we stink! The people in advertising, on the other hand, are concerned with truth. Is White being ironic when he describes us or them? Contemplation of the piece does not bring good cheer, for the more one reads, the more likely it seems that White says what he means about us, while being ironic about them.

All of which leads back to the truism that to find the meaning of a word, it should be read or heard in a sentence, preferably a paragraph, better yet in a story or a society. This is especially true of the words used by salesmen, for they bear some relation to the use of words in the piece by E. B. White; that is, like irony, the words of the salesman don't have their usual meaning. The salesman differs from White, however, in that White wants the reader to understand what he says, to be startled into awareness by the mechanics of irony, while the salesman must keep the secret of his irony.

Richard Warren Sears, the founder of Sears, Roebuck and Company, took a famously ironic view of the meaning of words. At the end of the nineteenth century, he started a mail order business, advertising sewing machines for just one dollar. As the dollars came in, Sears sent the merchandise out, but the promised sewing machine was nothing more than a needle and thread. Should SEWING MACHINE have been italicized, enclosed in quotation marks? "What," one might ask, "is the meaning of a word?"

The Federal Trade Commission (FTC) takes the position that the meaning of a word can be found in the understanding of the unsophisticated in an increasingly unsophisticated country. Not mere literacy, but sophistication will have to be the measure, for those who are merely literate cannot be expected to grasp the distinction between truth and irony. They will apparently continue to send their money to the inheritors of the mantle of Sears, among them those who advertise MAKE BIG BUCKS AD-

---

[2] Reprinted in E. B. White, *Writings from the New Yorker,* ed. Rebecca M. Dale (New York: HarperCollins, 1990), p. 151.

DRESSING ENVELOPES AT HOME. Seven dollars will actually bring the unsophisticated a fifty-cent supply of envelopes and a bit of advice. The sales pitch itself, while intending to fleece the rubes, has in it the ironist's scorn. In other words, the salesman says, "How could anyone fail to know?"

Irony provides him with an alibi. He speaks to anyone or everyone, but only those whom he despises will fail to understand the irony in his speech. SEND ONE DOLLAR IMMEDIATELY! he shouts, and some dollars will be sent. GENUINE ZIRCON! Why, a sane man is sure to laugh! And the others. . . . A fool and his money are soon parted, as everyone knows.

No word has been more thoroughly deformed than *Free!* (always attended by an exclamation point!). Publishers Clearing House and American Family Publishers both run sweepstakes promotions advertised as Free! Nothing to buy! They must, because requiring a purchase would constitute an illegal lottery. But how free is Free! After several rounds of mailings, Publishers Clearing House sent a notice, which began, "Dear Friend: I don't know how to break the bad news nicely—so I'll just speak plainly. THIS MAY BE THE LAST BULLETIN WE CAN MAIL YOU FOR SOME TIME . . . unless you order or at least write to us for more." The notice to a "Dear Friend" goes on to make the legal turns required to keep the sweepstakes from becoming an illegal lottery, but the message is clear.

American Family Publishers writes more informally, following the salutation "Dear Friend" with a comma rather than a colon. But it has an even more forceful message: "We really regret it, but we simply cannot afford to keep on writing to groups of people who never buy magazines. If you do not order now, or write to stay on our list, you may be among the first to go. Those who are dropped now will miss out—there's no guarantee of another chance for them."

The communication from these giants of magazine vending cannot be mistaken. When they said no purchase was necessary, they were only kidding. There is no such thing as a free lunch in America. Like all of the salesman's clichés, Free! has the nature of a line spoken by a burlesque comic in a Samuel Beckett play; it is as obscene and intimate as a leper's wink.

Such irony appears everywhere in the language of selling. TEN DOLLARS CASH BACK, the advertisement says, adding in small type below, "Certificate applies to your next purchase." Cash? The question arises again: Should the word be italicized, enclosed in quotation marks? What is the meaning of a word?

Salesmen have been accused all through history of lying about their wares. The Aztecs complained about the tortilla sellers in the marketplace of Tlatelolco. Shakespeare said, "lying . . . becomes none but tradesmen." But it wasn't the salesman's misrepresentation of his goods that bothered the Aztecs or the Elizabethans. The complaints really had to do with price, for one could see the merchandise, touch it, try it on, and, if need be, taste it. Only with the widespread use of packaging did language become the thing, and the only thing, the customer could buy. Only then did the salesman of packaged things turn from logic, price, and desire to language.[3]

The obvious deformations arose from the need to distinguish among invisible (inside the package), similar, or identical yet competing products. Uneeda Biscuit pioneered, and hundreds, thousands of others followed: Rinso, Duz, Spry, Joy, Lux, Wheaties, Cheerios, Kleenex, Contact, Raid, Dial, Bold, and so on. At first, the deformations were related to the products, from the imperative Uneeda Biscuit to the descriptive Rinso White. Any connection between Joy or Bold and grease and grass stains, however, strains the imagination; perhaps the words have some totemic value, like the animal names given to cars.

The aim of the salesman is to deform the language in a proprietary way. Many companies, Procter & Gamble, for one, realizing the utility of stealing a word from the language by deforming it, have sent computer-generated lists of words off to Washington to be registered in the company name.

But the name was only a beginning. Once the contents of the package were named, they had to be described, and that is when the more serious deformations began, when the words started to get worn down to meaninglessness. *New* became so battered that the FTC finally limited its use in advertising to the first six months of the life of a product. The salesmen, undaunted, began making infinitesimal changes in product formulations, known in the pages of *Good Housekeeping* as New! Improved!

Low, high, light (lite), and such seemingly straightforward notions as fat have all been deformed beyond recognition. A low-fat frozen meat

---

[3] Complex things should be considered packaged even if they do not come in a proper bag or box. An automobile, for example, is essentially a package and, if anything, more mysterious than a package of biscuits; similarly a washing machine, a computer, and even a wristwatch. A television receiver, on which the end result can be observed, presents a different situation. Consider, for example, the problem of demonstrating the qualities of a television picture in a television commercial which will be broadcast and reproduced on the screen that the marketer hopes to replace; the language of the commercial cannot make a picture of the thing.

dinner may have ten times as much fat as a serving of spaghetti in a sauce of tomato and fresh basil, with or without a drop of olive oil. How is one to know? The local market has a sign in the window: "fresh" ground turkey. We have no way of knowing what the butcher means by fresh. Perhaps it is the ground-up remains of an old turkey, but not a frozen turkey? Perhaps the turkey was frozen, then thawed and ground up this morning? Perhaps the turkey was killed this morning, then cleaned and ground up only moments before being put in the meat case? What is the meaning of *fresh*?

And was it a *quality* turkey? Was it ever a *quality* turkey, before or after it was frozen or not frozen and ground up, whenever it was ground up, whether that was soon or long after it was killed? What qualities of turkeyness did it have?

And did the butcher who dealt in turkeyness of some kind of freshness now or in the past have a relationship with me when I saw the sign in the store window? What is a relationship? Can a salesman and his or her customer have a relationship? In chapter 14, when stockbrokers or customer's men or registered representatives or account executives are discussed, the question of the use of relationships in selling will arise, for it is one of the great connotative deformations of contemporary selling.

Older deformations have all but forced words out of the language. *Fine* is lost forever. *Good* has been so deformed that children say BAAAD to mean good. In the legal view of the marketplace, *best* holds a unique position among deformed words; it means nothing at all. Anyone can say his or her product is the best, and the Federal Trade Commission will not quarrel with the statement. Once the word *best* is applied in a specific way, as in, "The best mileage of any mid-size Japanese car made in Ohio," the seller must be able to prove the statement to the satisfaction of the various arbiters of truth: the FTC, the continuity clearance departments of television networks, the advertising departments of certain magazines and newspapers, and so on.[4] The best of everything has no such requirements.

---

[4]   The wisdom of these arbiters of truth and meaning may sometimes be questionable. I recall the following conversation over a statement by a physician that a very high percentage of cases of testicular cancer in young men could be cured. I've forgotten the exact number, but after five years the number of recurrences in cases diagnosed and treated "in time" was heading down toward less than 10 percent. The head of the commercial continuity clearance department of a television network flatly rejected the copy. The network was close by, so in the company of our general counsel and his assistant for network clearances, I went to see the woman. I asked what she needed to pass on the copy.

"Evidence," she said.

To many promoters of salesman's language, these deformations have an inventive, a "creative" character. S. I. Hayakawa compared advertising to poetry. Wallace Stevens, who knew something more about poetry, said, "The incredible is not a part of poetic truth."

Nevertheless, deformations do catch our attention. Grammarians noticed that Winston would have done better to taste good *as a cigarette should*. People who live along the seacoasts must have been shocked into awareness upon finding that Tide was a detergent. Ordinary language, once praised by Claude Hopkins and David Ogilvy, may no longer serve the salesman. In that way, the salesman shares some of the aims of the poet, especially the wish for concise yet heightened expression. But Emily Dickinson and the woman who sells stocks or shoes or soap have nothing more in common than wishing and brevity. Dickinson sought the poetic truth of her life, of our lives, a truth more affecting and more deeply comprehensible than the truth of fact. The salesman strives for a new banality, not merely banality, but a new and proprietary banality; not a birth of language in poetic expression, but a death of words in the chamber of repetitions.

W. H. Auden offered this explanation of the cliché in his essay "Notes on the Comic":

> The human person is a unique singular, analogous to all other persons, but identical with none. Banality is an illusion of identity for, when people describe their experiences in clichés, it is impossible to distinguish the experience of one from the experience of another.
>
> The cliché user is comic because the illusion of being identical with others is created by his own choice. He is the megalomaniac in reverse. Both have fantastic conceptions of themselves but, whereas the megalomaniac thinks of himself as being somebody else—God,

---

"One of the physicians who approved the statement won the Nobel Prize in medicine for his work in cancer research," I said. "Among the others are Sir Richard Doll of Oxford, who discovered the connection between cigarette smoking and cancer; a fellow from Stanford who invented magnetic resonance imaging; and Joe Fortner, a surgeon and department head from Sloan-Kettering, who is the one making the statement on camera."

"Those are just opinions," she said.

I asked whether she thought we had an ulterior motive, that perhaps we were intending to market testicular cancer or to use it in a promotion, such as, Buy this car and we'll give you a free case of testicular cancer.

In the end her supervisor approved the copy, and it went on the air.

Napoleon, Shakespeare—the banal man thinks of himself as being everybody else, that is to say, nobody in particular.[5]

Thus the salesman is the poet in reverse, deforming words, phrases, the very structure of language—its grammar—into clichés. If he were a character in a play, he would be a comic figure, but the reality of the deformation of words through distortion and repetition, the transmogrification of words into clichés, which mean nothing in particular, produces the ear-splitting silence of a ruined life.

3. Transition

When Jerry J. Siano, an art director from Philadelphia, was named chairman of the board of N. W. Ayer, the agency's publicists were invited to a meeting to discuss the image of the new chief executive. The charge to the publicists, including a new man who had just taken over the agency's public relations operation, was to find a way to raise Jerry's stature in the industry. It was not an easy assignment. The new chairman was a garrulous man, with a penchant for obscenities and an art director's distrust of words. However, like many high-pressure salesmen, he was given to tirades.

After a brief discussion, the publicists agreed that Jerry's image would be helped by identifying him with a cause. Since he is a generous man (and I don't mean that facetiously), the idea appealed to him. The next step was to select a cause.

The new man suggested literacy. He even made a little speech about it. Literacy, he said, was important, noncontroversial, sure to be good for the image of the chairman and the agency.

"Literacy!" the chairman shouted, "Fuck literacy! There's too fucking much literacy already. Too fucking many words, not enough pictures. Fucking people going home every night reading books when they should be watching fucking television. That's what's wrong with this country, too much fucking literacy!"

---

[5] *The Dyer's Hand* (New York: Vintage, 1968), p. 379.

4. Images

When I was a young man, I made a silent lie, a wordless, prizewinning deception. It was a television commercial for Spare Tire, which was described to me as an aerosol can containing a latex compound and enough air under pressure to seal a small hole and reinflate a flat tire. In the commercial, a man walked into his garage, saw that a tire was flat, took a can of Spare Tire from the glove compartment of his car, sealed and reinflated his tire, got into his car, and drove off. There was actually one line of copy, as I recall, something to effect of "One flat tire, one minute, one can of Spare Tire."

The commercial won many prizes, the product sold very well, and customers were pleased with it, as long as the can remained in the glove compartment. When they tried to fix a flat with Spare Tire, they found that the latex and the air ran out of the same little hole that caused the flat in the first place.[6]

The case can be examined from many vantages. Roland Barthes might be most interested in the relation of texts and images, for the words of the commercial illustrate the text, in a reversal of the old form.[7] His analysis would be helpful; semiotics applied to this instance of selling would be interesting and revealing. The power exerted by language would surely be demonstrated by the response of the audience to the commercial. But the distortion of the image as language is the issue here. Every image shown on film, frame by frame, was true, in the sense of picturing what was in front of the lens. But the sequence of images was a lie. A flat tire was shown, a can of the product was connected to the air valve, and in sequential images, the tire was inflated. The mysterious contents of the package performed a function, proved their value before our very eyes.

Doubting Thomases could not, in biblical fashion, demand to be shown the hole in the tire, for each image, as well as the sequence of images, was immutable, and each image was a surface under which secrets lay. And unlike words, the images were far less susceptible to interpretation. In the language of images the lie was perfect, irrefutable.

---

[6] The commercial was done as a freelance project. I never saw the product demonstrated, and I did not attend the filming of the commercial. I believed the manufacturer's claims, which makes of me both a fool and an accomplice.

[7] See the section on text and image regarding the news photograph in *Image-Music-Text*, trans. Stephen Heath (New York: Hill and Wang, 1978).

Images used in selling function like packages, as surfaces containing mysteries within. Unlike words, which call to consciousness the variety of imagination and the questioning aspect of intelligence, images are fundamentalist preachments, salesman's proclamations, deformations of reality for which the customer has no recourse in intelligence. Pictures, like packages, can be put to the test of experience only after the sale.

The power of the package, the image behind whose skirts reality hides, is so great that it can overcome reality even when reality is available to the customer. This was demonstrated by the designer Marget Larsen, who was asked by a small baker of sourdough French bread if she thought it was worth doing something with the plain white bag in which the loaves were delivered. She did indeed. Larsen added red and blue stripes to the bag, connoting the French national flag, and the locally baked bread suddenly had a more Parisian flavor and vastly increased sales. Although the customer could still see and smell the bread and even test the thickness and crispness of the crust by squeezing the bread within the bag, the image revised the contents in the customer's mind, for the image is the dogma of perception.

If the images employed by the salesman were accurate representations of reality, they would return the marketplace to the time before the package. Instead, the images have the ironic character of the trompe l'oeil style; they fool the eye (into seeing something unreal as if it were true). As the photograph on the package or the demonstration of the knife that will cut through steel becomes more idealized, more convincing, more appealing, it moves further from the reality of the product, so that when the package is opened or the mailman delivers the set of knives, the irony of the images becomes ever greater.

The difference between the trompe l'oeil style of art and the deformation of reality in the salesman's images starts with the intent of the image maker. Trompe l'oeil was a matter of craft and wit; the viewer was expected to participate in the joke. Such irony is sweet. The salesman's images, presented as the bald truth individually and in sequence, often produce another form of irony, and the more the product diverges from the image, the greater and more irritating the irony.

As a style of decorating and painting, trompe l'oeil evolved into surrealism, the opposite of verisimilitude; and so, too, the salesman's images, which teach the eye, with savage irony, to disbelieve the represented world.

5. Debt

*The United States itself is the leader of a new, hard, materialistic civilisa-
tion . . . whose priests are the instalment-seller and the advertising expert.*

—*The Economist*, 1935,
quoted in the *OED Supplement*

The great American boom of the 1920s was largely the work of the
deformers of language, the salesmen. They had to change one critical word
from a pejorative to a description of the modern way of life: *debt*. It had
been the father of usury, the cause of untold suffering, the vilest of economic deeds. Anti-Semitism had fed upon it. Bankers had been shamed by
their use of it. Generations had been told that it was the godless road to
perdition. Even so, it was clear to the salesmen in the United States at the
beginning of the twentieth century that there would be no great boom
without great debt. But who wanted to be a debtor? And who wanted to be
a debt collector, a usurer in the eyes of God?

Installment buying had to be divorced from debt.

The task fell to the salesmen, and, as if by magic, debt became credit.
The great negative became the mark of virtue, of honor, of esteem, even of
acclaim. The former debtor became a person who had credit, judged by his
economic superiors to be worthy, stable, truthful, decent, hardworking.
More than that, credit implied a secure future; the assignment of it was
cause for optimism. No more promising diploma could be put into a person's hand than a long mortgage or a contract for payments on the installment plan.

Credit, which no longer had anything to do with debt, increased at a
phenomenal rate during the 1920s. Martha Olney, an economic historian,
calculated that purchases of major appliances on the installment plan rose
from 20 percent at the beginning of the decade to 75 percent in 1929.[8] But
that was only the beginning. Total consumer credit, not including home
mortgages, rose at an even more astonishing pace after World War II, going
from a little over $23 billion in 1950 to more than $800 billion in 1990, an
increase of 3,400 percent.[9]

[8]   Quoted in *Fortune*, December 16, 1991.
[9]   Federal Reserve Board of Governors, cited in Louis Rukeyser, *Business Almanac*
(New York: Simon and Schuster, 1988).

The United States of America had a debt, but consumers had credit. One was bad, and the other was good. It was, in the end, as simple as that.

6. Numbers

Top Banana to his Stooge: We'll divide the money in half. Here, that's one for you, and one for me.
And two for you, and one, two for me.
Three for you, and one, two, three for me.

—Burlesque routine

What weighs more: a pound of feathers or a pound of gold?

—Children's trick question

In the United States, which has been obsessed with the quantitative since its citizens discovered statistics at the end of the eighteenth century, numbers have always been considered more reliable than words or even pictures. "Two and two is four," Americans are fond of saying, as if it were the foundation upon which all truth must rest. And until the middle of the twentieth century, it was probably as good a touchstone as any.

The reliability of numbers began to suffer when researchers started telling the public about statistics based on probability rather than on counting. In 1935 Elmo Roper produced what he called the first "scientific" public opinion poll.[10] By 1960 Louis Harris, working for the Kennedy campaign, applied the techniques to politics.

One way to judge public opinion polling is by its intentions. Most major public opinion polls are tacked on to polls paid for by advertising agencies and corporations. A few are sponsored by print and broadcast news organizations, but those are now every bit as interested in selling as the corporations that own them. In most instances, it is fair to say that a public opinion researcher is a salesman (someone must pay for the poll) who sells to salesmen (advertising agencies or marketing departments) who sell to salesmen (clients in the form of companies or product managers or a board of directors) who sell to the public. It is unlikely that any number generated and transmitted under such circumstances can retain its integrity.

[10] Earlier polls, beginning with the first one funded by the Russell Sage Foundation, were also touted as scientific.

For many years questions about polling were centered on the validity of the sample, the assumption being that numbers did not lie, if the numbers were correct; in other words, as long as no one argued that two and two made five, polling was an accurate representation of the nation. Human beings were, like everything else in America, quantifiable.

A few people complained that polling conflated opinion, depriving the nation of its diversity as great factions of opinion were formed: Democrats think this, Republicans think that; men think this, women think that; blacks think this, whites think that.[11] Only recently, as people like Ross Perot began using polling results to support their sales messages, did the press begin to look at the nonnumerical aspect of the numbers; that is, knowing the number is not enough; one must consider the question and the possible answers, since polling data is rarely gathered from open-ended questions.

For most people, however, the sanctity of numbers remains unsullied. An opinion poll is the proof an advertising agency provides to the advertising department of its client, which in turn provides the numbers to its product or division management, which must report to the senior management of the organization. If the numbers are wrong, blame cannot be assigned, as in the cases of hundreds of new products that fail every year, even though they went into general distribution only after surviving the rigors of consumer clinics, focus groups, and various kinds of test markets.

How can the numbers be wrong in such simple tests? First, into each question a little ambiguity seems always to find its way. And then the sampling techniques never quite turn out as hoped. Interpretation of the data is just that: interpretation. And every presentation of the interpretation of the data containing a slight sampling error in the population asked to deal with slightly ambiguous questions requires a listener who may hear something slightly different from what was intended.

The product that looked like a sure thing, according to the numbers, fails.

To make such mistakes, each salesman—the one who first thinks of the new product, his research firm, the new product group supervisor, the product clinic group, the test market organization, and the executive in charge of the entire set of operations—must construe the numerical results

[11] Browns and Asians were rarely mentioned. Some surveys include more specific groups now, but the cost of sampling will soon drive most of them toward more broadly defined factions, perhaps whites and people of color.

of the tests to present reality as he thinks it will match the desires of his supervisor, who is his customer. Of many such weddings a disaster is created.

The failure, of course, comes in the confusion of the numbers of selling with the numbers of science. Nothing could be further from science than the polls the salesman sells. Yet, the salesman always presents numbers as if they were as neat as arithmetic and as certain as gravity.

Numbers also provide a way for the salesman to increase prices by ratcheting down quantity. Anyone who buys canned coffee may have noticed over the last few years that the one-pound coffee can now contains only twelve or thirteen ounces of coffee. Given that the price per can has remained stable, the price per pound has increased by between 18.75 and 25 percent.

The masters at ratcheting down quantity, as well as quality, are the Schoolmen of Procter & Gamble marketing groups. Irwin Landau, editor of *Consumer Report,* found that P&G had reduced the size of a roll of Bounty paper towels from 85 square feet to 60 square feet, all the while keeping the price stable. Landau noted in a *New York Times* op-ed piece that P&G had effected a "disguised price increase of 41.7 percent."

For the salesman any number will do, as long as some number can be generated. Once he has the number, the salesman has gotten past the problem of reality. Numbers have no reality; they are merely information, language, not even nouns, but adjectives intended to describe the world, like photographs, film, or the paper, plastic, or pasteboard covering foodstuffs. A number is a package in which reality can be hidden, like a soapbox, a soup can, or complexity. Nothing about a number is absolute, not even in a mathematician's dreams. The seductive surface of a number can be attached to anything. Given such a relative thing, an adjective with limitless range, the quantity of deaths, the quantity of births, the possibility of war and the likelihood of love, the measure of sweetness and the strength of light, the salesman finds himself, at last, in control.

Every set of adjectival numbers is a language of its own, attached only to the language that produced the information that generated the numbers. There are no limits to the salesman's power to use numbers to describe the popularity of Chrysler cars or Ross Perot's ideas, the contents of a coffee can, the price of an insurance policy, the cost of a mortgage. By manipulating the situation that generates the numbers, the composition of the test group, the nature of the questions, the conditions during which the test was done,[12] and so on, almost any numbers can be generated on any subject.

Since these numbers appear alone, as conclusions, and rarely, if ever, in the company of their means, let alone the motives that gave birth to them or the ends that are expected of them, the most sophisticated customers cannot judge their validity. For the rest of the market, the half who cannot read and the three-fourths who cannot understand difficult concepts, "figures never lie." Thus, for the majority in the land of the majority, salesmen are, after all, like gods and poets, free to use language to invent the world.

[12] A room was filled with the aroma of freshly brewed ground coffee, then people were brought into the room and asked to taste a cup of coffee and decide whether it was prepared from freeze-dried or freshly ground coffee beans. Since the sense of smell is so connected to the sense of taste, very few people could tell the difference in that setting between ground and instant coffee. The advertiser concluded that his instant coffee tasted "as good as ground coffee."

11

The Oversold Economy

The control or management of demand is, in fact, a vast and rapidly growing industry. . . . In everyday parlance this great machine, and the demanding and varied talents that it employs, are said to be engaged in selling goods. In less ambiguous language it means that it is engaged in the management of those who buy goods.

—JOHN KENNETH GALBRAITH[1]

It worries me when we give these rebates. When a guy takes a rebate and puts it in as a down payment, then he uses it to get a car he probably couldn't have afforded without that rebate, I worry about that. It's a big concern. It was a big struggle. I was never really satisfied that that was what we should do. They convinced me that the value would be there. Even with an additional down payment the guy would be able to make the payments and handle the thing. But I never felt good about it.

—ROGER B. SMITH,
former chairman of General Motors

When he was in college, he met a girl who told him a line from a poem by Theodore Roethke: "My heart holds open house." It was a perfect picture of his father, he thought, and he told her so. She asked him if he loved his father. He did not answer with the full stop of a yes or no; instead, he told her who his father had been and what he had made of their home in the great mosquito breeding ground known as New Jersey.

She laughed, for she liked his ruefulness, the way it made him seem

[1]   Galbraith's ideas, published in *The New Industrial State* (Boston: Houghton Mifflin, 1967), were greeted with disdain by the conservative economists of the time. Robert M. Solow led the attack with a review in the *Public Interest* (Fall 1967) in which he denied the power of selling, by putting forth the "innocence" or competitive position held by the cigarette manufacturers and once a comfort to me.

older, worldly, like a balding man or someone already divorced. If they had known some private place, a borrowed room, a secret woods, any wall to secure their modesty, they might not have talked so much or listened so hard, but it was a long time ago, when lovemaking was still linked to talking, so he told her about his father.

No weekend, no evening, was ever lonely in his father's house. Visitors came from every part of the country, young ones and old, married women and spinsters, even a bachelor or two, a prissy one from Denver and a man with wet white bread jowls who lived in Illinois. Some of the women wore too much makeup, and as far as he could remember, all of them smoked cork-tipped cigarettes. He noticed that under the table the women slipped their feet out of their shoes, and more often than not had trouble getting their feet back into them at the conclusion of the meal.

Some of the women were beautiful. He remembered one in particular who had softly curled white hair and skin like very fine paper. The younger women tended to be less finely made, and more than a few of them were fat. The visiting began when he was a baby, before he entered kindergarten. It went on for as long as he lived in his father's house. And it continued while he was in college, and afterward.

All of the visitors were customers, buyers who came east from Texas and Oklahoma, Colorado, Nebraska, South Dakota, North Dakota, Wyoming, Montana, Idaho, Nevada, New Mexico, Arizona, Kansas, Missouri, and Illinois—the territory. They brought gifts with them, arrowheads made by the Cheyenne, fresh corn, buckskin, pottery, beadwork, jerky, turquoise, silver buckles, and moccasins sewn from the skin of a deer. They were like dream people come to New Jersey from the American past.

In his father's house, they were always welcome. They could stay overnight, if they so desired, although few of them did. They could eat and drink and laugh late into the night, which was the ritual of evenings at their home in New Jersey. His father liked them all, welcomed them all, and they were glad to be there, for, as he knew when he heard the line from the poem, his father's heart held open house.

He would have married the girl who told him the Roethke line, but she had a slightly crooked arm, a flaw that he was too frequently compelled to touch, and it drove him from her as if it were a disease.

Nonetheless, he remembered her, carrying the sound of her delicacy with him all through the Wharton School, and into the firm, as his father called it, when he, too, became a salesman. The merchandise was ladies' ready-to-wear, which his father preferred to call *prêt-à-porter*. And the territory was very small to start: Alabama, Mississippi, and Louisiana. As he had learned to do at the Wharton School, he asked for more, and was promised Georgia, then Florida, if he proved he was a salesman, like his father.

Since he lived in a studio apartment in Manhattan and did not have a wife who would welcome all the acquaintances and customers of his life on the road, he could not hold open house. He invited people to restaurants, and always paid with a credit card, for he was careful with his accounts.

As his father aged, the company accommodated him, or so it seemed, by reducing the size of his territory, sparing him a city here, a state there, cutting back the number of airports and hotels, because they could sap a man's strength and dampen his enthusiasm for the new fall fashions and the exciting spring styles. Fewer people came to the house in New Jersey, but there was no change in the demeanor of his father's heart or his mother's smile. At the last moment, just before they sat down to dinner, she still lifted the halter of the apron over her head and fluffed and patted her feather-cut hair back into place.

His father retired gladly. He had wanted to turn over his territory to his son, but it was too late for that. The pupil had excelled the master, the son of the man whose heart held open house had become the marketing director of the firm. Salesmen now reported to the sales manager, who reported to him. At the retirement party, held in the private dining room of a restaurant on the outskirts of Maplewood, a father received a gold watch from his son.

To maintain the competitive position of the firm, the new marketing director reduced the size of the territories and lowered the draw, while raising slightly the commission paid to salesmen. He was generous with expense accounts, but he ruled that home entertaining was not an acceptable expense, because it was inefficient. A salesman, he said, should work out of motels.

When the recession of 1991 sharply reduced the gross revenues of the company, the president laid the problem in the lap of marketing. "We're doing everything right," the marketing director said, referring to his focus groups, fashion clinics, computer-guided regional breakouts, and in-store-tested designs. The president showed him what was known in the company as "the Bible," a computer printout provided by the comptroller's office. He flipped over the pages until he got to the end. Then he tapped his finger on the last line. "Not good," he said. And nothing more. In his style of management, silence was a goad.

With no guide but his years at Wharton, the marketing director was overcome by loneliness. He went to his office, closed the door, and sat among the echoes. When the telephone rang, he did not answer. Instead, he looked out the window, over the rooftops to the river. The ugliness of New York repelled him. He wished for the sparkling disguise of the city on winter afternoons, he prayed for odorless frost and clean snow.

Denver.

Santa Fe.

Cloudcroft.

Aspen.

Cheyenne.

Ruidoso.

Cornfields, wheat fields, frozen ponds, ice blue rivers, trees bending under the snow.

He telephoned his father. It was too late, the old man said, then relented. He recalled the old days, the gentlewomen of nostalgia, the spinsters vacationing with their nieces, the grandmothers at the end of their endless patience. Did he know Mrs. Goldfarb who did the buying for the Bluebell chain? He could give her a call. And Amy, did he remember Amy, the little thing who used to play the piano when she came for dinner? And Mrs. Miniver? That wasn't her name, but she was such an English lady, that one who had lost her husband in the war, such a lady! And Rowena Gordon, the buyer from the new discount chain that's had such a success, did he remember her, she used to bring him sweets from her sister's candy shop in Little Rock?

I was not a salesman to them; they were my sales force, the father said, my confidants, all the wisdom I ever had was tied up in them. In my house there was a school: I was their pupil and they were mine. From them I learned the market, to them I gave the news.

"Relationship selling," the son said.

His father hung up.

The afternoon oozed away, evening began. The marketing director saw the rose of pollution forming in the west, across the river, somewhere in America, in the territories where the salesmen worked. He strained to see beyond the stone gray teeth that stood on the palisades, into the green country where evening would come late for him. He peered into the daylight that rolled west for more than two thousand miles, past Chicago and St. Louis and Tulsa and San Jose. He imagined the endless rolling rose of the sky; he saw the soul of the market revealed there. Something had gone wrong in America; he could feel it now, it was in the air. An abatement had taken place, an appetite had died. The civility of shared hungers was no more. His father had retired just in time. A man's heart could no longer hold open house. There was nothing left but war.

1.

The task force was convened quickly, although not without some care. It was to be a mix of Young Turks and solid old-timers, people from Bell Labs, long lines, operating companies, and one outsider for leavening. One of the members, Raymond W. Smith, has since become chairman of Bell-Atlantic. Another, Kim Armstrong had come to AT&T straight from the staff of Philip Hart, the liberal U.S. senator from Michigan for whom the Senate Office Building is named. I was the outsider, more or less; N. W. Ayer had been AT&T's advertising agency for a very long time.

We held our first meeting in November. A preliminary recommendation was to be delivered by Christmas. The occasion for the haste was the worst thing that had happened to AT&T since the Telecommunications Act of 1934 permitted it to act as a regulated monopoly. The Department of Justice, under the administration of Gerald Ford, a duck born lame in the presidency, had brought an antitrust suit against the company.

Since the relatively obscure *Carterfone* decision had allowed the attachment of non-Bell equipment to the Bell System Network, a group inside AT&T had been looking at various ways to reconfigure the company after an antitrust action. But that was a company secret. To the outside world, including all but a few of its own employees, the Bell System was taken entirely by surprise. When AT&T's chairman, John deButts, came to a meeting of the task force, he ranted against President Ford, to whom he had lent Ed Block, "one of my best people," and insulted the U.S. attorney general, with whom he had gone hunting only a week before the announcement of the suit. He said that the attorney general couldn't "shoot the side of a barn." That was all he had to say to the task force charged with developing a public position for AT&T in response to the suit.

After two weeks of listening to lawyers and scientists and lobbyists and various executives on the subject of antitrust, the task force agreed on several things. The first was that AT&T's policy of "social pricing,"[2] would

[2]   AT&T used high rates for long-distance and business services to subsidize local telephone service. Originally, the system had been used to increase penetration of telephone

most likely end with the breakup of the company. The second was that AT&T would no longer be able to fund basic research of the kind that had won seven Nobel Prizes for Bell Labs. The third was that the marketing of telephone equipment in the form of "fancy phones" and so on would bloom while the great basic changes envisioned by scientists at Bell Labs would be delayed. In short, the breakup of the system would favor technology and marketing as opposed to science and social justice.

The first conclusion of the task force was that AT&T should hold on to Bell Labs and the "switched network," everything up to the jack or plug in the wall. The rest of it should be put up for grabs. We presented the notion to Alvin von Auw, AT&T's gray eminence. Alvin puffed on his pipe for a moment, then revealed that AT&T had been working on exactly such a scenario for some time. He also thought it was a good idea, but he said it would never come about. For one thing, deButts wanted to hold on to AT&T exactly as it was.

With no room to maneuver, the group turned to trying to understand the company. AT&T was gigantic. It had a million employees, assets the equal of a medium-sized country, and it was so diverse that one could hardly grasp all the aspects of it. The company's great virtue, the sense that it really was a public service, also led to its worst vices, in the form of lobbying regulators and wasting money; it was at once wonderful and corrupt.

To deal with the nature of AT&T, I brought a wise man to the meetings in the form of one of his books. My copy of John Kenneth Galbraith's *The New Industrial State* was seven years old by then, dog-eared and disfigured by underlinings and notes in the margins, but it still offered the best explanation of American contemporary business, at least as I knew it, and a brilliant description of AT&T, the classic "planned industry." As the task force reexamined AT&T in light of Galbraith's insights, the need for reliable supplier and customer markets, the advantages of the vertically integrated business, the efficiencies of industrial organizations that could plan confidently, a schism developed inside the group. Ray Smith, the intel-

---

service in the United States. As the number of households with telephones neared 100 percent, the pricing structure took on more and more the character of a redistribution of resources from the rich to the poor.

Social issues were very important to people inside this quasi-public company. One fellow at New Jersey Bell discovered that AT&T's policy of requiring high deposits from people in low-income areas and little or no deposit from people in affluent neighborhoods was essentially racist. He demonstrated that rich people were often "deadbeats," while poor people kept their bills low and paid them on time. The policy was changed; henceforth deposits were based on an individual's past payment history.

---

lectually adventurous financial man from Bell of Pennsylvania, was politically conservative. Galbraith and his ideas were unacceptable to him.

On several occasions Smith and I argued for hours, until we were both parched and exhausted. The arguments were always polite, never ad hominem. In the end, we agreed to compose a simple statement of the virtues of AT&T as a "planned industry," and to give the statement to a polling organization to find out how the public responded.

Galbraith would have been pleased to know that the majority of the people in the test group liked the idea of AT&T as a planned industry and opposed any antitrust action against such a company. The results were immediately carried to AT&T senior management. John deButts said the words *planned industry* sounded like Communist Russia; they were not to be used in connection with the Bell System.

In the end, AT&T was unable to mount a serious effort to convince the public that it should not be broken up, for the company could not reconcile its true nature with the politics of the golf course and the social club. Local rates did indeed rise, while long-distance and business rates fell. Bell Labs has greatly reduced its expenditures on basic research, and information in "the information age" is, so far, largely disorderly and thus inaccessible in a confusion of competing sources; everyone keeps waiting for the invisible hand to come along and make it right.

Meanwhile, the world that Galbraith saw so clearly in *The New Industrial State* has largely disappeared. "The mature corporation," he said of the time when the salesmen seemed to be in control, "has readily at hand the means for controlling the prices at which it sells as well as those at which it buys. Similarly it has means for managing what the consumer buys at the prices which it controls." In this situation, he wrote, "the producing firm reaches forward to control its markets and on beyond to manage the market behavior and shape the social attitudes of those, ostensibly, that it serves. For this we also need a name and it may appropriately be called The Revised Sequence."

Galbraith had seen the salesman step out of his traditional role as mediator, and take control. In cooperation with the state, the mature corporations ruled the lives of citizens in economic and social matters; the entrepreneur had been replaced; freedom suffered an unsubtle constraint. There was no prescription in Galbraith's book. He ended almost with resignation at the "accepted facts of life" he had described. Yet, there were hints all through the work that he believed things do not stay the same. With a sly and slightly progressive smile, he spoke of people "looking back" at this time.

What no one, not even Galbraith, could imagine in 1967 was that less than a quarter of a century later the economy that had been regulated by the salesmen would have become oversold.

By oversold I mean the condition in which people realize they have been convinced to buy goods or services they did not need or want and cannot afford. Many economic factors enter into overselling, but without debt the oversold condition would be uncommon, if not impossible. Since being oversold, as defined here, includes awareness of economic imprudence, the mood of the oversold customer is regret, accompanied by anxiety about the future and remorse over having acted imprudently.

The point where personal debt becomes imprudent has always been more a moral than an economic question, although debt has some logical limits. Bankruptcy is an indication of either imprudence or bad luck or both, but short of bankruptcy when does personal borrowing become imprudent? Economists often use consumer debt as a percentage of after-tax income to gauge the severity of indebtedness. In 1960, when the United States was just coming fully under the sway of salesmen, consumer debt was equal to 60 percent of after-tax income. By 1990 consumer debt had increased by half, to slightly more than 90 percent of annual after-tax income.

The cause of the oversold condition can be understood by comparing the role of the salesman in classical economics to the work of the salesman after the pipeline was filled following World War II. Let us say that Adam Smith's rule of natural liberty, including his exceptions for common decency and public works, prevails in the market. Then the salesman has only to act as a mediator to relieve some of the rough spots inherent in a complex system, because in Adam Smith's world, supply dances with demand and prices are related to equilibrium. The salesman's role in a system of classical laissez-faire economics is useful, but ancillary. The invisible hand does most of the work. Mere rationality does the rest.[3]

In the revised sequence described by Galbraith, the salesman replaces the invisible hand. Galbraith says this situation came about because the large

---

[3]   The standard laissez-faire argument for some distribution of wealth—how many beds can a rich man sleep in during a night, or how many toilets can he use during a day—notes that any market, no matter how small, can be efficient, but concedes that the greater efficiencies of the division of labor cannot be used for very small markets. What may appear to be morality on the part of the classical economists is only an acknowledgment of the rules of exchange, like a scientist noting that engines obey the laws of thermodynamics.

corporations wanted to be able to plan against their supplier and consumer markets. That may be part of the cause, but the rise of the salesman was more likely a response to the dangers of overproduction in the 1950s.

If the markets had been allowed to find equilibrium in the classical fashion then, as in the 1930s, another Depression was almost certain to occur. Instead, the corporations revised the sequence, as Galbraith says, but I think they did it to avoid what they believed was economic and (with the history of Europe after World War I in mind) political catastrophe; the salesman emerged as the savior of last resort. The rescue was brief and perhaps illusory; allowing salesmen to become the determining economic factor, the key to planning, was not a permanent solution to all economic problems. Had the salesmen achieved a lasting regulation of markets and secured ever-increasing profits through the efficiencies and control of planning, the market would never have become oversold and the declines of IBM, General Motors, RCA, U.S. Steel, and so many other giants would probably not have occurred.

Galbraith gave the corporations credit for shrewdness they did not possess and attributed powers to the salesmen that they could not maintain. The revised sequence was a desperate measure, a corporate existential act, for no businessman knew how it would turn out, and no businessman, not even the chairman of AT&T, the paradigmatic planned industry, dared to recognize planning for what it was. Galbraith was proposing something much closer to socialism than to salesmanship.

Overproduction was not the basic problem. Had output been maintained at rational levels, fueled by increases in population, productivity, and occasional invention, growth would have been slower, but the need to sell would have been reduced. Instead, the corporations "grew the business" by increasing production every time the salesmen brought demand into equilibrium with supply. If there was no money to buy the products newly wed to desire, the customer was simply made more honorable, reliable, decent, and hardworking; that is, he was given more credit.

When Ronald Reagan was elected president of the United States, and he gave the country into the care of the salesmen, his patriotic sentiments and enfeebled mind accorded the nation and all of its worthy (meaning middle- and upper-middle-class) citizens the greatest honor and most optimistic future: unlimited credit.

One of the many errors made by Reagan's huckster economists was the failure to understand their own laissez-faire economics: No man, no matter how rich or how white, can sleep in more than one bed or sit on more than one toilet. By redistributing wealth to favor their own class, Reagan's policies had made the job of the salesman in America virtually impossible: Large numbers of people could not afford a new bed or a new flush toilet, while others who could easily buy a hundred beds or a thousand toilets suddenly came to the realization that they had more beds and toilets than they wanted, let alone needed.

Toilet makers and bed manufacturers, who had spent decades believing they could continually increase production and depend on the salesmen to find a way to market their goods, found out that the salesmen had already done their job too well. The market was oversold.[4]

2.

Although it is far too early to make a final analysis of the oversold condition and the long-term effects of economic regret, the salesman's Pyrrhic victory over the customer appears now to occur in seven steps:

A. Domination

Selling becomes the determining factor in the economy, with business relying on the salesmen to find markets for as much as they can produce, no matter what the quality or the price of the products. For a time the sales-dominated economy seems to work. A different economic culture develops around it, optimistic, but cautious. The transaction, the sale, becomes the focus of the economy. Whatever supports the transaction is acceptable. Finally, the transaction, which happens now, today, at this moment, takes interest and investment away from the future, and focuses it on the instant.[5]

---

[4]   Of course, an entire economy does not become oversold at the same moment, nor do all businesses necessarily become oversold. Some businesses will continue to expand in an oversold economy, and some new businesses will be formed. The oversold condition itself will provide opportunities for some aggressive marketers of products and services; for example, when corporate layoffs force more people to work at home, someone will have to provide the computers, fax machines, desks, and chairs to the growing home office market. When people stop replacing their old cars, trucks, refrigerators, washing machines, and so on, those manufacturers suffer, but the makers of replacement parts and the owners of repair shops prosper.

The oversold condition does not apply to all persons in a giant economy, just as it does not apply to all enterprises. Nor does economic collapse appear to be a likely result. An oversold economy is simply exhausted. Its occasional spurts of growth will be brief and disruptive.

[5]   Two flagrant examples: Martin R. Himmel was trained in the advertising department of Vitamin Corporation of America, then started his own company, which bought and

B. Regressions

The oversold condition begins with a movement away from a creative culture to a timid, market-driven culture in which there is still some innovation, but an almost complete lack of invention.

A growing concentration of wealth in the hands of a few people limits the size of markets.[6]

The economic contribution of invention declines because of a fall in R&D expenditures throughout the economy. One example of this comes from the drug industry. The U.S. Senate Special Committee on Aging reported in 1992 that research spending in the drug industry had increased by 13.5 percent the preceding year, while spending on marketing costs increased by 15 percent. Sales and marketing costs in that year equaled 25 percent of all sales.

In another case Ford, which slowed its research and development spending in 1990, said in its annual report for that year, "The competition for market share flowing from overcapacity constrains normal pricing for products and lowers profit margins. Margins are further reduced by higher marketing costs to cover sales incentives and low financing rates. For example, since 1988 Ford's marketing costs in North America have nearly doubled."

Dozens of R&D studies have been published demonstrating that research expenditures fell faster than development costs. The National Science Foundation discovered that overall research expenditures were even lower than most studies showed, explaining that U.S. expenditures for research were boosted by the huge amount foreign companies were spending for research in the United States.[7]

"rejuvenated" products that had become nearly defunct, using huge amounts of advertising to sell them. Himmel brought back Compoz sleeping pills, Psorex dandruff shampoo, and Porcelana fade cream, but his true successes were Ayds for dieters, Doan's Pills, and Lavoris mouthwash. According to his obituary (*New York Times,* November 26, 1991), Himmel said he spent fully 50 percent of his gross revenues on advertising, claiming "it created cash, which bought more ads, which created more cash."

Danny Abraham, who previously owned Dexatrim, now runs a more profitable weight reduction business, Slim-Fast. *Forbes* magazine (December 9, 1991) said, "If Abraham is unwilling to tie up capital in manufacturing, he is lavish with money for advertising and promotion. In 1990 he spent around $100 million promoting Slim-Fast and a new thicker shake with extra fiber called Ultra Slim-Fast—about 15% of sales (at retail)—much of it in high-profile television campaigns."

6   In colonial America the gentry assumed they had to live luxuriously to provide work for tradesmen and others who did not own land, but noblesse oblige is no longer a factor in the United States; the rich tend to be social and economic conservatives.

7   The National Science Foundation estimated that 13 percent of the money spent on

If there was any doubt about the relative positions of the United States and foreign companies on the subject of research, Fujitsu cleared it away. On December 16, 1991, the Japanese maker of computers and communications hardware boasted in a full-page advertisement in the *Wall Street Journal,* "This year we'll spend more on R&D than most of the Fortune 500 will make in sales." Fujitsu had reason to brag. The preceding year, *Business Week* noted, AT&T cut research and development spending by 8 percent and IBM by 6 percent. Adjusted for 5 percent inflation, the declines amounted to 13 percent and 11 percent, respectively. "Once again," *Business Week* commented in its 1991 "Quality" issue, "overseas rivals outpaced the U.S. in [R&D] spending growth."

According to the National Science Board's 1992 report on research, the trend of falling R&D budgets began at the height of the Reagan era boom in stock and real estate prices. The rate of annual increase in R&D spending, adjusted for inflation, was 6.9 percent between 1980 and 1985. During the next five years it fell to only 1.2 percent. As a percentage of gross national product, the National Science Foundation reported, U.S. nondefense spending was slightly less than 2 percent in 1989, while the Japanese had passed the 3 percent mark.

Moreover, the percentage of R&D money going to research rather than to development in the United States, which is very difficult to gauge, had fallen, according to most estimates. Line extensions replaced new products; engineering replaced research. In a market-driven economy, as opposed to an economy based on the vast increases in wealth that can be created by invention, research had less and less place.

From 1988 to 1991 business investment in the United States averaged 11 percent of the gross domestic product (GDP), according to *Business Week* (April 18, 1994). Over the same period, Japan invested 20 percent of its GDP. By the end of 1994, the magazine estimated, with obvious pleasure, the gap would have narrowed to 12.5 percent for the United States compared with 17 percent for Japan, which was in deep recession.

C. The Keynesian Orgy

There is no need to repeat here the litany on debt spending used by the United States to keep its economy vital and its citizens feeling prosperous during the last quarter of a century and especially during the eighties and

industrial research in the United States in 1989 was for work done here by foreign companies. The dollar amount of foreign research in the United States that year was 10.3 billion.

early nineties. Reagan and Bush used up the credit line, and then some. John Maynard Keynes, on whom all blame for deficit spending is heaped, surely never imagined a debt spree like the one engaged in by Reagan and Bush. No prescription for curing the results of the ailment exists, nor is it even known for certain whether a nation can recover from such an enormous debt without some major disruption to its social and political fabric.

D. *Inability to Raise Prices*

An oversold economy faces the problem of demand standing still or falling slightly, which means that the intersection of price and demand comes either at the same or at a lower price. For U.S. companies the competition from overseas has lowered demand for their products much further. In the auto industry, for example, transaction prices fell precipitously when rebates, interest rates below market, extended warrantees, and so on are deducted from the selling price.

The advertising industry, which profited by being the instrument of overselling, saw the end of price increases in its own business at the end of the 1970s, as commissions were cut by many major advertisers and abolished completely by others. But the industry refused to apply its own experience to the economy as a whole, or even to its own clients. It held on to the idea of the ability of the salesmen to regulate demand, largely through branding, the attachment of certain information to a single brand as opposed to a commodity.

In a book written in 1989 and reprinted in 1990, *The Value Side of Productivity,* the American Association of Advertising Agencies wrote,

> A brand's image or franchise is reinforced by usage, experience, its pricing, distribution, and packaging.
> Here's a box. Doesn't mean much, does it, until we put three letters on it—IBM. Now, even if you don't know what's inside you know that the item is well made, it can be serviced or replaced easily, it's reliable, it's been well thought through, and best of all you won't be fired for buying it! A brand image at work!

At the time, the company's stock was selling for about $140 a share, and it stood as a genuine American industrial colossus. Only three years later, the stock was selling for $42 a share, the chairman of the company had resigned, and huge layoffs, plant closings, and organizational changes were implemented in an attempt to save the corporation.

IBM had oversold its customers in every imaginable way. It had in-duced small customers to pay too much for machines that offered little more than those three letters, and it had convinced large customers to buy hor-rendously expensive mainframe computers when the same work could be done by several smaller, much less expensive linked computers. As early as the mid-1970s, the marketing director of Sperry-Rand had learned of IBM's propensity to oversell its customers. He described pharmacies in small towns in the South that owned huge IBM computers to do the work of a logbook and prescription file. Although Sperry did not have the resources to make a run at IBM, others did, especially the Japanese. In an oversold market the leading overseller, IBM, could not maintain its prices, let alone raise them.

P&G faced the inability to raise prices at the end of 1991. Having spent years trying to use coupons to force distribution and sales that could not be accomplished through advertising or the use of hardball selling techniques, discounting, and case allowances to get fronts and dump bins and end aisle displays for its less popular products, P&G took to cutting prices. Durk Jager, a P&G executive vice president, told the *Wall Street Journal,* "If our pricing strategy calls for parity pricing on certain brands, we'll obviously execute it." He went on to explain that P&G was cutting back on promotional spending in order to lower prices.[8] Jager said nothing about the corollary to a company's inability to raise prices; P&G waited a full year before announcing plans to close plants and reduce employment around the world even though the company showed a large profit on its balance sheet.

P&G is not a charming company, nor is it often pleasant to do busi-ness with it, either as a customer or as a supplier, but no one has ever accused Procter & Gamble of stupidity. The company apparently recog-nized that its markets had been oversold, and responded with its usual icy rationality.

E. Limited Growth

The oversold condition of the market, the cautious nature of the culture, the failure to produce major inventions, and stagnation of income, population, and employment make the growth of mature industries almost

[8]   November 7, 1991.

impossible. Most businesses have no way to move beyond the replacement level in an oversold market. And they must struggle to maintain even that state of equilibrium with tepid demand.

After the automobile industry sold the idea of the two-car family in the United States, it saw the possibilities for growth in the three-car family, which its marketers believed would comprise either cars for the husband, wife, and child or a third vehicle devoted to recreational purposes. As it turned out, planned obsolescence could not sustain demand; after overselling the market for nearly twenty years, the auto industry could not even maintain the replacement level of the two-car family. The business cycle was sure to give it a brief burst of sales here and there as many old cars simply wore out and had to be replaced, but the auto industry was unlikely ever to return to its former size and rate of growth.

Although the car business was among the first to learn the lesson of laissez-faire economics, that no man can use more than one toilet at a time, other industries geared to growth soon followed. The makers of computers and other electronic office equipment have, at this writing, just encountered the wall of the oversold market. Many of them, including Apple, have announced layoffs, closings, and lowered expectations.

Rather than admitting to expectations of economic growth only slightly ahead of population growth, the salesmen—including most business and financial writers and the authors of those books that predict the future several years after it has come about—have deformed the language again, this time with a grab bag of words beginning with the Latin prefix *re* (meaning "anew" or "again"), as in reinvent, reengineer, and restructure.

F. Shrinking

Businesses go through a period of trying to raise profits through efficiency, because they cannot raise prices or increase sales. Greater efficiency is the obvious answer to the dilemmas of an oversold economy, but businesses would have increased efficiency in the past, if they had known how. There is nothing left for them to do but lay off people and close plants, desperate moves known for the sake of morale and the stock market as reengineering or reinventing the corporation.

The pattern is made of a thousand instances: Procter & Gamble closes plants around the world and lays off thousands in a market infiltrated by cheap store brands. Employment at General Motors falls from over a million to less than 700,000. Anheuser-Busch, plagued by low-cost competitors, complains about increased taxes on beer and announces that it is increasing its marketing budget and laying off 10 percent of its salaried employees. IBM cuts its work force by 30,000, then 10,000 more, and still more to come. Independent sales representatives suffer huge cutbacks and dismissals because they can be terminated on thirty days' notice, with no severance pay. A report from the American Management Association for the year ending in June 1993 says the cutbacks will continue unabated for at least another year. Many businesses, having learned the cost of laying off full-time employees, begin hiring temporary workers. In 1993 the average workweek in America hits a record high as employers find it is less costly to pay overtime than to hire additional workers.

The big question for companies doing business in an oversold economy is whether to cut costs while the business is still profitable, like P&G and AT&T, or to wait, like GM and IBM, until cost cutting becomes a matter of survival. More and more companies cut costs sooner rather than later, hoping to avoid the drastic measures of depression economics. But the cost of reengineering is very high; severance packages and all the other costs associated with closing plants can amount to billions of dollars.

Fewer people and plants do not necessarily produce true increases in productivity, either. After a wave of massive layoffs in 1993, there was a sudden increase in productivity in the United States.[9] Makers of end products also learned to simulate real increases in productivity by forcing cost reductions on their suppliers, who in turn forced cost reductions on their suppliers. Many employers negotiated more advantageous labor agreements. Only a few corporations demonstrated new production techniques that markedly increased efficiency and output. As corporations lay off people and cut benefits, phantom increases in productivity continue, but in an oversold economy nothing really gets better; the economy stumbles back toward equilibrium through attrition.

The people who retire early or get fired become the permanently oversold. Even if they find work again, they are destined to suffer a lifetime of economic regret and anxiety. And if they have no luck, and find only

---

[9] More than 200,000 jobs were cut by only ten large companies: General Motors, Sears, Roebuck, Boeing, Philip Morris, Procter & Gamble, Martin Marietta, Xerox, U.S. West, Pratt & Whitney, and RJR Nabisco. American Airlines, IBM, and others also announced cuts to be carried out over several years. Challenger, Gray & Christmas, a Chicago-based outplacement company, reported 192,572 people laid off in the first quarter of 1994, the highest first-quarter total since 1989.

part-time or low-paying work or no work at all, they will be regretful, anxious, and broke.

G. Political Struggle

An excruciating decline eventually culminates in a political struggle between the Promethean and the market-driven forces.

The oversold economy suffers from weariness; its desires have been exhausted, as well as its credit. The economic regret woven through the population is accompanied by awareness of the salesman's role in creating national and personal indebtedness, the waste of resources and élan in useless consumption. No cataclysm occurs, but the mood of regret is finally not acceptable in the United States, for the national character was formed—and still quite recently—by optimists: boosters, tinkerers, soldiers, merchants, salesmen, and more than a few geniuses.

At some time in the future, the people comprehend the economic and psychological forces of an oversold economy, and demand a remedy. Two powerful forces then compete for the right to return the mood of the country to optimism: One group, calling itself the party of the people, argues that the market must determine everything. The other group, the party of progress, contends that the nation must be led by the genius of invention. The contest has a uniquely American character, resembling the conflict between Jeffersonians and Jacksonians rather than that between socialists and capitalists.

A third group, the free traders, contends that the solution lies in expanded trade, largely with developing economies. The assumption of this group, that the historical pattern of exploitation will be repeated, proves false. After a brief success, the developing economies begin to take as much as they give, perhaps even a bit more. Once the free-trade solution fails, the contest between the marketers and the inventors intensifies.

During such a struggle, both sides employ the best salesmen they can find. As their main contribution, the salesmen deform the language: Those who work for the marketers give conformity the name of prudence; among the inventors risk is called conviction. All the while, the median age of the population continues to rise, which means the outcome of the struggle depends neither on economics nor on politics but on the resilience of the human spirit. No one knows what will happen under those conditions, since no one can predict the duration of economic regret, but in America the odds still favor a rebirth of enterprise and dreaming, if the citizens are able at this late stage to transform the nature of their dreams.

PART
3

In America,

whoever is not a salesman

lives alone.

12

Transactional Man

. . . the development of commercial society . . . , with the triumphal victory of exchange value over use value, first introduced the principle of interchangeability, then the relativization, and finally the devaluation of all values.

—Hannah Arendt

He had a fat, pimply face, and he carried a small pistol in the right front pocket of his raincoat whenever he went up to New York City. He was not a bigot, and he was not frightened, but he knew something about the city from having lived there as a young man, and he did not want to be defenseless in the streets.

On this trip he planned to stay for only a few days before continuing on to Africa, the Middle East, and the Pacific Rim countries, the Tigers. It was to be a very long trip, fraught with political and linguistic difficulties, perhaps some physical danger, and he did not relish the idea of having to leave the pistol in the company apartment in United Nations Plaza.

Before he left home, his wife fixed him a dinner of chicken gizzards, mashed potatoes, and greens, and offered to have sex with him in his favorite way, even though it was not pleasing to her. He ate the gizzards and greens and took full advantage of his wife's offer.

Later, before he went to sleep, she warned him about AIDS in Africa and venereal diseases in Asia. He told her she left him no choice but to make a pig of himself in Tel Aviv. She missed the joke, but he let it pass without trying to explain. After nearly fifteen years, he was used to everything about her but the way she still put her hair up in curlers and wrapped her head in toilet paper. When she got herself up that way on his last night at home before the trip, he just giggled, and said, "Damn! You look like a fool from the planet Pluto!"

It was late afternoon when the car picked him up at the airport and drove him to United Nations Plaza. He showered, fixed himself a drink, and sat down on the couch that faced east overlooking the river. On every coffee table, night table, occasional table, and end table, even on the breakfast room table, there was a package of one of the company's brands, cork tip, filter, straight, short, king-size, slim, or one of the targeted brands for women.

He chose the old brand, the original. The package touched his memory. As a boy growing up on the edge of tobacco country, he had been in awe of the company's buyers. They were always big men, like hunters or sheriff's deputies; straight men, like ten-penny nails. He had seen how one of them punished a mean dog. The man caught it in the belly with the steel toe of his work shoe, then stomped it until the dog split open. It was a big dog, bigger than a hound, and it died with a little squeal, like a puppy. When the tobacco man was done with the dog, he walked over to some high grass near a fence and wiped the blood from his shoe; then he took out a pack of the company's famous brand, wet the end, and lit up. The tobacco buyer never glanced back at the dog, which looked to the boy like one of the animals he had seen lying by the side of the state highway.

Now the boy had become the tobacco man, vice president of the company. He had gone to the University of North Carolina, then New York City, and home again. But first, one summer, he had sold term insurance house to house. A crew leader dropped them off one by one in a North Carolina town, nothing half so big or fancy as Asheville, just one damn town or another, all the same, one as poor as the next; dropped them off with empty pockets and nothing to eat or drink; not shit, not nothing, not even a goddamn dime to buy something in a store so's they'd let a boy take a piss indoors. And the dogs, the goddamn dogs! If only he'd had the pistol in his pocket in North Carolina! The sun was so hot some summer afternoons, it could have been Nigeria. And the damn dogs everywhere. Why would a decent God-fearing woman home alone with her kids and woes buy a term insurance policy from a college boy with pimples and wornout shoes?

He sold nothing for ten days. The leader called him a damn fool, a country boy, a farmer, a pussy, a cornholer, and a cocksucker and every other name he could think of. Then one afternoon, standing in the kitchen part of a two-room tarpaper and green pine shack, the boy talked to a great big woman about love instead of death; he put security into her enormous strawberry red hands, and then she took to him, she loved him, she remembered to him how her daddy died, and what they all suffered, and how she had sworn on an old white leather-covered Bible that she would never do her children that way. She would have bought anything from him.

After that he never mentioned death again. He did not believe in death. Even now he carried a pistol in his pocket to ward off death.

He opened the package of shorts, took out a cigarette, and wet the end, like an old country boy, before he put it in the corner of his mouth. The flavor of the tobacco was good, but it seemed a little dry to him; it burned too hot. He wondered how long the package had been lying there on the coffee table. Sales figures showed that very few people smoked shorts anymore, even in the South. He questioned the numbers. How did they show up in real life? A picture formed in his mind of an old deputy sheriff, big damn pistola on his hip, wearing a straw hat turned down in the back to keep the sun off his neck and smoking a king-size filtered cigarette. It made him laugh.

While waiting for the last dampness of the shower to evaporate, he wore nothing but Jockey shorts and a T-shirt. His bare feet rested on the cocktail table. The toes were straight, but his skin was very white and often cold to the touch. The toenails curled severely at the ends, making them difficult to trim. He knew the meaning of the signs. Some was folklore, some was science. The sight of his toes translated into a tremor of unease in his bowel. He wished he had put on a pair of socks or slippers.

A call from the concierge desk interrupted; a messenger was coming up. He put out the cigarette, and went to the bathroom to get one of the terrycloth robes. The delivery was of marketing material to prepare him for the African leg of the trip. He went back to his place on the couch, and settled in to read. As he looked down at the folders in his lap, he could not help noticing the bulge of his belly. Not good, he thought, not in combination with the marmoreal toes, the dead man's toes.

He opened the first folder. He and his staff had targeted Nigeria. While they all but controlled the market for high-quality cigarettes consumed by Europeans and a few cosmopolitan Nigerians, they had less than 10 percent penetration of the market for low-price product, sweepings. He smiled. The chemically rich sweepings couldn't be sold in the United States; virtually everything sold in the Third World was get-rich-quick money, added at the margin. But there was a catch.

As a market, Nigeria presented a problem the industry hadn't seen in the United States for generations: Most Nigerians had never smoked a cigarette.

He turned himself around on the couch, put his head against the soft, padded arm, and got his feet up. The robe fell open, displaying the white legs and dead man's toes. It always surprised him that the hair had fallen off his legs. He began reading a presentation from the Nigerian advertising agency recently affiliated with the company's main U.S. agency. It was entitled "Trialing: A New Approach to the Nigerian Market."

Page after page detailed the problems of teaching Nigerians to smoke: Cost. Disposable income. Culture. Communications. Islam. Ibos as a separate social and cultural group. Cigarette lighters. Matches. Ashtrays. Multiple problems of smoking among barefoot people. Flammability of wood and thatch dwellings and furnishings.

There were many photographs of native Nigerians. Some were scarified. Others leered at the camera. To illustrate the difficulty of installing vending machines, there were many photographs of back-street taverns, whorehouses, and workmen's hangouts. He thought of the pistol. He could tell the Nigerian ad agency that he needed a pistol. They would get one for him; after all, he was their client, potentially their biggest client. Why the hell shouldn't a man carry a pistol in a country where half the damned population didn't have a mailing address and the other half couldn't read what came in the mail?

Nigeria! The speed of his heart changed. It was the excitement, he thought, the anticipation of triumph. He would march on that country like a Roman legion; he would step to the sound of a mechanical drum. His heart beat faster, out of control, like a lion running. He could not stop. He came fully conscious, frightened. To end the moment, to slow his heart, he relaxed the muscles of his neck, and let his head fall back onto the heavily upholstered arm of the couch. The papers tumbled onto his belly. His hands tingled. The robe and the T-shirt lay oppressively on his chest; they were a weight on his heart. He breathed heavily, as if he were fleeing down a back street in Lagos. It was night. There were coruscations in the air. Fireflies. Everything was made of thatch. Trees covered over the narrow roadway, the trail, the passage into darkness. He strangled in a sigh. The pistol was in his hand.

1.

Interview with Chris Calhoun

My favorite salespeople are like the flamboyant attorneys who, with another slight tick of the dice, would have been actors. They view the customer as a sucker, absolute sucker. They're getting over. Yeah, getting over, putting one over on them. They don't have to sell anything, or even make any money; the motivation is just the sell in itself. I mean, it's just the getting-over part.

It's very much like car salesmen that I've known. The person that they really wanted to sell was not the guy who came in deliberately looking for the brand new Caddy, even though that was the best commission. The most fun to sell was somebody who'd taken the wrong turn on the freeway and was going in there to turn around.

Even if they bought a thousand-dollar car, it was much more fun to sell that person. That's really getting over. The person was lost, had no idea they were shopping for a car, turned in there by mistake, and they left buying a car. This guy made seventy-five bucks, but he's got a story, he's on a high that cannot be matched. That guy really got over.

Getting over. I don't know if it's a sales thing. Getting over, put one over. Bluffing his way into a club, getting on a plane with no ticket . . . he got over, you know. For a lot of the people that's the real high.

I'm not of the school that these corporate psychologists go to; they're instilling something phony. The real sales motivators today, these psychologists that go out and speak to IBM salespeople or Met Life, they have to make people believe. There's a great deal of guilt that these salespeople have. They do get jazzed, but they're not open enough about it; they're not deliberately going out to get high. They do get excited about the sale, but at the end of the day the majority of the people come back and say, "That guy didn't really need another insurance policy. He's maxed out. What I sold him, he's gonna be paying a premium on, and his extra benefits are infinitesimal."

There's a certain type of salesman that's not troubled by that, is excited by that, that he went back one more time and got blood out of a stone, sold something they just didn't absolutely need. Now, you're supposed to do that. All salespeople are supposed to do that.

Interview with Eileen Bresnahan

I think you have to be pretty scrupulous about the way you run your business, because a middleman is not the cat's meow. A forked tongue! One thing I've always applauded myself for is not becoming sleazoid, because it is very easy; the corruption factor is definitely there. There are a lot of defective personalities in the garment business, a lot of curious egos.

When I first became a textile broker, I used to joke that I was fascinated by how people slid around on the ground with no legs. I was interested in these creatures, because I came from a world where mercantile was not in my vocabulary. My mother's family were farmers. My father's father was a barber. After a very minor publishing experience, I thought, at least I'm getting to see a little of human nature in action. These people were gritty, yes, very gritty, but some of them are incredibly interesting.

I'm not defined by my work. It defines me in terms of my time. It defines me in terms of what I think about when I wake up in the middle of the night. I have to have a different approach based on the personality of the person I'm dealing with. I cannot be the person that I generally am, pretty much unedited, and sometimes boisterous and a little sarcastic. I have to be very careful. I'm not creating multiple personalities, but you have to be considerate of the kind of personality you're dealing with.

Interview with Roger B. Smith

I remember as I child I had one of those red velvet autograph books, and you took them around and you got your favorite teacher to write something in it. And your best pals and the little girlfriends all wrote something in it: Roses are red, violets are blue, like that. I remember my father wrote something in mine. He said, "Personality and brains have to be marketed for you to get anywhere. Your job through life will be to be a salesman." And you know, I looked at that and I thought, "Oh, hell, it doesn't even rhyme. Oh, Dad!"

Never showed that to anybody. I think I left it in the back part of the book. You know, it took me a while to figure out what he was saying.

I'm serious when I say, "Everybody has to be a salesman." You don't get people to go along with your ideas, you can't be a leader without being a salesman. The chairman's got to sell the board on his ideas; the union leader's got to sell the employees on the idea of giving up a day's wages a year for what he gets in return for belonging to the union.

But let me give you an example I know. A young fellow I was talking to the other day, he is selling California Closets. These people come in and they partition off this and put a few drawers here, so you hang all your suits up here, your long stuff here; you got socks in drawers. It's really a very good thing.

He was telling me he advertises, he goes in home builder shows, he's in the phone book, there's word of mouth, five or six ways he gets leads. People call up and say, "Hey, I saw your ad in Sunday's paper and, boy, it's just what I need. Could you have your designer (that's what they call them) come out and design a California Closet for my home?"

Now, here these leads are, coming in twenty, thirty a day, and this young man's got five women. Now, here's the gamut: He's got this one over here, he calls her a lead-eater. She goes out and she closes 20 percent of her leads—they're all random out of a box—and on this end over here, he's got what he calls a winner. She gets her leads out of the same box as this gal, and she closes 80 percent of her deals.

His problem is it costs him, let's say, two hundred bucks worth of advertising to get a lead. Well, this lead-eater is killing him, right? What he wants, he wants to get rid of her and get this winner over here—see?—that's closing 80 percent of the deals. And I say, "Look, is one tall and one skinny and one a gorgeous blonde with big hooters or something?"

He said, "No, you couldn't tell the two apart walking through a door."

I said, "Well, what is it that makes this gal a super salesman and this gal no good?"

He said, "Damned if I know. I tried to tell this gal to be more aggressive, and she gets thrown out of the house. This gal over here, I've been with her, I don't know what happens, but all of a sudden we go out, we get the orders. She closes that deal."

Now, there's people just like that in car sales. You go to any dealership, you'll find their lead salesman, he doesn't get any more leads than the worst guy, but he closes, he's got that salesman's ability to find out what is it that'll make Earl Shorris buy the car.

I'll tell you what I think, but I really don't know. I think what happens is they're able to present their case in such a way that they convince the guy that, number one, he needs the product and, number two, that this product is a good value. But more, the thing is that now is the time for him to make the decision. And I think it's that last thing, the closer, where you say to him, "Lookit, if you sign up now, I can give you a hundred-dollar discount today, but only today. Tomorrow I can't give you the discount. Earl, you look to me like the kind of guy I can really talk to, and I want to tell you, this is a deal, this is a real . . ."

So, I think they size up their people, and say, "Look at that guy's red tie. I wonder what that means. It means he's aggressive, so maybe he wants to be challenged."

So, I say, "Earl, you can't beat this deal. I've got a deal for you here, you can shop all over and if you find a better way to get this, I will personally give you fifty dollars out of my own pocket."

Or they look at you and they say, "This guy, that won't hit him, he'll go out and buy somebody else's car and I'll have to pay him fifty dollars."

See, they're able to analyze what it is by talking to people that finds their little linchpin. And I don't think they could do this if they came in and you never opened your mouth, but just listened, see? They have to converse with you well enough to size you up and know where your button is. And they've got to push that button to get you to do it.

I'm going back to the California Closet girl. I don't think this gal is able to size up the people to know what makes them tick, to understand what it is that will make that person say yes. And I think this gal here, the 80 percent, when she's talking to people, she analyzes them, she figures out, maybe she goes right away and says, "Hey, this guy's not gonna do anything without talking to his wife. I'm wasting my time. Or Boy! I know what it's gonna take this guy: He's stuck on the price. A hundred bucks'll get him. I'll give it to him. And close the deal. Or this guy isn't real sure that this is good quality. I'll give you a three-year written guarantee to show you this thing is really good. No extra cost!"

They know what it takes to come across and get that thing done. It's the deal, yes. The sizing up, though, what it takes to get that button pushed; everybody does that. You got to know what it takes to get him to buy into something.

2.

William Barrett had just completed *The Illusion of Technique* when we first talked about business and technology.[1] He was sixty-five years old, and it had been a long time since his famous work, *Irrational Man*. He said in the new book that rocks, trees, home, the eyes of his aged dog, loss, and the likelihood of death instructed him: Questions about God and freedom in a man-made world were on his mind. Like many philosophers, he was concerned mainly with negative freedom, freedom from. *The Illusion of Technique*, published in 1978, ends with Barrett's fears for China and what was then the Soviet Union.

In Barrett's view, Being and technology battled for supremacy. He wrote at length of Heidegger, for whom technology destroyed Being, man's connection to nature. But when we talked, Barrett had no doubt that man would continue to accept technology and allow himself to be ruled by it. That was the way of the world to him; he made an observer's concessions to what he considered practical life.

Unless I misunderstood our conversations, Barrett no longer believed that an individual could or should overcome the coercive force of economic organization; he had abandoned such dreams of freedom; the technology he accepted included the one known as management. Late-twentieth-century capitalism, in his view, was about as good as the real world was going to get. Like many deists, he poured himself a drink, and hunkered down in sorrows and existential loneliness to await the end.

Twenty years earlier, in 1958, Barrett had joined Mary McCarthy and W. H. Auden in praising *The Human Condition,* a new work by their friend Hannah Arendt. Barrett and Arendt were only acquaintances, but they had philosophical connections through their interest in Kant and Heidegger. Arendt looked back from Heidegger to the classics and politics. Barrett looked forward, concentrating more on technological thinking and ontology. Totalitarianism concerned them both.

[1] Barrett was part of a project I had organized to develop an interdisciplinary appraisal of the future of nuclear power in the United States. The project was funded by the Edison Electric Institute. Among the other participants were Richard Cloward and Frances Fox Piven, sociologists; Gloria Levitas, an anthropologist; Andrew Hacker, a demographer; Arnold Rogow, a lay analyst; and Herbert Gans, another sociologist. Although we had this business together, Barrett and I began our conversations as writers do, in the mire of gossip, for we were then both published by Loretta Barrett (no relation) at Anchor Press. Since he and I liked and admired Loretta, it was a nice beginning.

The great difference between them was that Arendt, a Jew who escaped from Germany before World War II, still had faith in what she called "the *vita activa*," by which she meant direct activity between human beings "without the intermediary of things or matter." This plurality, she said, is *"the* condition . . . of all political life." She closed *The Human Condition,* her book on the *vita activa,* with a sentence from Cato, "Never is he more active than when he does nothing, never is he less alone than when he is by himself." To Arendt, as to Cato, thinking was action.

By 1986 the author of *The Illusion of Technique* had moved deep into pessimism. His new book was called *Death of the Soul: From Descartes to the Computer,* and he ended it with this gloss on Scripture: "What shall it profit a whole civilization, or culture, if it gains knowledge and power over the material world, but loses any adequate idea of the conscious mind, the human self, at the center of all that power?"

It was the same question Arendt had asked in 1958, but the mood had undergone a remarkable shift. Had the world changed so much between 1958 and 1986? To move from Arendt's neoclassical faith in politics and thinking to Barrett's sense of consciousness lost betokens a great decline in human self-esteem. Was it warranted? Was this expression of the aging of a man the exact analogue of an economy in its late maturity? And if the shift of mood was warranted, was God, politics, or technology the cause?

The self-image of man at this stage in history and pluralism will never again be complete in simple, for the mirror in which the species sees itself has curious properties. Nothing that has ever been reflected on its surface disappears—and I am speaking not of history but of what is alive in the world now. Each image appears atop all the others, like so many transparencies piled upon the light of the mind. One seems always to be foremost, brighter than the last and all the images that went before, but not alone. A picture of this progression cannot be drawn, but it has been imagined, it can be told.

Since the stages are well known, I will review them very briefly:

Primitive Man

At first, man could not distinguish himself from the world. He was like sunrise or a tree, for the world seemed to him a circle, continuous and inclusive. We call such thinkers primitive, and we separate them from ourselves by their inability to write, which limits memory, but not mind. History has little importance and immortality is beside the point in a circular conception of the world: Whatever happens happened before and will happen again.

Homo Religiosus[2]

With *homo religiosus*, man becomes immortal; that is the "glad tidings" of Christianity. The concept is less clear in Judaism, more certain in Islam, subject to elegant variations among Buddhists. Kant's three questions—What can I know? What ought I to do? What may I hope?—are answered for *homo religiosus* by the teachings of his religion, which are enforced by the varieties of immortality—paradise, hell, and so on.[3]

Homo Sapiens

The religion of ancient Greece did not answer Kant's questions well enough to satisfy the people. For one thing, the gods had too many human qualities; they couldn't be trusted. This failure of religion left the Greeks in a quandary, because they had already been separated from the rest of the world by their sense of wonder; a primitive world view was no longer possible for them. They had to find an alternative way to live. Philosophy provided the answer. Thinking in the classical world turned on the struggle to find a secular way to deal with questions of epistemology, ethics, and ontology.

Homo Faber

After the epistemological and theological battles of the Renaissance had been fought and won largely by the scientific point of view, the Enlight-

---

[2] I have followed the tradition of describing these reflections in mock-Latin phrases. It's a handy way to deal with the question of names for them, but the practice should not be understood to place the reflections or the naming of them in time. *Homo faber* and *animal laborans* both belong to the nineteenth century, yet the activities existed long before.

[3] Karl Jaspers noted that Kant asked a fourth question—What is man?—in two passages. Paraphrasing Kant, he wrote, "Fundamentally, one might subsume the first three questions under the last. The fourth question . . . means that Kant does not start from God, being, the world, the object, the subject, but from man, for man is the area in which all the rest become reality for us." Karl Jaspers, *The Great Philosophers,* ed. Hannah Arendt, trans. Ralph Manheim, vol. 1 (New York: Harcourt, Brace & World, 1962), p. 92.

enment reconsidered man and discovered the toolmaker. For the first time, man did not see himself as a part of the world or even as a response to the world; *homo faber* is the inventor, the one who uses the natural world as raw material from which to make a new world of his own design. He is not immortal, but his creations may last forever.

Among the tools made by *homo faber* are language and logic. That is why *craftsman* does not serve as a translation of *homo faber*. Craftsmen use tools; *homo faber* makes tools. The extent of his influence is therefore limitless: Tools can be used to make tools that make tools, extending the reach of *homo faber* with each new iteration, until he uses the entire world. That is what Heidegger meant when he said technology holds the world in standing reserve.

Only one of Kant's questions interests *homo faber:* What can I know? He answers with Cartesian method, which enables him to design the repetitive certainties of technology. The other questions do not engage the toolmaker: He does not care about what he ought to do, because he is obsessed by the question of what he is able to do. As for ontology, it does not interest him either, because it applies to nature, the raw material for *homo faber;* his world begins as the natural world ends.[4]

Animal Laborans

Meanwhile, man does not grow like the grass or sit like a stone; he lives. And the curse of Eden, as promised, describes the nature of his life; he toils. This creature who lives by toil, *animal laborans,* was described by Marx in his *Economic and Philosophical Manuscripts:*

> His work is not voluntary but imposed, *forced labor*. It is not the satisfaction of a need, but only a *means* for satisfying other needs. Its

---

[4] Henri Bergson, who is credited with having coined the term *homo faber,* argued that intellect is practical, not speculative. He carried this notion very far in *The Creative Mind,* in which he said that the intellect breaks the world down into its constituent parts. The theory worked easily enough for static objects, but he had a problem with motion. His answer for that was a cinematographic technique of the mind, like the film technique (of Muybridge) in which motion is broken down into its parts, with each part shown on a separate frame.

The comparison to the methods of modern technology is unavoidable. In fact, Bergson said that the best way to understand the human intellect is to look at the great success of technology.

To deal with human values, which lay outside his definition of the intellect, Bergson turned to mysticism.

alien character is clearly shown by the fact that as soon as there is no physical or other compulsion it is avoided like a plague. . . .

We arrive at the result that man (the worker) feels himself to be freely active only in his animal functions—eating, drinking and procreating, or at most also in his dwelling and in personal adornment—while in his human functions he is reduced to an animal. The animal becomes human and the human becomes animal.[5]

The view of man as a laboring animal grew out of Marx's reading about the conditions of factory work in nineteenth-century England, conditions created by *homo faber,* whose tools built and organized the factories that alienated man from his labor. In that sense, *animal laborans* was the creation of *homo faber,* like any other tool. Feuerbach's answer to this desperate, dying life, his "philosophy of the future," was a new form of immortality, the limitless future of the species-being; man had only to submerge his own desires and ambitions in the community of men, and he would live forever. Marx agreed, and carried the idea forward.

But the man who saw himself as Marx's *animal laborans* could not really hope to control his own life, to have a sense of ethics. As *animal laborans* he could know nothing other than pain and animal urges; he became the consumer, the one who could not tolerate discomfort or stop eating. Ethical and ontological questions could be answered only by giving himself up to his species. In the terminology of existentialism: If he wished to be, he had to abandon the uniqueness of his being (by merging with the species).

Never before in history, not even in the world of the primitive mind (to which Marx related *animal laborans* by depriving him of the human sense of distinction from the rest of nature), had man been so meaningless a creature. Capitalism took everything human from him, using him as it used the ox of the field. But the value of his labor, multiplied by the technological triumphs of *homo faber,* could be converted into capital; there was at last in human history a true surplus of labor.

In the intersection of *homo faber* and *animal laborans,* enormous wealth was produced, but the majority of human beings had to be consigned to the life of *animal laborans.* They did not make tools, they served

---

[5] From *Karl Marx: The Essential Writings,* ed. Frederic L. Bender (New York: Harper & Row, 1972), p. 74.

---

as an adjunct to the toolmakers and the system of tools, technology; they were part of the standing reserve. The situation was not only morally unsatisfactory but contained within it, as Marx said, the seeds of its own destruction: overproduction, stockpiling, and economic collapse.

Of course, the system did not collapse—or, to give the Marxists the benefit of the doubt, has not yet collapsed. Some of the errors of distribution were corrected by unionization, others by the action of government in concert with industry, and yet others by the activities of salesmen.

The Great Depression very nearly caused the collapse of the system. And in the 1950s the Western nations once again faced the danger of overproduction, but this time the economies were rescued long before they reached the brink of collapse. The act of saving them produced a new concept of man, one whose influence was to grow immensely over the next half of the century, until it became the foremost concept of its time: *homo vendens, sales*man, the mediator.

Homo Vendens

The facts behind the concept of *homo vendens* may need to be rehearsed briefly here. Perhaps one comparison will serve. In 1993 the private U.S. business with the largest number of employees was still General Motors, but the business with the next greatest number was Wal-Mart. Moreover, General Motors was shrinking while Wal-Mart was growing. Since the late 1950s *homo vendens* had been increasing his dominance. By 1990 the contest was over; he had superseded the other conceptions of man.

Of course, selling did not begin after World War II, and mediation dates back to the earliest human ideas: the phrase *homo vendens,* like its predecessors, is intended to mark the enthroning rather than the beginning of a concept. In addition, the naming of the concept makes it easier to speak of.

In our time *homo vendens,* the *sales*man, has such a widely recognized influence on American society that the concept, although not the name, will seem familiar to many readers. The only difficulty might come from confusion generated by the attention paid again recently to the consumer society.[6] To help clarify the distinction: A mediator may be a consumer in other

---

[6] See, for example, Michael Schudson, *Advertising: The Uneasy Persuasion* (New York: Basic Books, 1984), and William Leach, *Land of Desire* (New York: Pantheon, 1993). See

phases of his life, but mediation is not consumption, just as it is not production.

Homo vendens is an outcome of his own history, the most recent creation of the toolmaker and his laborers. *Homo vendens* may hold some of the attitudes toward the world of his inventor, but he does not himself destroy and re-create the world. One must go back to the mediators of mythology, the coyote and the raven, those scavengers that eat flesh but do not kill, to be reminded of the essential difference between the salesman and the toolmaker. The toolmaker kills nature; the salesman works with the toolmaker's product. As a person, *homo vendens* must find ways other than those of the toolmaker to deal with epistemology, ethics, and ontology.

He bears more relation to *animal laborans,* but the salesman cannot, by definition, look forward to the Marxist communitarian solutions proposed for the laborer. The sense of an animal existence, the value of life itself over any action in life, including thought, informs the salesman, but does not define him. He covets his pleasures in an animalistic way, he is a consumer, but consumption according to his animal urges does not make a salesman of him.

The mastery of *homo faber* and his tools over things and other men, technology, made a salesman of man. His role in the cycle of production and consumption was to equalize the pace of the one with the other. Every time technology increased the pace of production, *homo vendens* had to increase the pace of consumption. In this role he suffers three forms of isolation: from other men, from meaning, and from history.

Isolation from Society

A mediator, by definition, may not belong to one side or the other. He neither makes nor buys goods or services. But this does not give him a political life. He cannot do politics, because he does not act directly with other human beings; "things or matter" always come between them. In other words, his actions in the world cannot ever be purely human. *Homo vendens* lives in the world with other men, but not among other men; he conceives of others as his business, he values them as his business; business is the matter between them. Today it is an automobile, tomorrow a dozen

---

also works by Christopher Lasch, the corporate authorship of *Habits of the Heart,* Michael Schudson's essay "Delectable Materialism," in *American Prospect,* no. 5 (spring 1991): 26–35, and so on.

oranges, the next day the laundering of a shirt or dress. Business is always about things, never about thinking, which cannot be manufactured or consumed; it is never so purely human that it can be political.

When *homo vendens* executes his function in the world, he maintains his distance from those in the current transaction and all future transactions. The agonistic character of selling contributes to his isolation: The salesman competes with the customer for control of information and desire, and he competes with all other salesmen for control of the customer's wealth and desires. Nothing is excluded from the contest: Books compete with bread, shoes compete with salt, restaurants contend with the rent, and in desperate situations the drugs that maintain life may take the place of dinner. Because he is a potential mediator in all of these contests, the salesman lives in isolation from his colleagues as well as from his customers.

The salesman hunts, and the hunter has no home, further isolating him from the political world, for politics, from the Greek *polis,* belongs to home, meaning not merely place but association. Without a home, a person has nothing to defend and no place in which to build. In that sense, every salesman is a traveling salesman, no matter where he is and with whom he fosters transactions.

Isolation from Meaning

In his role as mediator *homo vendens* facilitates exchanges by providing information that weds desire to things. Since he understands that the thing-in-itself cannot be known, he attempts to learn the mind of the customer, including the customer's desires. Once he understands the rules behind the customer's perception and appreciates his desires, the salesman conforms the information about the thing for sale to the customer's desire, and the transaction takes place. To do this successfully the salesman has to follow the disciplines of his calling: Primarily, he cannot make judgments.

To judge means to apply a set of standards to a thing or act, to value it. *Homo vendens* operates on the principle that all value is exchange value, and as such is set by the market, no one else. The market determines the value of time, not merely for *animal laborans* but for everyone. People trade most of their human life for food, shelter, and the trinkets of the dime-store culture. How much time for how many meals or geegaws, how many hours of happiness for how many T-shirts, compact discs, and frozen dinners, depends entirely upon the supply and demand of life and things. In the market anything may be exchanged for anything else, as long as a transaction price can be agreed upon. Neither the utility of the thing nor its other intrinsic qualities (beauty, durability, happiness, economy, healthfulness, and so on) can change the judgment of the market. Nothing has value in itself. If no one wanted to buy the *Mona Lisa,* it would not be worth a dime. If there were more than enough happiness to go around, the price of happiness would fall. Similarly, the Hope Diamond and the Taj Mahal. By the same reasoning, in a peaceful world weapons would be junk.

Surrounded by relative values, with no influence on the setting of those values, the salesman lives apart from the meaning of things and acts. After all, how can he know what something means if he cannot judge it, but must wait for others to do so, and then accept whatever they say as if he were a blank slate? Moreover, he must accept the judgment of the market as it happens: yes one day, no the next; good in the morning, bad in the evening. Even after it has been inscribed, the blank slate has no permanence; the judgments by which *homo vendens* lives change constantly. What meaning can be assigned them other than impermanence?

Condemned to endless and ever-changing tolerance, separated from judgment, *homo vendens* responds to relativism by negating all meaning. He has no choice, no other way to respond, for to accept meaning imposed by others, with no hope of affecting it, would be to live as an intellectual chattel, a slave to other men's opinions. Yet the salesman's alternative results in an equally inhuman condition: By denying the value of value, making everything relative, he reduces life to a process over which no one has control. Unlike the nihilists of the preceding century, the salesman does not conclude that everything is permitted; he sees everything as worthless—that is, what is done or not done has no importance.

Once he arrives at such a conclusion, *homo vendens* is set loose, not free, but disconnected, isolated. He suffers a loneliness unimaginable even to the nihilist, for the nihilist lived in response. He rejected something. Permission, even in the nihilist credo, must be granted, implying a judgment by some force, some group, some set of rules from which permission can be secured. In the world of *homo vendens,* permission no longer matters, transactions matter; nothing else on earth or in heaven, not love or money, nothing can truly be said to have value but the transaction itself.

Again, meaning has no place: How can the worth of a transaction be judged apart from what is transacted? How can an act have meaning if it has no content? And how can it have content if everything is interchangeable?

Homo vendens lives in a world in which all acts, as well as all things, have been emptied of content. Business demands it; transactions must not be impeded by the intrusion of meaning. Nothing can be allowed importance in his world other than the inconstant forces of the market, and the promiscuous will of desire. To do his business *homo vendens* must deny all that is authentic, intrinsic, meaningful. Once he has rid himself of those impediments, he can proceed to achieve the velocity required of a salesman in a nation of salesmen.

Isolation from Immortality

Since all value depends on the judgment of an inconstant market, transactions must take place in the instant of meeting among the desire of the customer, the information provided by the salesman, and the price set by the market. The transaction itself has no permanence, no moment; it is an occasion.

The parts of the occasion include the customer, the product or service, and the market (aggregate demand and supply, and so on); the salesman stands outside the occasion, vital to it, but not a participant in it. He cannot find an eternal home among his species, for he is an antagonist in their midst; he leaves no irreversible mark, either as a scar upon nature or as an unforgettable thing; and he cannot count himself among the gods. *Homo vendens* exists in the occasion of his work, and disappears; his death is in the doing. The product and the customer continue, but the occasion leaves no remains.

An utterly mortal man, without politics, *homo vendens* has nothing to guide him, either in this life or in the next. He lives apart from Kant's three questions for thinking; he sells.

13

The Moral Life of *Homo Vendens*

The characteristic doctrine was one, in fact, which left little room for religious teaching as to economic morality, because it anticipated the theory, later epitomized by Adam Smith in his famous reference to the invisible hand, which saw in economic self-interest the operation of a providential plan.

—R. H. TAWNEY, *Religion and the Rise of Capitalism*

A great man . . . rather lies than tells the truth; it requires more spirit and will. There is a solitude within him that is inaccessible to praise or blame, his own justice that is beyond appeal.

—NIETZSCHE, *The Will to Power*

A society . . . , whose members were unable to distinguish truthful messages from deceptive ones, would collapse.

—SISSELA BOK, *Lying*

She did not expect the job to go well. Nothing ever did. She was not lucky.

When the agent telephoned, and gave her the pitch, she thought for a moment that her luck had changed. It can happen. It happened to Herve Villechaise, and not for just a week or a year but for many years, until the suffering became unbearable, and he killed himself. She had pains too. A similar problem in the chest. When she had a cold, which seemed to be more often now, the coughing caused an ache that reached into her soul.

For that reason she asked the agent to write something in the contract about the costume. She didn't mind dressing as a potato—in fact, the idea appealed to her sense of theater—but she didn't want the weight of the costume to add to the strain on her lungs. The agent promised that it would weigh no more than five pounds, including the mechanism that controlled the eyes. So she went down to Philadelphia for the interview.

The man at the advertising agency looked normal enough, although he seemed to have too much white hair for such a young person, and he chewed incessantly on a wooden toothpick that he kept in the corner of his mouth, like a B-movie tought guy. She felt uncomfortable with him. Perhaps it was his height; he was very tall, like a basketball player, and his hips waggled when he walked. She wondered whether he was a pervert, and she asked herself whether that would be good or bad for getting the job.

Her first task, the advertising agency man explained, was to convince the sales force at the potato chip company that she could charm people in grocery stores by appearing in the guise of one of the cold-weather potatoes that made theirs the best-tasting, crispiest chips. If that meeting was successful, she would work in supermarkets around the East Coast, along with many other little people in potato costumes, promoting the chips made from cold-weather potatoes. It would provide steady work for months, perhaps years. And if the idea was successful, there was a shot at a television commercial.

She said it was a good offer and she was glad to have it. The tall man from the advertising agency said he thought she was cute, just right for his campaign, and he telephoned the costume company to come right over to the agency and measure her. She was paid four hundred dollars and expenses for each fitting.

While the costume was being made, the man from the advertising agency taught her what to say in her role as the cold-weather potato. She did not feel comfortable with the lines he wrote for her, but she did not complain. During her thirty-one years she had been forced to do many things to earn a living. But the man from the advertising agency gave her the creeps.

It made her laugh to think of him as strange, almost freakish. She was forty-three inches tall, with bandy legs, a bulging forehead, and a chest problem that was more difficult to live with every day. Yet, there was something worse, deeper, wrong with him. He was so nervous. If he touched her, even to shake hands, she felt a chill and got gooseflesh.

Her husband, who was normal size, had lost his job at the beginning of the recession, and nothing had come along since. He got a few days of work here and there in a retail store or a garage, but he wasn't cut out for retailing, and the garages were overloaded with mechanics who had been laid off by the defense plants around Bridgeport. She did what she could to earn money, to keep their nucleus of a family off the streets. The problem was her size; there were only so many ways a forty-three-inch woman could earn enough to pay the rent.

Since she did not consider herself lucky, she expected the potato project to fall through at any time. But it went forward on schedule. The costume was delivered to the advertising agency, and she took the train from Bridgeport to Philadelphia for her last fitting before the presentation to the salesmen.

This time the man from the advertising agency was stranger than ever. She thought he was hyper, not like people who do cocaine, but hyper like some kids who are allergic to chocolate or something, hyperactive, nuts. And he kept touching her, helping her to pull on her gloves and asking if she needed help with the tights.

When they found that the eyes were out of sync, he said they were haywire, which is what her mother had said about her thyroid system. She told him she didn't like the word, and he apologized, like a gentleman instead of a nut who wanted to touch her arms and legs while she was getting her costume on. But then he got so close to her while he was fooling around with the eyes that she thought he might really have some intentions. A lot of people did.

A person from the costume company came over in a cab and adjusted the cloth strap that fit around her head, enabling her to control the eyes by leaning her head to the left or right. The problem was that she had let her head go forward inside the costume, and the strings that controlled the eyes got off their tracks.

The advertising agency man gave her a check at the end of the fitting and rehearsal, just as he had after every session. He told her that if the session with the salesmen from the client company went well, he would pay her a bonus. Then he invited her to lunch at a restaurant not far from his office. He offered to take her hand as they walked over, but she did not want to touch him. At the restaurant he met several acquaintances, to whom he introduced her. They were all in the advertising or film business. She gave each of them a business card. "If you ever need a little person . . . ," she said.

On the day of the presentation, everything was different. The man from the advertising agency was very curt with her. He complained that she was late. He did not like the timbre of her voice or the way she walked or controlled the eyes of the potato, and he was particularly unhappy with the way she recited her lines. They rehearsed again and again, until her legs were weary and her chest hurt.

She did not feel lucky about her chances to succeed as a cold-weather potato. The little touches of frost on her costume looked like mold or disease. The eyes were out of sync again. Her chest hurt. When she was in serious pain, she had trouble talking. She carried a small vial of Percodan, which the doctor had prescribed, but she was afraid to take such a strong painkiller before an important presentation; what if she forgot her lines?

While the salesmen gathered in the meeting room for the presentation, she waited in a green room, which was outfitted with a small loudspeaker so that she could listen for her entrance cue. She waited until the last minute to climb inside the potato costume, because it tended to make her sweat after a while, and she did not want to have the sweat on her arms or legs show through the tights and long brown gloves.

The voice of the advertising agency man came over the loudspeaker. She could not tell by the sound whether he had the toothpick clenched between his teeth, but she could hear the nervousness underneath his rapid patter. "And now for the pièce de résistance," he said, pronouncing the last three words with an elaborately French accent. "We intend to hire fifty midgets in potato costumes to wander the aisles of supermarkets up and down the Eastern Seaboard, telling women shoppers about the fantastic flavor of the chips made from cold-weather potatoes. And now I want you to meet one of the living potatoes who will persuade the women shoppers, charm their children, flirt with their husbands; that's the kind of absolutely terrific potato she is. Gentlemen, she's a *hot* potato!

"Just imagine! You're in a supermarket, you're bored, going through the same routine, standing there, looking at the shelves full of potato chips, trying to make up your mind . . ."

It was her cue. She stepped through the door into the presentation room. There must have been a hundred salesmen in the audience. As best she could see through the peepholes in the costume, they were all prosperous looking, a lot of them middle-aged. And there was the man from the advertising agency. His back was turned to her, just as they had rehearsed. She walked across the floor to where he stood, and prepared to tap him on the hip to get his attention.

". . . yes, trying to make up your mind when someone unexpected comes up to you and cheers you up . . ."

He did not know where she was. In his anxiety to encounter the potato, he turned around just as she reached forward to tap him on the hip.

Instead, her hand touched his crotch. The salesmen laughed. After the hours of presentations by various members of the marketing and research staff, they longed for laughter, a mistake, a pratfall, anything, so the first funny sight of the day seemed uproarious to them. They howled with laughter. They cheered and applauded and howled like beasts.

The man from the advertising agency and the cold-weather potato were transfixed by the waves of laughter. They waited for minutes until it subsided. Then the agency man went on with the rehearsed routine: "So you see how charming and memorable it can be. Now, we have a little dialogue between the customer and the cold-weather potato."

He turned to her, leaning forward slightly and speaking in loud, precisely enunciated sentences: "Why, hello there. And who are you?"

"I'm the cold-weather potato," she said in a tiny voice strangled by the growing pain in her chest.

"Well, isn't that adorable! And tell me, what's going to happen to you, cold-weather potato?"

"I'm going to be skinned and sliced up and then fried in scalding hot oil."

What had seemed during rehearsal to be nothing more than a recital of the advertising campaign sounded bizarre in the presentation room. The salesmen could hardly believe what they were hearing. The sound of the tiny suffering voice describing its horrible fate filled the salesmen with revulsion. "Get it off the stage! That's disgusting! You asshole!"

"It's all over," the advertising man whispered to her, "go back to the green room."

"No," she said, shaking her head vehemently inside the costume, causing the strings that controlled the eyes to come off the track, "I want to do the rest of my lines."

She turned to the audience, with her huge potato eyes rolling wildly and the sweat running down her thighs and arms, soaking through the fabric, and in the loudest voice she could bring out of her aching chest, she said, "And then people just like you are going to take me piece by piece and put me in their mouths and chew me all up and swallow me. And that's the story of my life."

The reaction was much worse than before. Some of the men in the audience stood up and jeered. Others walked out of the room. She did not know how to regain their interest, their attention, and she needed the job, she needed the contacts.

Several people grabbed her arms and pulled her to the green room.

Once inside, two men from the advertising agency offered to help her change out of the cold-weather-potato costume. They opened the Velcro fasteners on the side of the potato-shaped costume, and lifted it off her body. She wore only underwear, but they did not look at her, not even at her breasts or the great space between her thighs. She was no longer a woman to them, no longer a person.

After she had changed, the advertising agency man came to talk to her.

"I can hear them on the loudspeaker," she said. "They're having a cocktail party or something."

"Yes."

"I'd like to join them."

"You're not invited."

"I need the money," she said. "I want to go out there. A lot of guys like little people. You know what I mean? I can make four, five hundred dollars a trick. People do things with us, certain things. And they'll pay a lot for it. So I want to go out there and give my card to a few of those guys."

"You're a rotten little whore," he said.

"Yes," she said, "I'm a whore and a freak, and I need money, so I'm going out there."

She started for the door, but he grabbed her arm. "No, you're not; you've made enough trouble for us already. You ruined everything. You fucked up, you goddamn little whore. You're not getting paid for today, not after the way you fucked up. And you're not going out there!"

"Yes, I am!" She fought to twist her arm out of his grasp.

He called for help. Two other men from the advertising agency rushed in. "She's a whore," he told them; "and she wants to go out there and solicit our clients. We've got to get her out of here."

The three men picked her up and carried her out of the building. They put her into a car, and locked the doors. One man sat in the back seat with her, while another one drove. "We'll take you home," they said, "all the way to your house in Bridgeport."

She closed her eyes, and nodded her acceptance of their offer, her concession of defeat. She was not a lucky person. It is not good luck to be born with one's ductless glands gone haywire. She comforted herself by thinking of home. The men in her husband's plant in Bridgeport did not revile her; in some sense they revered her, as among ancient cultures little people had always been revered, for they were believed to have been favored by the gods, given special powers and insights, the ability to do magic.

1.

Every season someone publishes a survey of public attitudes about the kind of work people do. Most of the studies ask the opinion of a thousand or fifteen hundred carefully randomized respondents, producing more or less statistically valid data, depending upon the definition of random, the questions asked, and so on. But there have been so many surveys about occupations, and they have been so consistent on the question of salesmen and sales-related occupations, that in the aggregate they have gone beyond mere probability to achieve the truthfulness of counting.

One survey, published in 1991, sought to find the "sleaziest ways to make a living"[1] in the view of the American public. Seven of the top (bottom?) occupations in that category involved selling. Only criminal activities and television evangelism were considered sleazier than selling, and one of the criminal acts, drug dealing, is a form of selling, as is TV evangelism. The twentieth occupation on the list was prison guard.

Of the twenty most admired ways to earn a living, not one was directly related to selling, according to the survey.

The low esteem in which salesmen are held has not been news for several thousand years, but the choice of words to describe the character of salesmen and their ilk indicates what people dislike most about them. Both *Webster's* and the latest *OED* say that *sleazy* or *sleaze,* when applied to a person, denotes low moral standards. Sleazy fabrics are insubstantial, sleazy surroundings are sordid, and sleazy persons are unethical. No matter that the salesman makes a major contribution to the economy, no matter that selling may be all that stood between the United States and another Depression following World War II; it does not even matter that selling as a form

---

[1]   James Patterson and Peter Kim, *The Day America Told the Truth* (New York: Prentice-Hall, 1991).

Another survey done May 16–18, 1991, by the Gallup organization asking people to rank different fields according to honesty and ethical standards showed five of the lowest seven rankings belonging to salesmen, including "advertising practitioners." The most ethical people, according to the respondents, were druggists, clergy, medical technicians, and medical doctors, all of whom were thought to have high ethical standards by half or more of the respondents. At the bottom were real estate agents, thought to have high ethical standards by 17 percent; stockbrokers, 14 percent; insurance salesmen, also 14 percent, advertising practitioners, 12 percent; and at the very bottom, as one would expect, car salesmen, 8 percent.

of mediation plays an indispensable role in the interplay of people and things that we call culture. Selling fails the test of public morality. Insurance salesmen, street peddlers, and stockbrokers were sleazier than prison guards in the view of the American public at the beginning of the last decade of the twentieth century.

That is what the survey of the sleaziest occupations says. That is what all the surveys say. But there must be something wrong with the surveys. There are customers in the stores. Someone opens the door when the insurance salesman knocks. And even though the cold call comes in the middle of dinner, somebody listens.

The response points to a disjunction in the mechanism of learned response, failure at a level far more basic than reason. A dog, a bird, a common earthworm, can learn not to go where it will be stung. But human life is apparently too complicated for the iron rules of self-preservation. The customer will not punish the salesman for his sleazy acts, not by ostracism or by ordinance. The rule of *caveat emptor,* first challenged in Roman law, then in Scots and British law, and finally eliminated almost entirely in American protections for the customer, has survived; it may not be the law, but it is still the reality of selling, the license of the salesman, his almost perfect liberty. The disjunction between what the customer knows and how the customer acts makes it so.

With little or no constraint directly from the customer and a set of commercial laws that can be fairly characterized as weak and largely ineffectual, the moral life of the salesman becomes the salesman's choice: *Homo vendens* invents himself, and the range of his invention is enormous, even in matters of life and death.

Here are two examples: One is a businessman, the other is a physician. They demonstrate the antipodes of ethics. Not that businessmen and physicians are antipodal, as the physician will explain; the actions of the men, not their occupations, separate them.

The story of the businessman, Charles M. Harper, appeared in the business pages of newspapers at the end of May 1993. Harper, the chief executive of a large commodities company, Conagra, was sixty-five years old, getting ready to retire, when he was invited by Henry R. Kravis of Kohlberg, Kravis, Roberts and Company, the buyout specialists who helped set the tone of business in the 1980s, to become CEO of an even larger corporation.

Harper had made his reputation by his response to a heart attack suffered in 1985. First, of course, he quit smoking, and then he turned his experience with cardiology into a hot, new business. He invented Healthy Choice food products, a line of low-in-everything prepared foods. It was a brilliant salesman's response to new knowledge: The heart attack made him aware of the desires of his customers (good health, longevity, and the pleasures of eating), and Harper produced a line of food to match it. But he didn't just produce diet foods, like those on the market. He was a man, to judge from photographs, who liked to eat. So he introduced the food at the Plaza Hotel in New York, with a great fuss about the flavor, as well as the low-in-everything contents.

Harper's new job also related to cardiology. Kravis had put him in charge of RJR Nabisco, which sells $8 billion a year worth of tobacco products. Did Harper believe there was a connection between smoking and heart disease when he accepted Kravis's offer? One can only surmise from the way he behaved following his own heart attack.

David Blumenthal, a cardiologists in New York City, is also concerned with selling and cigarettes. Blumenthal tries desperately to persuade his patients not to smoke. He uses the intellectual approach first, he says, and if that doesn't work, he tries to get family members to intervene, and if he can't sell a patient on giving up smoking by any other method, he said, "I beg. And what I mean by that is: To show them how much I care, I indicate to them that my recommendation is beyond the mere science of it; it is a personal thing. In other words, we're past the science, we're up to friends; you are my friend."

The son of a physicist, David Blumenthal did not learn the rules of selling at home. In his role as mediator between his patients and acts that invite death, Dr. Blumenthal is in exactly the same relation to smokers as Harper is. But Blumenthal begins from the other pole of the moral life: He knows that if he can't convince his patients to follow his advice, they may die.

"You know," he said, "the worst thing in the world for a doctor is to offer advice you believe in and have somebody not accept what you say. So one of the things I'll do is—you see Cornell, Johns Hopkins, Phi Beta Kappa, all this on the wall—so at least they'll say, 'He's a pretty smart guy. If he tells me something, at least it's worth listening to.'

"It doesn't always work, but it's one more thing that I do. I guess the other thing I do, to an extent, is rather than just tell you what I think, I'll tell you why. It won't be overly technical, but I will cite papers to patients insofar as laymen can understand. In other words, I will give the *New York Times* version of a paper. So I won't just say, 'You should have a catheterization.' I'll start with who should have a catheterization, you know, what the data is, what supports this, what supports that . . . and try and give them at least a reasonable scientific framework. Again, in part, to sell them on what I want to tell them. So, I guess I use intellectual stuff. I try and tell somebody I'm smart, I'm thoughtful, and therefore you should listen to me."

He says that doctors sell to each other as well as to patients. He sells by delivering papers to his fellow physicians on the practice of cardiology. He also sees referrals promptly and reports his diagnosis soon. He concedes that it is a form of selling, the only kind he is willing to do. And it has worked well for him. In a published survey of the best cardiologists in New York City, his peers included the doctor who sells by knowing as much as he can and doing his job as well as he can. If it is correct to say that David Blumenthal is even in part a salesman, he represents the ethical antipode.

Although his brother is a salesman, and he likes and admires his brother's talent for sizing people up in an instant and making them like him, the idea of selling bothers David Blumenthal. Even the word concerns him when it is applied to his work. "I don't call it selling," he said. "I would say persuasion. It doesn't differ from selling, in a sense, except clearly for me *selling* is a pejorative term. There's no question that in my own view selling implies the attribution of disproportionate value to something that does not have that much value.

"I can't help it. That's the way I view the term. I don't like the idea of sales that's out of proportion to the value of what it is that you're providing. I think everything's got an intrinsic worth. When you portray that excessively, I'm put off tremendously.

"There have been, over the years, people like that at New York Hospital, and I would not have sent them anybody under any circumstances. The term for a private physician of that ilk (a salesman) is a *slick*. When you talk about a slick, everybody knows what that is. *Slick* is a very pejorative term; it means someone who is really after the buck, who has a fancy office and a fancy practice and a fancy car and is doing the bare minimum to take care of the patients, but is very eager to improve revenues to the absolute maximum.

"I'm thinking of a specific case: A woman I was asked to see in third opinion—she ultimately became my patient—a lovely, older woman in her eighties, who needed valve replacement—did fine—the sweetest lady, a fabulous person. She had seen doctor so and so. He did a physical and he did an echocardiagram—absolutely indicated.

" 'Then,' the patient told me, 'I had the stress test.' Now, a stress test in the disease she had, critical aortic stenosis, basically is, in most circumstances, contraindicated. It is positively hazardous, not in every instance, but basically hazardous. At the time he did the stress test, he knew she had to be catheterized, so the information to be derived was absolutely zero. I mean, there was not a chance on earth that he could get a piece of information out of that test that would help him in any way, shape, or form. There's only one reason on earth he did that test.

"That's a slick. Is this guy well dressed? You bet. Does he have a tan all the time? You bet. Nice suits, nice this, nice that, second family, all the stuff, you bet! That's a slick."

If Blumenthal and the "slick" represent the antipodes in medicine, Emerson Foote of the Foote, Cone & Belding advertising agency and later chairman of McCann-Erickson Inc. and Charles M. Harper represent the antipodes in marketing and sales.[2] In 1948 Foote resigned the American Tobacco Company account, depriving his company of 20 percent of its gross billings and probably far more of its bottom line, since cigarette accounts are among the most profitable an agency can handle. Sixteen years later Foote confronted the ethics of selling cigarettes again. He resigned the chairmanship of McCann-Erickson, because the company handled cigarette accounts. Foote's famous statement about cigarettes and advertising stands as one of the ethical peaks of selling: "I am always amused by the suggestion that advertising, a function that has been shown to increase consumption of virtually every other product, somehow miraculously fails to work for tobacco products."

The other pole in the advertising business is richly represented by such agencies as Ogilvy & Mather, founded by David Ogilvy, who gave up tobacco farming in Pennsylvania to enter the advertising business. His agency, which produced many commercials for the American Cancer Society, sells Philip Morris tobacco products around the world.

Ogilvy, Harper, and the "slicks" described by Dr. Blumenthal share a special trait of the salesman—hypocrisy. Ogilvy works for the American Cancer Society, Harper sells healthy foods for heart patients, and the slicks

---

[2]   H. R. Haldeman, John Ehrlichman, and other salesmen who were connected with the Watergate scandal seem to me a special rather than a representative case.

claim to follow the Hippocratic oath.[3] Perhaps hypocrisy disarms the public, opens the door for the insurance salesman, and sends the customer to the used-car dealer. Perhaps it keeps the public from ostracizing salesmen. According to Sidney R. Bernstein, former editor of *Advertising Age*, hypocrisy was the best tool business could have used to keep customers from demanding laws to regulate advertising.[4]

Public response to unethical behavior makes ethics extremely difficult for salesmen, because it sets no limits. Not only does the public fail to ostracize unethical salesmen; it appears to reward them. Charles M. Harper and David Ogilvy are rich men. Ogilvy is more famous than his former rival Emerson Foote, and Harper has achieved far more influence than Dr. Blumenthal over the cardiological fortunes of his fellow citizens. If morality is rewarded and immorality punished, it must be in the next life. In this world salesmen are free.

Given such complete liberty by his customers, *homo vendens* must decide what ethical position he should take, why he should be ethical, and what rules, if any, he ought to follow. Finally, he must decide how to behave when selling and morality come into conflict.

2.

When *homo faber* held sway in the world, the ethics of the salesman could be more or less ignored. The salesman was a secondary factor, at best, the slightly comical mediator between shortages and desire. In such a world,

---

[3] They are not alone. Prudential Securities agreed to the largest fines in the history of the retail brokerage business after the Securities and Exchange Commission judged that it had deceived its customers about some kinds of limited partnerships, churned their accounts, and so on. The day the story broke, October 22, 1993, Prudential published a full-page newspaper advertisement admitting that it had misled some customers about the stability of limited partnerships, but neglecting to say anything about churning accounts, failing to manage its employees, and so on, all misdeeds for which it had been fined. In other words, Prudential attempted to deceive the public in the course of its mea culpa on the subject of deception!

Even more astonishingly Prudential was hoping to attract new customers through its mea culpa campaign. See chapter 14, note 1, for the further adventures of Prudential Securities.

In the past, charges of fraud or the mishandling of accounts had closed E. F. Hutton and the firm associated with Michael Milken, but had no apparent effect on Salomon Brothers or Shearson or other large firms, which had also faced charges of misconduct.

[4] See chapter 3.

---

ethics could be given into the care of the invisible hand, and men could go about their business of tearing a new existence out of nature.

Before God became dead (Nietzsche) or indifferent (the existentialists), the vestiges of *homo religiosus* hiding in every person had an important role in determining the behavior of the salesman. This world was not the place where final things were played out; there was some fear of the divine. Behavior was judged according to the rules of Judeo-Christian or Muslim or Buddhist ethics. Limits were imposed from above by supernatural beings whose prescriptions and judgments could not be challenged except by profound revolt.

In the world of *homo vendens*, however, neither of the religious concepts, the invisible hand of this world or the imagined hand of the next, is in control. The primary actor, the salesman, must choose the ethics of his domain. First, he must choose whether to have a moral life at all. If he decides that morality has a role, he then faces many options, and none is simple, for most of his actions will place one moral concept in conflict with another.

For a definition of a moral person, we can use the one given by John Rawls in *A Theory of Justice:* "Moral persons are distinguished by two features: first they are capable of having (and are assumed to have) a conception of their good (as expressed by a rational plan of life); and second they are capable of having (and are assumed to acquire) a sense of justice, a normally effective desire to apply and to act upon the principles of justice, at least to a certain minimum degree." Rawls goes on to say, "There is no race or recognized group of human beings that lacks this attribute," by which he means "the capacity for moral personality."[5]

Whether *homo vendens* chooses to live within Rawls's "race or recognized group of human beings" is the question to be considered here, first with some specific questions and then by comparing the life of *homo vendens* to the requirements of some ideas about ethics.

What ought the salesman to do?

Ought he to sell? Under what conditions?

Ought he to follow other rules of conduct? Professional or religious, for example?

What happens when selling and other rules of conduct conflict?

How does he answer the metaethical questions? For example: If *homo*

[5] (Cambridge: Harvard University Press, 1971), pp. 503–4.

vendens seeks the good, what is the good? Or what is happiness? And how is pleasure defined?

Does the universe have a center, and is *homo vendens* standing there?

Does the salesman have a duty to fulfill? And if so, who said so? And to whom does he have this duty?

Motives, means, or ends—which does *homo vendens* put first? A system of morals begins with that question.

If the salesman put motives first, it would be his duty to do the right thing, as Kant said, even if it meant the end of the world. If he put ends first, he would follow the utilitarian principle of Hutcheson, Bentham, and Mill, which is to produce "the greatest good for the greatest number." Unfortunately, *homo vendens* does put ends first, but not ends as we generally know them: The end a salesman seeks is a sale. That leads to a problem. A sale is a transaction, and a transaction is a means rather than an end.

Perhaps the problem reads more clearly as a metaphor: If life were constructed as clearly as a simple sentence, motives would be the subject, means the verb, and ends the object. In that case, the object of the actions of *homo vendens* would be a verb.

The problem with a verb as an object is that it can be applied to many nouns. It describes an exchange; the result of it depends on the nouns it acts on. If the verb were one that could be valued, such as *kill,* which many people believe immoral under any circumstances, or *love,* the ethical system could be built around the value of the verb. But *sale* is not such a verb; like an operational sign in arithmetic, it has no moral content. One may sell nutritious bread at a fair price to people in ordinary circumstances or rancid meat at an outrageously high price to starving children. Both activities qualify as sales; the moral content is determined by the nouns (described by the adjectives).

At this point, it would seem easy enough to say that the ethical salesman sells bread and the unethical salesman makes a marriage between starving children and outrageously expensive rancid meat. But what if there were no food available other than rancid meat, and the salesman could get it only by paying outrageous prices to black-market operators?

How much control does the salesman have over the things and persons involved in the sale? Should he refuse to sell the overpriced meat on ethical grounds? How shall we define overpriced in a time of shortage? Is black-market meat more or less overpriced than the thirteen ounces of coffee in a one-pound can on the supermarket shelf? Should he refuse to sell the rancid meat if his refusal would cause the children to die of starvation?

Homo vendens deals in transactions. The nouns originate elsewhere and rest not with him but with his customers. What is the ethical condition of the transaction, of interchangeability? In the case of the salesman, we are speaking not of some grandiose Nietzschean "transvaluation of values" but of something more desperate and more difficult to deal with, the devaluation of value into exchangeability. What meaning can be assigned to the process of exchange other than exchangeability?

Has the salesman escaped judgment?

What ought the salesman to do? Should *homo vendens* sell only things that people need?

If he did that, in the world left to him in economic trust by *homo faber* and *animal laborans,* a monumental worldwide depression would result. Governments would collapse; whole societies would be thrown into chaos. Perhaps the upheaval would eventually result in a revaluation of things, a new measure of happiness, but that would occur only, if ever, in the long run, when, as Lord Keynes noted, we are dead.

If *homo vendens* cannot be eliminated, replaced, or redirected on moral grounds, perhaps a hedonistic ethics can solve the problem: Should *homo vendens* sell only things that give people pleasure?

The salesman comes very close to ethical hedonism now. If pleasure were defined as the satisfaction of desire, the salesman would be a pleasurer. But people desire many things that don't fit comfortably into the category of pleasure: knowledge, love, moral qualities, to borrow a few from G. E. Moore's argument against ethical hedonism. Aren't those also intrinsically good? Is freedom intrinsically good, and is freedom a form of pleasure? Even more difficult questions arise in the real world. If the onerous labor of three persons is required to provide pleasure to one, is the amount of pleasure in the world increased or decreased? Should the total amount of pleasure be judged positively, or should the amount of pleasure in the world be whatever is left over after the subtraction of the suffering?

When *homo vendens* becomes the seller of opium dreams and crack cocaine highs, he satisfies desire and gives people pleasure: "In Xanadu did Kubla Khan / A stately pleasure-dome decree. . . ."

By fiddling with the definitions of pleasure and intrinsic goodness, including certain moral acts, excluding such notions as freedom by consigning them to Western thinking rather than to intrinsic goodness, one can defend hedonistic ethics. But to make Xanadu the ethical norm offends the moral personality, which is not merely a Western idea but a universal attribute of rational animals. The consumer society, Xanadu, exists, but is not congruent with the notion of an ethical society, not because ethics precludes consuming but because it includes other aspects of human life.

The categorical imperative—"Act according to a maxim which can become a general law"—of Immanuel Kant, which Bertrand Russell claims is nothing more than the Golden Rule, may limit some of the salesman's methods, but it would have no effect on the salesman's idea of an ethical life. The test of the categorical imperative for the salesman is not complicated: Would he sell, if the act of selling were to become a maxim for everybody to follow?

The answer is equally uncomplicated: *Homo vendens* believes that selling is the duty of man in the modern world. It is the act that he wills to be universalized. He answers Kant with a resounding "Yes!"

It is, however, not an answer to the full meaning of the question, for the categorical imperative does not live lonely in the world; it was born of something, and it is a member of the family of a moral construct. In the last chapter of this book, *homo vendens* will be viewed within the greater framework, and it will be seen whether the maxim he wills is to his benefit in his human life. For now, it is safe to say that the salesman comforts himself with the Golden Rule by applying it to selling, as if the question were put to the act of addition, subtraction, or multiplication. Naked, orphaned from the world, it becomes the ideal philosophy for *homo vendens*.

Would the salesman lie, cheat, or steal in the course of selling, if he followed the categorical imperative? Certainly not! Salesmen lie, but selling is not lying, even though it may lead to lying, as Sissela Bok pointed out: ". . . a company may set . . . high goals for production or sales. When economic conditions become adverse, it may be next to impossible to meet these targets without moral compromises. If the incentives for achieving the goals . . . are felt to be too compelling, the temptation to lie and to cheat can grow intolerable."[6]

[6] *Lying: Moral Choice in Public and Private Life* (New York: Pantheon, 1978), p. 245.
In contrast to Bok's steady, stolid view of the subject, J. Huizinga, in *Homo Ludens* (Boston: Beacon Press, 1955), p. 52, writes,

> To our way of thinking, cheating as a means of winning a game robs the action of its play-character and spoils it altogether, because for us the essence of play is that the rules be kept—that it be fair play. Archaic culture, however, gives the lie to our moral judgement in this respect, as also does the spirit of popular lore. In the fable of the hare and the hedgehog the beau role is reserved for the false player, who wins by fraud. Many of the heroes of

Kant makes powerful arguments against lying in any situation. Saint Thomas Aquinas opposed lying, but he had an uncharacteristic soft spot about some kinds of lies, including the kind "which *saves a man from death*" or from "*unlawful defilement of the body*." He concluded "it is evident that the greater the good intended, the more is the sin of lying diminished in gravity." Utilitarians also have a somewhat softer view of lying than Kantians, although there are no systems of ethics which welcome liars and lying.[7]

Utilitarian ethics, on the whole, would seem most welcoming to *homo vendens,* since Hutcheson's "greatest good for the greatest number" describes what most philosophers of selling, beginning with Adam Smith, would call the goal of modern capitalism.[8] There is, of course, the problem of defining the good or happiness. *Homo vendens* believes happiness comes from buying things, happiness not only for the buyer but for the maker, the seller, and everyone connected in an economic way with the thing he sold.

---

mythology win by trickery or by help from without. Pelops bribes the charioteer of Oenomaus to put wax pins into the axles. Jason and Theseus come through their tests successfully, thanks to Medea and Ariadne. Gunther owes his victory to Siegfried. The Kauravas in the *Mahābhārata* win by cheating at dice. Freya double-crosses Wotan into granting the victory to Langobards. The Ases of Eddic mythology break the oath they have sworn to the Giants. In all these instances the act of fraudulently outwitting somebody else has itself become a subject for competition, a new play-theme, as it were.

The hazy border-line between play and seriousness is illustrated very tellingly by the use of the words "playing" or "gambling" for the machinations on the Stock Exchange.

This pattern is often repeated in modern selling and politics. Whatever the real truth might be, the Clarence Thomas Senate confirmation hearings were played out as a contest between tricksters. Thomas, aided by the sharks and snakes on the Republican side, now sits on the U.S. Supreme Court, having bested the buffoons and boozers on the Democratic side. Anita Hill's role remains a mystery, at least to me.

Many business dealings, especially hostile takeovers of corporations, are played according to the ancient rules of morality rather than those embraced by Bok. In the struggle for the Paramount Corporation, the bidders enlisted outside forces, Southern Bell and Advance Communications among them, just as Medea and Ariadne were enlisted to help Jason and Theseus.

If Huizinga's view now seems too playful, almost light-headed, it must be remembered that he completed his work more than half a century ago, when the world was hungry but games were still sweet.

[7]   Ruth Benedict taught us in *Patterns of Culture* not to make such generalizations, but the treacherous behavior of her Dobu islanders hardly qualifies as a system of morals, and a broken culture is more suited to the study of anger or despair than ethics. She is no more convincing than the lunatic fringe of multiculturalism on the possibility of human beings without "the capacity for moral personality."

[8]   For some reason, perhaps to avoid the appearance of human kindness, they prefer to say, "A rising tide lifts all boats."

Under no circumstances will he accept the notion that selling could hurt anyone, so he will not abandon his belief in the value of selling even if utilitarianism is turned on its head and the good is defined as that which causes the least suffering.

Again, the salesman concentrates on the transaction, not on the product or the person who buys it. He can sell cigarettes, alcohol, firearms, unhealthy food, unsafe cars, products made by slave labor in China, as well as bread and books, all under the same ethical umbrella of the sale itself. Utilitarian ethics do not apply to the transaction per se.

The transaction has no shadings, no gray areas. A sale is either made or it isn't; transactions take place or they don't. The alternative to selling is not good selling or slightly better selling. No alternative exists other than stasis, an end to commerce, exchange, activity, the death of society. On utilitarian grounds activity is better than death; selling is thus not the greatest good, but the minimal good, and not for the greatest number, but for anyone and everyone. The world so defined rests on the shoulders of *homo vendens;* now that he has taken control, the villain of ancient morality has become the savior of the last days of the twentieth century. But what system of morals does he embrace? What are the rules of the game? How should *homo vendens* live?

3.

Within the transaction, the activities of the salesman can be held up to moral scrutiny. Does he lie? Does he cheat? What ethical rules apply to the deformation of words, images, even numbers?

John O'Toole, president of the AAAA, which publishes a code of ethics for advertisers, wrote,

> It is not in the nature of advertising to be journalistic, to present both sides, to include information that shows the product negatively in comparison with other entries in the category. . . . Information is selected for journalism—or should be—to provide the recipient with as complete and objective an account as possible. Information is selected for advertising to persuade the recipient to go to a showroom or make a mental pledge to find the product on a store shelf.
>
> Advertising, like the personal salesman, unabashedly presents products in their most favorable light.

Prior to heading the industry's trade organization, O'Toole sold Kent cigarettes, presenting them, of course, in their most favorable light.

O'Toole had no qualms about describing the ought of journalism, but his industry exerted influence on journalists to keep them from behaving as they ought, according to the *New England Journal of Medicine*. In an article published in January 1992, the *Journal* found that in its very broad survey of magazines "as the percentage of advertising revenue from cigarettes rose, the probability of discussing the hazards of smoking fell." Dr. Kenneth E. Warner told the Associated Press, "My sense is that the publishers and editors are genuinely afraid they will lose advertising revenue if they discuss the hazards of smoking."[9]

Similar pressures have been applied by the automobile industry, public utilities, whoever sells, in their efforts to keep what are known in the trade as "exogenous factors" from entering the transaction. In that way selling becomes like a trial in which the lawyers for one side try to keep certain evidence from the jury.

Salesmen invite comparison to lawyers because of this similarity in their methods of argument. The best of lawyers, a man who wrote frequently and well on moral questions, Marcus Tullius Cicero, offered advice that has often been used in the marketplace: "It is sometimes the business of the advocate to maintain what is plausible even if it be not strictly true." The author of a famous essay *On Duties* was not at all shy about his deceptions. Cicero said to one of his clients: "Let me tell you that it was I who produced the necessary darkness in the court to prevent your guilt from being visible to everyone."

From Cicero's comments and the remarks about the courts in Plato's early dialogue the *Euthydemus*, it would appear that lawyers and salesmen are one and the same when it comes to the conflict between truth and persuasion. I put that idea before James Shorris, who had been a prosecutor in the Frauds Bureau of the Manhattan District Attorney's Office.[10] He

---

9   The story confirmed what everyone in the business world knew. I remember getting a telephone call from Louis T. Hagopian, chairman of N. W. Ayer, asking whether Ayer had anything to do with a statement by the electric utilities trade organization comparing radiation from cigarette smoke with emissions from nuclear power plants. George Weissman, then CEO of Philip Morris, which owned a company represented by Ayer, had telephoned Hagopian demanding to know. The threat from the enraged CEO of the cigarette company was clear: If Ayer was involved in an attack on cigarettes, 7-Up was going to change advertising agencies.

10   James Shorris, my younger son, is now in private practice in Boston. Although there

agreed that lawyers sell, explaining that law firms now have marketing departments and even use marketing techniques for jury selection, although the lawyer as salesman was not a role that particularly pleased him. As an illustration of lawyers selling, he pointed to several instances in brochures distributed by law firms in which assertions were made that "would not be admissible in a court of law."

He drew a distinction, however, between the lawyer as salesman and the lawyer in the courtroom, where American jurisprudence requires the lawyer to adhere to the forms of the law. There are both civil procedures and criminal procedures that must be followed (as every law student learns), and the attorney who fails to follow these forms risks losing his case.

On the other hand, selling follows no forms; it has no procedures. The customer is not guaranteed the right to counsel, nor is there an adversarial procedure presided over by an impartial judge to be certain the customer is treated fairly. The proof of the distinction between the law and sales rests on the recourse of the customer who thinks he has been wronged by a salesman: He goes to a lawyer.

Sales need not be unethical and the forms of the law too often result in injustice, blurring somewhat the distinction between the results of the two practices, but the likelihood of a fair and honest outcome has been enhanced in the case of law by a historical refinement of the forms, while selling has been made less equitable through the development of science-based psychological marketing methods.

In law the forms may be considered expressions of ethical behavior, although a lawyer who practices according to the forms will still have to face many ethical questions. He will have to decide whom to represent and what to do with clients who lie and what to charge, and so on and on, but he will not prosecute the undefended and he will not withhold evidence or tutor his witness in perjury. "The law has justice and order as its ends," said the former prosecutor, "and uses the forms that regulate argument to assure it of achieving those ends in many, if not most, instances." *Homo vendens* submits to no forms; he roams free, as ruthless as success requires; where he prevails, there is a commerce without rules.

---

are few direct quotations in his comments, he has read and corrected my reporting of his views.

4.

In its classical form, the study of economics is ethically neutral, like the natural sciences. Surely, the law of gravity is neither good nor bad, but ethically neutral. Economists like to think of their work, too, as descriptive rather than prescriptive. No scientist ever says we need a little more gravity to make us good persons, nor do economists prescribe a more intimate relationship among supply, price, and demand to increase our happiness. As science and economics live apart from the world, observing and describing it, they impose no values upon their work.

Now and then science has brought trouble down on its head by describing the world, Galileo being one of the great examples. Since economics may be viewed from the left or the right, economists have also suffered because of their claims to scientific neutrality. The salesman had similar difficulties in the early part of his career: The punishment of the serpent in paradise was terrible and relentless. Neither the Old Testament or the New offers the slightest hope that the salesman might be forgiven for introducing man to knowledge or causing him to lose his innocence.

Like the scientist, the salesman suffered less as he became more important to the life of the time. Moving from subsistence societies to large-scale agriculture and trade to the time when he was finally set free by the vast increase of productive capacity in the nineteenth century, the salesman gained more and more distance from the censure of ancient ethics. Now that the salesman has been given responsibility by the technological enormities of this century to maintain economic order, *homo vendens* has emerged, and he can, like the scientist, determine much of the ethical agenda.

Homo vendens does this by declaring selling an ethically neutral act. Since it is merely a mechanical function relating one customer to one thing, the sale is a verb of exchange, and what are the ethics of interchangeability? One could as soon say gravity is good or bad, nasty or nice. *Homo vendens* lives apart from the world judged by ethics or, as Nietzsche might have said, beyond ethical judgments. The only thing that concerns the salesman is the sale itself, which is no thing, a transaction, an exchange. Since nothingness as a desired end would be absurd, a comic suicide, ends cannot determine the ethics of *homo vendens*. Utilitarianism cannot apply. Nor will a sale suffice as a motive; exchange cannot be valued, only the exchange of a particular thing. And that is not what the salesman intends; his interest does not extend beyond the sale, which is to him like sunlight and oxygen, life's necessity.

The great salesman of the last quarter of the twentieth century was Michael Milken, a Wall Street financier who was convicted of insider trading, fined, and sentenced to a brief stay in a minimum-security federal prison.[11] The cost to the nation of his junk bond schemes has been estimated conservatively at tens of billions of dollars and by some accounts at hundreds of billions. The ultimate cost to individuals because of lost funds for the commonweal is inestimable.

Milken's activities are reprehensible by any ethical standard, yet the convicted felon, barred from the securities business for life, has become a model for *homo vendens*. According to the *New York Times*, students at the University of California at Los Angeles crowd his classroom, wanting to learn from the man the reporter James B. Stewart called a "genius salesman." The *Times* quoted one student who said Milken is "the smartest man in the country." And Milken has begun to describe himself as a martyr in the cause of *homo vendens*, comparing himself to "Galileo and other penalized visionaries proved right by history."[12]

Michael Milken the salesman represents his time as few other men

[11] Shortly after the Milken scandal broke in the newspapers, his chief public relations man asked if I would come by his office to talk about a public relations problem. I had known and liked Ken Lerer for many years, so I went gladly. After I arrived, he told me that his new client was Milken. Lerer was concerned about the treatment of his client in books and in the press in general. He spoke at some length about Milken's personal life, his love for his children, and so on. He also talked about a charitable foundation Milken had established. At the time, Lerer appeared to believe that Milken could earn more credit with the public by giving away money than by making it.

It soon became clear that this traditional means was not the most effective way to handle Milken. In the era of *homo vendens*, Milken the salesman was a better product than Milken the philanthropist. After Lerer resigned the account, Milken's new handlers changed the information about their product (Milken), producing a hero salesman instead of a reluctant philanthropist.

I had no advice to offer Lerer.

How Ken Lerer, whom I met when we both worked on former U.S. Attorney General Ramsey Clark's Senate campaign, could become Milken's chief salesman is the subject of this chapter. How I came to be a "vendor" to General Motors and a worker in the campaign of the man who brought a federal antitrust suit against GM, fits under the same heading.

[12] *New York Times*, October 16, 1993.

have. He epitomizes the code of *homo vendens,* which holds that selling is beyond judgment, ruled by no moral law. To the exemplary practitioner, the genius salesman, selling has the intrinsic worth of necessary things; it is as essential to the conduct of human life as speech or thought. Therefore the one who does this work transcends ethics to become the hero of our time, *homo vendens,* the indispensable outlaw.

14

The Social Life of
Homo Vendens

You're born.
You suffer.
You die.

Fortunately,
There's a loophole.

Billy Graham Crusade in Central Park

—Advertisement
prepared by Bozell, Jacobs

Wolfefogel was brilliant. That he worked beneath a low ceiling in a basement room before an audience seated on the flimsiest of metal folding chairs made no difference to him. After his introduction, at the precise instant when the applause came to a peak, in that cradle of enthusiasm, the moment of hope, he stepped into the room. He moved quickly, a man of straight, sturdy stride, who drew the attention of the audience as if he were the only light in the room, and not a reflected light, a source, a brilliance among the shadows.

His pale brown hair was combed upward from the temples, not for a mask of baldness as it might have been in other men, but a crown of hair combed upward equally from both sides so that it appeared Mephistophelean, magical, like a crown of flames. He was, in his suit of brown serge pin-striped with blue, his burnished ocher wingtip shoes, his thin brown stockings carefully clocked, his eighteenth-century rectangular eyeglasses rimmed in wire of gold, magnetic.

He smiled, and opened his hands, spreading them slowly, like a flower opening in the time-lapse grace of a nature film. The gesture was so welcoming, so warm, so utterly ingenuous that it brought a sigh from the audience.

Then Wolfefogel spoke.

"Mercedes-Benz," he said.

And a long moment later, after the image of lumbering luxury had come and gone in the minds of his listeners, he spoke again.

"Caviar."

He did not wait so long before he spoke the next time, because he knew that his audience could not taste the Sevruga sturgeon eggs that lolled on the palate of his imagination.

Wolfefogel leaped at them with a string of words:

"Single malt scotch whisky. No blends. I don't drink blends, you don't drink blends. Single malt, Mercedes-Benz, Sevruga, Beluga, is what we earn."

He looked at them for a moment, stark now, suddenly aggressive, suddenly business.

"Rolex. You wear Timex. I wear Rolex." He raised his arm. The brown serge pin-striped sleeve and white shirt cuff fell back, revealing a wristwatch.

"Oyster."

"Ladies and gentlemen, everyone in this room who would like to be rich, I have a number for you: twenty-four thousand. Write that down. Think about it! Every five years, whether I do anything or not, whether I live here in this difficult city, this unwelcoming climate, or I spend my time on the beach in Miami or Acapulco, I make twenty-four thousand dollars from people I never met who bought things from people I do not know, often in places I have never seen. Twenty-four thousand. And that's just my income from automobiles. And I earn that if I quit today and never work another moment as long as I live.

"And ladies and gentlemen, fellow entrepreneurs, I'm not in the car business."

From the audience of people who wanted to be rich, Wolfefogel chose a face. It was fat, as gray as an overcooked pork shoulder. He found the eyes of the face, locked them to his gaze, and said, "Have you ever gone on holiday—vacation—with your wife?"

The eyes opened wide; they showed a shimmer as of tears. Wolfefogel had chosen correctly. The man was either divorced or widowed. Wolfefogel congratulated himself. "Stand up!" he told the man, sinking the barb of conquest deeper. "Tell us about your vacation. Where did you go?"

A formless man rose in place. He wore a blue suitcoat and a white shirt, but the collar button of the shirt was not closed and he did not wear a tie. His neck was ringed with rolls of flesh between his collar and his chin. It was the kind of neck that chafed easily on hot days, requiring cornstarch or baby powder, perhaps a kerchief, a slightly yellowed handkerchief rolled up and knotted at the side. "Hawaii," the man said.

Wolfefogel nodded. "I was in Hawaii two months ago. I had a double at the Royal Hawaiian for fifty-five dollars a night. Where did you stay and what did you pay?"

The man put his hand to his face, laying it beside his ear.

"It speaks louder than words," Wolfefogel said.

The man remained standing, his hand now seemingly attached to his cheek.

"You may take your seat," Wolfefogel said, and the man lowered himself back down onto the folding chair.

From then on, the man watched Wolfefogel with exceptional focus. He did not blink his eyes or move his hand from his cheek. He appeared to have been hypnotized. Wolfefogel moved on; he would use the man later.

"The secret of success is levels and savings. Levels and savings. One night, at a dinner party, you let the word out that you spent a hundred and ninety-five dollars for a full week at the Acapulco Queen Hotel. Before the evening is over, every person will ask you how you got a fifteen hundred dollar package for a hundred and ninety-five dollars. And then you say, 'Purchasing Power, the secret of enjoying life in an age of unconscionable profits.' From that moment on, they will ask you, they will interrogate you, they will drag the information out of you. No matter how reticent you are, they will find out everything you know about the advantages of the Benjamin Franklin Philadelphia Purchasing Power Club."

He looked again at the man with his hand still held to his cheek. "That, dear sir, is how you get Beluga, Sevruga, Mercedes-Benz. . . . Oyster."

While the period put on the litany by the name of the wristwatch created a silence, Wolfefogel scanned the audience, then he tensed himself, crouching slightly, like an animal about to leap.

And shot out a finger at the crowd!

"Money!"

They looked up at him, waiting, literally breathless.

"Levels!"

He saw the puzzlement in their faces, and he allowed himself to relax. Now that he owned them, he could talk. "You get twenty dollars per car. Now, what kind of commission is that? It isn't even noticeable. Twenty dollars off a twenty thousand dollar car. How can that be twenty-four thousand? Levels. You have five executive levels, each one has five people, and each one of them has five people, until you get to the last level, where they have ten; that's six thousand. Say one in five buys a new car. That's twelve hundred cars times five years equals twenty-four thousand dollars every five years, and you didn't do a thing for the money. That's levels. The secret of capitalism. They do the work, you get the money. Levels. Five executive levels. Start now, and by the time you've come to my stage in life. . . . Sevruga, Beluga, Mercedes-Benz. . . . Oyster!

"Do you understand?"

He looked at the pork-faced man. The hand was gone from his cheek, but his eyes still belonged to Wolfefogel. This was his man. A relationship had been established.

The audience grew restive as Wolfefogel explained the details of the organization. They wanted to hear about the money, not the work. When he feared he might lose them, Wolfefogel spoke of his own background: "Twenty years in financial services. I became a consultant on leveraged deals, hedges, new products. Then I met Howard Henry. And I saw that financial services had been a waste of time. Yes, I had a car and a condo and a boat in the water, but I worked for every cent. I had to break my back. Why? Consulting. High fees, but no levels. You can't make real money without levels.

"Not in real estate, not in speculation, not in medicine or law. Levels! And that's what I'm here for. To meet people who will climb the ladder of levels."

Wolfefogel was winding up to the close. "Sevruga, Beluga, Mercedes-Benz. . . . Oyster!" he said. "It's yours for he taking. Condos, powerboats, diamonds, and gold. The cash that keeps on coming. Cash, cash to the person who understands the ladder of levels.

"Take the first step. Climb the ladder. Become an executive of the

Benjamin Franklin Purchasing Power Club. The lady at the back of the room will accept your applications now. Use a personal check or credit card to cover your application fee. If you're not adjudged executive material, your application fee will be returned. I wish you luck. I know you'll succeed. I have faith in you. I believe in you, and I look forward to working with you. Join us now. And never forget what you're climbing the ladder for. Sevruga, Beluga, Mercedes-Benz. . . . Oyster!"

Wolfefogel was brilliant. They played him off with applause, even a cheer. Yet everyone did not rush to the little table at the back of the room near the stairs that led to the street. There were some, a few, and most of them said they wanted to take the application home to fill out. Only the man with the overcooked pork face stood at the table filling out his form, working over it as if it were physical labor. Sweat broke out on his forehead, the rolls of flesh that ringed his neck turned wet from the exertion.

He touched the ballpoint pen to his tongue at the beginning of every line. The ink left purple marks.

Soon the basement room was empty except for the Wolfefogels and the pork-faced man. Wolfefogel moved up close to the man. "I am Wolfefogel," he said. "At your service."

The pork-faced man said, "Pleased to meet you."

"We are going south from here," Wolfefogel said. "We would be pleased if you would accompany us."

"May I?"

Wolfefogel smiled. "This is my wife, Mrs. Wolfefogel. And you are . . ."

"Krause, Karl."

"A famous name."

"We are not related."

"A pity," Wolfefogel said. "But there are some who believe he was demented. The magazine, the relentless satire. Ahhh, Vienna!"

"You are Viennese," the pork-faced Mr. Krause said.

"Yes and no. And you?"

"German, although from generations back. My mother was actually more Irish.

"You don't look Irish."

"I have a German neck."

Mrs. Wolfefogel interrupted. "We must go soon, dear. They close the hall. It may rain. I heard thunder." Her fingers, fat and white, fussed among the unused applications, flailing like impassioned tentacles. Her body lolled inside a summer dress, hiding behind the salience of her breasts. She chewed ceaselessly on something tucked into the corner of her mouth. It could not have been tobacco in such a dainty fat woman; was it merely rumination?

"To horse!" Wolfefogel cried, picking up his brown umbrella from behind the table, and raising it like the sword of a gentleman officer of some forgotten century.

"Horse?" asked Krause.

"We shall board a bus, my friend, and we shall be pleasured by air-conditioning during this long ride on this hot, hazy, humid metropolitan night." He turned to his wife. "Is that not correct, my dear?"

"Taxis smell," she said.

Mrs. Wolfefogel gathered up her papers and stuffed them into a brown imitation leather folder; then they headed up the stairs and out onto the street, three musketeers, with Mrs. Wolfefogel, lumbering on swollen ankles, in the middle.

As they boarded the bus, Krause reached into his pocket for the fare, but Wolfefogel stayed his hand with a commanding gesture. "You are my guest," he said, producing three tokens.

They sat across from each other on the front seats. Krause and Mrs. Wolfefogel on one side and Wolfefogel himself on the other. "Is this not comfort?" Wolfefogel asked. "I despise taxis, those pigs, they want to save a thimbleful of gas by not turning on the air-conditioning."

Krause agreed.

Other people on the bus could not help listening to the words that came rolling out of Wolfefogel, who sat on the edge of his seat, magnificent in his brown suit with the blue pinstripe, his stockings elegantly clocked, now revealed by the bent knee, and his ringed fingers curled over the handle of the brown British bumbershoot. "What is your current occupation, Mr. Krause?"

"Looking."

"Ah, yes, as in looking for work."

Krause smiled.

"We shall have to get you a cravat, Mr. Krause."

"Karl."

"Karl."

At midtown they alighted from the bus and walked two blocks in the steaming summer night to Wolfefogel's hotel. "You'll come up," he said to Krause.

There was no question; Krause was commanded. He went with the Wolfefogels into the small commercial hotel, down the corridor to the self-service elevator, and up to their room. In the closeness of the elevator they touched each other. Krause caught his breath at the sensation of the Wolfefogel's arms pressed against his; he understood it for a symbol.

Once inside the tiny room, Mrs. Wolfefogel went into the bathroom "to freshen up" while the men sat at the round table against the far wall. "You can write out the check while we talk," Wolfefogel said.

"I have nothing in the bank. I'm looking."

"Your credit card will do."

"Canceled. All."

"Have you come up here under false pretenses, Mr. Krause?"

The pork-faced man's cheeks swelled into pouting. Tears tumbled from his eyes and rolled down his face. "As soon as I get on my feet . . ."

"You're tying my hands, Mr. Krause. The fee is modest, perhaps trivial: two hundred and fifty dollars. But the question of faith is not trivial. We have rules. As much as I would like to, I cannot put up the fee for you."

"Indigent," Krause said. "I sleep in a room in the back of a widow's apartment. She takes my possessions. Each week that I cannot pay the rent, that I cannot put up a dollar for food, she takes more. Last week, the hi-fi. Can you imagine a life without Mozart?"

"Krause, before you were looking, what were you?"

"I was married."

"Your work, Krause, your occupation."

Krause put his hands over his face. A muffled voice came forth: "When I was a young man, I was so handsome, the Adonis of The Bronx they used to say. I sold my face, my physique."

"You were a model?"

"Sales."

Wolfefogel rose from his chair. He thrust his chin forward in a sign of command. He wore his hair like a flaming crown. With a barely perceptible click he brought the heels of his polished ocher shoes together: "Dismissed!"

Krause looked up, displaying the most pathetic face. The pork roast had grown tired, beset by rot, softening at the edges. "I beg of you . . . ," he said.

Wolfefogel turned his back to Krause, executing the move with military precision. From the corner of his eye, he saw the pork-faced man struggle to his feet and drag himself to the door. With his hand on the knob, holding on hard, as if to keep himself from falling, Krause made one last appeal. "If I still had a watch . . . ," he said. "But the old lady has taken everything. I live on baked apples and hope. Wolfefogel, for God's sake."

"Dismissed!"

After Krause had gone, Mrs. Wolfefogel came out of the bathroom. She had rouged her cheeks and powdered her nose and chin. She looked quite nice, but for her teeth, which were marked by a dark line of lipstick, so that when she opened her mouth it appeared to be filled with blood.

"Have we money for the room?" Wolfefogel asked.

She shook her head.

1.

Most people agree that love and friendship are the perfection of social life. We cherish these relations because so long as they exist, they are pure; that is, they have no end but humanness. According to the old rules, which were set down by saints and poets, one does not love for gain nor maintain friendship for profit. These rules remain, a remembered liturgy, but intimate alliances have another meaning to *homo vendens.* For the moment, let it suffice to say that he is a jealous lover.

2.

. . . it is necessary for a prince to possess the friendship of the people; otherwise he has no resource in times of adversity.

—MACHIAVELLI, *The Prince*

Not far from the town of Princeton, the state of New Jersey becomes beautiful. The slums of Newark and the slaughterhouse and chemical stench of Secaucus have been left far behind, and the landscape outside the car window has turned bucolic. The farms have the look of wealth about them, and the crossroads stores sell things that only the affluent know. Far back from the state roads, in the seclusion of hills or groves of trees, large corporations have set their headquarters or research operations or training centers. In one of these, which Merrill Lynch calls its corporate campus, the purest of all salesmen, stockbrokers, learn a new way to sell.[1]

The new method, which was probably learned from observing lawyers, product managers, and the marking habits of dogs, was forced upon the "full-service" brokerage firms, like Merrill, by the establishment of discount brokerages that appeal to younger customers. While Merrill executives deny that the discount brokers had any effect on their business strategy, a book entitled *Share Ownership,* published by the New York Stock Exchange, showed that by the end of the 1980s the use of full-service brokers was heavily concentrated among older investors. Of those over sixty-five, almost 64 percent used full-service brokers. When all customers were considered, the number declined to 56 percent. Among those people the New York Stock Exchange characterized as baby boomers, 27 percent used discount brokers exclusively. Merrill's choice was clear: become a discount brokerage or change the character of selling.

As the market leader, Merrill was in the best position to try to hold on to its historically profitable business by redefining the nature of the sale. And as a company dealing with highly abstract products, it could rework the sales proposition, for few other businesses have such power over the product they sell as the money business.

It may be useful to digress here for a moment to compare the role of the salesman in the money business to the salesman in any other endeavor. Sales depend on salesmen according to the degree of abstraction involved: Everyone knows that an onion will decorate a hamburger and bring tears to

---

[1]   I chose Merrill Lynch because it is the market leader and the only major firm that puts forth a clear strategy in its public statements. I would be hard-pressed to discern anything of similar clarity from the public pronouncements and advertising of Smith Barney Shearson or Dean Witter. Only Paine Webber among the larger firms describes a strategy like that of Merrill, using the slogan "We invest in relationships."

Prudential Securities, troubled by a scandal involving the sale of limited partnerships to its clients, uses relationship selling as part of the campaign to restore its image. Its effort to produce information that would marry more easily with the desires of customers included an advertising campaign in which Jeff Daggett, a Prudential broker, appeared on television to say, "I tell rookies a good relationship evolves from prospect to client to friend." The *New York Times* (February 17, 1994) reported that Jeff Daggett's relationship with Monsignor Maximos Mardelli, a Roman Catholic priest, did not progress according to plan. Monsignor Mardelli has filed complaints against Daggett and Prudential with the National Association of Securities Dealers and sued for $750,000. In the lawsuit the priest alleges that he asked for his money to be managed conservatively, and that Daggett invested it instead in a risky limited partnership that collapsed. William Ahearn, a Prudential spokesman, argued that the suit was filed after the commercial appeared and had all the ear marks of an incident arranged to garner publicity.

the eyes of the cook, but a salesman can make a share of stock sound like a ticket to paradise. A house in which to live has the value of plumbing, walls, a roof, and heat to keep out the cold, but a house on which to speculate has the value of tomorrow, which has no walls and provides no heat, and so must be considered largely on the future the salesman conjures up.

But a house, even a speculative house, is as solid as sand compared to a pure financial instrument. Who has ever seen a Eurodollar? How many people keep stocks and bonds in a safe-deposit box or under the mattress? And what would a stock be worth if the certificate were put into its owner's hands? Its par value? The breakup value of the company? Ten, twenty, a hundred times the earnings of the company? None of those formulas applies. A stock or bond or Eurodollar is valued in the transaction; more than anything else (but fraud) financial instruments are of the salesman's doing.

Financial instruments have no other reality, money has no other meaning; wealth is now largely an electronic instant of agreement between buyer and seller, the salesman's brief success. It is a never-ending dance of bid and ask, buy; bid . . . Every transaction becomes the basis for the beginning of the next transaction. Without the salesman to mediate the transactions, financial markets would collapse, resulting in economic chaos. Although it may seem a dire and unlikely consequence, that is what would happen in the world of *homo vendens,* for wealth, once the creation of capitalists through the labors of their employees, now comes into the world through the work of salesmen, who bid up the value of abstractions as if they were things of intrinsic worth.

On the other hand, wealth once disappeared through consumption, dinner, or decay (and it still does), but now dies into oblivion on a salesman's word. A prediction, often incorrect, can reduce the economic worth of the world by billions. And if a great salesman has a nightmare, the wealth of nations can turn to ashes in a day.

Because money does not exist, any more than tomorrow or the day before time began, the sellers of the abstractions of finance, including money, are the purest salesmen, the least impeded by reality. From time to time the people who sell money get rich or go broke, but for the most part they struggle to earn a living by describing the futures of abstractions in an unpredictable world.

The Merrill Lynch corporate campus mainly serves those people who struggle to earn a living in the brokerage business. They were the people at risk, the foot soldiers whose methods required a change of strategy, because a full-service broker who simply buys and sells financial instruments charges two, three, five times as much as a discount broker for the same service. To save them, and thereby to save themselves, the managers of Merrill had to change the way they approached their customers.

Merrill calls the new approach "relationship selling." The package goods business calls it "branding." Lawyers speak of it as "client relations."

Relationship selling is taught by Merrill Lynch in classes held at the conference center and through the use of videotapes bicycled around the offices of the firm. The program operates at three levels: At its most basic level it trains new brokers; after they have learned the basics of the business, it helps them to "break through" to higher levels of production; and it also teaches the new method of selling to older, well-established brokers.

The project operates under the direction of Madeline A. Weinstein, First Vice President, Director of Human Resources and Training, and Dolores Gibson, Vice President, Manager of Financial Consultant (FC) Training. They work in the tasteful splendor of a school and administration building attached to a conference center/hotel. No university on earth, not Harvard, Oxford, Lomonosov, or the Collège de France, has such quarters. The very buildings themselves teach the students the first lesson of selling, which is that the rewards of eristic far exceed those of philosophy.

Weinstein, who asks that she be called Maddy, presides from behind a delicate, crescent-shaped desk. She is a tall, slim, almost thin woman, with straight blond hair cut into deep bangs. There appear to be two of her, perhaps three—each persona distinct and appealing. One displays the salesman or social worker's sudden intimacy, speaking in a soft voice, inquiring, thoroughly empathetic, looking at the world through soft, maternal eyes. Another speaks in the softly demanding voice of the executive, not harsh, but sure, in command, fatherly, full of compliments for subordinates, literally patting them on the back to reward work well done. A third persona appears in videotapes, an uncertain one, neither here nor there, perhaps not a persona at all, merely what remains after the persona has been rehearsed away.

She put the new approach to selling in the context of the business: "The broker sells himself and the firm and a strategy. Ours is a strategy for consultative selling. You want to know various things about the client. The broker must understand what the client or prospect needs."

Although she sells the company strategy, she mixes the argument with sudden admissions of fact: "Are there stock jockeys out there? Of course there are, but we don't think that's the best way to sell. We're doing advanced training, retooling to change from stock jockeys.

"If you're going to help somebody, you need the information. The steps are to gather the information and make appropriate recommendations. Good relationships are important. You have to like your clients. They have to be comfortable with you; otherwise, they should go to Schwab." Before she gives customers away, she adds that Schwab (the discount broker) "has relationships with financial planners who do what Merrill is doing."

Weinstein offers two theories of the sale:

"1. Very smart people in the presence of good information will act on that information.

"2. The buyer buys your belief in the product, the recommendations of the financial consultant."

Then she shows how the FC can use the strategy to sell, dividing the process into three discrete steps:

"Step One: I care. I will work hard. I am smart enough to do a good job.

"Step Two: Develop a strategy and then sell it. If the client says no to the strategy, the FC has two options:

"A. Go with the client's decision.

"B. It's too uncomfortable (very high risk, for example).

"Step Three: Sell specific recommendations as part of an asset allocation mix. Use Merrill research."

She advises them to do this largely in person, not by phone. "For example," she said, "I can't imagine how you could trust me, unless we do it right."

Weinstein, leaning forward slightly, sipping coffee, gracious, with the charming straightforwardness common to successful executives, constantly reinforces her argument with allusions to the realities of the broker's trade: "The core of the business is this: The end result is doing the right thing for the client. However, we are in business to make a profit. The firm makes money by buying and selling securities. We want to sell products, but we want to sell the right product mix. The way to do this is to have a relationship over time; the transaction will follow."

No broker exemplifies the Merrill strategy better than Stanley Heilbronn, a measured man, part of the breed of educated New Yorkers whose clarity and precision of speech and mind were once the hallmark of the city of rising expectations. One senses that he has always done what most people think is right: Stanley Heilbronn played football in school and served in the military during the Vietnam War. He takes calls from clients on the weekend, and the word *sell* makes him slightly uncomfortable.

We spoke by telephone early in the morning, before his day began. This is what he said about his business:

"What I learned early on was that I enjoyed interacting with people. And the selling I thought was different from selling a pair of shoes or a computer. What you're selling are concepts; what you're selling is trust. I think that's a major difference in our industry compared to other industries.

"In my case, my selling—if you want to use the word *selling*—comes at the early stages of the relationship and is a continuing part of the relationship.

"The sense of selling in this business is somewhat different from selling in other businesses. Here, at least the way I run my operation, I'm constantly meeting with my clients. I'm constantly reviewing their needs, constantly trying to understand where their assets should be allocated, what's appropriate for my clients. So there's an ongoing learning experience every time you speak to a client, every time you visit with a client.

"When it comes to the point of selling or recommending a specific stock or bond, I think most of the work has been done prior to that.

"What I've tried to do over the twenty-seven years that I've been in this industry is for my clients to develop a high level of trust and confidence in me. The way I reach that point is by trying to understand as much about my clients as I can, and that involves sitting down with my clients, speaking to them about their needs, understanding their risk tolerances, understanding what their future plans are.

"In a way, you're selling knowledge by asking questions and developing more information flow from your clients. So it's an ongoing process. The bottom line is your clients are relying on you, and if they're convinced that you are honest, that you have their well-being in mind, and that you're professional and meet their needs, then I think the last part of recommending a bond, a stock, a mutual fund becomes mechanical. You develop a relationship, and the relationship makes the sale easy.

"It's generally viewed that performance is the single most important criterion for people doing business with people like myself. And while it's important, it's not the number one, number two, or number three generally. It's the confidence that people have that you'll communicate with them, that you understand their needs, that you're going to do the right thing for them, that you're going to service their portfolio, that you're going to service their problems. That doesn't mean that you want to lose money, but performance is not their only criterion for walking in and doing business with me."

Although he describes relationship selling exactly the way the corporation prefers to have it known, Stanley Heilbronn does perform for his clients. He is a "value" investor, a believer in diversification, a man who does not buy the kinds of stocks that lose their worth overnight. He was unable to recall a single client whose losses were such that the client had to change his style of living, and he spoke at length of large profits in technology stock mutual funds and of the wisdom of having put many of his clients into Latin American stocks before the rest of the world discovered the continent.

As an example to other Merrill brokers, Heilbronn occupies a powerful position. The man who puts relationships ahead of performance generates more commissions from individual clients than all but a handful of brokers in New York.

How deeply Merrill Lynch believes in relationship selling can only be measured by how it rewards its brokers. For example, a company that truly put the well-being of its clients first might reward brokers according to the increases in the portfolios of their clients. Or it might pay bonuses to brokers according to how much their clients professed to love or trust or simply like doing business with them. In that case, relationship selling would be about relationships first and selling second.

A look at the training tapes Merrill bicycles around its offices gives a slightly different view from Heilbronn's or Weinstein's and a very different view from that of Dolores Gibson, the pretty, carefully made-up former schoolteacher who runs the training program. Brokers are advised to set goals for production, to use their time wisely. The client-interviewing process Merrill calls "profiling" turns out to be a way to "gather assets." Weinstein and a young Merrill broker, Saly Glassman, star in the tapes. Weinstein loses some of the appeal of the timbre of her voice and the gentleness of her selling manner on the tapes. Glassman seems more like a money machine than a person. She speaks of quantitative goals, and always the basics of the brokerage business: time management, profiling, prospecting.

If relationship selling has anything to do with the welfare of the other person, it did not appear in the tapes. The relationship was merely a means to selling a product, "dropping the ticket." Glassman reveals the business goal of relationship selling as she explains it to her audience: "I could be the best stock-picker in the world, but if I don't establish a relationship, the client won't stick with me." Her view of the final sale, which she admits has "some excitement" about it, conforms exactly to Heilbronn's: "By the time you make a recommendation on a product 90 percent of the selling has been done, and it's just a question of closing on the transaction."

Can it be that the advent of the discount broker had no effect on Merrill's plan? Can it be that Weinstein makes an error in argument when she talks about the cost of an investment advisory service for Schwab customers, saying it simply replaces the service Merrill customers get from their Financial Consultants? According to Gibson, the change in the business in the 1980s was not the beginning of the discount brokerage houses. "A bigger variable," she said, "was the sophistication of the consumer. There was an incredible proliferation of information on financial matters." She went on to talk about tuning around the television channels and finding people talking about real estate investment trusts (REITs) and sophisticated swaps.

When I suggested to her that knowledgeable customers might be more comfortable using the minimal service of the discounters, she smiled, and kept on talking, the pretty teacher in the perfect suit, with the delicate scarf at her throat, lecturing, following the lesson plan. She spoke of meeting and getting a new client, the essence of relationship selling: "A good match of personality, style, philosophy. I would have to tell you something you would identify with. I think that the sale is a process and that there are a series of sales that have to take place along the process. The sale doesn't happen when you drop the ticket. How do you know when it happens? When you fall in love!"

3.

The relationship the broker hopes to create bears more than a little resemblance to the psychoanalyst's connection to the patient. Like the broker, the psychoanalyst does not want to be judged solely on the basis of performance. The relationship begins with taking the history of the patient, what the Merrill brokers call "profiling," and continues for many years, with the analyst gaining new information about the patient at every session. Dolores

Gibson's description of the sale also applies to the analyst. Falling in love may not be the same as transference, but her use of the phrase may not be the same as falling in love. In all three cases the connection is deep, more emotional than rational, and difficult to terminate.

While the motives of the psychoanalyst, the stockbroker, and the lover differentiate them, one from another, the differences sometimes do not hold. Vast numbers of people have languished on the couches of sleepy old men talking and talking, getting nowhere at $25, then $50, now more than $100 an hour. The psychoanalyst encourages this world without end, in part because he is an economic creature who does not want to lose his income. Like the stockbroker, he has many affairs, and true love does not enter into any of them, which is not to say that both the psychoanalyst and the stockbroker do not frequently help their clients, but to point out that relationships of the pocketbook can never be the same as those of the heart.

Religion would be the most effective form of relationship selling, if religion and selling were merely variations on the same process. But they are not. Religion only seems like a form of selling, because it uses some of the same methods and because some priests describe themselves as mediators between man and his God. The similarity ends there. Selling and religion have different ends and produce different effects in people.

One triumphs in the transaction, whatever it may be; the other wants an exclusive arrangement for both the worldly life and the immortal soul of the convert. On the surface, proselytizing seems the most like selling, but at a deeper level it uses an entirely different method. Although a mediator begins the process of conversion, either by argument or by the sword, the convert eventually deals directly with his newfound god. In the case of profound conversions, no one mediates between the convert and what he believes is the only way to heaven; the salesman lives within.

Selling works by exploiting the desires of the customer; no salesman can create desire. Religion begins with existing desires—for inner peace or immortality or, in some cases, for material goods—and converts them. It would, in fact, be fair to say that religious conversion is the conversion of desire. A person may come to desire peace more than prosperity, eternal life more than worldly existence.

It is hardly necessary to look to saints or zealots to find these results.

People who convert to Islam or join the Church of the Latter Day Saints must give up alcohol and in some sects even Coca-Cola. Jews and Moslems are not allowed to eat pork, while many religions of the Indian subcontinent do not permit their followers to eat meat at all. The Moslem women of Iran and Saudi Arabia wear veils in public, the Mennonites of both sexes wear only black, Orthodox Jews must not shave their beards, and some Jewish sects insist that women shave their heads after marriage.

Those who enter the priesthood undergo even greater changes of desire. Roman Catholic priests, nuns, and monks take vows of celibacy. Some Hindu holy men as well as some Roman Catholic priests and monks take vows of poverty. Certain Hindu sects insist that holy men live as mendicants, begging for food and sleeping in the street. Bloodletting, using a thorn to pierce the foreskin, was required of priests and rulers in several meso-American religions.

The list of suppressions and conversions of desire goes on, virtually without end. The shamans of the Dinka had to submit to being buried alive when they grew old. Self-flagellation remains common in religions throughout the world. Untold numbers of followers of Western, Eastern, African, and Native American religions have given their lives for their religion, from the Jews who leaped from the cliff at Masada to the self-immolation of Buddhist priests during the Vietnam War. The evidence is overwhelming. Religion and selling differ in the most profound way: One changes desire, and the other seeks merely to satisfy it.

Man's desire to overcome his anxiety about eternal things and his desire for anything of this world, including his own comfort and safety, belong to different categories. It is worth repeating that no one ever walked across a continent to go to war on behalf of the videocassette recorder or chose to die on the cross for suits by Armani or scents by Chanel.

With conversions in the reverse order, from religious asceticism to worldly hedonism, the thesis still holds true. The monk who succumbs to his passion for dancing girls has also undergone a profound change, a change of desire. Even the person who moves from religious orthodoxy to a more liberal form of worship undergoes a conversion of desire, accepting a different route to paradise. When the putatively devout succumb to temptation, as in the cases of television evangelists who take up with prostitutes, the revelation may be the result of exposure rather than evangelism. When the truly devout turn to earthly ethics, it is difficult to know whether reason has had a victory or virtue has suffered a fall, but the corruption of angels,

like Swaggart and Bakker, has nothing to do with religion. It is pure buf-
foonery, like a burlesque house comic reaching into his baggy pants to
discover his manhood.

In only two situations do religion and selling mingle. The most common confusion occurs when members of God's flock become his customers, asking for divine help to furnish the living room or trade in the family
car or escape the loneliness of city life. There is nothing novel in this. People
have always prayed for earthly goods (the Bible certainly contains evidence
of it), but God's customer base seems to have grown very large in our time:
According to a Poloma and Gallup study, "Varieties of Prayer," 42 percent
of all prayers offered up by Americans ask for material things [2]

Religion and selling overlap more and more frequently now in their
means of communication. The sales pitch for Billy Graham used as the
epigraph for this chapter was prepared by an advertising agency. Grey Advertising, Ayer, and other agencies have also produced advertisements and
radio and television commercials for religious organizations. In Northern
California, Richard Southern and Robert Norton, who had been in the
financial marketing business, formed Crossroads Church Growth Consultants, which produces demographic studies and other marketing information for mainline liberal churches, then advises them on how to operate
the churches to conform to the needs of their target market. Evangeli-
cal churches have been using marketing techniques for more than a decade.

Since few relationships outside the immediate family are more intimate
than those between a person and his religion, the use of sales and marketing
techniques to win church membership may indicate something about the
nature of social relations for *homo vendens*. The language of the advertisement for Billy Graham reveals how much religion has changed since God
tested Abraham by instructing him to sacrifice his son Isaac or Dostoyevsky
wrote of redemption through suffering. In the advertisement religion has
become a "loophole," like a weakness in the law to be taken advantage of by
those on the slippery edge of ethics.

> You're born.
> You suffer.
> You die.

[2] Quoted in *Newsweek,* January 6, 1992.

Fortunately,
There's a loophole.

Billy Graham Crusade in Central Park

The beginning of the copy could have been lifted from the Book of Job: "Man that is born of woman is of few days and full of sorrow. He cometh forth like a flower, and withereth." But there is no poetry in the soul of *homo vendens;* he sings a peddler's song. Life has been reduced to six words: "You're born / You suffer / You die." Metaphor has been cast aside. The salesman sets out the terms of a deal.

Compare the offer in the Book of Job to Graham's deal. There are no loopholes for Job. His story may be the quintessential life without a loophole, yet Job must keep his faith. No lesson could be more clear about the duty of man to his God, the rules of his religion, or the nature of the creature religion creates. Monotheism established a relationship so powerful and so exclusive (in the place of many gods one true God) that it caused the Hebrews and their descendants, the Christians and Moslems, to abandon animal desires in favor of the ethics of Sinai.

When religion turns into relationship selling, the preacher no longer hopes to change desire. Instead, he makes a deal, offering new information about the fundamentals of human existence, conforming the pattern of life to existing desire. Unlike Job, Billy Graham's followers can negotiate for a better deal.

The Reverend Graham's advertising agency has followed the rules of marketing very carefully. The advertisement announces Graham's concession to the dominance of *homo vendens:* Human existence, for those who follow him, can be freed from the seemingly immutable pattern of birth, suffering, and death: "There's a loophole." The journey from *homo religiosus* to *homo vendens* is complete.

To expand religion's clientele of exclusive relationships, a new God has been created, One who bows to the desires of the market. Performance, which played no part at all in Job's relation to his God, has been brought into the relationship to close the sale. And why not? As Stanley Heilbronn, the master of relationship selling, said, "Performance is not number one, but nobody wants to lose money."

4.

First of all, strategies are devised to assault the competition, not the consumer. Secondly, the word is not only a military term, but a sports term as well. In fact, it is much more applicable to advertising in its football sense. Advertising strategies are either defensive or offensive. They are conceived to achieve gains at the expense of the opposing team (the competitive product) a yard (or share point) at a time. When they are successful, the paying fans in the stands get their money's worth and come back for more.

—JOHN O'TOOLE

In this late season of the American economy, when the salesman can no longer depend upon an expanding market, *homo vendens* has of necessity become a killer. The agonistic character of the American in business—learned, as Veblen said, on the playing fields, but also in the streets and barrios—has been intensified in the weary world of the end of the century. Crows and coyotes, the mediator's metaphors, attack each other now, wanting all that remains of a dwindling supply.

It seems a strange thing to say, but the methods of the killer, who cannot physically destroy his competitor, are limited to varieties of love. Having studied the preacher and the lover, the monopolist and the elitist, the salesman has fixed upon relationships as a killer's best tool. He has become the monogamist of the marketplace.

Ironically, *homo homini lupus* comes to mean the personification of toothpaste and the rote expressions of consideration and concern. As in the fable, the wolf dresses up in the costume of gentle love to get his prey.

The first and continuing effort to create a monogamous relationship between the product and the customer was branding. It came about with the advent of packaging machines and national distribution at the end of the nineteenth century. At the same time, the development of the web offset press made it possible to print vast numbers of magazines at high speed. The magazines and the manufacturers supported each other in the effort to establish brands, to create a brutal monogamy in the marketplace.

Peter Kim, director of research and planning for J. Walter Thompson, said that "a product is a physical thing, while a brand has no tangible, physical or functional properties. Yet it is just as real as the product. Disembodied, abstract, ephemeral, it exists like a myth in the imagination of its consumer." Kim goes on to say that many of the critics of advertising "as well as some of its practitioners, fail to understand the fundamental truth that advertising is not always about what a product 'does,' but rather about what a brand 'means.'

"A brand's equity therefore refers to the latent capacity of a brand to influence the behavior of the beholder by evoking a specific set of thoughts, feelings, sensations, and associations."

He concludes with an exegesis of the word *latent,* explaining that it implies "the potential to continuously and regularly influence the behavior of those who behold the brand, routinizing their purchase behavior and thus stabilizing the demand for an existing product, or expanding their purchase behavior to create demand for new products."[3]

In an expanding market the business of brands works well and can be practiced gently. When markets stabilize, the meaning of "share of market" changes. It no longer denotes a steady part of a growing whole. Instead, a steady share implies stagnation or retreat. Branding, which despite Kim's puffy rhapsody, really means little more than giving something a proper name, is insufficient. The very idea of selling has to undergo a change, passing from the realm of commerce into the social life of man. Like religion, it must have an exclusive relationship, but unlike religion it cannot solve the mortal anxiety of man; it can only entangle itself in desire, as lovers do.

Ted Levitt, former editor of the *Harvard Business Review,* described the ideal involvement of buyer and seller with absolute precision. He wrote of relationship selling as a "marriage" rather than a "momentary flirtation."[4] Levitt and other marketing experts, many of them not nearly so sophisticated as he, believed they had found an answer to the failure of American industry to hold on to its market share in the face of competition from overseas.[5]

---

[3]   All of Kim's statements come from direct and indirect quotations in a AAAA pamphlet, *It Works,* by Bernard Ryan, Jr., (copyright 1991).

[4]   *The Marketing Imagination* (New York: Free Press, 1983).

[5]   I cannot give a definitive answer about the effectiveness of relationship selling, but I have participated in some conversations about it. In the late eighties, when General Motors was suffering a serious decline in its share of the domestic market, a meeting was called in Detroit to consider the problem.

We met in a small conference room—two well-regarded inside consultants, an economist and an engineer/lawyer/psychologist, and a vendor—to discuss the marketing crisis that had gripped the corporation. The economist wrote a number on the blackboard: fifty

Instead of better cars and electronic equipment at acceptable prices, the salesmen and his customers "fell in love" and entered into "marriage," the killing of the competition by exclusion. Friendship and love, which had been the perfection of social life, the ends to which man had always aspired, became a means, the tools of this commerce of exclusion, this jealous commerce in which no competitor could be tolerated. *Homo vendens* no longer held his social life apart from business; he used affections. The sentiments of which happiness had been made now had an economic end.

In addition to every thing being interchangeable and so devalued, every affection had to be interchangeable as well. Love could no longer be limited to those for whom *homo vendens* had no wish but human happiness; the salesman and his customers had to fall in love. Lovers became interchangeable; one customer, one salesman, was like another. In the salesman's view every person with the price of a product was a prospective lover. The priceless sentiment lost its unique position, and the value of love fell to the price of the product.

Other sentiments, other relationships, also served as a means of making the transaction. Friendship was as good as love for the salesman's purpose. Any affection would do, as long as it led to the exclusivity of marriage. In the world of relationship selling, all sentiments, all attachments—love or fondness, affection, friendship, mere amity—fell into the same category. They lost their intrinsic value. Now that they were interchangeable, determined by the market, the value of such sentiments as love or friendship became so unstable that it could not be predicted from day to day, moment to moment. Nothing endured. *Homo vendens* was set afloat. He had no social anchor; he could not depend upon anything to inform his heart.

If love as a means could have been limited to the marketplace and the

---

million. "That is our greatest asset," he said, "the cars we have out there now, our customer base." The engineer/lawyer/psychologist nodded, for the credo of the corporation had been spoken; relationship marketing had been the main idea of General Motors since the days of Alfred P. Sloan.

And it had worked. I remember traveling through West Virginia, Arkansas, and Texas, interviewing General Motors customers in the early 1970s, when the relationship still held. It was astonishing to find that even a vendor's connection to General Motors was enough to win the immediate respect and admiration of people all across the American South. People welcomed me into their homes as if I were the family doctor or the minister of their church.

Fifteen years later, as the outsider in that little meeting, I had to say of the fifty million cars on the road, "No, it's your greatest liability. The cars are no damn good, and everyone knows it."

Some marriages end in divorce.

inner life of *homo vendens* had remained the same, the effect might have been different. He might have become a two-part person, half of him still ruled by human emotion, capable of love as an end it itself. But the same emotion cannot have many lives, many definitions. Love cannot mean one thing in the morning, another in the afternoon, and yet another at night. Once *homo vendens* put love to work, using it to kill his competitors, he could no longer rescue his human life from devaluation.

It was his decision to make all affections, all objects of affection interchangeable, to establish relationships with customers as if they were lovers, yet he cannot have failed to notice the deterioration of the sweetness of life. He must have felt the loneliness of the agonist, the interminable chill. A return to the separation of human life and the pursuit of the transaction will beckon soon, if it does not already engage his thoughts, but the world of *homo vendens* moves forward like a train hurtling down a track. New worlds, new times, are more probable than a return to the past. The dominance of selling is unlikely to end in a relinking with old values. Even the idea of intimate, human life becomes a problem for the imagination when a relationship described as love or marriage has no purpose but to destroy the competition, when fidelity is the instrument of murder.

Homo vendens has made, perhaps of necessity, a life in which the sorting of things and thoughts, human discernment, has become difficult, perhaps impossible. When God bows before the will of the market and reasonable men can suggest the marriage of a person with a box of breakfast cereal, the social context of the affections has been lost; order is in jeopardy.

This flirtation with anomie[6] would be a difficult problem, but manageable, a shopkeeper's dilemma writ large, were it not that at the end of the day, *homo vendens* must go home to his own life. With love used up, and friendship, too, and loyalty, fidelity, even gentle amity, what is possible, what can his relationships be?

---

[6]   The concept comes from Emile Durkheim's *Suicide* (1897): "... society's influence is lacking in the basically individual passions, thus leaving them without a check-rein. . . . But economic anomy is not the only anomy which may give rise to suicide. . . . [D]omestic anomy [results] from the death of husband or wife." *Suicide: A Study in Sociology,* trans. John A. Spaulding and George Simpson (Glencoe, Ill.: Free Press, 1951), pp. 258–59.

David Riesman, from whom I first heard the word when I was his student, used it much less narrowly, almost as a synonym for *maladjusted.*

Here, the word, now commonly spelled *anomie,* is employed less imaginatively to mean "normlessness" or "lawlessness," following the original *anomia,* as used by Herodotus.

15

The Human Life of *Homo Vendens*

Man is the measure of all things.
—Protagoras

Although it was his last day and he had been fired, the Dutchman arrived early, for there was still much to do. With only eight hours left—nine if he worked through lunch—he would have to press. He stopped at the reception desk to pick up the type proofs that had been delivered during the night, peeked inside the envelope to be sure everything was there, then walked back to the production manager's office to see if the illustrations and retouched photographs had come in.

He did not like the way they had fired him. Two weeks' notice was not much, and he thought the terms were harsh: "You can leave today or you can work out the two weeks. I can only pay you for the days you work."

The choice had not been difficult: He liked the work, and he needed the money.

At first, he planned to spend most of the two weeks job hunting, but then the catalog came in, and as he had explained to his wife, "You know how I love Christmas."

She had no choice but to smile. It was part of the bargain of their marriage: Christmas and selling were sacred. One was his hobby, the other his calling.

He unwrapped the package of illustrations, using a razor to cut the masking tape that held the brown paper in place. The boards were big. He liked an artist to work big so that when the work was reduced there was lots of detail in it. Catalogs needed detail. And faces. People had to see the joy of Christmas connected to the products; they had to be given to understand that at Christmas time goods and goodness were connected. Goods brought happiness, he had often said, especially at Christmas.

When people talked about the commercialization of Christmas, he frowned. They did not understand. He loved the toys of Christmas and the glitter of Christmas, and to those who were critical of his views, he extolled Easter sales, back-to-school sales, Thanksgiving Day sales, Columbus Day coat sales, and summer white sales, too. "In sum," he always said, "things make people happy, and what's wrong with happiness?"

He studied the cover illustration, which he had sent back to the artist four times. It still did not please him. He telephoned the artist, a dour man, with a long lower lip and the watery eyes of an old dog. The answering machine came on. "I'm not here," it said, followed by a beep.

After pausing for a moment to gather his words, the Dutchman said, "Thank you for the work. I think we're getting close, but I need to talk to you. You have to put more joy in the children's faces. Can you come in today? I'm leaving at five to pick up a car in Jersey and take the family away for a few days."

Next, he looked at the bill that accompanied the photographs he had sent out for retouching. They had charged him for spotting, which should have been done by the photographer. He drew a circle around the charge and wrote a note instructing the bookkeeper to deduct the amount from the photographer's bill.

All day the pieces of the catalog kept coming in wrong. The display type was too big. What he called "the miracle of the computer" happened: There were typographical errors in the final proofs that had not been in the readers. The client telephoned, wanting to change one of the items. Half an hour later, the client telephoned again, wanting to put the original item back in, while keeping the new item. The Dutchman took the problem to the art director, who threw up his hands and swore he was going to quit.

"Listen to me, young fella," the Dutchman said. "When you've been fired from a few jobs the way I have, you won't be so quick to lose your temper."

"Jesus, I'm sorry," the art director said, "but I can't stand this fuckin' place. These Limey bastards who own this place are fuckin' killin us." He smashed the remains of a cigarette into the top of a film can that served as an ashtray. "I can't fuckin' stand it. Look how skinny I am! I'm wastin' away. My old lady says my dick is bigger around than my leg!"

The Dutchman stood over him, a huge presence in the room, a slow-moving symbol, more like a sculpture than a man. "I was once the deputy director of a house owned by a Tokyo outfit. You don't know how bad it can get."

"Worse than this?" the art director said, standing up and loosening his belt buckle as if he were going to drop his pants. The Dutchman smiled, but he did not laugh. He was a big man, not so heavy as he had been when he was young, although he still moved and spoke at the measured pace of a person who does not fit easily into his own domain. He wanted to laugh, but laughter did not suit him; it made him look foolish, like an ox dancing. He smiled.

By noon the Dutchman had a headache. The air in the office was stale. The odor of crotch sweat came up out of the fabric seats and cotton padding of the chairs. He checked his watch to see if it was time to take his pill. Whenever he forgot the pill the rhythm of his heart changed, and he got a headache. It was too early, but he took the pill anyway. Stress, he told himself. The doctor had told him that stress was the heart's worst enemy. "Stress, tobacco, and fat, in that order," the doctor had said.

The Dutchman ordered a turkey breast sandwich-hold-the-mayo from the deli. He did not specify the kind of bread he wanted, because he planned to eat only the meat. An account executive he had worked with on his last job told him he could cure his headaches by giving up starches. So the Dutchman sat at his desk proofreading the type for the third time and picking pieces of white meat off the bread with his thumb and forefinger. To avoid soiling the type proofs, he wiped his fingers with a napkin after every bite. It made eating a slow process, but he put up with it. Camera-ready art was expensive.

At two o'clock the illustrator came in. "Asshole," he said for a greeting, "it's your last day. Why are you breaking balls?"

"It's important."

"Are you out of your mind? It's a fucking catalog!"

The Dutchman leaned forward, resting his arms on his desk, looking straight into the tired, watery eyes of the illustrator. "You've heard this from me before," he said. "I'm sure you're tired of it by now. But the truth about our work should be part of the way we live. Selling is the lubricant of our economic system, my friend. Unless each of us does his job, the system will break down. So let's not pretend it's monkey business."

"You're a big, ugly Dutchman," the illustrator said, "and I love you like a goddamned brother, but you have no sense of humor."

"As you say, my friend, as you say. But let's not waste time, please. I have to be out of here by five; then I have to get a bus to Jersey to pick up a Hertz car."

"To Jersey? What's the matter, they wouldn't rent to you in Manhattan?"

The Dutchman looked down at his desk: "I've lost my job. I thought I told you."

"You'll get another job."

"Meanwhile, I must be careful," the Dutchman said. "It's less than half the price of renting in the city."

They argued for nearly forty minutes over the face of a small girl in the lower right-hand corner of the cover illustration. The Dutchman insisted on more joy in the girl's expression, while the illustrator fought to keep it the way it was. They could not agree. "Schmuck! You're fired!" the illustrator said again and again. "Why are you breaking my balls?"

In the middle of the argument the Dutchman's wife telephoned. She asked how the day was going.

"Just fine, dear. I think the catalog will really move goods. The photographs are terrific, the illustration just needs a little more work."

"You won't stay late?" she said.

He shook his head, as if she could see him. He had worked late every night for the last sixteen days. "Absolutely not," he said.

"I don't want to make you nervous, honey. B-u-u-u-t," she said, drawling out the conjunction, "if you don't pick up the car on time, we won't get to the hotel for dinner."

"Don't worry, dear. I wouldn't be late for my best customers."

They said good-bye, and he turned back to the illustrator. "You will fix it," he said, "won't you."

The illustrator washed his face with his hands, rubbing his eyes hard as his fingers passed over them. "If you weren't such a pain in the ass, you'd be running your own shop by now. Why don't you get wise, give a little. You're a talented man, a terrific writer. Learn to go along. You've got to go along to get along."

"Does that mean you'll make the change?"

"Yeah. I'll send it back on Monday. Who gets the board?"

"They haven't told me," the Dutchman said.

"Pricks." The illustrator started to leave, then turned back to the Dutchman, and grabbed his hand. "Take care of yourself, for God's sake. Gimme a ring next week. I'll buy you a turkey sandwich-hold-the-mayo."

"Can I count on you to do our card?"

"Why the hell should I do a Christmas card for a church I don't even belong to?"

"Thank you," the Dutchman said. "I'll get the copy to you in plenty of time."

The day was disappearing, and the catalog was falling apart instead of coming together. The art director couldn't fit the extra item into the format without reducing the pictures and resetting the type for the entire spread. The printer telephoned to say he had looked at the latest version and couldn't bind in the black-and-white insert and hold to the estimate. "Why not use a blow-in card?" he asked.

"You mean a fall-out card?" the Dutchman said.

"Save the jokes for Monday; I'm exhausted," the printer said.

"Today's my last day."

"No kidding? What happened? Do you have something?"

"Not yet."

"I'll ask around for you, kid. Stay in touch."

In the middle of the afternoon, the office manager came in to give the Dutchman his paycheck. He said nothing as he handed a white business envelope across the desk. The Dutchman opened it, took out the check, and looked at the number. There was nothing extra. "It's been a long week," he said to the man who had fired him.

The man did not respond. He wished the Dutchman luck, and turned away. Neither man offered his hand in parting.

For a long time afterward the Dutchman could not think about the brochure. He closed his eyes and stretched out his feet and made a series of snorting sounds, the sighs of a drowning man. He sank slowly into the warm muck of self-pity, descending past jobs lost, arguments regretted, the destruction of his chest, the disaster that had befallen him between jobs. He remembered how they tore his chest open to tinker with his heart, leaving him with such pain that morphine failed to quiet the fire.

After that it had been so long between jobs. What had they seen in him, the prospective employers, the head hunters, the counselors? Did they see in the gray of his face and the dull surface of his eyes that he no longer offered excitement, only middle age, a ragged heart, and devotion to the happiness that salesmen create? Finally, after the money in the bank was gone and the stocks had been sold and the little place they had built in the Catskills had been auctioned off, the catalog job had come along. He remembered the blunt questions during the interview: Can you take it physically? How can I be sure you haven't lost your touch?

He should have known, he should have known.

"Oh, God!" he cried aloud, and was embarrassed, afraid someone had heard him in his pain. Was there anyone he had not telephoned the last time he was out of work or the time before? Could he use the same mailing list? "Yes," he said aloud, more comfortable speaking to himself now, "serendipity."

The telephone roused him, dragging him up out of the comforts of old pain, of suffering grown mild in memory. It was his wife. "Will you be on time?" she asked.

"Yes, dear. I'm just waiting for a new C-print and some type. It shouldn't be too long."

"I hope you're getting ready," she said. "It's nearly five."

"Yes, yes. And dear, I got my check. Nothing extra."

"Oh, honey, you didn't expect anything from those people."

He said that he couldn't talk long. There was still a lot to do. She told him that she loved him.

"You're my best customer," he replied. Before he hung up he listened for the sweet chimes of her laughter.

The type came in all wrong. The art director had not marked the tissue properly before sending it out, and the type house had followed his instructions. Now they were in trouble. All the measures were too wide.

"Can you cut it apart?" the Dutchman asked.

"Aw, fuck that!"

"It's six copy blocks; you could do it in an hour."

"I could fuckin' cut my throat with the fuckin' knife, but I'm not gonna do that either."

"Please, I have to pick up a car in Jersey."

"So go ahead, asshole. What do you think? They'll put a stop payment order on the check? Forget about it!"

"I'll stay just until we get the type out."

It was after six o'clock when they finished marking up the type. Three of the six blocks were too long. And the problem wasn't just windows; they were too long by a full line. The Dutchman had to rewrite the copy, and the art director had to do a tissue. In two instances more characters had to be cut and new tissues had to be made. Nothing went right; everything took longer than he expected.

At six twenty-five the art director called the type house for a pickup. The traffic manager said she wouldn't have anybody until Monday. "Monday!" the art director screamed. "Monday! You wait till Monday, it's the last fuckin' job you'll ever get out of this shop!"

"You want us to fix it over the weekend, get yourself a cab, bring it down. I'm going home."

"I'll go," the Dutchman said.

He telephoned his wife to tell her that he was leaving. "I just have to stop at the type house on my way to the bus."

"Oh, honey, why does it have to be you?"

"It's important," he said. "The Christmas brochure."

He had forgotten to clean out his desk, which took nearly half an hour. By the time he packed his things into his briefcase and two small boxes and said good-bye to the art director, it was after seven. Friday night was always a difficult time to get a taxi, and the traffic going crosstown was terrible, as usual. He arrived at the type house at seven-thirty. Fifteen minutes later he went downstairs and got a taxi to the Port Authority Bus Terminal.

There was a line at every ticket window. Panhandlers approached him from all directions, whining, demanding, threatening. While they milled around him, pushing each other like crows fighting over carrion, he tried to choose a line. The panhandlers blocked his path; they would not permit him to move. He put coins in their hands until he ran out of change, trying always not to touch them, dropping the money into their filthy palms. "God bless," he said to each of them as he moved toward the nearest line, using his briefcase and the boxes filled with his belongings as a shield, "God bless." And they blessed him in return.

The line moved slowly. Someone was fighting with the ticket clerk, trying to give a personal check. The Dutchman wished he had left the office earlier. If it hadn't been a Christmas catalog, he might have thrown up his hands, but the sales of Christmas were special, important. Although it was late now and he was forced to hurry, he was glad he had done his job.

He noticed a few people getting out of his line and going over to another. He changed lines, too. But the other line did not move any faster, and he was now at the end instead of the middle. New panhandlers greeted him. When he turned away from their entreaties, having spent all his coins with the beggars at the other line, they cursed him. A tall, very fat woman wearing two coats pushed her face up close to his. Dark brown drool ran out of the corner of her mouth. The stench of her breath sickened him. "I can't wait till you're in my shoes," the woman shouted into his face. "You'll see, you'll see, God will get you, you stingy son of a bitch."

The eight o'clock bus left without him. He had to run up two flights of stairs to catch the eight-fifteen. Once aboard the bus, he began to count the minutes. He followed the second hand on his watch, calling out the name of the new minute each time the hand passed twelve. Several people on the bus glanced over at him. He didn't mind.

When the bus pulled into the station in New Jersey, it was after eight-thirty. The Dutchman grabbed his briefcase and the boxes from the overhead rack, and pushed his way through the crowd to the front of the bus. As soon as his feet touched the ground, he started running toward the Hertz car rental office. It was only a few blocks, but they were long and slightly uphill, going away from the river.

At first, the air felt cold coming into his lungs, then it started to burn. He ran crazily, lurching from side to side. Three blocks. Four. He could not catch his breath. Five blocks. He saw the yellow sign, and slowed down to a trot. When he entered the office, he felt comforted, warm. His breath came easily again. The fire diminished in his chest. He rang the little metal bell on the counter to summon the clerk. While he waited, he took his driver's license and credit card out of his wallet and laid them on the counter. After a minute a tiny woman in a yellow blazer came out from behind a partition. She could barely see over the top of the counter. "May I help you?" she asked.

"Yes ma'am," he said. "I reserved a car." He pushed the driver's license and credit card toward her, "Under this name."

She picked up the cards and studied them for a moment, comparing the picture on the license to his face. "Oh, I'm terribly sorry," she said. "We released that car at seven-thirty, and it was rented."

"Well then, I suppose I'll have to take something else."

"We don't have anything else," she said. "Its a foliage weekend. Yours was the last car."

"Is that the honest-to-goodness truth?"

She nodded.

"Cross your heart?"

The woman smiled at the childlike question.

He fell down suddenly, and without making a sound. When the tiny woman came out from behind the counter, she found him crumpled among his things, looking pale, but otherwise quite comfortable. For a moment, she thought he was playing a trick on her.

1.

It is evening, the order book has been put away, *homo vendens,* perhaps a commuter riding home on a train or a traveler settling down in a motel at the edge of an unfamiliar town, closes his eyes for a moment, and in the mirror of darkness glimpses his human life. Who is he? How does he value himself? What is it about him that offends?

He may sniff at his own body, contemplate shaving again before dinner. If *homo vendens* is a woman, she may study the clarity of her eyes or the shape of her waist. They are interchangeable, the man and the woman; they sell, and it is selling that defines them.

They consider themselves useful. In the courtship of mind and matter, they are the dancing masters. It has always been so, since Eden, since Prometheus, coyote, and crow. The man or the woman sees a blemish, an unexpected hair, sweat, colonies of bacteria growing in a bodily crease; could that be the offense?

Nothing is wrong. They have exceeded their quotas, loved their children, buried their parents. What about them offends? It must be an error of judgment, they say to themselves, but in the revelations that come in the blink of an eye they read the signs of unhappiness. Something is wrong.

Homo vendens bears the burden of the sadness of the age; he has no dignity.

What is meant by *dignity?* It languishes in the modern vocabulary, an uncommon word, one that feels obsolete now at the end of the century, a souvenir of royalty or the nobility of savages. The word is more likely to be used today to describe the bearing of a horse than the value of a person. Yet, this seemingly archaic idea (or is it merely a sense of propriety?) completes the definition of selling, for the loss of dignity is the human consequence of the ascent of *homo vendens*.

Dignity has several meanings, and there is some interplay between them. The older definition—at least the more common one—dates back to Cicero, and has about it the sense of decorum. Sometimes this Ciceronian definition includes the notion of self-respect in its immediate family, but more often it has to do with being held in esteem by others, with stateliness, gravity, composure. Such dignity belongs to Roman senators and the faces that appear on currency. It has to do with seriousness of purpose, perhaps with power or wealth, certainly with success. Old people have this kind of dignity, unless they are poor.

Homo vendens likes to confuse this dignity of decorum with the other, more profound forms. He comforts himself in that way, with a salesman's trick.

A second kind of dignity lives mainly in documents, a dignity of grand promises made by the authors of constitutions, treaties, and other lofty statements of principle.

The third kind of dignity has to do with intrinsic worth. It sounds like the dignity of documents, but differs from it in that, with some thought, one can discover what the third kind of dignity means. The great proponent of this kind of intrinsic dignity was Immanuel Kant. He said that man was not a means but an end in himself, a person rather than a thing. And he said dignity was beyond price. His ideas were clear and flattering to human beings, but his sense of intrinsic dignity is not often discussed, because this kind of dignity does not appear on the surface of life. No one can point to the intrinsic dignity of a person; it has to be inferred from a whole series of observations, which is why the question has not been raised in this book until now, after all the stories have been told and all the observations have been made.

When the question of dignity has been concluded, it will be seen that to live in the dominion of *homo vendens* amounts to a human calamity, for the loss of one's intrinsic dignity comes at the end of a chain of loss, and is profound. History argues that for many people a life without dignity may not be worth living.

It should be said here that while the salesman's ability to take away the dignity of others is new, a lack of dignity has always been connected with salesmen. At the end of Eden, God did not punish the trickster/salesman by destroying him, as he did the citizens of Sodom and Gomorrah. He chose instead to condemn the serpent to spend all eternity crawling on his belly, eating dust; in other words, to live without dignity.

Dressed in fur or feathers as the metaphor of Neolithic cultures, the trickster/salesman was a comic figure, utterly without dignity, the butt of a thousand jokes. Religions reviled him, philosophers distrusted him, everyone was wary of him, he was the epitome of cheating, the identical twin of usury, yet like the serpent, he was not destroyed, for the necessity of the mediator was never denied. His punishment by God and man was the loss of dignity. It was the best, or rather the worst, they could do.

In his role as mediator, the trickster/salesman/usurer/cheat was involved in virtually everyone's life, but he was not a danger to the dignity of his customers, because he was despised. The salesman was merely a means, but his customers were more than that; they were persons. When he dealt with the poor, the salesman's effect on dignity was negligible, for the history of the poor is a history of living like things, used by the rich, a means to their wealth and comfort. Only once, in the brief flower of social democracy in America, did the salesman have a different effect on dignity.

At the beginning of the nineteenth century, the use of paper money and the need to develop the country beyond the Atlantic Coast produced a new salesman and a new citizen, one who was part of a great mass of men. Dignity, which had previously belonged only to the gentry and the clergy, was given to this great mass. Not to each, not as individuals, only to all, as a mass, a public, the *demos* of democracy.

For a moment in history the shopkeeper and the department store owner, the drummer and the booster, the insurance agent and the adman, gave the nation the newborn's sense of optimism and dignity. Everyone sold something to everyone else. One man's dollar was as good as another's. Public opinion, the choice of goods or ideas, was the most powerful force in the country, and the public was everyman. It was the salesman rather than the authors of proclamations who elevated the poor to the status of persons.

The rough social democracy of the new country was its major theme until the Great Depression quieted America's exuberant sense of dignity. War restored dignity in another form: it produced once again the soldier's sense that dignity lies in death or the risk of death or, more precisely, in the willingness to die, for there can be no greater realization of man as an end, of life beyond any price, than the soldier's decision to go to war. As William

James famously noted, there is not as yet a moral equivalent.

But dignity decays quickly in the ensuing peace. Although no one made a very good record of it, not in novels or movies, not even in one great short story, the soldiers came home from Europe and the Far East to be priced again, as things are priced, without a dignified person's sense of himself.[1] Some of them became salesmen, for selling was in many ways like war. It did not require much education or training, and it had a similar rhythm of long waits and quick, intense action. Salesmen and soldiers diverged mainly in the realm of ethics, for soldiers can bring themselves to die only for goodness, while salesmen do their work in a special place beyond good and evil.

Homo vendens emerged as a heroic figure, the one who could save a country from sinking back into depression after the war, but he did not have dignity. If ever a man had his price, it was *homo vendens*. He knew. All salesmen know they must sell themselves before they have the authority to manipulate information. However, it did not entirely please them to sell themselves, for soon after salesmen began to dominate the American culture, they went in search of some form of dignity. Early on, the founders of the Benton & Bowles advertising agency left the business for publishing and statesmanship. Other successful salesmen sought dignity through philanthropy and art collecting. Walter Annenberg and Henry Kravis still do, but they are anachronisms; they belong to the world before *homo vendens*.

2.

In a nation of salesmen, one seeks to achieve dignity by becoming more of a salesman, making a virtue of the pricing of everything. Lee Iacocca, Donald Trump, Victor Kiam, and dozens of others force themselves into the world, flouting the Ciceronian rules of dignity by public displays of crassness. James Carville, Jerry Della Femina, and David Ogilvy seek dignity by burrowing ever deeper into the world in which every person is a means. It would be a misunderstanding of their motive to describe them as apologists for the undignified state of *homo vendens*. They have not accepted any of the

---

[1]   Several books and movies dealt with the subject: James Jones's *Some Came Running*, Sloan Wilson's *Man in the Grey Flannel Suit*, and the movie *The Best Years of Our Lives* remain among the best known.

earlier definitions of dignity; on the contrary, they want to sell a new definition in which other measures—celebrity, wealth, power, fame, or even
notoriety—replace the stateliness of Ciceronian dignity and the priceless
character of intrinsic dignity.

One can hear the desire for dignity and the salesman's approach to it in
the how-to books for salesmen. J. T. Auer wrote this advice to salesmen in
The Joy of Selling, "We are members of an elite group and can be proud to
be working in the noblest and most interesting profession in the world: that
of salesperson." He went on, "After you close a sale, feel good! If you are
satisfied with yourself, don't be shy about it. Tell the world! Be proud of
your success!"

These soldiers of the new definition aim to enjoy the position of
keeper and controller of others. They want to hold human society in standing reserve, as Heidegger said technology holds nature in standing reserve.
To establish what they define as their own dignity, they must make a means
of all the rest of humanity, putting people to use just as *homo faber* put the
raw materials of the earth to use.

Even when presented with the opportunity to treat other human beings as ends rather than means, *homo vendens* will find a way to put a price
on them. Elmer Johnson, a salesman who was for a brief time general
counsel and executive vice president of the General Motors Corporation,
demonstrated this trait in a conversation about laws making seat belt use
mandatory. Johnson, who touted himself publicly as an "ethicist," listened
to the case for GM to support such laws. It was explained to him that this
minor act would undoubtedly save many lives and prevent many serious
injuries and that it would cost GM virtually nothing to announce its support
of laws requiring drivers and passengers to use the belts already installed in
cars. There was no moral or economic risk. Johnson's response was "What
good will it do the corporation?"

Presented with virtually the same proposition, Mark Green, who was
then Ralph Nader's business partner, said that Nader could not advocate
seat belt use, because his support of the idea would delay passage of a law
requiring air bags in cars. When he was advised that tens of thousands of
lives could be saved by seat belt use during the ten to fourteen years it would
take to replace the fleet of cars on the road in the United States, Green
maintained Nader's position. "Ralph," he said, "wants air bags."

One salesman was like another: Human beings were no more than a
standing reserve, priced according to the market. Yet, both men sought to

dignify themselves by connecting their work to ethics, when in fact neither man could even grasp the meaning of a life beyond price. They were concerned with how to sell, not how to live.

Whoever thinks about how to live, the question of ethics, comes to think about dignity. But dignity is not something to be found in the world. It was not bestowed on man; it can only be created by him. That is why the twentieth-century philosopher Karl Jaspers said of Kant, "He begins from man," because dignity, upon which Kant built his ethical system, begins from man.

It is around dignity that the little schoolmaster of Königsberg[2] constructed his case for the autonomy of human reason, arguing that man may obey only those laws he himself makes, then insisting that he must obey them, that it is his duty. "The dignity of man consists in this capacity to legislate universally on condition that he obey his own legislation."

Here then is the connection of dignity to freedom. Human beings can do what they ought to do. They are free to be dignified; they are free to be human. When man has dignity, no one can buy him, no one can use him. Everything begins from him, from his own reason; he is the ruler of himself, the possessor of his own mind.

Like some latter-day Sophist, Kant measures the universe by you and me. How could so important a creature as man have a price? He cannot be compared to the world; he is the measure of worldly things.

Free. Beyond price. More than that.

Is the proper description of the ideal state of man contained in a pun? Coincidence? An error of language? Free and free. The measure of all things controls himself, judges himself, governs himself. He cannot be for sale. Since he controls, judges, and governs himself, it is unlikely that he can be bought. What of him is left to sell?

The tension between man and salesman must finally be recognized as a struggle for dignity. *Homo vendens* wants for himself the Ciceronian dignity of Caesars and senators, which in our time has degenerated from decorum to renown. He does not want to think of how he also lives in society, in a context of others, one of many. He does not want to think that making a

---

[2] The philosopher Johann Georg Hamann's phrase. Hamann attended Kant's lectures in the 1780s.

Kant's biographers say he was a tiny man, with one shoulder higher than the other. He worried about his diet and his health, and was careful to obey a government order not to speak his views on religion.

means of the rest of the world also makes a means of him.

Homo vendens deals with his condition by shutting his eyes, like a child, thinking that whatever he does not see does not exist. In the dark the tiger of apprehension and the spider of remorse disappear; he imagines himself apart, safe. When he opens his eyes, he immediately encounters his price, and realizes that someone is using him; the illusion dies in the light.

Homo vendens longs to return to the darkness, to his lonely pleasure, but a man alone cannot be renowned, just as he cannot be free. The salesman covets both lives. He wants to use others without being used. He wants to be famously alone. That is the salesman's antinomy, his stumbling place. He does not understand that one person alone cannot have dignity, just as one person alone cannot be free.

Dignity occurs only among others, but not under the tyranny of others. The mass of individuals, the public, which gave men dignity at the end of the eighteenth century, when politics was still fresh and full of meaning in the American mind, has become the dictatorship of the market, the tyranny that refuses men their dignity now.

When men use others as a means, when the market dictates the imagination and the act, the dream life as well as the day life of men, the true meaning of dignity comes clear. Kant did not pin his ethics on decorum; by *dignity* he meant "free." He could not tolerate man as a means, in the grasp of others, even in the grasp of God. He begins with man, with possibility; that is what is meant by freedom, that is the ethical question the triumph of *homo vendens* raises, not the process of the transaction, but the ability to be free.

The surrender of freedom is the sadness of the age:

Under the dominion of *homo vendens,* man is no longer free to know the world. The salesman now informs him. In the mix of mind and matter, perception, the information comes not from the senses encountering reality but from the salesman. Man has lost the world.

By conceding the world to *homo vendens,* human beings enter into an agreement in which everything exists as part of a transaction. A man is interchangeable with a thing; he no longer determines his own worth; a price can be put on him. Man has lost his humanity.

When *homo vendens,* who recognizes himself as merely a means, makes all men into a means for his use, he takes away their freedom. Man has lost his nobility.

Under the conditions of a life dominated by *homo vendens,* an abstraction of desire, the unthinking market, initiates action. The world no longer begins from man; he has forfeited the autonomy of his own reason. Man has lost his mind.

Do I mean to say that Americans are lunatics, living in chains? Of course not. But freedom is a fragile thing—it must be initiated every day—and thinking is the hardest part of making men free. A creature who lives in a world described by his own senses and invents the rules by which the game of life should be played is always in danger of throwing up his hands and letting someone or something else do the work. All through history someone has been waiting for weariness to set in so that he can take over, sometimes with a gun, at other times, as now, with a word.

A transaction has no ethical content. As Huizinga said of play, it in itself lies outside morals. The ethical problem at the end of this century is not about selling; in the dominion of *homo vendens* the problem is tyranny.

Response

Enlightenment is man's exit from his self-incurred tutelage. This tutelage is man's inability to make use of his understanding without direction from another. Self-incurred is this tutelage when its cause lies not in lack of reason but in lack of resolution and courage to use it without direction from another. Sapere aude! (Dare to know!) "Have courage to use your own reason!"—that is the motto of enlightenment.

—IMMANUEL KANT[1]

An alternative to the domination of *homo vendens* is no longer an easy choice, for the economy of the world is built upon the belief that the tutelage of the market has been inculcated in virtually everyone in the United States, and is working its way into the cultures of the rest of the world. Sudden change would be catastrophic, disrupting markets, throwing millions of people out of work.

---

[1] The opening lines of *What Is Enlightenment?* I have used the translation provided by James Haden for Ernst Cassirer's *Kant's Life and Thought* (New Haven: Yale University Press, 1981) (almost identical to Lewis White Beck's translation). Carl J. Friedrich's version in the Modern Library edition substitutes *immaturity* for *tutelage,* divorcing the idea from Kant's notion of critique and his concern with freedom.

Man the customer, the thing the salesman puts to use, can not be made suddenly to disappear, replaced overnight by enlightenment's daring thinker. The cost of such a revolution would be too high. The tutelage of the market must continue. But for how long and to what extent?

This question of the quality of our existence was raised in earnest by Socrates, who asked what kind of life was worth living. Long before the Enlightenment, he spoke in defense of reason. He abjured the unexamined life, choosing instead to die. Have courage! was also his advice to the world.

The choice in our time is not to die but to think, for in thinking freedom begins, and freedom is the antidote to *homo vendens;* it is the parent of autonomy. But how can thinking begin? What are the ingredients of the antidote?

A plan for thinking that is as simple as the instructions for assembling a table or a toy cannot be written. In an earlier time, Wonder was considered a beginning; merely to separate oneself from nature was then sufficient to trigger thought. But now we accuse each other of being too alienated from nature to understand its importance; we can no longer be awakened by the surprise of finding ourselves in the world rather than merely a part of it. Thinking must begin from a different occasion.

The source of Wonder now can only be astonishment at our own existence. This flash of awareness has been described by many writers, but rarely in a comprehensible way. It is the sudden recognition of one's own being, according to some. The sensation of one's physical presence in space, according to others. Or it may be the experience of being within Being.

But I think it is not so arcane or complicated an idea. Wonder appears at the instant when a person sheds the modesty imposed upon him by others and recognizes the truth that everything must begin from man, not all men, but any man, any woman. At that moment he bestows upon himself the dignity of creators. He becomes the mother and the father of the world, yet guided by a sense of limits, for he is uplifted by the joy of creation and burdened by the responsibility of freedom, a creature who has chosen—out of recognition of the worth of his own being and beginning—to think.

Thinking will create difficulties, discomforts, dislocations. The free man, the person who refuses to rule himself according to the tutelage of the market may choose different satisfactions: time instead of things, happiness instead of wealth. If so, the productive capacity of nations will have to be diminished or production will have to be described in a different way, revalued, like something brought out of a long sojourn in darkness and suddenly exposed to the light. Wisdom could become more valuable than widgets. Professors and poets would become the wealth of nations. It is not a mad scheme I propose; even now, there are wise men saying that knowledge is in many ways more valuable than things. I have even heard them say so in the suites of great corporations. They are not merely asking the question. It is the system of valuation that impedes them now. And they are neither fools nor revolutionaries. They have won Nobel Prizes and made fortunes.

If they are correct about the revaluing of the world, they may be predicting great upheavals. Perhaps the economies as we know them will not survive the light. An end to the domination of *homo vendens* poses enormous risks. What if the desire to possess beautiful things were better satisfied by grace than by gold? Under the rules of the autonomy of human reason, a rich man might be one who has enough, and poverty would describe the lonely. If man could rid himself of the self-incurred tutelage of the market, if he were free and questioning, if he practiced in his daily life even a modicum of the rigorous critique the philosophers prescribe, the weight of *homo vendens* would be lifted from him by the miraculous lightening of laughter.

The danger of thinking cannot be overstated. But neither can its contribution to joy. *Homo vendens* will come to the end of his dominion. A tremendous clash of values will precede his demise, and then a clamor of freedom to announce that the renaissance may begin.

After chance, necessity:

butterflies, roses, apples,

symmetries, salesmen,

and song.

Acknowledgments

After Starling Lawrence put his mind to it, this book became better organized and more accessible. Reading and responding to his editorial notes was a conversation with a brilliant, feisty, meticulous, and often funny friend.

During my thirty years as a day sleeper, many people were tolerant and helpful and more than a few were not. In retrospect, I am as lucky to have known the rivals and enemies as the friends. Tolstoy knew what he was talking about when he said that all happy families are alike.

Among the tolerant were King Harris, Dudley Burchard, Ed Wong, Pete Dailey, and Al Haas in San Francisco; and Bob Dunning, Neal O'Conner, Lou Hagopian, Ed Block, Waldo McNaught, Tom Mullen, Jack McNulty, George Pruette, Bob Kingsbury, Tony DeLorenzo, and Carmen Macksoud in New York and Detroit.

I am grateful to the people in my group at Ayer who did the work while I drowsed, and especially to Sirje Helder, who managed the group on a day-to-day basis.

Charles Simmons and I talked about many of the ideas in the book. His advice on life and letters is as funny as *Powdered Eggs* and as wise as *Wrinkles*.

Roberta Pryor is the nicest tough guy in town. Patricia Chui is the cheeriest apprentice famous-editor in North or South America.

Sylvia Shorris looked up now and then from work on her own book to wish this one Godspeed.

Index

Index